AF560671

# BANK MARKETING

# BANK MARKETING

*By*

**Dr. Bidhu Bhusan Mishra**

&

**Dr. Prakash Chandra Mishra**

DISCOVERY PUBLISHING HOUSE PVT. LTD.
NEW DELHI-110 002

First Published – 2008

Reprinted – 2024

ISBN: 978-81-8356-347-5



**Bank Marketing**

*Published by:*

**DISCOVERY PUBLISHING HOUSE**
4383/4B, Ansari Road, Darya Ganj
New Delhi-110 002 (India)
*Phone*: +91-11-23279245; 23253475; 43596065
*Mobile*: +91 9811179893 / +91 9871656464
*E-mail*: discoverybooksindia@gmail.com
orderdphbooks@gmail.com
namitwasan9@gmail.com
*web*: www.discoverypublishinggroup.com

*Printed at:*
Infinity Imaging Systems
Delhi

# FOREWORD

Banks are the most important institutions in the financial systems of any country. They play the catalytic role in the economic development of a country. Banking sector is probably the most important financial sector not just in terms of turnover, profit and employment, but also in its paramount impact on all spheres of the economy. The Five-Year Plans in India always call for tremendous efforts for resources mobilization by all concerned. Since the banks are the major repositories of public savings and purveyors of credit, they have been increasingly called upon to mobilize and channel their resources for meeting plan objectives

The crucial contribution of the banking industry in ushering the desired socio-economic development in India by canalizing the savings of the community to various productive sectors is beyond any body's doubt. In order to meet the ever increasing expectations of the society from the banking system, it is utmost important that the banking industry should keep pace with changing needs of the society. During the last two decades, more particularly after liberalization of Indian economy, Indian banks have undergone unprecedented qualitative and quantitative changes. After nationalization of commercial banks in India (1969 and 1980), the emphasis of the banks have changed from "class-banking' to 'mass-banking'. Now the question before the Indian banks to maintain the balance between the twin contrasting objectives of profit making and social banking.

The recent years have witnessed significant development in international banking Competition, dis-intermediation, new services and unique promotion schemes are some of the emerging features of changing international banking scenario. The globalisation of financial markets has been facilitated by the progressive removal of controls and barriers to move capital across the borders (unification of currency and trade pacts among the European economy). This process has been further accelerated by the development of technology particularly in the field of telecommunication, information technology and electronic banking system. India is not far behind in this regard. It has made its laws flexible and liberal, allowed foreign banks to operate and progressively loosen the hackles in the path of smooth functioning of the banking sector. Now commercial banks in India are provided operational freedom and will be held accountable for their own results.

With changing scenario the expectations and needs of the customers are also changing. Customers need more and more benefits from their bankers. Their loyalty is also changing very fast from one bank to another. In the present environment, bankers are operating in a buyers market, where they are at the mercy of the customers. Customer oriented banking is the need of the hour, in the face of fierce competition from other banks and non-banking organizations (NBFC). The future success of the banks depends upon identifying new profitable segment in the market by recognizing new needs and designing new schemes to meet the needs at a profit to the banks. Through better marketing approaches, the bank can increase the number of customers and the size of the deposits. A successful banker must no longer guess his customers' needs and provide services, which he hopes, will meet those hypothesized needs. Rather the needs and desires of the customers must be researched and services should be provided, which will satisfy these needs and desires.

# PREFACE

Indian banking has witnessed a paradigm shift after the financial sector reform in 1991. The banks realised that profit will be under pressure with the introduction of prudential norms and asset classification. There was a clear shift on the emphasis from growth to profit; and on a clean, transparent and healthy balance sheet as opposed to the large-sized ones of the earlier years. As the foreign exchange and money markets were gradually deregulated, competition intensified; the net results of the bank will be under tremendous pressure. Now the banks are looking for new avenues to meet the challenges posed to them.

Today, banks can look back with satisfaction by having responded effectively the challenges put before them from time to time—whether of social control or of reforms. In future, the banks will have to adjust their system of functioning, venturing into new areas, improve efficiency levels by inclusion of trained and skilled manpower and restructure their organisations. Then only, they can face the challenges of the future more confidently and proactively.

In the changing banking scenario of 21st century, the banks have to have a strong identity to provide world-class services. The banks are now have to be of world-class standard, committed to excellence in customers, shareholders and employees' satisfaction, and to play a leading role in the expanding and diversifying financial sector.

The banks have to change their thinking; and have to put the new innovations in the field of banking and customers' satisfaction at top of the list of priorities. It has rightly been said that

"Customer–the Crown Prince of Today and Monarch of Tomorrow". Bank marketing is the creation and delivery of financial services suitable to meet the customers' needs at a profit to the bank. The need for bank marketing also arises due to increasing sophistication of bank customers, improvement in technology, and increased cost of meeting the customers' needs. Today all the banks including foreign banks operating in India offer many innovative financial services. Customer service is the primary end of any bank. A customer always wants something and expects that the bank should come up to the level to fulfill those needs. Again, the more you provide, still more the consumer needs.

Quality is a buzz word in marketers' dictionary. Poor quality places a firm at a competitive disadvantage. Service quality is about meeting customers' needs and requirements, and how well the service level delivered matches customer expectations. Service quality in banking implies consistently anticipating and satisfying the needs and expectations of customers.

The success of any corporate initiative in customer services depends mainly on the men at the counters, their commitment and concern for customer needs, which can make or mar the growth of the Bank. This is where the bankers have an important role to play. It is necessary that the customers should be made educated on new products and services introduced by the bank. A personal touch is therefore vital to carry the conviction. Further, in a highly competitive environment, retaining existing customers is as important as mobilising new ones. It is to be remembered that 'customer is just everything in a service industry like banking'.

The service-marketing triangle is built with employees, technology, and the service strategy as the corner points and customers at the heart of that triangle. This make the task of marketing services more complicated and stressed the marketers to be more customers centric. Service companies should, therefore, pay particular attention to the product—planning stage of their marketing programmes. For marketing of services, especially in the Banks, the marketing manager must understand the nature of the characteristics of services and the manner in which they impinge upon the marketing strategy.

The present study aims at providing better understanding of the customers' needs, which will help in designing a better marketing strategy to retain existing customers and attracting new customers. The study is a unique one, as no such study has been done earlier on customers of the banks in Orissa. The main objective of the present study is to understand the banking behaviour of customers of Orissa. The study is mainly based on field survey and is exploratory in nature. The sources of data are mainly primary. Data are collected through three tailor-made questionnaires, i.e., Customer Survey, Banker Survey and *Servqual,* with a view to measure the perceptions about the quality of service delivered to the customers. I am sure this book will be of immense use to the bankers, students of M.Com, M.B.A. and the researcher scholars in the field of banking and service marketing.

**Prof. Girija Prasad Acharya**

*Former Principal, Revenshaw College*
and *Director, Govt.*
*Text Book Press, Bhubaneswar*

# ACKNOWLEDGEMENTS

I am afraid if my humble endeavour would have culminated into a presentable thesis had I not been privileged with the unstinted help, support, guidance and counselling from a wide variety of persons and organisations at all stages of my work. I therefore, feel so much indebted and obliged to all of them that I find every conceivable expression grossly inadequate to express my heartfelt gratitude to each of them.

First of all, I take this as an opportunity to sincerely and profoundly thank to my guide Dr. Prakash Chandra Mishra, Reader and Former HEAD, P.G. Dept. of Commerce, Berhampur University for his sustained interest in the work. His valuable guidance, constant inspiration and thorough reviews provide me many constructive suggestions. I am also greatly indebted to his family members who rendered all love, affection and cooperation during my course of work.

I am indebted and grateful to my teacher Prof. Ranjan Kumar Bal, Professor, P.G. Dept. of Commerce, Utkal University his kind encouragements and help and advice, which they have so willingly offered. His valuable guidance and constant inspiration has been the lifeline through which the present research has passed from the conception to the completion stage. I am also greatly indebted to his family members who rendered all love, affection and cooperation to me.

I also express my profound gratitude to my colleagues in the Dept. of Business Administration, Utkal University for their help and encouragement. I am fortunate to have an extremely capable and useful friend Sri Minaketan Sarangi, Asst. Director,

Dept. of Planning and Coordination, Govt. of Orissa for his constant help and cooperation, who deserves to be thanked for his warm feelings and comraderie. I am also thankful to my friend Sri J.N. Panda of P.N. College, Khurda for his help and cooperation. I make a special mention of my friend Dr. S.K. Tripathy and his wife Supriti for their support and encouragement.

I take this as an opportunity to thank all the respondents who have spared their valuable time in providing me the data for the research, otherwise it would have been impossible to complete the task in time. I thankfully acknowledge the role of my teachers, well wishers, friends and relatives for their inspiration and encouragement.

I shall fail in my duty if I do not express my gratitude to all those authors I have consulted for my work. I have sincerely tried to acknowledge them when ever a specific idea made that possible. But it is just possible, there might have crept into this work and certain ideas of others which might have become so identified with my line of thinking and presentation that separate acknowledgement could not have been possible. I however, put on record my deep scence of gratitude to all those who have helped me shaping my ideas.

I appreciate the cooperation rendered by the Librarians of IIM, Ahmedabad; Xavier Institute of Mgmt. Bhubaneswar, Parija Library, Utkal University; Seminar Library, Dept. of Business Administration Utkal University, IBS, Bhubaneswar and few publishing houses.

I shall be partial if I do not put on records of my thanks to my two young brothers Bibhuti and Umasankar who have sacrificed their pleasure of holidays to help me in completing the research work. It would not be fair if I do not mention my thanks to my wife Jayashree and my two kids Brajesh and Rajesh who uncomplainingly let the research work disrupt their life-cycle. I take this as an opportunity to thank my brother Bimal, a bank officer, two sisters and sister-in-laws for their constant inspiration and support.

I owe a deep sense of gratitude to my beloved parents, whom I believe will be the happiest persons in the world seeing their son's labour bringing fruits. It is, indeed, they who had inducted me into this pious mission of teaching. Finally, I am grateful to the ALMIGHTY without HIS blessing nothing will happen on this earth.

**Bidhu Bhusan Mishra**

# CONTENTS

# CHAPTER–1

# INTRODUCTION

## THE PROLOGUE

The twenty-first century will go down in the business history as the era of profuse attention to customer expectations and to profitability through higher customer retention. The purpose of a business is to create and to keep a Customer (Levitt, 1960). The success or failure of a business depends on what of customer relationship it practices. In the modern world of competition, growing consumerism, and information explosion, the one single element that stands out as the factor of success is the customer. After all, customer is the life-blood of a business. While defining the purpose for which business exists, Peter Drucker had said; "With respect to the definition of business purpose and business mission, there is only one such focus, one starting point; and it is the *customer*. A business is not defined by the company's name, statutes, or Articles of Incorporation; rather it is defined by the needs and wants of the customers. The customer buys a product or service to satisfy his needs. To satisfy the customer is the mission and purpose of business".

Realisation has already dawned on organisations that customer retention is more crucial than acquiring new customers (Gopalakrisnnan, 2005). Growing competition and technological innovations have created tremendous awareness among the customers and their expectations are growing at a rocketing speed day by day. In order to retain even the existing customers, products require constant upgradation keeping in mind the developments happening elsewhere. The problem is more so with globalisation, where the organisation is required to keep themselves abreast of the developments worldwide.

It is worth quoting the father of our nation, *Mahatma Gandhiji* who on the occasion of inauguration of Union Bank of India on 11$^{th}$ November 1919, defined customer and that still holds good today. His words are: "A Customer is the most important visitor on our premises. He is not dependent on us; rather we are dependent on him. He is not an interruption on our work. He is the purpose to it. He is not an outsider on our business; he is a part of it. We are not doing him a favour by serving him. He is doing us a favour by giving an opportunity to do so".

The last decade of the 20$^{th}$ century is truly the decade of customers. Two major developments in India which triggered customer revolution are: first, the process of liberalisation and globalisation, second, the invasion of information technology (IT) and large scale disintermediation. These developments have unlashed competitive forces and the sellers' market has been transformed into a buyers' market. Organisations are made to run for their business not only by attracting customers; but more importantly by retaining existing ones. The ever-changing IT is also helping in extending the range of delivery systems and transforming the fixed point of transaction into multi-point delivery system right up to the customer door-steps. Retaining customers have become more challenging with new configuration of service quality.

Indian banking has witnessed a paradigm shift after the financial sector reform in 1991. The banks realised that profit will be under pressure with the introduction of prudential norms and asset classification (Gopalakrishnan, 2005). There was a clear shift on the emphasis from growth to profit; and on a clean, transparent and healthy balance sheet as opposed to the large-sized ones of the earlier years. As the foreign exchange and money markets were gradually deregulated, competition intensified; the net results of the bank will be under tremendous pressure. Now the banks are looking for new avenues to meet the challenges posed to them. They have realised that they had no option but to address the needs of the customers effectively to survive in the highly competitive market. Customer loyalty programmes are gradually made an integral part to face new challenges. The awareness has dawn that prompt, efficient and speedy customer service alone will tempt the existing customers to continue and induce new customers to try the services offered by an organisation. A lot of initiatives have already been taken up by the Indian banks in the present century to improve customer service. But results are available only in few urban and metropolitan centres. The Indian Banks have miles to go to capture the recent trends and to be at par with their Western counterparts.

In the changing banking scenario of 21st century, the banks have to have a strong identity to provide world-class services. The banks are now have to be of world-class standard, committed to excellence in customers, shareholders and employees' satisfaction, and to play a leading rôle in the expanding and diversifying financial sector (Balachandran, 2005). There has been a tremendous change in the way of banking in the last few years. Customers have also rightly demanded world class quality services from the banks. With multiple choices available, customers are not willing to put up with anything less than the best. Banks have recognized the need to meet customers' aspirations. So it is an urgent drive to move the bank up in the high tech ladder.

The banking industry is the repository of savings of a nation contributed by millions of people (Industry Snapshot, 2004). Thus a bank plays an intermediary role between savers and borrowers. Hence the margin of a bank arises out of the difference in interest paid to depositors and charged to borrowers. The Indian Banking Sector has been undergoing rapid changes. Regulatory, structural and technological factors are significantly changing the banking environment (Angur, Natarajan and Jahera, 1999). N. Vittal, the Central Vigilance Commissioner, in his talk delivered at BECON, Calcutta, 2001, highlighted that monetary and credit policy, macro economic policy, foreign investment policy and overall market environment are all putting pressure on the bank's margin. He put more emphasis by expressing that the main problem of Indian Banking system is nothing but, the non-performing assets (NPA).

Hence in the emerging environment two aspects become important: monetary and credit policy is for better corporate governance and the macro-economic policies for innovativeness and developing competitive edge.

The banking industry in India comprises scheduled commercial banks (SCBs), co-operative banks and regional rural banks (Shainesh and Sharma, 2003). The SCBs in India are classified as Public Sector Banks, Private Sector Banks, and Foreign Banks. The major commercial banks can be grouped into State Bank group, nationalized banks, foreign banks and other private banks. Further the private banks can be separated as newly formed and old private banks. Private sector banks gradually expanded the usage of banking services through Automated Teller Machines (ATMs), home banking, Internet banking and tele-banking. The three major external forces that affect competition in financial services industry are: increasing internationalization, change in the regulatory environment, and the accelerating impact and pervasiveness of information technology (Sachdev and Verma, 2004). There are three major tasks that a market oriented manager in financial service must accomplish. First one is identification of the key strategic success factors and building unique strategy of own accordingly. Secondly, the ability of making a system capable of creating and implementing plans built around the company's strategy. Thirdly, the manager must have the ability to use the free market forces in its departmental base and infuse and defuse it throughout the organization (Sachdev and Verma, 2004).

The banks have to change their thinking; and have to put the new innovations in the field of banking and customers' satisfaction at top of the list of priorities. As Tom Peters puts it → If you satisfy customers, you will make a lot of money. There must be a commitment to excellence and a willingness to put the customers first. They must be customer oriented and customer centric to make their dreams come true. It has rightly been said that "Customer – the Crown Prince of Today and Monarch of Tomorrow".

The success of any corporate initiative in customer service depends mainly on the men at the centres –says D.T. Pai, Chairman of Syndicate Bank (Pai, 2000). In his words, "Their commitment and concern for customer needs can make or mar the growth of the organisation. This is where the banks have a very important role to play. It is necessary that you educate the customers on new products and services being offered by the Bank. A personal touch is therefore vital to carry conviction. Further, in a highly competitive environment, retaining existing clients is as important as mobilising new customers. The mere realisation on your part that customer is just every thing in a service industry like banking will surely pave the way for customer delight in the months to come" (Pai, 2000).

Today, knowledge is power and the upgradation of skill and knowledge will enhance the quality of decision making at various levels and significantly improve the customer service in the banking sector. Advanced information technology (IT) ushering in the new millennium is bent upon delivering rapid changes demanding a repositioning by both individuals as well as industry as a whole. Those bearing apathy to learning and up-dating respective knowledge and marketing skills are bound to loose their ground. The growing vastness of the whole complexity is so enormous that imitating others too, may prove increasingly difficult in future, live alone the expedition to innovation. Thus, adoption of professional management practices with a vision is the need of the hour influencing the basic stance of organisational culture. At this backdrop, the banks have to link their job enrichment training programmes to individual potential development, individual promotions to his marketing ability, leadership placement to business advantage simultaneously keeping an eye on vibrant status of the bank as an organic whole (Divanji, 2000). In a nutshell, the bank has to optimally utilise the men and means at its disposal.

Indian banking system is transforming itself towards more commercial and customer oriented banking system, a clear departure from the time it was expected to play only social and developmental role (Raju, 1999). The marketing and technology orientation is throwing up new opportunities for the banking system. Cataclysmic structural reforms in Indian economic system following the Government's policy of economic liberalization and tumbling of trade barriers coupled with metamorphic liberalized policy in the financial sector in lines with Narasimhan Committee recommendations leading to replacement of regulated, over administered banking industry by greater degree of operational autonomy, triggered by competitive environment in the financial sector in the country with market forces deciding the future of banking and other financial institutions (Debasish, 2003). Public sector banks (PSB) having being recognized as harbinger of economic development and enjoyed hither to monopolistic position with over 80 per cent of market share are facing tremendous challenges stemming out of liberalization and globalization.

The banking industry in India has undergone a radical change in the last two decades. When the 90s saw the revamping of Banking industry and setting up of new generation private sector banks, the first decade of the 21st century will precedé a little further (Samal, 2005). Now the banking has become too open and competitive. The basic focus and direction has changed from a level of whatever business available to get every thing possible. Even the flow of business movement has changed from Customer's door bank to Banker's customers' doorstep. Earlier, a common man was thinking whether he can open a bank account and now every day one finds a sales/marketing trainee of some private bank approaching you (a big customer) with host of offers and requesting you to be their customer. Earlier, no banker easily agreed to nurse a small customer more so a small borrower. Now every bank boasts of being a retail bank. Today retail loans are sold and marketed like any other product (Haldipur, 1998). Every thing is now being sold under the umbrella of banking. Now banks are over enthusiastic to sell so called third-party products and substantial amount of fee based income by using their banner and services through existing customer relationships. They sell both life insurance and non-life insurance products in the name of Bank-assurance. They sell all mutual funds and issue credit cards. Bank's ATMs are now refilling mobile pre-paid cards of several companies. Banks have created a separate department to handle utility bill payments. Banks offer online railway ticket booking through internet. Recently, HDFC Bank has declared to sell gold bars through their counters and is going to issue co-branded credit cards with idea Cellular.

## INDIAN BANKING SYSTEM

The banking system is an integral sub-system of the total financial system. The Banking Regulation Act, 1949 defined banking as "accepting for the purpose of lending or investments of deposits of money from the public, repayable on demand or otherwise, and withdrawal by cheque, draft, order or otherwise". The Reserve Bank of India (RBI) is the apex body of the Indian Banking system and the nerve centre of the Indian financial system. The financial system functions as an intermediary and facilitates the flow of funds. It represents an important channel of collecting small savings from the households (surplus sector) and lending to the corporate sector (Khan, 2003).

Excessive government control and the inherent weakness of the banking system were realized in the late 1980s, which led to the reforms of 1991. The financial system was completely dependent and inefficient, and the situation was ripe for drastic reforms. During 1990 to 2000, the annual average growth rates of deposits and advances 16.1 per cent and 14.8 per cent respectively. The net profit of the banking system grew from Rs. 555.3 crores to Rs. 7306.4 crores as on March 31, 2000. The net profit of public sector banks stood at Rs. 15, 558 crore as on March 2005, recording a decline of 6 per cent over the previous year (IBA Bulletin, August 2005). The aggregate deposits of the commercial banks for 2004-05 (April-September) grew at 5.4 per cent compared to the previous year of 7.4 per cent and the advances grew at 9.3 per cent compared to 0.9 per cent in the previous year (Banking Trends and Progress, 2003-04). The Narasimham Committee has recommended many guidelines to strengthen the banking system in India. Slowly, the covers of protection were removed from the public sector banks and they are left to the market forces. Now most of the bankers have recognized the importance of the customers and in retaining them.

In late July 2004, a spasm of panic throbbed through the minds of millions of Indians when RBI ordered a three month moratorium on all accounts of the Global Trust Bank (GTB). The collapse of GTB has raised the issue in the minds of the customers: just how safe is my bank? Are public sector banks safer than private entities? If my bank goes under, how can I reclaim my money? (Outlook Money, August 2004). This indicates that the survival of the banks depends on customers' faith and confidence. In the latter part of the same year, it merged with Oriental Bank of Commerce (a Public Sector Bank). The customers have suffered a lot for the failure of GTB. In the same year (i.e., 2004), a foreign bank named Muscat Bank merged its Indian operations with Centurion Bank. Now Centurion Bank is planning to acquire Bank of Punjab as a step towards restructuring and growth. Many other banks are also planning to merge/consolidate to become strong and vibrant. The Finance Minister Mr. P. Chidamberam while addressing the 'century celebration' of Bank of India has indicated the consolidation of Banks in near future (*Times of India*, July 2005).

While supporting the financial and economic structure of our country, banking itself has undergone evolutionary process and revolutionary changes during last 25 years. The nationalisation of 14 major commercial banks in July 1969; followed by another six in April 1980 added new dimension to the role of commercial banks as catalysts in promoting the economic growth of India. The banks were called upon to shoulder new social responsibilities and there was a major change of the traditional concept of 'class banking' to the new concept of 'mass banking'. The post-nationalisation period witnessed spreading of commercial banks to unbanked rural and semi-urban areas reducing the density of banking coverage by reaching to the door-steps of common-man and diversifying the credit towards priority sector. Consequently, banking has seen massive growth in terms of size, business and profitability.

The mid-eighties saw the commercial banks consolidate the gains of expansion. At that point of time, 90 per cent of the commercial banks were in public sector and operated under protection regime and closely regulated by RBI. Banking sector becomes dependant and inefficient in the early 1990s because of the continuing financial profligacy of government with close control on its vital functions. It was a situation that called for drastic changes in the banking and financial sector to regain its vitality. In 1991, the Narasimham Committee recommendations were a milestone in the direction of reforms and brought about a total transformation in the banking sector. The reform process has seen several banks posting losses and some of them having their capital base eroded completely. But after initial pangs, banks are eventually coming to a surviving position in a competitive market and are looking a lot healthier than they were in the years of total control. The public sector banks registered a strong turnaround from the net loss of Rs. 371 core in 1995-96 to a net profit of Rs. 3100 crore in 1996-97. There after, they continued to be in profit and some of the weaker banks also have gained strength.

Today, banks can look back with satisfaction by having responded effectively the challenges put before them from time to time – whether of social control or of reforms. In future, the banks will have to adjust their system of functioning, venturing into new areas, improve efficiency levels by inclusion of trained and skilled manpower and restructure their organisations. Then only, they can face the challenges of the future more confidently and proactively.

## BANKS TO BRACE FOR COMPETITION

At a recent public meeting in Bangalore, Union Finance Mister asked bank employees to prepare themselves for an increased competitive environment. (TOI, 6th July 2005). He also hinted upon the consolidation of Indian banks to make them bigger banks of global size. 'Our biggest bank, State Bank of India, is ranked 82$^{nd}$ in the world'. The message was clear that there is no room for community banks, which are trying hard to be alive in the highly competitive environment. However, many old private banks insist that there is enough room for them to exist. Many of them focused on branch expansion and technology upgradation to prolong their existence. The competition according to them is still a number game. 'On one hand, there is a talk about consolidation, but on the other, government expressing the need for increased competition, which needs many players' (Banking Annual, *Business Standard*, 2004).

Cherian Varghese, CMD, Union Bank, said consolidation would benefit the consumer in the long run. The intense competition in the industry has kept the operational cost high, but consolidation would push this down. A lower operational cost would also enable banks to pay a slightly higher interest rate on deposits without affecting the current lending rate. Many public sector banks are not ready to accept this argument and are trying hard to enlarge their footprints outside their base and gearing up for the Basel II era (Banking Annual, *Business Standard,* 2004).

The New Private Banks entered into the banking business in India in the mid-nineties after the banking sector is opened for private participation. Till then public sector banks dominated the banking scene with reach and trust. As financial products are more or less similar, private banks can not compete on that front. Thus, private banks used service differentiation to take on public sector banks. The various service differentiators used by the *Private Banks* are as follows:

*Differentiating Offer:* The private banks offer some services by adding some special features to the offer. Free ATM services, home pick-up of cheques and demand drafts, free online banking services, sending account details through SMS are some of the feature those are added to the base product. These features can only provide them temporary advantage, but they can easily be replicated by the competitors. Thus, such benefit of differentiation could not last long as the public sector banks also followed the same route.

*Differentiating the Delivery of the Service:* By differentiating the mode of delivery, banks can differentiate their services. This can be done in three ways – people, physical evidences and the process. A bank can hire competent people and train them properly to deliver better customer service. It must be ensured that its personnel are responsive to the needs of the customers and take care of the individual needs. The employees need to understand customer needs and provide service accordingly. They also need to be courteous and patient while providing the service. Banks can also train their employees to deliver exceptional service to customers by customizing their products.

The banks can differentiate their services by creating an attractive physical environment. Ambience forms one of the key cues a customer considers in judging the qualities of the service provider. Therefore, banks should provide a good ambience to make customers feel comfortable. They can build facilities with air conditioning system, luxurious decor, and clean surroundings.

Differentiation also can be achieved through the process. Processes include the way a customer has proceeded to complete his transaction. Customers will prefer the banks, which provide them hassle free services. Banks can differentiate themselves in this regard by reducing the burden of the customer. This can be achieved by reducing the number of documents required to be furnished by the customers and also the time to process those documents. The internal processes should also be streamlined to provide quick and efficient service to the customers.

*Differentiating the Image:* Service can also be differentiated on the basis of the image. This can be achieved through branding and promotion. ICICI bank has been able to build a successful brand image in the minds of its customers. The bank roped in Amitabh Bachan as its brand ambassador to enhance its image.

## RECENT PERFORMANCE OF THE BANKS IN INDIA

In 2004, the Business Standard annual ranking provides that the public sector banks are far from the inefficient, stodgy, and stereotypes as they are perceived to be (Business Standard Annual Banking Survey, 2004). Both, the 'Best Bank of the Year'-Vijaya Bank and 'the Best Banker of the Year' – Mr. B.D. Narag, Chairman of OBC, are from the public sector. The message from the rankings also seems to be that size by no means is everything in banking, and there is plenty of scope for smaller players. Kotak Mahindra Bank has topped the list in terms of productivity and growth, Bank of America is seen to be the safest, Vijaya Bank tops the profitability, and HDFC Bank is the most efficient (BS Banking Annuals, 2004). The same year also, public sector banks continue to fly high, bagging six of the top 10 slots in the banking survey for 2003-04. Private Banks accounted for three slots, while the list includes a lone foreign bank. Public sector banks are doing what they have never done before to cater to the needs of individual customers. Today customer is the key (Bhattacharya, 2005). SBI has opened 69 'Personal Banking Branches' in different cities in India to cater to the needs of retail customers.

Foreign banks are no more keen to enter into Indian market. In fact, some have already left, and some are leaving or planning to leave within few years (Verma, 2002). There were 42 foreign banks operating in India, three of which have already closed their business and anther five are likely to shut down their shops in next three years (A & M, Feb. 2002). The market that global banks want to enter, however, is China (Verma, 2002). The expectations of banking sector reforms in Chinese market has a special advantage; what get announced, gets done. In contrast, India had offered to reform the banking system in early 1990s through its Banking Bills, it is in parts and proposes to recapitalise public sector banks via a reduction of Government's stake in them without shedding control. The public sector banks those have gone for public offer, have not furnished the details of kinds of shares being offered. Lack of privatization in itself is not the only complaint; what has been of greater concern is the non-performing loans of Indian banks — says Naina Lal Kidwai, Vice-Chairman, J.M. Morgan Staney (A&M, February 28, 2002).

## BANK CONSOLIDATIONS AHEAD

Consolidation stands for synergising business/regional strengths to cross the domain of Indian banking into the International arena converging global benchmarks (Sinor, 2005). The process of consolidation of banking institutions is very complex as different banks are operating in different systems with specific customer base. For smoothening the pace of change, it is necessary to examine the regulatory, legal, accounting, HR and technology related issues. Consolidation will provide banks new capabilities, technologies and products, help to overcome entry barriers, ensure immediate entry into new markets and lower operating costs through consolidation of resources (Purwar, 2005). Consolidation through mergers and acquisition may be required in future. Mergers and acquisitions in the domestic banking sector should be driven by market related parameters such as size and scale, geographical and distribution synergy, and skills and capacity (Singh, 2005).

Banks have had an easy time in the last few years, when steadily falling interest rates ensured that all banks had to do was to park their money in government securities and book the treasury profits that fell in their laps. This year the bond yields have moved up sharply and banks will have to go back to the hard work of making money on their loan books. The windfall treasury profits had also enabled the banks to make provisions for and write off their non-performing assets (NPAs), and bank balance sheets are now much stronger. But going forward, the turn in the business cycle could on the one hand add NPAs, while on the other banks would have less leeway to make provisions. With corporate sector looking to expand their capacity after a long investment drought, credit growth is set to zoom. Moreover, as the loan book increases, banks will also need more capital, and they will have to access the capital market. Also looming over the landscape is the brooding presence of Basle – II, which threaten to separate the men from the boys in the banking industry (editorial – Banking Annual 2004, BT).

Consolidation in the financial sector is an open challenge across the globe. Our thirst for global aspirations will compel us to invent invisible synergies of this dictum more visible in the near future (says Mr. P.S. Shenoy, Chairman, Indian Banks Association, 2005). A spiralling wave of consolidation across the globe has herald a sea change in the nature of financial sector as a move towards Basel – II norms. Consolidation is gaining its strength from competition that emanate not only amongst the banks but also from other segments of the financial sector.

The change in the business environment for banks is conducive for mergers and acquisitions (M&A), as banks try to squeeze out value through economies of scale and operation. To protect the interests of depositors in the recent past, few mergers have taken place. It should aim at helping the merged entity to become stronger and develop ability to withstand market shocks (Singh, 2005). Perhaps, more importantly, banking consolidation has received the blessings of the Government, which owns three-fourth of the banking industry in the country. It's therefore logical to think for consolidation of banks for best of their performance. In the west, the US banks have gained from consolidation in the 1970s and they surpassed the one-time strong banks of German and Japan. Now the Germany banks are toiling for their survival. The stories also in India are not new. The merger of New Bank of India with Punjab National Bank (PNB) some years back is a success story and it had helped PNB to rise to become the second largest bank in the public sector. Similarly, another success story is the recent takeover of Global Trust Bank by Oriental Bank of Commerce (OBC), where the former has gone to the drains. In future, information technology (IT) will play a major role in the programme of bank consolidations, as they can provide similar platforms for merger. Apart from that about 19 cases of mergers and amalgamations have taken place in the banking sector in India (Agarwal, 2005).

## SERVICE QUALITY PERCEPTIONS IN BANKS

Customer service is the primary end of any bank. A customer always wants something and expects that the bank should come up to the level to fulfil those needs. Again, the more you provide, still more the consumer needs. Service quality is about meeting customers' needs and requirements, and how well the service level delivered matches customer expectations. Service quality in banking implies consistently anticipating and satisfying the needs and expectations of customers (Howcroft, 1991). Raddon (1987) while emphasizing the importance of service quality in banks reported that 40 per cent of those customers switching financial institutions in the USA did so because of service problems. Improving quality in the eyes of customers paysoff for the companies that provide it. Data from the Profit Impact of Market Strategy (PIMS) research show that a perceived quality advantage leads to higher profits (Buzzell and Gale, 1987). Berry and Parasuraman (1991) also hold the view that high quality service gives credibility to the field sales force and advertising, stimulates favourable word-of-mouth communications, enhances customers' perception of value, and boosts the morale and loyalty of employees and customers alike. Heskett et al. (1990) observed that across a wide range of businesses, the pattern is the same: the longer a company keeps a customer, the more money it stands to make.

Increased competition, slower growth, and mature markets are also forcing many businesses to review their customer service strategy. Many businesses are channelling more efforts to retain existing customers rather than to acquire new ones. There is enough evidence that demonstrates the strategic benefits of quality in contributing to market share and returns on investment (Adrian, 1995; Bateson, 1995; Berry and Parasuraman, 1991; Buzzel and Wiersema, 1981; Reichheld and Sasser, 1990) and lowering manufacturing cost and improving productivity (Garvin, 1983; Kotler, 1999; Leonard and Sasser, 1982). Maximizing customer satisfaction through quality customer service has been described as "the ultimate weapon in all industries, when competitors are roughly matched, those that stress customer service will win." (Davidow and Uttal, 1989).

In today's competition in Indian banking industry, customers have to make a choice among various service providers by making a trade-off between relationships and economies, trust and products, or service and efficiency (Sachdev et al, 2004). Customers are increasingly aware of the options on offer in relation to the rising standards of service (Krishnaveni et al, 2004). In this context, expectations rise and customers become more critical of the quality of service. Service quality, customer satisfaction, customer retention and delight are now the major challenges in gripping the banking sector in India. Again, the deregulation in this sector created a great change in present scenario. In addition to the service diversification, the idea of customer satisfaction and formulation of marketing strategies to drag the customer towards the banks are now the key issues in order to survive (Aurora et al, 1997). Level of customer satisfaction is becoming the major target of banks to increase the market share. More specifically, the cost of retaining existing customers by enhancing the products and services that are perceived as being important is significantly lower than the cost of winning new customers (Krishnan et al, 1999). Customer satisfaction is nothing but an outcome of purchase and use resulting from the comparison of the rewards and costs vis-à-vis customers' expectations and actual performance of the product purchased in relation to the expected consequences (Anderson et al, 1994; La Barbera et al, 1983). Customer satisfaction is a measure of extent the existing bank is fulfilling the general expectations of a customer and how far and/or close does the existing bank come to the customer's ideal bank in his mind (Beerli et al, 2004). Customer satisfaction can be viewed as the future intentions of customers towards the service provider, which is more or less related to the attitude (Levesque T. et al, 1996). Recently, there has been a keen interest, especially in banking, where banks are looking at the life time value of the customer base rather than focusing on the cost of transactions (Ambler, 1995). Customers perceive services in terms of the quality of the service and how satisfied they are overall with their experiences (Zeithaml and Bitner, 2003). Satisfaction is the consumer's fulfilment response (Oliver, 2003). Customer satisfaction is influenced by price, product quality; service quality and brand image (Wirtz, 2002).

**Service Quality; The Key Factor in Satisfying Customers' Needs**

Parasuraman et al (1988) developed an instrument, called *Servqual* for assessing customer perceptions of service quality in service organizations. They gave a distinction between service quality and satisfaction by saying that perceived service quality is a global judgment, or attitude, relating to the superiority of the service, but satisfaction is linked to a specific transaction. It can be used in assessing customer expectations about and perceptions of service quality delivered by different banks. In a nutshell, customer perceived service quality is based on five factors, viz. core service/ service content, human element of service delivery, non-human element of service delivery (or, systematization), tangibles of service (service spaces), and social responsibility (Sureshchandar et al, 2002). The researchers suggested an instrument known as service quality index (SQI) to be used for the measurement of customer perceived service quality levels. The quality perceived in a service is a function of the gap between customer's desires/ expectations and the perceptions about the service that is actually received (Parasuraman et al, 1985). Gani and Bhatt, (2003) conducted a survey on banks in India in the area of customer expectations and perceptions in relation to service quality dimensions. The study gave the idea that the service quality of foreign banks figures high while as the service quality of Indian banks is comparatively low. Each bank has to match the expected service and the perceived service to each other so that customer satisfaction is achieved. Customers generally perceive a difference in the aspects of service quality which are influenced by employee actions. The frontline employee's perceptions of service climate are linked to the customers' perceptions of service quality (Shainesh et al, 2003; Krishnaveni and Divya Prabha, 2004). Here the six dimensions about the service quality taken are, competence, convenience, customer-orientedness, promptness of service, modernization, and communication. The results revealed that the service qualities still have to be improved and customers expect more monetary concessions in service charges. Customers would feel happier if any improvement in the service is made.

As electronic banking becomes more prevalent, nowadays customers are evaluating banks based more on their "high-touch" factors than on their "high-tech" factors in most of the developing economy like India (Angur et al, 1999). The unique selling proposition (USP) defined by Kotler (1997) of a bank still appears to be personal banking services. Angur et al (1999) conducted an empirical study to examine the performance of alternative measures of service quality proposed by Cronin and Taylor (1992), in India.

The internal perspective of service quality measurement is defined as zero defect-doing it right at the first time; where as external perspective gives the aspect in terms of customer perception, expectation, satisfaction, attitude and delight (Sachdev et al, 2004). The researchers found that in case of banking sector, the perceived performance is below "would be" level of performance in respect of reliability, responsiveness, assurance and empathy dimensions of service quality. Banks seem to have performed better in case of tangibility dimension.

Hallowell Roger (1996) conducted a research on customer satisfaction, loyalty, and profitability and found that as compared to public sector, private sector bank customers' level of satisfaction is comparatively higher. The operationalization of customer satisfaction in banking sector is somewhat hazy, and it should be operationalized along the same dimensions that constitute service quality (Sureshchandar et al, 2002).

Just as people cannot live without eating, companies can't survive without having satisfied customers (Gould, 1995). The author put more emphasis on the fact on making some of the customers much more than just satisfied. Service providers should exceed customers' expectations by considering three selective dimensions, viz. value, service, and dealing with complaints. Arora and Malhotra (1997) gave some idea about factors determining customer satisfaction, the level of customer satisfaction and some marketing strategies in both private and public sector banks in India.

A financial firm needs to focus on satisfaction with its offered product line in order to reap maximum gains in overall satisfaction (Krishnan et al, 1999). After making quality attribute analysis, the authors gave the idea that, in order to improve overall customer satisfaction, priority for the bank is the allocation of resources to increase the perceived quality of their product offerings. The researchers identified four quality attributes as being critical to determining satisfaction with product offerings, viz. product variety which creates customers to consolidate services at one place, ease of opening and closing of accounts, competitive interest rates and fees, and lucid information on all products and services. The research also suggests that the satisfaction with the quality of automated telephone and branch services and financial reporting have a significant impact on overall satisfaction, mainly for different customer segments.

According to Liang et al (2004), the service quality attributes are of two types; one is product related, and the other one non-product related. These two types of attributes may create the perception of functional benefits, symbolic benefits or experiential benefits among customers. The empirical research shows that there is no positive association between experiential benefits and customer satisfaction. But, the results strongly highlighted the fact that customer satisfaction positively affects customers' trust and commitment on service provider, which in turn affects customers' behavioural loyalty. There are many controllable variables, which can be considered to know other variables' effect on customer satisfaction and repurchase intentions.

In most of the regional rural banks, customer satisfaction refers to the customer judgment on marketing of bank products and/or services in rural settings by comparing pre-purchase expectations with accumulated experience with the banks having maximum transactions (Sharma et al, 2004). The customers having low income residing in rural areas are showing "just satisfactory" attitude towards all the rural banking services, where as those having higher income show "above average". In both the cases the level of satisfaction goes in descending order concerning to 4Ps' of marketing mix, viz. product, place, price and promotion respectively. The study suggests 5 steps of strategic action for rural banks, namely identification, measurement, creation, maintenance, and monitoring customer satisfaction by keeping higher level of rating in measurement scale.

**Employee—Customer Contact**

In the year of 2003, James Thomas Kunnanatt conducted a research study upon the behaviour and performance of branch managers of commercial banks in India to find out whether managers in tough competitive environments display type A behaviour pattern (TABP) in day to day transactions and also to know whether differences in managerial performance have any relationship with the distribution of type A behaviour among managers. The variable of "performance effectiveness" is defined as the degree to which a manager achieves the deposits and advance targets assigned to the branch under his/her charge. The second variable, "type A behaviour pattern" of the managers is measured by using the Lifestyle Questionnaire – a modified version of the Bortner Rating scale. The result of the study showed that the high – performing managers possess significantly more scores on certain TABP than their low-performing counterparts. The low performing managers are found to be showing relatively less type A behaviour, because they just do not want to be super performers at their bank. This study perhaps helps the regulators and policy makers in banking sector in dictating the lifestyles of the employees and executives living in the emerging economies.

There are so many examples demonstrating the unique determination of customer satisfaction variables by employees' characteristics (Mittal and Lassar, 1995 cited in George B.P et al, 2004). George and Hegde (2004) put much more emphasis on employee-customer contact in banks, particularly those in the frontline. According to the researchers, human capital is among the most major drivers of service performance. Employee satisfaction indirectly affects the customers' value perceptions about the overall quality of the product and the reliability of the service provider, thus giving clues to future transaction behaviour as well as relationship building.

**Service Quality and Profitability**

The profits of public sector banks in India are always under the pressure of the policies set by the authorities, not by the bank's management and hence the scope to improve the performance of the banks is limited (Bhatt et al, 1995). After the financial sector reform in 1991, capital restructuring, transparency and profitability have brought in most important and significant changes for banks in India (Satyanarayana, 1995). In public sector banks, a large degree of autonomy has been granted to the management of individual banks with overall control of the government. In the changing scenario of the Indian Banking Sector, a long-term analysis of total factor productivity (TFP) growth can provide some useful insights into the relationship between economic regulations and the banking sector's productivity growth (Bhattacharya et al, 1997). In order to survive in a fast paced dynamic environment, now banking firms are putting more stress on key success drivers, like better utilization of resources, process of delivering quality service to the customers and performance benchmarking. According to Mukherjee et al (2002), performance of a bank is generally conceptualized as the degree to which the bank is able to utilise its resources to generate business transactions, and is measured by their ratio, which is known as efficiency. In this concern, the concept of "efficiency" is generally used to benchmark "performance" of banks in use of multidimensional performance measurement. Analyzing productive efficiency in Indian Banking Sector is interesting especially after deregulation creating to trigger competition and enhance resource use efficiency (Kumar S. et al, 2002). Profits, in banking terms refers to the excess of interest spread over burden, whereas profitability is a ratio of net earnings to the total funds used (Debasish, 2002). A branch in a particular bank can be considered as a decision-making unit (DMU), whose efficiency is computed as the ratio between sum total of weighted outputs and weighted inputs (Choudhari et al, 2003). Performance management activity in a bank consists of three steps, viz. setting of performance standards, measuring and reporting performance, and evaluating performance (Mallya, 2003). All the banks in India can be evaluated on the basis of some key performance indicators published annually by RBI bulletin and hence they can restructure their strategies for future growth (Madhumathi et al, 2003).

**Performance Analysis**

The profitability of commercial banks depend on so many factors categorized as endogenous and exogenous (Bhatt et al, 1995).The authors define the endogenous factors as the representative of control of expenditure, banking business expansion, timely recovery of loans, and productivity; whereas exogenous factors include direct investments and directed credit programmes. Productivity of a bank can be measured in several ways, but the authors emphasized the ratio of credit to the establishment expenses. In their study, authors have highlighted how the productivity of banking system has been improved after the formation of Narasimham Committee (1991) and Chakravorty Committee (1984).

Apart from various classifications of banks in India, banks can be classified as category "A", "B", and "C" based on the profitability position (Satyanarayana, 1995). Author has suggested various strategies for enhancing the profit levels. According to him, the activity of deposit planning and monitoring should be replaced by profit planning system. All the bank units should treat themselves as profit and or centres. Banks have to be positioned in a better manner in the market by employing the technique of benchmarking. Each bank has to be cautious in diversification strategy. Management of banks at the Board level should be stopped if necessary. Lastly, author has suggested the capital restructuring strategies, particularly for "B" and "C" category banks.

Since most of the public sector banks in India are not free from economic restrictions, the objective of unconstrained profit maximization can not be applied for these types of banks and hence in order to measure the productivity, cost function analysis is appropriate in this situation (Bhattacharyya et al, 1997). According to authors, a long-term analysis of the total factor productivity (TFP) growth of public sector banks in India can give important insights in the context of government regulations and bank's productivity growth. The optimization problem of a public sector bank should have cost minimization as the objective function, given the output/input constraints. In India, deregulation activity contributed a lot for high rate of TFP growth creating a competitive environment.

The average efficiency results by ownership showed that, private banks have the highest efficiency figures with least variation, where as foreign owned banks have least average efficiency and maximum variation in India. The public sector banks in India are more efficient than foreign banks because of the larger customer base and widespread operational network as compared to small niche markets and less stable corporate resources in foreign banks (Mukherjee et al, 2002). According to authors, the identification of strategic groups in banking based on performance analysis can help individual banks in benchmarking with respect to competition.

The frequency with which an efficient bank shows up in the reference set of other inefficient banks represents the extent of robustness of the bank among the whole set of efficient banks; higher the frequency, the more robust it is (Chen and Yeh, 1998; Kumar et al, 2002). The research study conducted by Kumar S et al, 2002 revealed that, the technical efficiency in Indian public sector banking sector is found to be around 17 per cent, indicating the wider scope of improvement given the same inputs. The return on asset (a measure of bank's profitability) is a function of four broad parameters, viz. Liquidity of the bank (L), Return Performance (RP), Expense Parameters (EP), and Operational Efficiency (OE), (Debasish, 2002). Choudhari et al (2003) took bank data published in *"Business Standard"* magazine, December 2000 of 27 public sector banks to measure performance efficiency for different indicators, like profitability, productivity, liquidity, etc. The result showed that, Corporation Bank and Oriental Bank of Commerce are more efficient and can be used as benchmarks for improving the efficiency of other inefficient banks. The study on branch performance measurement system (BPMS) conducted by

Mallya (2003) revealed that around 80 per cent of the banks studied are implementing the standardization and comparison concept in their performance measurement system. Most of the banks are giving more importance to the routine process component of the service. Public sector banks need to redefine the customer service parameter in order to compete with the new Private sector banks.

In the dynamic age of today, there is a need to keep a constant touch with some of the key performance indicators published annually by RBI bulletin, so that all the banks can be evaluated on the basis of these key performance indicators and banks can restructure their strategies for future growth (Madhumathi et al, 2003). In their research study, the authors have identified 18 bank performance variables in terms of financial ratios published by RBI for the year of 2000-02 and concluded by saying that, most of the public sector banks although having wider access to customers, should go for investment in IT based infrastructure. All the private sector and foreign banks, although putting more emphasis in customer focus and quality, should spread their service branches geographically.

## THE PROBLEM TO BE INVESTIGATED

The recent years have witnessed significant developments in international banking. Competition, disintermediation, new services and unique promotion schemes are some of the emerging features of changing international banking scenario. The globalisation of financial markets has been facilitated by the progressive removal of controls and barriers to movement capital across the borders (Unification of currency and trade pacts among the European economy is one such example). This process has been further accelerated by the development of technology particularly in the field of telecommunication, information technology and electronic banking system. India is not far behind in this regard. It has made its laws flexible and liberal, allowed foreign banks to operate and progressively loosen the hackles in the path of smooth functioning of the banking sector. Now commercial banks in India are provided operational freedom and will be held accountable for their own results. Now the customers are also more informed and learned to choose a better bank for themselves. Again, on the managerial side, the Narasimham Committee has made a strong plea for full autonomy of the commercial banks in India with Reserve Bank of India as supervising and controlling authority. It has focused on overall competitive efficiency and profitability of the banks. As a consequence, the Indian banking which was operating in a highly comfortable and protected environment till beginning of 1990s has been pushed into the choppy waters of intense competition (Raju, 1999). At this backdrop, the major problem before the commercial banks, more particularly the public sector banks in India which were operating in a sheltered regime after nationalisation, is their long-run survival and forging way ahead by retaining their valued customers.

## SIGNIFICANCE OF THE STUDY

The financial reform process initiated in 1991, poses lot of challenges before the banking sector in India as never before. After nationalisation of commercial banks in India in 1969 and 1980, the ownership of major commercial banks was taken over by the Government. Then, the Government decided the agenda for action, directing the flow of credit and even determining the pattern of credit flows to specific sector (Joshi and Joshi, 1998). After nationalisation, competition was restricted and the banking sector was insulated from world financial markets. Over a period of time, the prevailing environment created a mindset, where one began to look for guidance for every thing. There was a comfort among the bankers when approval, guidance or confirmation of actions taken was received from the higher authority. The banking personnel have completely lost their vigour and stopped thinking and operating like business organisation.

A country without efficient and profitable financial markets suffers from multiple disadvantages in a more open world. When India opened up its financial markets in the early 1990s, the weaknesses in its financial sector were exposed. It was not able to attract foreign investment, suffered worst in real interest rates in an attempt to attract capital, riddled with the threat of capital flight and erosion of tax base. Another significant aspect is the gradual weakening of the financial base of the banks and over loaded with non-performing loans. In matters relating to adoption of technology and handling difficult issues like credit proposals and personnel matters; the public sector banks face the thorny path. The situation was further worsening with increasing competition because of the entry of new players and the impact of changing environment. In issues like changing the attitude of personnel and developing strategies for survival of both the strong and weak banks are more justified. All banks look back in order to learn from the corporate failures of the past while designing their future strategies, more so for the public sector banks.

With the entry of new generation tech-savvy private banks and the expansion of operations of foreign banks, the banking sector has become too competitive. The 'one for all' and 'all for one' syndrome is being given a go-by. To deal with the emerging situations, bankers have to shed a lot of old ideas, change in practices, develop customer loyalty programmes, and adopt a distinct approach to meet the challenges ahead. In a fiercely competitive market, non-price factors like customer service become more important (Kotler, 2003). Hence, it is desirable for banks to develop a customer-centric approach for future survival and growth. The awareness has already dawn that prompt, efficient and speedy customer service alone will tempt the existing customers to continue and induce new customers to try the services offered by a bank. Indian banks have already taken lot of initiatives in this regard. Further, it has been realised that Indians banks have miles to go to capture the recent trends and to be at par with the Western counterparts. As a result, many banks have introduced new customer friendly measures like 24-hour banking, 7-day and anywhere banking, internet banking, extended business hours, ATM network, etc. It is important to continuously build on this goodwill in the months to come.

In the light of the research findings, interest in service quality is, thus, unarguably high. Poor quality places a firm at a competitive disadvantage. If customers perceive quality as unsatisfactory, they may be quick to take their businesses else where. Thus, it is clear that service quality offers a way of achieving success among competing services, particularly in the case of firms that offer nearly identical services, such as banks, where establishing service quality may be the only way of differentiating oneself. Such differentiation can yield a higher proportion of consumers' choices and, hence, mean the difference between financial success and failure.

The success of any corporate initiative in customer services depends mainly on the men at the counters – said Mr. Pai, the Chairman of Syndicate Bank (Message to GIANT – in-house Journal Sept. 2000). Their commitment and concern for customer needs can make or mar the growth of the Bank. This is where the bankers have an important role to play. It is necessary that the customers should be made educated on new products and services introduced by the bank. A personal touch is therefore vital to carry the conviction. Further, in a highly competitive environment, retaining existing customers is as important as mobilising new ones. It is to be remembered that 'customer is just everything in a service industry like banking', will surely pave the way for customer delight in the months to come.

## OBJECTIVES OF THE STUDY

The main objective of the study is to analyse the data collected from the customers and bankers to understand their banking behaviour. The study has been conducted with the following specific objectives in view:

1. To analyse the present banking scenario of India *vis-à-vis* of Orissa;
2. To understand the factors that influence the customers' choice of one bank over the other;
3. To examine the expectation and perceptions of the customers regarding banking services;
4. To know whether the banks are at, above or below the perceptions of their respective customers in terms of quality;
5. To make a comparative study of perceptions of bankers relating to the service quality of the offers; and
6. To suggest, on the basis of study results, ways and means for improving service quality in banks with a view to make overall banking service more effective and efficient.

## RESEARCH DESIGN AND METHODOLOGY

Research design is the blueprint for the collection, measurement and analysis of data to arrive a conclusion. The study is mainly based on field survey and is exploratory in nature. The sources of data are mainly primary and data are collected through three questionnaires tailor-made for the purpose to collect the data from bankers and customers.

### Sample Profile

The present study has been conducted in the state of Orissa. The banks operating in Orissa were purposely selected for the present study. Data have been collected using a structured questionnaire and the respondents were approached personally. In order to seek fair and frank responses on quality of service in banks, both bank customers and officials were interviewed regarding the importance of service quality. Further, discussions were made on alternative services offered to customers, knowledge of costs and benefits of retaining customers relating to attracting new ones, bank's performance and future growth. Respondents (bank officials and bank customers) were asked to give their opinion about the level of quality of service delivered/received on a seven-point Likert scale (ranging from one indicating strongly disagree to seven indicating strongly agree).

The sample for the study comprises of 337 bank customers. While choosing a bank customer, the method of random sampling was followed. Principal demographic characteristics like age, level of education, level of income, occupation and geographic location of the bank were taken into consideration. All these characteristics have an important bearing upon bank customers' evaluation of service quality. In the same way data were collected from 157 bank officials constitute the sample for the study. Data for the study were collected by using three instruments; namely Customer Survey, Banker Survey and SERVQUAL with a view to measure the perceptions about the quality of service they are delivering to their respective customers. Bank officials were purposively selected for the present study as they play an important role in administering banking regulations besides marketing of bank services. While choosing bank officials, the method of judgement sampling was used. All other important factors' about bank officials like type of the bank, size of the bank and location of bank were taken into consideration while approaching the bank officials to fill up the questionnaires.

**Tools and Techniques for Data Analysis**

The data collected through various instruments are entered into an Excel spread sheet and then transferred to SPSS data sheet for further processing. Cross tabulations are made to understand the underlying relationships among the variable under study keeping the broad objectives in mind.

**T-Test**

To test whether or not the observed differences of two sample means drawn from independent populations are significant; is tested through t – test. The use of t – test is made when population standard deviation for either population is unknown or when one or both samples are small ($n_1 < 30$ or $n_2 < 30$). For using t – test following assumptions are required.

(i) Independent samples are drawn from two normal populations.

(ii) Population variances are unknown but equal.

The hypothesis may be stated as:

$H_0 \quad : \quad \mu_1 \quad = \mu_2$

$H_1 \quad : \quad \mu_1 \quad = \mu_2$ (Assuming a two-tailed alternative)

The test statistic is

$$t = \frac{(\overline{X}_1 - \overline{X}_2) - (\mu_1 - \mu_2)}{sp = \sqrt{\dfrac{1}{n_1} + \dfrac{1}{n_2}}}$$

with $n_1 + n_2 - 2$ degrees of freedom, where *sp* is an estimate of product standard deviation given by:

$$sp = \sqrt{\frac{(n_1 - 1)s_1^2 + (n_2 - 1)s_2^2}{n_1 + n_2 - 2}}$$

For given level of significance, the corresponding t-value with $n_1 + n_2 - 2$ degrees of freedom is obtained from t-distribution. If computed t (absolute value) exceeds tabulated t, the null hypothesis is rejected.

**Chi-Square Test**

The analysis of association between two cross tabulated variables by computing percentages can be carried out by using chi-square ($\chi^2$) tests of independence, which are categorised into two or more groups. This may be examined by testing the following hypothesis.

$H_0$ (Null Hypothesis) : The two variables are not related.

$H_1$ (Alternative Hypothesis) : The two variables are dependant.

To test the hypothesis, $\chi^2$-test of independence is applied. The observed frequencies are obtained from the survey data, whereas the corresponding expected frequencies are computed under the assumption that the null hypothesis is true. The contingency table for the expected frequencies for any cell ( *ij* ) is found as:

$$E_{ij} = \frac{R_i * C_j}{G}$$

where;

$E_{iij}$ = Expected frequency corresponding to the cell in the $i^{th}$ row and $j^{th}$ column

$R_i$ = Total of observed frequencies corresponding to the $i^{th}$ row

$C_j$ = Total of observed frequencies corresponding to the $j^{th}$ column

G = Grand total of frequencies

The chi-square is computed by using the following formula:

$$\chi^2_{(r-1)(c-1)} = \sum \frac{(O_{ij} - E_{ij})^2}{E_{ij}}$$

where;

$O_{ij}$ = Observed frequency of the cell in the $i^{th}$ row and $j^{th}$ column

$E_{ij}$ = Expected frequency of the cell in the $i^{th}$ row and $j^{th}$ column

and (r – 1)(c – 1) indicated the degrees of freedom where r stands for the number of rows and c for the number of columns.

For given levels of significance, the computed chi-square value is compare with the tabulated chi-square value. In case the computed chi-square is greater than the tabulated chi-square value, the null hypothesis is rejected to conclude that the variables are dependant.

**Correlation Coefficient**

The degree of association between two variables is computed by using correlation coefficient, denoted by 'r'. A measure of linear correlation coefficient between two variables X and Y is measured by correlation coefficient, the formula of which is given as:

$$r = \frac{\sum (X - X) - (Y - Y)}{\sqrt{\sum (X - X)^2} \sqrt{\sum (Y - Y)^2}}$$

where,

X = Sample mean for the variable X

Y = Sample mean for the variable Y

n = No. of observations in the sample.

This measure can assume any value between – 1 to +1 and is independent of units of measurements. The correlation coefficient can be computed for interval and ratio scale data. To test the significance of population correlation coefficient, we may use t-test described below:

$H_o$ (Null Hypothesis): There is no correlation between the two variables

$H_a$ (Alternative Hypothesis): There is correlation between the two variables

The test statistics used to test the hypothesis is given by:

$$t_{tn-2} = \frac{r\sqrt{n-2}}{\sqrt{1-r^2}}$$

where; r = sample correlation coefficient

N = sample size

**Factor Analysis**

How do customers evaluate banks? They often consider many variables for this purpose. Among these variables a customer measures a few which are more related to each other than they are to others. Factor analysis allows us to look at these groups of variables that tend to be related to each other and estimate what underlying reasons might cause the variables to be more highly correlated with each other (Jeff Miller, 2003).

Factor analysis is a general name denoting a class of procedures primarily used for data reduction and summarization. It is a multivariate statistical technique in which the whole set of interdependent relationships is examined. It is applied in several steps. At first instance the underlying dimensions that explain the correlations among a set of variables are identified. Then a smaller set of new uncorrelated variables are identified to replace the original set of correlated variables. After that a smaller set of salient variables are identified from a large set for use in subsequent multivariate analysis.

**Factor Analysis Model**

In factor analysis each variable is expressed as a linear combination of underlying factors. The amount of variance a variable shares with all other variables included in the analysis is referred to as community. The co-variation among the variables is described in terms of a smaller number of common factors plus a unique factor for each variable. These standardized, the factor model is represented as:

$$X_i = A_1F_1 + A_2F_2 + \ldots + A_nF_n + \ldots + V\ U$$

Where,

$X_i$ = $_i^{th}$ standardised variable.

$A_{ij}$ = Standard multiple regression coefficient of variable$_i$ an common factor$_j$.

F = Common Factor.

$V_i$ = Standardised regression coefficient of variable$_i$ an unique factor$_i$.

$U_i$ = The unique factor of variable$_i$.

m = Number of common factors.

The unique factors are uncorrelated with each other and with the common factors. The common factors themselves can be expressed as linear combinations of the observed variables.

$$F_i = W_1X_1 + W_2X_2 + W_3X_3 + \ldots + W_kX_k.$$

where,

$F_i$ = Estimate the $_i^{th}$ factor.

$W_i$ = Weight or factor score coefficient.

K = Number of variables.

It is possible to select weights or factor score coefficients so that the first factor explains the largest portion of the total variance. Then a second set of weights can be selected, so that the second factor accounts for most of the residual variances. This principle could be applied to select additional factors. Thus, the factors can be estimated so that their factors scores, unlike the values of the original variables, are not correlated. Further, the first factor accounts for the highest variance in the data, the second factor the second highest, and so on.

To test whether the problem is a suitable case for factor analysis or not, two conditions must are applied. They are:

(i) Bartlett's test of sphericity: A test statistic used to examine the hypothesis that the variables are uncorrelated in the population; where approximated value of Chi-Square must be significant; and

(ii) The Kaiser – Meyer-Olkin (KMO) measures should be more than 0.5.

## SCOPE AND LIMITATIONS

The present study on "Attitude and Perception of Customers towards Bank Marketing in India" is confined to the bankers and customers of commercial banks operating in Orissa. The sample for the study was 337 customers and 157 bankers, may not be a proper representation of the population. Because of paucity of time and cost, the study is done with a small sample base, hinders the generalisation of the results. Though the samples are selected through a random method, but due to non-cooperation from the respondents, finally data are collected from a purposive sample to represent the customers in age, sex, education, income and occupation variations. The data from the customer of private banks are mostly form urban areas, as they are only operating in seven cities/towns of the State. Similarly, the conservative attitudes of the female and aged respondents restricted proper representation of these groups in the sample. Lack of earlier researches in this field in Orissa, restricted the scope and direction of the present study. This is an one-time study having no reference to earlier studies, hence, relevance of the findings are limited without cross references.

## CHAPTERISATION

The present study is divided into seven chapters. The first chapter introduces the topic of research and outlines the objectives of the study, relevance, research design and methodology along with a brief review of existing literature. Chapter II makes a critical examination of the trend and progress of banking sector in India with special reference to Orissa to assess the role of banks in development of India. Chapter III deals with the theoretical aspects by defining marketing in banks in the context of growing need for attaining customer satisfaction and retaining the existing customers. It also examines concept service quality and its relevance in customer satisfaction.

Chapters IV, V, and VI are the analytical chapters based on primary data collected through different instruments. A detailed analysis of the customers' profile along with their perceptions and expectations relating to various banking parameters are presented in Chapter IV. The next chapter deals with the views of the bankers relating to various aspects of banking, the difficulties they encounter, assessment of customer satisfaction, analysis of competition, and the strategy for the future. Chapter VI defines and measures customer satisfaction by using the instrument known as *Servqual* by collecting the data from the customers. The last chapter is devoted for presenting the main findings of the study, suggestions for the future and concluding notes.

## REFERENCES

Ninan, Oommen A. (2005); "Future Shape of Banking", *The Hindu*, October 24, p. 17.

Agarwal, Shyamji (2005); "Consolidation in Banking Industry Through Mergers and Acquisitions", IBA Bulletin (Special Issue), January, Vol. XXVII, No. 1, pp. 100-105.

Angur, M.G., Nataraajan, R. and Jahera, J.S. (1999); "Service Quality in the Banking Industry: An Assessment in a Developing Economy"; *International Journal of Bank Marketing*; Vol. 17, No. 3; pp. 116-123

Armstrong R.W and Seng T.B. (2000); "Corporate-Customer Satisfaction in the Banking Industry of Singapore", *International Journal of Bank Marketing*; Vol. 18 (3); pp. 97-111.

Arora, Kalpana (2003); "Indian Banking – Managing Transformation Through Technology", *IBA Bulletin;* Vol. XXV, No. 3, March.

Aurora S. and Malhotra M. (1997); "Customer Satisfaction: A Comparative Analysis of Public and Private Sector Banks"; Decision; Vol. 24; Nos. 1-4; January-December; pp. 109-130.

Balachandran, M. (2005); "Strategic Model for Re-positioning of PSBs), *IBA Bulletin*, Vol. XXVII, No. 8 (August), pp. 5-8.

Beerli A., Martin J. D and Quintana A. (2004); "A Model of Customer Loyalty in the Retail Banking Market"; *European Journal of Marketing*; Vol. 38; No. 1/2; pp. 253-275.

Bhatt P.R. and Ghosh Rita (1995); "Profitability of Commercial Banks in India"; *Indian Journal of Economics*; Vol. 76(30); October; pp. 203-214.

Bhatt, Atul (1991); "Bank Marketing, Market Research and Indian Banks", *Prajnan*, January-March, pp. 45-55.

Bhattacharya, T.S. (2005); "Marketing and Personal Banking", *Business Standard* (August ), p. 2.

Bhattacharyya Anjana, Bhattacharyya Arunava and Kumbhakar Subal Customer (1997); "Changes in Economic Regime and Productivity Growth: A Study of Indian Public Sector Banks"; Journal of *Comparative Economics*; Vol. 25; pp. 196–219.

Banking Annual, *Business Standard* (2004); "Banking Round Table on Consolidation of Indian Banks Ahead", pp. 18-24.

Chidamberam, P. (2005); Addressed the Press on "Bank Consolidation Ahead", *Times of India*, July 6, 2005.

Choudhari Sanjay and Tripathy Arabinda (2003-2004); "Measuring Bank Performance: An Application of DEA"; *Prajnan*; Vol. XXXII; No. 4; pp. 287-304.

Davis, J.L. & Cohn, J. (1989); "Marketing of Financial Services in a Fragmented Market", *Journal of Bank Marketing*, (Jan.-Feb.), p. 25.

Debasish Sathya Swaroop (2002-2003); "Prime Discriminators of Profitability in the Indian Commercial Banks"; *Prajnan*; Vol. XXXI; No. 4; pp. 301-312.

Dhananjayan, G. (2005); "Services Marketing: Integrating People, Technology and Strategy", *Marketing Mastermind*, February, pp. 17-23.

Divanji, J.Y. (2000); as ED's Message to *GIANT- House Journal of Syndicate Bank*, Vol. XLII, No. 3 (July-September), p. 4.

Gani A and Bhat Mushtaq A (2003); "Service Quality in Commercial Banks: A Comparative Study"; *Paradigm*; Vol. VII; No. 1; January-June; pp. 24-36.

Garg, I.K. (1994); "Perspective on Banking in the Emerging Environment in India", *State Bank of India Monthly Review*, Vol. XXXVI, No. 9, September, pp. 466-476.

Garg, I.K. (1998); "Future of Banking in India – Key Issues", *State Bank of India Monthly Review*, Vol. XXXVII, No. 9, March, pp. 151-158.

Gavini, A.L. and Athma, P. (1997); "Customer Service in Commercial Banks – Expectations and Reality", *Indian Journal of Marketing*, Vol. XXVII, Nos. 5, 6 & 7.

George Babu P and Hegde Purva G. (2004); "Employee Attitude Towards Customers and Customer Care Challenges in Banks"; *The International Journal of Bank Marketing*; Vol. 22; No. 6; pp. 390-406.

Gopal Sundaram, C.R. (2001); "The Emerging Challenges for Banking Industry", *IBA Bulletin;* Vol. XXIII, No. 3, March.

Gopalakrishnan, S. (2005); "Customer Service and Grievance Redressal Mechanism", *The ICFAI Journal of Banking Law*, Vol. III, No. 4 (October), pp. 29-30.

Gould, Graham (1995); "Why It is Customer Loyalty that Counts (And How to Measure it)"; *Managing Service Quality;* Vol. 5; No. 1; pp. 15-19.

Haldipur, R. (1998); "The New Face of Retail Banking", *Indian Management*, (November), pp. 19-27.

Hallowell Roger (1996); "The Relationships of Customer Satisfaction, Customer Loyalty, and Profitability: An Empirical Study"; *International Journal of Service Industry Management;* Vol. 7; No. 4; pp. 27-42.

Industry Snapshot (2004): Private Sector Bank Industry; Report; October.

Jha, S.M (1989), "Innovative Marketing for the Banking Services", *Pigmy Economic Review*, pp. 01-08.

Jha, S.M. (2003); *Bank Marketing in India*, Himalaya Publishing House, Mumbai. pp. 1-5.

Kamath, K.M. (1979); "Marketing of Banking Services: Special Reference to Branches in Bombay City of Syndicate Bank", Unpublished PGDM Thesis, NIBM, Pune.

Karlapudy, P.C. (2005); "Managing Services in the New Millennium", As Quoted in Dhananjayan, G. (2005), "Services Marketing: Integrating People, Technology and Strategy", *Marketing Mastermind*, February, pp. 17-23.

Khan, M.Y. (2003); *Indian Financial System*, Vikash Publishing House, New Delhi.

Kothari, C.R. (2004); *Research Methodology – Methods and Techniques*, New Age International Publishers (P) Ltd., New Delhi, pp. 233-245.

Krishnan M.S, Ramaswamy V., Meyer Mary C and Damien Perception (1999); "Customer Satisfaction for Financial Services: The Role of Products, Services, and Information Technology"; *Management Science;* Vol. 45; No. 9; September; pp. 1194-1209.

Krishnaveni, R. and Prabha D. Divya (2004-2005); "Measuring Service Quality in Banking Sector: With Special Reference to Motor and Pump Industry"; *Prajnan;* Vol. XXXIII; No. 1; pp. 47-55.

Kumar Sunil and Verma Satish (2002-2003); "Technical Efficiency, Benchmarks and Targets: A Case Study of Indian Public Sector Banks"; *Prajnan;* Vol. XXXI; No. 4; pp. 275-300.

Kumar, Pawan (1999), "Private Sector Banks in India", *Indian Management*, (October), pp. 18-20.

Kunnanatt James Thomas(2003); "Type A Behaviour Pattern and Managerial Performance: A Study Among Bank Executives in India"; *International Journal of Manpower;* Vol. 24; No. 6; pp. 720-734.

Leeladhar, V. (2003); "Branch Banking—Its Future in India", *IBA Bulletin;* Vol. XXV, No. 3, March.

Levesque Terrence and McDougall Gordon H.G (1996); "Determinants of Customer Satisfaction in Retail Banking"; *International Journal of Bank Marketing;* Vol. 14, No. 7; pp. 12-20.

Levitt, Theodore (1960); "Marketing Myopia", *Harvard Business Review* (July-August); pp. 45-56.

Liang Chiung-Ju and Wang Wen-Hung (2004); "Attributes, Benefits, Customer Satisfaction and Behavioural Loyalty—An Integrative Research of Financial Services Industry in Taiwan"; *Journal of Services Research*; Vol. 4; No. 1; April-September; pp. 23-57

Lovelock Christopher, Wirtz Jochen and Keh Hean Tat (2002); "Services Marketing in Asia: Managing People, Technology and Strategy"; Prentice Hall; Singapore; pp. 173-188.

Madhumathi R and Kumar Lakshmi (2003-2004); "Multifactor Evaluation and Forecasting of Bank Performance in India"; *Prajnan;* Vol. XXXII; No. 4; pp. 317-331.

Malhotra, N.K. (2002); *Marketing Research: An Applied Orientation*, Pearson Education, New Delhi, pp. 585-601.

Mallya Prita D. (2003-2004); "Performance Management Systems in Banks"; *Prajnan*; Vol. XXXII; No. 3; pp. 243-256.

Mukherjee A., Nath P. and Pal M.N (2002); "Performance Benchmarking and Strategic Homogeneity of Indian Banks"; *International Journal of Bank Marketing*; Vol. 20, No. 3; pp. 122-139.

Murthy, NRN. (2003); "Reinventing Banking in India", *Bank Quest, The Journal of Indian Institute of Banking and Finance*, Vol. 74, No. 3, July-September.

Pai, D.T. (2000); "Moving Towards Customer Delight", *GIANT- House Journal of Syndicate Bank*, Vol. XLII, No. 3 (July-September), p. 1.

Pai, M.R. Banks and Customer Service, Bombay: All India Depositors' Association (Bombay Branch), 1976.

Parasuraman A., Zeithaml V.A and Berry L.L (1988); "SERVQUAL: A Multiple-Item Scale for Measuring Consumer Perceptions of Service Quality"; *Journal of Retailing*; Vol. 64; No. 1; pp. 12-40.

Prasad, B.R. (2001); "Improving Strength and Competitiveness of Indian Banks—Some Strategic Issues", *IBA Bulletin;* Vol. XXIII, No. 3, March.

Purushottaman, A. (2004); "Relationship Banking Holds the Key to Beat Competition in the Emerging Banking Scenario", *Bank Quest, The Journal of Indian Institute of Banking and Finance*, Vol. 75, No. 1, Jan.-March.

Purwar, A.K. (2005); "Consolidation Through Mergers and Acquisitions—Future Landscape of Indian Banking", *IBA Bulletin (Special Issue)*, January, Vol. XXVII, No. 1, pp. 5-8.

Raju, B.Y. (1999), "Looming Challenges to Banking", *Indian Management*, (November), pp. 21-27.

Ranade, M.P. (1985); "Marketing of Deposit and Allied Services to Non-residents", Unpublished PGDM Thesis, NIBM, Pune.

Sachdev S. B and Verma H.V (2004); "Relative Importance of Service Quality Dimensions: A Multi-sectoral Study"; *Journal of Services Research*; Vol. 4; No. 1; (April-Sept.); pp. 59-81.

Samal, S.R (2005); Interview Given to Students of IMIS, Bhubaneswar on 'Future of Indian Banking" *IMIS Newsline*, Vol. 10, No. 4 (August).

Satyanarayana K. (1995-1996); "Capital Restructuring and Profitability of Banks"; *Prajnan*; Vol. XXIV; No. 1; pp. 35-49.

Shainesh G and Sharma Tanuja (2003); "Linkages Between Service Climate and Service Quality—A Study of Banks in India"; *IIMB Management Review*; September; pp. 74-81.

Sharma R.D. and Kaur Gurjeet (2004-2005); "Strategy for Customer Satisfaction in Rural Banks—A Case Study of Shivalik Kshetriya Gramin Bank, Hoshiarpur"; *Prajnan*; Vol. XXXIII; No. 1; pp. 23-45.

Shastri, R.V. (2003); "Towards a New Banking Order", *IBA Bulletin;* Vol. XXV, No. 3, March.

Shenoy, P.S., (2005); Given in the Foreword of *IBA Bulletin*, January, Vol. XXVII, No. 1.

Sinor, H.N. (2005); Given in the Editorial of *IBA Bulletin*, January, Vol. XXVII, No. 1.

Singh, Dr. Dalbir (2005); "Consolidation in the Banking Industry: HR Challenges, Consequences and Solutions", *IBA Bulletin*, January, Vol. XXVII, No. 1, pp. 9-15.

Sureshchandar G.S, Rajendran Chandrasekharan and Anantharaman R.N. (2002); "Determinants of Customer-perceived Service Quality: A Confirmatory Factor Analysis Approach"; *Journal of Services Marketing;* Vol. 16; No. 1; pp. 9-34.

Sureshchandar G.S., Rajendran Chandrasekharan and Anantharaman R.N (2002); "The Relationship Between Service Quality and Customer Satisfaction: A Factor Specific Approach"; *Journal of Services Marketing;* Vol. 16; No. 4; pp. 363-379.

Swain, B.K. (2004); "Indian Banks in 2010: Emerging Scenario", *IBA Bulletin;* Vol. XXVI, No. 1, January.

Vittal, N (2002); "Challenges Before the Indian Banking Sector"; Talk Delivered at BECON; 16.01; Calcutta.

Chance, William A. (1975); *Statistical Methods for Decision Making*, D.B. Taraporevala Sons & Co., Bombay.

Levin, Richard I. and Rubin, David S. (2002); *Statistics for Management*, Pearson Education, New Delhi.

Malhotra, Naresh K. (2002); *Marketing Research – An Applied Orientation*, Pearson Education, New Delhi, pp. 585-595.

Zeithaml, V. A. and Bitner Mary Jo (2003); *Services Marketing: Integrating Customer Focus Across the Firm*; Tata McGraw-Hill Publishing Company Limited; New Delhi; pp. 83-118.

# CHAPTER–2

# TRENDS AND PROGRESS OF BANKING SECTOR IN INDIA

## INTRODUCTION

India launched a programme of stabilization and structural reforms in 1991-92 with the prime objective of improving the productivity and efficiency of the entire economic system and imparting greater competitive and structural flexibility. Reform of the financial sector constitutes a crucial component of India's programme towards economic liberalization (Rangarajan, 2003).

India has long been characterized by a dense network of financial institutions. Since independence in 1947, an active promotional role has been played by the Government, led by the Reserve Bank of India (RBI) in setting up financial institutions. Today, in addition to the RBI, the banking network includes commercial and cooperative banks, national and state level development banks, and host of other non-banking financial institutions.

The commercial banking system has been progressively nationalized over the years, starting with the creation of State Bank of India in 1955 and subsequent nationalization of fourteen major commercial banks in 1969 and six more in 1980. Foreign banks, many of which have operated in India from colonial times, were not nationalized but there were restrictions on branch growth, and on entry of new foreign banks. After liberalization of financial sector in 1991, these restrictions were eased and foreign Banks today account for about 8 per cent of bank deposits. Since 1969, there has been a massive expansion in the scale and geographic coverage of the banking system.

**EVOLUTION OF BANKING**

The system of banking in its most simple form is as old as civilization. The genesis of modern banking can be traced to the Bank of Venice, which was established in 1157 A.D. and served as an institution for transfer of public debt. There are also references to "Monte" (meaning a standing bank or mount of money) in Florence in 1336. The primary function was exchange of money, receiving deposits and discounting bills of exchange, both for the citizen and for the foreigners. Successively in 1407, the Bank of Genoa was established. In the first decade of 17th Century, the Bank of Amsterdam was established. Most of the European banks those are now prevalent, which were initially planned to meet the needs of the merchant class. The concept of "Cheque" originated from the practice of this bank under which a depositor received a kind certificate entitling him to withdrawn, on demand, his deposits on transfer the money from one account to another.

The initial form of banking was granting credit to the people at an exorbitant rate of interest. As early as 2000 B.C. Babylonians had developed a system of Banks. In ancient Greece and Rome the practice of granting credit was widely prevalent. Traces of credit by compensation and by transfer orders are found in Assyria, Phoenicia and Egypt before the system attained full development in Greece and Rome. In Rome the bankers were called Argentarii, Mensarii or Collybisoe and the banks were called Tabernoe Argentarioe. Some of the banks carried business on their own account and others were appointed by the Government to receive the taxes. They used to transact their business on similar lines as those of the modern Bankers. These bankers were engaged in receiving deposits lending money, the money being lent on the security of land. Private individuals did much of the banking business.

Indigenous banking is an age-old tradition in India. The evidence of money lending operations was found since *Vedic* times. *Shresties* or bankers were in existence during *Buddhist* period

(Kumar, 1999) in all the trade centres and of their wide-spread influence in the life of the community (Panadikar, 1998). The principal activity was to lend money to traders, to merchant-adventures who went to foreign countries against the pledge of movable and immovable property. The rules and regulations concerning credit was first mentioned in the works of saint *Manu*. *Manu Sanghita* contains references regarding laws governing credit and the use of credit instruments in judicial proceedings along with concepts of interest on loans on bankers, customers, and even the renewal of commercial papers. Further, in his book there are references regarding deposits, pledges, and policies of loans and rates of interest, which was in existence in 2nd and 3rd century B.C. Kautilya's *Arthashastra* laid down the maximum legal rate of interest on secured and unsecured loans, which may go to the maximum extent of 240 per cent per annum depending upon the depending upon the risk portfolio.

*Hundis* or indigenous bills of exchange came into use from the 12$^{th}$ century, which appears from the writings of few Muslim historians, European travellers, and State records (Panadikar, 1998). *Ain-i-Akabari* indicated that indigenous bankers have played a prominent part in lending money, financing internal and foreign trade with cash or bills, and giving financial assistance to rulers during periods of stress. During the Mogul period, the issue of various kinds of metallic money in different parts of the country gave the indigenous bankers great opportunities for developing a profitable business of money changing. The most important of them is the appointment of mint officers, revenue collectors, and the bankers in various parts of the empire. Many of them wielded great influence in the country, and those among them known as the *Jagat Sheths* (world bankers) in the 17th and 18th centuries, possessed great power as private bankers. The indigenous bankers, however, could not develop a system of obtaining deposits from the public and paying the interests regularly. The reasons seem to be that many of them had combined trade with banking business. This combination reduced the stability of their banking business, and produced an unfavourable reaction upon banking development in India. The inexperience of Indians of financing the trade and commerce was also exploited by the Britishers.

Therefore, although the East India Company established connections with these bankers, borrowed funds from them and for the first few years collected a portion of land revenue through them, the English Agency Houses in Calcutta and Bombay began to conduct banking business besides their commercial business.

The English Agency Houses began to serve as bankers to the East India Company, the members of the services, and the European merchants in India. They financed the movement of crops, issued paper money, and paved the way for the establishment of joint stock banks. The earliest of these was the Hindustan Bank, which was established in 1770 by one of the agency houses in Calcutta and its business was closely connected with these houses. But it was wound up in 1832, when the firm of Alexander and Company, with which it was intimately connected, failed. The Bengal Bank and the General Bank of India were established about 1785. The latter was voluntarily liquidated in 1791 owing to inability to earn profits, and the former failed a little later owing to a severe run upon it caused by the temporary reverses inflicted upon the company by Tipu Sultan. These Banks were chartered by the East India Company, and were followed by banks established under the Acts of the Indian Legislature. The latter may be divided into two groups, the first consisting of the three Presidency Banks amalgamated into the Imperial Bank of India in 1920, and the second, of the Indian joint stock banks.

The Bank of Bengal, the first of the Presidency Banks, was established in 1806 as the Bank of Calcutta, and received its charter as the Bank of Bengal in 1809.The East India Company became a share holder of the bank by contributing £100,000 which was one-fifth of the banker's capital and obtained the right to appoint three of its directors. In 1803 the bank was allowed to issue notes, and in 1839 to open branches and to deal with inland exchange, but not in foreign exchange. The Banks of Bombay and Madras were established in 1840 and 1843, with a share capital of Rs. 50 lakhs and Rs. 30 lakhs respectively, out of which the East India Company provided Rs. 3 lakhs in each case and obtained the right to appoint to appoint some of their directors. Their secretaries and treasurers were members of ICS. Both the Banks are allowed to issue notes up to a certain amount. The bulk of the shares of all the three banks were subscribed by the Europeans. In 1862 their right of note issue was taken over by the Government, and as compensation they were given the use of Government balances in the Presidency towns free of charge.

## NATIONALISATION OF COMMERCIAL BANKS

The first phase of nationalisation started with the nationalisation of State Bank of India in 1955. Then Life Insurance Corporation was created by nationalising the existing private insurance companies in India. In the late 1960's there was a feeling among the policy-makers and the Central Government that the Indian banks which have a vital role to play in economic growth had given little priority to the credit requirements of the small scale sector, agriculture sector and export sector. Nationalisation was aimed to give priority status to these neglected sectors, and this credit facility was to be rendered at considerably low interest rates. In the first phase of bank nationalization, fourteen major Indian banks with a minimum deposit of Rs. 50 crore each on the last Friday of June 1969 were identified and the Central Government acquired the undertaking of these banks. These 14 banks had a total deposit of Rs. 2741.76 crores.

The broad aims of nationalization of banks as stated in the preamble to the Banking Companies (Acquisition and transfer of undertakings) Act 1970 are to control the heights of the economy and to meet progressively and serve better the needs of development of the economy in conformity with national policy and objectives. The important objectives of bank nationalization can be stated as: widening the ownership base of the banks (publicly owned); provisions for adequate and cheap credit to neglected sector like SSI, exports and agriculture; induction of professionalism in bank management; encouraging a new set of entrepreneurs and streamlining the regulation regarding training and service conditions for bank staff.

On the 18th July 1970 the Central Government constituted the first Board of Directors for each of the nationalized bank. The scheme governing the composition and appointments of the Board of Directors is called Nationalised Banks (Management and Miscellaneous) Scheme, 1970. Under this scheme, each of the nationalized banks will have a board constituting directors of maximum 15 in number. The board should consists of representatives of the employees (two), depositors (one), officials of the RBI and Central Government (one each) and such other persons as may represent the interest of each of the following categories viz. formers, workers and artisans (one representative from each group). There will be whole time directors, of whom one shall be the managing director. The Government is empowered to appoint a maximum of 5 directors from amongst persons having special knowledge or practical experience in commercial banking. Compensation was paid to each of the 14 limited companies whose undertakings were acquired. A fixed amount was to be paid to each of the 14 nationalised banks within 60 days from the date the banking company applies for it.

Eleven years after the nationalization of fourteen commercial banks, the Government on April 15, 1980 took over six more scheduled commercial banks, each with demand and time liabilities exceeding Rs. 200 crore. These banks are: Andhra Bank, Punjab and Sindh Bank, New Bank of India, Vijaya Bank, Oriental Bank of Commerce and Corporation Bank. The decision to nationalize these banks was guided mainly by two considerations; first, to help in implementing the 20-Point Programme particularly in raising the share of advances to priority sectors from 33.3 per cent to 40 per cent over the period of next five years and secondly, to have effective control over the credit policy implementation of the banking system as a whole.

## GROWTH AND DEVELOPMENT OF BANKING SYSTEM IN INDIA

In order to understand present make up of banking sector in India and its past progress, it will be fitness of things to look at its development in a somewhat longer historical perspective. The past four decades and particularly the last two decades witnessed cataclysmic change in the face of commercial banking all over the world. Indian banking system has also followed the same trend. In over five decades since independence, banking system in India has passed through five distinct phase, viz.

| | |
|---|---|
| Evolutionary phase | (Prior to 1950) |
| Foundation phase | (1950-68) |
| Expansion phase | (1968-84) |
| Consolidation phase | (1984-90) |
| Reformatory phase | (since 1990) |

**Evolution Phase: Prior to 1950**

Enactment of the Reserve Bank of India Act, 1935 gave birth to scheduled banks in India, and some of these banks had already been established around 1981 were under the definition. The prominent among the scheduled banks is the Allahabad Bank, which was set up in 1865 with European management. The first bank which was established with Indian ownership and management was the Oudh Commercial Bank, formed in 1881, followed by the Ajodhya Bank in 1884, the Punjab National Bank in 1894 and Nedungadi Bank in 1899. Thus there were five Banks in existence in the 19th century. During the period 1901-14, twelve more banks were established, prominent among which were the Bank of Baroda (1906), the Canara Bank (1906), the Indian Bank (1907), the Bank of India (1908) and the Central Bank of India (1911).

Thus, the five big banks of today had come into being prior to the commencement of the First World War. In 1913, and also in 1929, the Indian Bank faced serious crises. Several banks succumbed to these crises. Public confidence in banks received a jolt. An important point to be noted here is that no commercial bank was established during the First World War, while as many as twenty scheduled banks came into existence after independence – two in the public sector and one in the private sector. The United Bank of India was formed in 1950 by the merger of four existing commercial banks. Certain non-scheduled banks were included in the second schedule of the Reserve Bank. In view of these facts, the number of scheduled banks rose to 81. Out of 81 Indian scheduled banks, as many as 23 were either liquidated or merged into or amalgamated with other scheduled banks in 1968, leaving 58 Indian schedule banks. The age-wise distribution of these 58 Indian scheduled banks is given in Table 2.1.

**Table 2.1: Age-wise Distribution of Indian Scheduled Banks**

| Sl. No. | Established During | No. of Banks |
|---|---|---|
| 1. | 19th Century | 2 |
| 2. | Pre-First World War | 14 |
| 3. | Inter-War Period | 21 |
| 4. | Second World War | 3 |
| 5. | Post-Second World War | 18 |
| | **Total** | **58** |

It may be emphasized that banking system in India came to be recognized in the beginning of 20th century as powerful instrument to influence the pace and pattern of economic development of the country. In 1921 need was felt to have a State Bank endowed with all support and resources of the Government with a view to helping industries and banking facilities to grow in all parts of the country. The Imperial Bank of India was formed to accomplishment of this objective by amalgamating the three Presidency Banks. The role of the Imperial Bank was envisaged as to extend banking facilities, and to render the money resources of India more accessible to the trade and industry of this country, thereby promoting financial system which is an indisputable condition of the social and economic advancement of India. Until 1935, when RBI came into existence to play the role of Central Bank of the Country and regulatory authority for the banks, Imperial Bank of India played the role of a quasi-central bank. It was by making it the sole repository of all its funds and by changing the volume of its deposits with the Bank as and when desired by it, the Government tried to influence the base of deposits and hence credit creation by Imperial Bank and by rest of the banking system.

Thus, the role of commercial banks in India remained confined to providing vehicle for the community's savings and attending to the credit needs of only certain selected and limited segments of the economy. Bank's operations were influenced primarily by commercial principle and not by developmental factor. Failure of banks was common as governance in privately owned joint stock banks left much to be desired.

**Foundation Phase: 1948-68**

The banking scenario prevalent in the country during the period 1948-68 presented a strong focus on class banking on security rather than on purpose. The emphasis of the banking system during this period was on laying the foundation for a sound banking system in the country. Banking Regulating Act was passed in 1949 to conduct and control operations of the commercial banks in India. Another major step taken during this period was the transformation of Imperial Bank of India into State Bank of India and a redefinition of its role in the Indian economy, strengthening of the co-operative credit structure and setting up of institutional framework for providing long-term finance to agriculture and industry. Banking sector, which during the pre-independence India was catering to the needs of the government, rich individuals and traders, opened its door wider and set out for the first time to bring the entire productive sector of the economy-large as well as small, in its fold.

**Table 2.2: Number of Commercial Banks during 1951-68**

| Particulars | December 1951 | December 1956 | December 1968 |
|---|---|---|---|
| Scheduled Banks | 92 | 89 | 71 |
| Non-Scheduled Banks | 474 | 334 | 210 |
| **Total** | **566** | **423** | **281** |

During this period, the number of commercial banks declined remarkably (Table 2.2). There were 566 scheduled and non-scheduled banks as on December 1951. Of this, 92 were scheduled banks and the rest 474 were non-scheduled banks. This number went down considerably to 281 at the close of the year 1968. The sharp declined in the number of banks was mainly due to continuous fall in the number of non-scheduled banks, which touched an all time low level of 210.

The banking scenario prevalent in the country up-to-the year 1968 depicted a strong stress on class banking based on security rather than on purpose. Before 1968, only Reserve Bank of India (RBI), State Bank of India (SBI) and Associate Banks of SBI were mainly controlled by Government. Some associates were fully owned subsidiaries of SBI and in the rest; there was a very small shareholding by individuals and the rest by RBI.

**Expansion Phase: 1968-84**

This phase witnessed socialization of banking in 1968. Commercial banks were viewed as agents of change and social control. However, inadequacy of social control soon became apparent because all banks except the SBI and its seven associate banks were in the private sector and could not be influenced to serve social interests. Therefore, banks were nationalized (14 banks in 1969 and 6 banks in 1980) in order to control the heights of the economy in conformity with national policy and objectives. This period saw the birth and the growth of what is now termed as directed lending by banks. It also has seen commercial banking spreading across the country with great pace; with which a number of poverty alleviation and employment generating schemes were sought to be implemented through commercial banks. Thus, this period was characterized by the death of private banking and the dominance of social banking over commercial banking. It was hardly realized that banks were organizations with social responsibilities but not social organizations. This period also witnessed the birth of Regional Rural Bank (RRBs) in 1975 and establishment of NABARD in 1982, which had priority sector as their focus of activity.

Although number of commercial banks declined from 281 in 1968 to 268 in 1984, number of scheduled banks shot up from 71 to 264 during the period. The number of non-scheduled banks registered perceptible decline from 210 to 4 during the period under reference. The rise in the number of scheduled banks was, as stated above, due to the emergence of RRBs.

The fifteen years following the bank nationalization in 1969 were dominated by the Banks' expansion at a path breaking pace. As many as 50,000 bank branches were set up; three-fourths of these branches were opened in rural and semi-urban areas. Thus, during this period a distinct transformation of far reaching significance occurred in the Indian banking system as it assumed a broad mass base and emerged as an important instrument of socio-economic changes. Thus, with growth came inefficiency and loss of control over widely spread offices. Moreover, retail lending to more risk-prone areas at concessional interest rates had raised costs, affected the quality of assets of banks and put their profitability under strain. The competitive efficiency of the banks was at a low end. Customer service became least available commodity. Performance of a bank/banker began to be measured merely in terms of growth of deposits, advances and other such targets and quality became a casualty.

**Consolidation Phase: 1985-90**

A realization of the above weaknesses thrust the banking sector into the phase of consolidation. This phase began in 1985 when a series of policy initiatives were taken with the objectives of consolidating the gains of branch expansion undertaken by the banks, and of relaxing albeit marginally, the very tight regulation under which the system was operating. Although number of schedule banks increased from 264 in 1984 to 276 in 1990, branch expansion of the banks slowed down. Hardly 7000 branches were set up during this period. For the first time, serious attention was paid to improving housekeeping, customer services, credit management, staff productivity and profitability of the banks and concrete steps were taken during this period to rationalize the rates of bank deposits and lending. Measures were initiated to reduce the structural constraints, which were then inhibiting the development of money market.

By this time about 90 per cent of commercial banks were in the public sector and closely regulated in all its facets. Prices of assets and liability were fixed by the RBI; prices of service were fixed uniformly by the Indian Banking Association (IBA); composition of assets was also somewhat fixed in as much as 63.5 per cent of bank funds were mopped up by CRR and SLR and the remained was to directed towards priority sector leading and small loaning; salary structure was negotiated by the IBA and validated by the Government. Thus, there was no autonomy in vital decisions. Commercial approach in operations and drive towards efficiency was almost non-existent. The result was that during this period, the banks ended up consolidating their losses rather than the gains.

**Reformatory Phase: 1991 and Onwards**

Continued financial profligacy of the Government coupled with close monitoring and control rendered the financial systems completely dependent and inefficient so much so that by the year 1991, the situation was ripe for drastic reforms. It was, however, precipitated by the unprecedented economic crisis, which engulfed the economy in 1991. For the first time in its history, India faced the problem of defaulting on its international commitments. The access to external commercial credit markets was completely denied; international credit ratings had been downgraded and the international financial community's confidence in India's ability to mange its economy had been severally eroded. The economy suffered from serious inflationary pressures, emerging scarcities of essential commodities and breakdown of fiscal discipline.

In the year 1991, another historic event took place in the annals of Indian banking with the appointment of a high level committee headed by Mr. M. Narasimham to examine the existing financial system and to recommend measures to improve its efficiency and effectiveness. Till that date Govt. of India (GOI) talks about control and social welfare for the banks. But as the financial viability of the banks were at stake, GOI for the first time talked about efficiency and effectiveness indicating a new phase of reforms for the Indian banks. The first out come of this was merger of a weak public sector bank New Bank of India with 'Punjab National Bank' in the year 1993 reducing the number of public sector banks to 27. In the same year, Reserve Bank of India issued guidelines as per the recommendations of Narasimham Committee for setting up new private sector banks in India. This has led to the establishment of new banks like Bank of Punjab, HDFC Bank, UTI Bank, ICICI Bank, etc. along with the existing private banks like Federal Bank, J&K Bank, Vyasya Bank, etc. Many of the private banks born at that phase has grown stronger and few of them are no more. (Global Trust Bank has merged with Oriental Bank of Commerce in the year, 2004).

The Government took swift action to restore international confidence in the economy and redress the imbalances by initiating various macro economic structural reformatory measures in the field of foreign trade, tax system, industrial policy and financial and other sectors. The objective was to improving the underlying strength of the economy and furthering the fundamental developmental objectives of growth with equity and self-reliance.

South-East Asia crisis, mounting non-performing loans (Rs. 40,000 crore at a point of time), over-staffing by 40 per cent (as estimated by GOI), lack of legal infrastructure for recovery of loans, duplication of branch network, over-banked geographical terrain calling for branch closure, etc. are some of the major developments at the end of 20th century. Some other crisis of the banking system are lack of autonomy rubbing of banks from quick decision making, completely outdated systems needing technological support and changes in the domestic and international scenario. Further, the need for review of recommendations of Narasimham Committee was felt for the Indian banking and financial system. At the back drop of these crises, the second generation of reforms start in the year 1998 with the constitution of Narasimham Committee II. It has made a series of recommendations those are being used as a launching pad to take Indian banking sector further ahead. The changes made during the last four decades have transformed the banking scene in the country beyond recognition. The banks have not only grown in size, but they have become robust by changing their scope of functioning and integrating themselves to the global changes.

Indian banking system has been subject to widespread structural reforms initiated since June 1991. This phase can be regarded as "second banking revolution". During this phase, reform measures such as introduction of new accounting and prudential norms, liberalization measure etc., are heading towards a truly competitive and well-structured banking system resilient from an international perspective. These have spurred the dynamics of Indian banking sector in all the fields. State Bank of India has become the first universal bank in 2004 followed by ICICI Bank. Now India is boasting of joining the bandwagon of universal bank elsewhere in United States, Europe, and Japan. The consolidated balance sheet of the scheduled commercial banks has shown substantial growth since the dawn of this century.

**Table 2.3: Summary of the Indian Banking Industry: (1990-91 to 2000-01)**

| Year/Bank Group | 1990-91 | | | 1995-96 | | | 2000-01 | | |
|---|---|---|---|---|---|---|---|---|---|
| | Pub. | Pvt. | Forg | Pub. | Pvt. | Forg | Pub. | Pvt. | Forg |
| No. of Banks | 28 | 25 | 23 | 27 | 35 | 29 | 27 | 32 | 41 |
| Total Deposits (Rs. Billion) | 2087.3 | 64.3 | 84.5 | 3908.2 | 361.7 | 306.1 | 8593.8 | 1349.2 | 591.9 |
| Total Credit (Rs. Billion) | 1305.7 | 49.5 | 50.6 | 2075.4 | 219.3 | 225.0 | 4146.3 | 672.1 | 429.9 |
| Credit-deposit ratio | 0.63 | 0.52 | 0.60 | 0.53 | 0.61 | 0.75 | 0.48 | 0.50 | 0.73 |
| Share of Total Deposits (%) | 92.1 | 4.2 | 3.7 | 85.4 | 7.9 | 6.7 | 81.6 | 12.8 | 5.6 |
| Total Income (Rs. Billion) | 240.4 | 10.4 | 15.3 | 536.7 | 71.8 | 74.99 | 1034.9 | 163.9 | 119.8 |
| Net Profit (Rs. Billion) | 4.7 | 0.4 | 1.5 | –3.3 | 15.9 | 7.4 | 43.2 | 12.3 | 10.2 |

*Notes:* PUB-Public Sector Banks; PVT-Private Sector Banks; Forg-Foreign Banks.

Table 2.4: Consolidated Balance Sheets of Commercial Banks in India

(Amt. in Rs. Billions)

| Sl. No. | Items | Public Sector Banks | | | | Private Sector Banks | | | | Foreign Banks | | | |
|---|---|---|---|---|---|---|---|---|---|---|---|---|---|
| | | 2003 | | 2004 | | 2003 | | 2004 | | 2003 | | 2004 | |
| | | Amt. | % | Amt. | % | Amt. | % | Amt. | % | Amt. | % | Amt. | % |
| 1. | Capital | 141.75 | 1.10 | 146.76 | 1.00 | 29.21 | 0.98 | 30.28 | 0.82 | 44.98 | 3.86 | 46.45 | 3.41 |
| 2. | Reserves and Surplus | 514.08 | 4.00 | 645.49 | 4.39 | 159.75 | 5.38 | 194.91 | 5.31 | 89.06 | 7.63 | 102.01 | 7.48 |
| 3. | Deposits | 10,791.67 | 83.96 | 12,258.38 | 83.38 | 2071.74 | 69.73 | 2685.49 | 73.12 | 693.13 | 59.41 | 797.56 | 58.51 |
| 4. | Borrowings | 224.25 | 1.74 | 307.36 | 2.09 | 421.40 | 14.18 | 403.66 | 10.99 | 229.04 | 19.63 | 253.89 | 18.63 |
| 5. | Other Liabilities and Provisions | 1182.36 | 9.20 | 1346.30 | 9.15 | 289.17 | 9.73 | 358.42 | 9.76 | 110.39 | 9.46 | 163.25 | 11.98 |
| | **Total Liabilities** | **12,854.11** | **100.0** | **14,714.28** | **100.0** | **2971.26** | **100.0** | **3672.76** | **100.0** | **1166.61** | **100.0** | **1363.16** | **100.0** |
| 1. | Cash and Balance with RBI | 651.67 | 5.07 | 842.42 | 5.73 | 163.99 | 5.52 | 217.26 | 5.92 | 45.57 | 3.91 | 72.78 | 5.34 |
| 2. | Balance with Banks and Call Money | 577.32 | 4.49 | 574.49 | 3.90 | 110.36 | 3.71 | 151.16 | 4.12 | 63.45 | 5.44 | 96.58 | 7.09 |
| 3. | Investments | 5,456.36 | 42.45 | 6,256.78 | 42.52 | 1073.23 | 36.12 | 1348.01 | 36.70 | 407.94 | 34.97 | 415.87 | 30.51 |
| 4. | Loans and Advances | 5,484.37 | 42.67 | 6,327.40 | 43.00 | 1389.49 | 46.76 | 1708.96 | 46.53 | 521.68 | 44.72 | 605.07 | 44.39 |
| 5. | Fixed Assets | 105.93 | 0.82 | 115.28 | 0.78 | 74.99 | 2.52 | 79.26 | 2.16 | 21.86 | 1.87 | 19.50 | 1.43 |
| 6. | Other Assets | 578.47 | 4.50 | 597.92 | 4.06 | 159.21 | 5.36 | 168.13 | 4.58 | 106.11 | 9.10 | 153.35 | 11.25 |
| | **Total Assets** | **12,854.11** | **100.0** | **14,714.28** | **100.0** | **2971.26** | **100.0** | **3672.76** | **100.0** | **1166.61** | **100.0** | **1363.16** | **100.0** |

*Source:* Report on Banking Trend and Progress, 2003-04, RBI.

It is evident from the above table that the commercial banks in India have grown substantially in period under study. The increase in deposits and advances indicate a favourable trend in the financial sector. The public sector banks continued to lead the tally with among the banking sectors. The number of Banks in Indian Private Sector and foreign banking sector has increased over the period 1990-01 i.e. from 25 to 32 private banks; and from 23 to 41 foreign banks. The annual growth of branch expansion during 1990-2000 was 1.1 per cent. The population served per branch was 15000 as at March-end 2000. During 1990-2000, the annual average growth rates of deposits and credit were 16.1 per cent and 14.8 per cent respectively. During 1990s, the growth of investments was 20.0 per cent as compared to 16.0 per cent during 1985-90 and 18.8 per cent during 1980-85. The net profit of the banking system grew by more from Rs. 555.33 crore as at March end 1990 to Rs. 7306.36 crore as at March-end 2000.

Public sector accounts for the highest share of total deposit and total credit during 2000-01 i.e. Rs. 8593.8 billion of deposits and Rs. 4146.3 billion of total credit. But the proportionate share of deposits by Public Sector Banks has declined from 92.1 per cent in 1990-91 to 81.6 per cent in 2000-01, while that of foreign banking sector has increased from 3.7 per cent (1990-91) to 5.6 per cent (2000-01). The total income for each of the three banking sectors has increasing substantially during the period 1990-01. The total net profit of public sector banks decreased from Rs. 4.7 billion (1990-91) to Rs. 3.3 billion (1995-96) and then increased to Rs. 73.2 billion in 2000-01. The net profit of both private and foreign banks also increased during 1990-01 i.e. from Rs. 0.4 billion to Rs. 12.3 billion for private banks, and from Rs. 1.5 billion to Rs. 10.2 billion for foreign banking sector. The total deposits of the public sector banks has grown from Rs. 10,791.67 billion to Rs. 12,268.38 billion, while the private banks from Rs. 2071.74 billion to Rs. 2685.49 and for foreign banks from Rs. 693.13 billion to Rs. 797.56 during 2003 and 2004. Similar trend is observed in all the parameters.

At the end of June 2005, the aggregate deposits of scheduled commercial banks stand at Rs. 1,789,864 crore registering a growth of 14.74 per cent over the previous year. Similarly, the aggregate bank credits have grown to Rs. 1,161,387 crore registering a growth of 32.37 per cent over the corresponding period of the previous year. The credit-deposit ratio was 64.89 per cent as on 24.6.2005. At the end of March 2004, the number of branches has grown to 457,158 thousands serving about 16,000 populations per branch. The CRR and SLR have reduced to 5 per cent and 25 per cent respectively to leave the banks with more loanable resources. The bank rate has been reduced to 6 per cent and the rates of interest on deposits have been made free so that the banks can go for cheaper source of funds.

## MAJOR DEVELOPMENTS IN INDIAN BANKING

The major developments that have taken place in the history of Indian Banking are described below in chronological order.

1967 Social Control.

1969 Nationalisation of 14 Major Indian Banks.

1974 Targets for Priority Sector Lending set.

1975 Norm prescribed for lending and fixing working capital limits.

1978 Demonetisations of high denomination notes.

1980 Nationalization of six more Indian Banks taking the total banks nationalized to 20.

1982 Establishment of National Bank or Agriculture and Rural Development (NABARD), Export-Import Bank of India.

1985 Introduction of MICR technology. Introduction of Health Code System for classification of bank loans.

1987 Banks allowed to commence mutual fund business.

1988 Establishment of Discount and Finance House of India, National Housing Bank, Service Area Approach adopted for rural lending programmes.

1989 Change of Accounting Year of Banks from January-December to April-March. Introduction of Commercial Paper and Certificate of Deposits. Cheque bouncing made a criminal offence. Loan concentration on ratios evolved.

1990 Access to call/notice money market enhanced. Establishment of Small Industries Development Bank of India. Loan writes off for agricultural borrowers.

1991 New formats for banks balance sheets introduced. Committee on the Financial System (Narasimham Committee) made far-reaching recommendations leading to introduction of banking sector reforms.

1992 Rupee became convertible effective March 1, 1992 for all approved external transactions. Branch Licensing Policy abolished. Auction of 364 days Treasury bills introduced.

1993 Norms for setting up new private sector banks announced Liberalisation of entry and expansion norms. Auction of 91-day treasury bills announcement. Securities Trading Corporation of India was set up. Foreign Currency Non-Resident Deposits Scheme introduced. Introduction of capital adequacy, asset classification, income recognition and provisioning norms for banks. Nationalised banks recapitalised. Norms for valuation of investments in Government securities on mark to market basis introduced in a phased manner. Debt Recovery Tribunals constituted for speedy recover of high value loan dues. The first merger among the public sector banks took place with the merger of New Bank of India with Punjab National Bank.

1994 Interest rates on loans over Rs. 2 lakhs deregulated allowing banks to fix prime lending rates. Banks allowed raising capital up to 49 per cent of equity from the capital markets by amending Banking Companies (Acquisition and Transfer of Undertaking) Acts, 1970/1980. Board for Financial Supervision was set up.

1995 Banking Ombudsman set up for customer grievance redressal. Cash credit system reformed. World Bank's Financial Sector Development Project assisted 8 banks in obtaining loans of US $150 million for modernization and automation. Measures initiated to introduce Electronic Fund Transfer, Electronic Clearing Service and Electronic Data Interchange in the banking industry.

1996 Measures taken to strengthen secondary market in government securities. Banks allowed purchasing PSU bonds in the secondary market. Limits for sanction of advances against shares and debentures enhanced.

1997 India's first shared payment network system (SWADHAN) became operational in Mumbai. Limited and conditional autonomy are given to public sector banks. Central Board of Bank frauds constituted to contain incidence of frauds in the banking industry. Norms for setting up of local Area Banks announced.

1998 Committee on Financial Sector Reforms (Narasimham Committee) reviewed the progress of the reforms and recommended blueprint for implementation of second-generation reforms. Norms for capital adequacy, reduction in the non-performing assets evolved. Internet rats on term deposits above 15 days deregulated. Banks allowed to offer incentives based on the size and tenor.

1999 Guidelines on asset-liability management issued for implementation by banks.

2000 Union Budget proposals contained bringing the government equity in public sector banks to 33 per cent without losing the character of the public sector.

2001 Recommendations of Narasimham Committee II came into force.

2002 Banks are asked to make provisions for NPA as per the revised guidelines; as a result many public sector banks posted heavy losses in their balance sheet.

2003 Reduction of CRR to 4.5 per cent of NDTL. The maturity period of fresh NRE deposits to be 1 to 3 years. Guidelines on Fair Practices Code issued. Revised guidelines issued to banks to identify wilful default. Detailed operational guidelines for the process of take-over of bank branches in rural and semi-urban centres are issued. The guidelines for accounting legal expenses in suit-filed accounts issued. Banks are given freedom to determine rates of interest on advances. Education loans up to the ceiling of Rs. 7.5 lakhs for studies in India, and Rs. 15 lakhs for studies abroad to be reckoned under priority sector advances. Foreign Banks operating in India are permitted to remit net profits on quarterly basis to the Head Office. A working group on flow of credit to SSI sector constituted. Each commercial bank is required to constitute an *ad hoc* committee to undertake procedures and performance audit on public services rendered by it.

2004 All branches maintaining currency chests are to provide customer services to the public more actively. Private sector banks are to ensure that no transfer takes place on any acquisition of shares of 5 per cent or more without prior acknowledgement of Reserve Bank of India. Banks are free to decide on all aspects relating to renewal of overdue deposits. Guidelines towards bringing about a certain minimum level of uniformity with regard to the content and coverage of the Best Practices codes (BPC) in banks issued. Revised norms with regard to Cheque Drop-Box facilities, delivery of cheque books over the counter and statement of accounts are to be issued. Banks are to ensure the compliance of three accounting standards (Nos. 24, 26, and 28) relating to discounting operations. Banks are to maintain the confidentiality of information provided by the customers for 'Know Your Customers' (KYC) compliance. The types of instruments those are to be included in Tier II bonds were widened. Banks are to take appropriate steps to increase credit flow to priority sector. Banks can open branches having no interface with customers, and which will attend exclusively to data processing. Banks are to formulate a comprehensive policy covering the three aspects, viz., immediate credit to cheques, timeframe for collection of cheques, and interest payment for delayed collection.

## STRUCTURAL CHANGES IN THE BANKING SYSTEM

Financial systems worldwide are undergoing structural transformation. Technological innovation, deregulation of financial services at the national level, external financial liberalisation, and organizational changes in the corporate world are some of the global factors driving the transformation. Banking and finance in emerging economies is also caught up in this change. In these economies, in addition to global developments, country-specific factors are motivating the structural shifts. Consequently, two separate directions of reform are evident. There is an expansion of the financial system due to vacation of policy interventions in entry, exit and operations, the application of new advances in information technology and in general, a greater emphasis on competition and market-based outcomes. There is also a strong drive towards consolidation in a quest for exploiting core competitiveness and for developing "niche" strategies.

In India, the primary force for transformation was structural reforms launched in the aftermath of the balance of payments crisis of 1990-91. It was recognized that a vibrant, resilient and competitive financial sector is vital for sustaining the reform process in the real sectors of the economy. Significantly, financial sector reforms in India were pre-emptive and proactive rather than a result of banking crises, as has been the experience of several emerging economies. Further, the momentum of change in the financial system has been the motivation for upgrading the technological infrastructure in Indian banking and finance rather than the other way round. In that sense, the Indian financial system has been a late entrant in the expressway created by the information and communication technology revolution. Competitive pressure – a major force of change worldwide – also has been reforms-driven rather than a driver of the transformation. Finally, a large measure of the impetus for change has come from reforms in the regulatory and supervisory regime and the aspiration to apply international best practices to the country-specific situation.

The role of the public sector banks has come under close scrutiny in the recent years. It is necessary to recognize that these banks have played a critical role in the development of the Indian economy in the period 1969-90, particularly in the spread of banking and monetisation of the economy, the mobilization of savings and their allocation by plan priorities. For all economies in the early and intermediate stages of development, credit markets face a persistent excess demand, reflecting the existing resource constraints. Moreover, market processes can well exclude the genuine credit needs of the weaker sections of society, which do not have the competitive strength to bid for funds in the market for bank credit. Public ownership in Indian banking was intended to address both concerns i.e. the rationing of credit in the face of excess demand not cleared by the market, and the channelling of bank credit flow to the economically disadvantaged sections of society. Over the period 1970-90, a massive expansion of bank branches occurred, and credit allocations ensured some equity in the distribution of bank credit.

At the same time, however, there was erosion in the financial health of public sector banks and deterioration in the quality of customer service. Within the ambit of financial sector reforms, therefore, the focus since the early 1990s has been on the viability, efficiency and competitiveness of banks and financial institutions. Liberalisation and deregulation has to go hand in hand with a greater emphasis on consolidation, productivity, asset quality and profitability. There is also an urgent need for Government to divest substantial shareholding to the public, so that these banks can respond effectively to changing market conditions. Under the present circumstances, improvement in the cost structure of the banks and work culture are important priorities.

In order to enable the public sector banks to deal with the new capital requirements as per international guidelines, re-capitalisation was initiated in 1993. The Verma Committee's recommendation that re-capitalisation of weak public sector banks be accompanied by conditionality relating to managerial and operational aspects of the banks' functioning was endorsed in the Union Budget; 2000-01. Accordingly, in 2001-02, Rs. 1300 crore was provided to one of the weak nationalized banks. Two of the weak banks have already turned around and are reporting profits and a capital adequacy ratio of 9 per cent. The last one is also going through a turnaround. Re-capitalisation is associated with a monitorable reform programme and operational restructuring to ensure that flow problems in a bank's performance.

Mergers have reflected efforts to reap economies of scale and scope through joint production of financial services and one-stop delivery wherever synergies in service supply can be exploited to lower costs of production. In general, these mergers have come about as a result of government efforts to restructure inefficient national financial systems. Market-driven consolidation is a relatively new phenomenon in these countries. A critical issue in almost all emerging economies is a reassessment of the ownership of the State in the financial system and a redefinition of the role of State-owned banks and financial institutions. The changing structure of the banking and financial systems in emerging economies has implications for systemic stability and the supervisory regime.

The major structural change in our financial system is the infusion of competition. The enabling conditions for a more competitive environment initially took the form of shifts in the policy regime. Statutory preemptions were progressively lowered, interest rates were deregulated and restrictions on entry and exit were eased. Financial markets were developed to enable financial intermediaries to deal in assets and liabilities of varying maturities and risk profiles. Activity restrictions were eased and banks can now undertake various types of activities reserved earlier for development financial institutions. Likewise, the term-lending financial institutions have been allowed to undertake working capital financing. Elements of this growing convergence have determined the pace and sequencing of the approach to universal banking in the recent years.

Within the banking system, there is heightened competition with the introduction of new generation private sector banks. In January 2001, revised guidelines were issued for entry of new banks in the private sector. Despite the preponderant share of domestic banks in banking activity in India, foreign banks have been a source of competition, at least potentially, given their use of sophisticated technology, risk monitoring analysis and exposure management. In recent years, the policy thrust has been to level the playing field for domestic and foreign banks. For example, foreign banks that were earlier allowed to operate only branches but not subsidiaries are now free to choose to set up either branches or subsidiaries under common banking regulations including lending norms. Foreign direct investment up to 49 per cent has been allowed in private sector banks and up to 20 per cent in nationalized banks. Guidelines have been issued for the entry of banks into insurance business either as joint venture participants or to take up strategic investment for providing infrastructure and services support without any contingent liability.

## TECHNOLOGY, PAYMENT AND SETTLEMENT SYSTEM

The information technology revolution has brought about a fundamental transformation ushering in, as Alvin Toffler describes it, the fourth wave. Perhaps no other sector has been affected by advances in technology as much as banking and finance (Jalan, 2003). It has become the most important factor for dealing with the intensifying competition and the rapid proliferation of financial innovations. It has enabled, in general raising the efficiency of financial intermediation in the face of ever-rising volumes of transactions, reducing margins and more empowered customer expectations. In particular, there are four or five key areas in which the financial system has experienced the benefits of the technology revolution: product development, market infrastructure, risk control and market reach. The interaction of technology with globalisation has contributed to the expansion of financial markets beyond national borders, heralding the end of geography. In the process, technology has changed the contours of three major functions of financial intermediaries: access to liquidity, transformation of assets and monitoring of risks.

The Indian financial system is quickly adapting itself to these developments and is acquiring a customer-centric focus. The proliferation of Automated Teller Machines (ATMs), networking of these ATMs and Shared Payment Network based ATMs is a feature that has been welcomed by the banking public. Other innovations already within the domain of banks and financial systems in India include Internet Banking, Electronic Funds Transfer and Anywhere/ Anytime Banking, all of which have a high level of technology embedded in the systems offering these services. Many of the older banks are migrating towards the implementation of Core Banking or Clustered Solutions which would contribute significantly towards increasing customer satisfaction. In all this, business process re-engineering becomes an essential concomitant to ensure best results in technology upgradation.

In recent years, the Reserve Bank has assigned priority to the upgradation of technological infrastructure in the Indian financial system (ibid, 18). Efforts have been made to modernize clearing and payment through MICR based cheque clearing, Electronic Clearing Services and Funds Transfer (ECS and EFT) and the Centralised Funds Management System. For the traditional paper-based cheque systems, introduction of cheque truncation and imaging of cheques is envisaged to reduce the time lags in realization of cheques. Substantial efforts have gone into developing what has been described as the 'plumbing' in the financial architecture-a modern, efficient, integrated and secure payment and settlement system for the financial services industry in India. Significant milestones in this path are the Negotiated Dealing System for transactions in government securities and the Clearing Corporation of India. In order to establish and efficient, cost-effective and dependable communication backbone, the Indian Financial Network (INFINET) has been set up. About 150 banks, primary dealers and mutual funds have become members. Structured Financial Messaging Solutions are being implemented for secure message transfers across members of the INFINET. Common inter-bank application software has been designed, taking into account the security requirements. The medium-term goal is the operationalization of Real Time Gross Settlement, which would enable real time funds transfer across different banks and thereby the optimal utilization of funds. Critical to the future of the payment and settlement system of the country is the ongoing research in the IDRBT on messaging systems, security and design specifications for RTGS.

Adequate security is a prerequisite for a modern, technology-intensive payment and settlement system, especially one functioning in a highly networked environment. Information Systems Audit is another area, which needs to be adequately addressed. Some progress has been made in defining what we need but implementation would require a system-wide collaboration to obtain the best results. It is with this objective that the Reserve Bank of India has recently circulated the recommendations of its Working Group on Information Systems Security for the Banking and Financial Sector among all banks and financial institutions. Legal changes to deal with electronic data interchange and legal wherewithal for participants in the payment system are on the anvil. These changes are intended to enable the benchmarking of our payment and settlement system against international standards such as the Core Principles for Systemically Important Payment Systems of the Bank for International Settlements.

The future of banking and finance hinges around exploiting the opportunities thrown up by the technology explosion. This requires the combined efforts of all participants in the financial system. In December 2001 the Reserve Bank of India set out its vision of the road ahead in the Document Payments System in India to share this vision with all participants and the nature and direction of reforms needed to achieve it. The collective goal should be to make use of synergies between technology and finance to maximize the benefits to society.

## UNIVERSAL BANKING

The universal banks are mega financial entities that offer commercial banking, investment banking, securities trading, insurance and other financial services. Different nations have different types of structure for the universal banks (Rao, 2005). While there could be risk mitigation and economies of scale and scope through diversification of revenue streams, some argues that there could be diseconomies as well. Further, issues like conflict of interest and too-big-to-fail arise through universal banking.

The Universal Banking has appropriately flagged the burning issues in a very topical area. It has been mentioned that the speed of consolidation in banking has begun to slacken, and the model of universal banking which was earlier being hotly pursued by the big banks is now considered as flawed (ibid, 5). It is also pointed out that recent events have brought to the fore the inherent conflicts of interest between commercial banking and investment banking being conducted within one bank. Further, despite the theoretical arguments in support of cross-selling of products such as insurance, there are few success stories possibly because this requires team building and selling skills, which all banks do not have.

Extending the above arguments to the Indian context, it is mentioned that the merger strategy to create size is likely to be witnessed here and is likely to result in the take over of the old private banks by public sector banks. I would first like to comment on the issue of mergers. The regulators are interested in seeing a banking sector which has a diverse array of well-capitalized and sound banks which have the skill and appetite to serve different segments of the population. However, we do not prefer any particular method by which this should be achieved and certainly do not promote mergers between public and private sector banks as the best solution.

Mergers, especially those between banks, are not easy. First, finding suitable partners is not an easy task and once this is done, getting agreement on a suitable swap ratio is equally difficult. Finally, all this requires the blessing of the regulators and is also subject to scrutiny at a later stage. If the merger is approved, then there is the vexatious issue of management control, which is always a bone of contention whether it is a merger or an acquisition. Compulsory mergers are not always a good solution because they invariably involve one weak bank and lead to a loss for the shareholders and the depositors and also have the potential to create a systemic problem.

## RE-ENGINEERING OPERATIONS IN BANKING

Banking has traditionally remained a protected industry in many emerging economies. However, a combination of developments has compelled banks to change the old ways of doing business. These include, among others, technological advancements, disintermediation pressures arising from a liberalized, marketplace, increased emphasis on shareholders value and macroeconomic pressures and banking crises in 1990s. As a consequence of these developments, the dividing line between financial products, types of financial institutions and their geographical locations have become less relevant that in the past. At the same time, the growing size of financial activity relative to the overall economic activity in a closely integrated world has implied that disruptions in the financial markets in any economy can engender contagion, which can spread rapidly and have adverse economic ramifications. Consequently, while traditional banking activity has continued to remain the mainstay of banking business, the greater globalisation of banking operations and expansion of financial activities in an increasingly market-driven environment have made risk management extremely critical and indispensable.

**Risk Management**

Risk is intrinsic to banking business. Of late, the management of risk has gained prominence. The growing sophistication in banking operations, derivative trading, securities underwriting, corporate advisory business, improvements in information technology, online electronic banking, provision of bill presentation and payment services have led to increased diversity and complexity of risks being encountered by banks. The major risks confronting banks and financial institutions are credit risk, interest rate risk, foreign exchange risk and liquidity risk.

**Banks' Entry into Insurance Business**

As part of the integration of financial services world over, new opportunities have emerged for banks to enter into the area of insurance, Banks' entry into insurance sector has opened up viable opportunities to enhance their non-interest income and improve their performance. Accordingly, those banks which satisfy the vital parameters set therein-minimum net worth of Rs. 500 crore, eligibility criteria in regard to net worth, capital adequacy, profitability, reasonable level of non-performing advances – would be allowed to set up insurance joint ventures on risk participation basis. Banks which are not eligible as joint venture participants, would be allowed to take up strategic investment up to a certain limit for providing infrastructure and services support without taking on any contingent liability provided these banks satisfy some of the criteria specified therein. With a view to providing the banks with another avenue for generating fee based income, any scheduled commercial bank or its subsidiary would be permitted to undertake insurance business as agent of an insurance company and distribute insurance products without any risk participation. Banks are required to maintain an 'arms length' relationship with insurance outfit and adopt a risk management framework where the risks of insurance business do not get transferred to the banking business.

**Credit Information System**

An efficient system of credit information is the prerequisite for management of credit risk. RBI/Government as well as credit institutions have keenly felt the requirement of an adequate, comprehensive and reliable information system on the borrowers through an efficient database system. Recognising the need for an effective mechanism for exchange of information between banks and financial institutions, the Finance Minister in his Budget proposals of 2000-01, indicated that the growth of fresh NPAs could be curbed through better institutional mechanism for sharing of credit information on borrowers among banks and FIs. It was therefore decided that Credit Information Bureau would soon be established on the recommendations of the Working Group constituted by the Reserve Bank of India to work out the modalities for setting up a Bureau.

**Credit/Debit/Smart Cards**

In India, credit card operations of banks have been de-regulated. Banks with a minimum net worth of Rs. 100 crores need not take prior approval of Reserve Bank for commencing this business, except for setting up of subsidiaries. They can introduce the same with the approval of their Boards. Further, based on a special study undertaken on the systems and controls on issue of credit cards, and recovery of dues there under, banks have been advised to adopt certain additional safeguards in the matter of recovery of overdues, sharing of information on credit card holders, fraud control etc. in order to ensure that their credit card operations are run on sound, prudent and profitable lines. Banks can introduce smart/online debit cards with the approval of the Board, keeping in view the guidelines issued by RBI. While banks need not obtain the prior approval of the RBI, the details of smart/online debit cards introduced are to be advised to RBI together with a copy each of the agenda note put to the Board and the resolution passed thereon. However, only banks with a net worth of Rs. 100 crores and above should undertake issue of offline debit cards and these banks should take prior approval of RBI. Banks are also allowed to issue smart cards (online/offline) and online debit cards to select customers who maintain accounts with the banks for less than six months subject to their ensuring the implementation of "Know Your Customer" guidelines. However, banks introducing off-line mode of operation of debit cards are required to adhere to the minimum period of satisfactory maintenance of accounts for six months. Banks cannot issue smart/ debit cards in tie-up with other non-bank entities.

**Retail Banking**

Today's banking is very different from the retail banks of 20 years ago. Consumers are prepared to buy financial services from non-traditional providers including entirely new providers and established retail companies with no history of financial services. Traditional financial service providers are, as a result, facing competition from entirely new sectors in their domestic market as well as from new entrants from overseas markets. In an environment of change, the traditional financial service providers have had difficulties. The large banks, in particular, have been described as the dinosaurs of the New Economy, too slow and inflexible to cope with the e-commerce revolution.

The new providers are certainly achieving remarkable levels of success. However, a recent study by KPMG – "Awakening Giants: How European Big Banks Will Win the E-commerce Revolution (2000)" – disagrees with the view that the new delivery channels mark the end for established banks. It argues that the large banks have three inherent advantages that will ensure their long-term survival in the retail banking-traffic, trust and multi-channel access. Some products are more suited to e-commerce than others. For instances, car insurance has proved particularly well suited and has become an intensely competitive e-commerce market. Other products, such as retail banking, have been slower to embrace e-commerce. Generally, simpler products and services tend to be better suited to retail delivery, partly because of the regulations often surrounding more complex products. The new delivery channels and the ease with which customers can switch between banks and other financial product providers have forced established providers to concentrate on customer service. The key to success in e-commerce is an understanding of how technology can help to build customer value. For example, the Woolwich has achieved considerable success in this area with its Open Plan Services innovation.

Gaining access to customer data, and the ability to use it, has helped many of the non-traditional financial service providers to enter the retail market. Supermarkets are particularly well placed to collect valuable data on their customers spending habits. Loyalty cards enable the chains to record exact spending habits and to detect changes in circumstances well before the customer bank. The e-commerce revolution has placed new stresses on the infrastructure of financial services organizations and increased their exposure to operational risk such as system failure, electronic frauds and damaged reputation. Security has therefore become the biggest worry for online customers and the biggest risk in terms of brand damage to the financial service provider. The key factors influencing the purchase of any personal finance product are trust, security and reliability; whatever may be the delivery medium. Any security breach breaks all three rules but, most significantly, it damages the brand.

Reportedly, new business models are emerging within the financial services industry and beyond that could radically alter operations of all companies in the future. Some of these models are like Vertical Portals (the ultimate access point), Aggregators/ Intermediaries (sites providing the consumer with large information), Speciality Manufacturers and Company Sites, etc. It is also expected that leading financial services firms of the future will be organized into three different models such as:

- Proprietary integrated companies owning the customer gateway and offering mainly own products.
- Non-proprietary integrated companies owning the customer gateway and offering a mix of home grown and alternative products.
- Others as niche players, specialists and low-cost/high-volume product providers. In this non-integrated model, the customer will be in control of the gateway.

The message from all advisers is that in order to compete in the e-commerce world, financial service providers will need to invest heavily in customer relationship management systems and in brand identity. In the fast-track Internet world, it may be the only way to survive. Over and above what has been said, the staff in the banks particularly the public sector banks must have an open mind and accept the fundamental changes brought about by the computers for better delivery of customer service and appreciate the more efficient way of accounting transactions and generating an array of MIS reports both for the bank management and the Regulator.

In this regard training and acquiring new skills becomes absolutely essential whatever be the age profile of the staff. I am very confident that in these transition times staff of the banks will rise to meet the competition and deliver the type of services demanded by the customer in the present and futuristic IT environment.

## FUTURE TREND OF BANKING SERVICES/PRODUCTS

Worldwide the banking system is changing very fast. The economic and financial news papers of today carry feature articles on the developments in Information technology and success stories of financial houses by using this new technology. The internet revolutions are poised to take the banking scenario by storm and the existing products being offered by Banks will undergo a drastic change. The e-concept like expectation-business, expectation-banking, expectation-cash, expectation-mail, etc. will be the mode of transaction in the future.

### Data Mining

The process of data mining involves sifting through all the voluminous data and eking out a pattern, which enables the bank to personalize its communication towards the customer as much as possible and banks can get a better understanding of what drives the customer relationship. It helps to increase the business by targeting the right customers and to make the right offers to customers. Worldwide, data mining is a big business. Software majors like IBM, I-flex and NCR Corporation are some who provide the necessary tools for data mining. Data mining is likely to gain ground in the Indian banking industry also. The objective will be to increase the existing customer base, enhance loyalty and bring the high net worth and elite class of customers to the bank's fold.

With a view to cross-selling products and services to each other's customers, data mining may be done in such a way that offerings by banks and cellular companies are customized. Hence banks and mobile telephony service providers may use data mining. With the roll-over of Internet banking, especially mobile banking, a foreign bank and some private banks are building data-profiles of their customers in association with all of its mobile service providers, viz. Hutchison Max, Airtel, BPL Mobile, Tata Cellular, RPG, Aircell, Cellphone and Command.

**Plastic Money—Credit/Debit and Smart Cards**

During 1980s, credit card was introduced followed by the debit card which was introduced a couple of years ago. Now there will be a new offering in India, which is a little bit more advanced i.e. a chip-based card (Smart Card). It is not only a payment instrument and a kind of electronic-purse (e-purse), it also serves a number of non-payment functions like storing driving licence, office ID, loyalty programmes and host of other information. In short, it can carry one's entire personal database. Smart card, which is essentially a pre-authorised card, has a microprocessor. While credit and debit cards have magnetic strips which have a limited memory and are susceptible to fraud once the card number is available. With microprocessor, smart card will offer a high level of security and information, as it cannot be tampered with. The RBI has already imposed stringent standards that issuers of this product will have to meet, because smart cards have the potential to be strong players in the payment services industry and could impact the entire monetary system. Hence, only the PSBs are likely to be permitted to issue smart cards.

Plastic money, in India, is replacing cash very fast. Card issuers are now counting on the debit card to ultimately do away with the use of cash. Debit card base in India was just 3 lakhs in March 2000; now it has shot up by 63 per cent to 4.9 lakhs during the first half of 2000-01. Spends on debit cards, as a result, have also rocketed by as much as 65 per cent to Rs. 825 crore from Rs. 500 crore in March. Credit cards also will be targeted on a specific group of customers. A PSB has recently introduced an internationally valid credit card, personalized and exclusively designed for doctors. This is the country's first credit card of its kind. Special features of this credit card are the availability of:

- Doctor's liability insurance of Rs. 4 lakhs free of cost, for the first year, as a special introductory offer.
- Special discounts on select medical equipment and discounted personal loans from GE.
- Balance transfer facility that allows cardholders to transfer their balances from other credit cards.
- Cash-access at over 6 lakhs Visa-plus TMs globally, teledraft facility, discounts on domestic and international air-tickets and hotels across India and purchase protection of Rs. 10, 000 up to 90 days.

Globally valid, this Card for doctors will be accepted at over 190 lakhs Visa International merchant locations worldwide. Another PSB is planning to launch four new credit cards, viz. Gold Card, International Card, Secured Card and Corporate Card. Under the Secured Card, customers will take credit against their fixed deposits, while the Corporate Card is being specifically designed to cater to the needs of employees of the companies who undertake frequent travelling. The Secured Card is being designed to satisfy the needs of the fixed deposit holders and other product will help reduce travelling cost of the companies. Gold Card and International Card will be having al features of these types of cards already issued by the foreign banks in the developed world. According to Gemplus India, total market size of smart cards in India would be around 14 million by 2002 and around 50 million by 2003. At the moment, there are about 3 million credit card users in India.

**Tie-Up Arrangements**

The new millennium will witness many tie-up arrangements between banks and utility services providers. The basic objective of these tie-up arrangements would be to cross-sell each other's products. The trend is already visible, as a Calcutta-based Telecom Company has just announced a tie-up with some foreign and private banks for mobile bill settlements. This facility will be made available to all its customers who have an account with any of these banks. In addition, the customers can also settle their bills online. As of now, utility payments seem to be the mainstay of Net banking followed by e-broking and funds transfer. Banks will be accordingly tying up with a host of utility providers like telecom, electricity and mobile phone companies across the country.

Some banks have already launched mobile commerce (m-Commerce) service for their customers in a tie-up arrangement with the cellular service providers. Under the M-Commerce service, the customer sends a short message to the bank and within a minute he receives a response on the screen. For a beginning, services such as, balance inquiry, stop payment, mini statement, cheque book requests, statement requests and change operative account requests are being made available. More services, such as, bill payment and fund transfer, shopping mail facilities, investment advisory and other services may also be introduced in the near future.

**Virtual Banking**

It is not interesting to know that in the developed world some banks are charging their customers a penalty for a branch visit? These banks are discouraging their customers for branch visit but encouraging them to do banking transactions through Internet, as this helps these banks in cutting transaction costs by a wide margin. From the bank's point of view, less number of customers' visit to branch will save the bank on office space, the salary of officers at the counter, besides other incidental expenses on air-conditioning and lights, etc. The customer will save on time and taxi fare for visiting the branch. Car owners will save on fuel, besides the hassles of looking for parking space near the branch.

With the deep penetration of Internet, now banks in India will also discourage their customers for visiting the branch. However, on this issue, there are other views also. Some banking experts think that this development may not appeal to customers in rural/semi-urban/urban branches, as customers at these centres want human touch, which staff at the branch only can provide. Indian customers' enticement for human touch will continue to dominate the banking scenario in the foreseeable future.

### Marketing Agents

With a view to increasing the amount of proactive selling instead of waiting for customers to come to the branch, banks will employ Direct Sales Agents (DSA). A bank might have the best of products and services, but if these are not sold, what is the use of such products/services? DSA help banks marketing their best products. Some foreign and new breed of private sector banks has already started employing DSA in the metropolitan areas. At these centres, customers do not have the time or the inclination to go to a bank. Substantial portion of business under consumer durable loan schemes today is likely to be generated through DSA.

### Point-of-Sale Terminals

Banks are likely to have large number of Point-of-Sales Terminals (POST), in circulation, for payment through debit cards. These POSTs, will be set up with a view to collecting good amount of revenues from the use of these POST terminals for payments through debit cards of other banks.

### Automated Teller Machines

ATM services, till date, have been confined to deposit and withdrawal from bank accounts by customers, but NCR Corporation India has included several value-added services on its ATMs, such as, utility bill payments, ticket reservations (airline and railway ticket booking) and the facility to deal in mutual fund units. The new ATM services will also include selling cinema tickets. Banks are, therefore, likely to try hard to install more and more ATMs. According to a survey, it is revealed that 40 per cent of ATMs have been deployed outside the bank premises. Even banks are entering into agreements with HPCL, BPL, IOC and IBPL, etc., for setting up ATMs at petrol pumps run by their franchisees in the major cities so that customers may use their ATM Cards on the way to their tours/journeys without any hassles. As a result, the number of installed ATMs is likely to be more than 4,000 by the next year as against 1,800 at present.

### Insurance Products

With a view to increasing the income from non-fund based business many banks will be foraying into underwriting insurance products and distribution of others' products.

**Loan Products**

Banks, in near future, will be structuring their loan products to suit their customers' need. Products like invoice financing and secured fixed rate note on the lines of asset-backed commercial paper may become a reality soon. In India, for decades, cash credit and overdraft have been the mainstay of working capital funding. Cash credit constitutes 70 per cent of the total bank credit with bill finance accounting for 10 per cent. With a view to boosting bill finance culture in India, low rate of interest as compared to demand loan and cash credit loan may be offered. Working Capital Demand Loan (WCDL), under the concept of Loan System for Delivery of Bank Credit, is likely to get momentum as many banks are now charging lower rate of interest on the WCDL portion of the working capital limits. Cash credit loan concept may ultimately lose its relevance in the new millennium. More and more tenor-based demand loans are likely to be provided to the customers without any strict monitoring system. Loan once disbursed will be repaid on due dates without permitting any operation in the account. A PSB has already introduced a product titled 'Line of Credit on Demand'. These types of liquid loan available to borrowers on request (as per sudden requirement) against assets already charged to the bank are expected to be a big hit with the trade and services category.

**Tech-Savvy New Banking Products**

Recently some of the foreign and new private sector banks have launched tech-savvy new banking products in India. Special features of some of these products launched very recently are given below:

- A private sector bank has launched an e-Age Savings Account for cellular phone users. Under the scheme, customers are being encouraged to access their accounts through direct banking channels, that is, off-site banking. The new service has been launched to meet the banking needs of the "technology-savvy mobile generation". A customer can now access his account through direct banking channels, such as, ATM, phone banking, Internet banking, mobile banking and the international debit card. This ultimately will minimize the need to visit the bank branch for routine banking transactions. In this way, the needs of the cellphone generation, which intends to bank while on move, are being fulfilled.

- A foreign bank has offered a unique type of banking service in India only after Singapore. Under this type of service a text message is sent to the customer's mobile phone or via e-mail, whenever any already defined incidents take place. Customers can choose from a range of account-specific notifications about which they want to be informed, including past-due-date reminders, overdrafts and credit cards. If, for instance, the customer has requested to be informed every time he has used over 70 per cent of his credit line on his credit card, the trigger is set when this event actually takes place and a message is sent out to the customer on his mobile phone or his e-mail. It is an Internet and mobile phone based alert service designed to provide customers with information whenever, however and wherever they want it. It is a completely personalized service and provides customers with the latest information regarding their accounts.
- With a view to wooing salaried class customers, a foreign bank has introduced a savings bank account scheme. Under the scheme, a host of unmatched services are being offered free of charge like providing an ATM Card, which can be used as a debit card with an access to tele-banking and Internet banking facilities. The special discounts and incentives across varied products and services are also being offered on an ongoing basis.
- A new private sector bank has launched a technology-driven package very recently. The product is packed with a range of services compatible with electronic banking and other add-on facilities to make it more user-friendly, attractive and unique. It is targeted at students, housewives and the salaried class. The user of this product can avail of facilities like a global e-banking, ATM and debit cards, mobile and Internet banking, round-the-clock customer care centres, 'anywhere banking' and 'doorstep banking'. The customers will also be able to avail of the facility of utility bill payment, which will be available only in a particular State. The bank has tied-up with National Insurance Company to offer insurance schemes at discounted premiums to all users of this product.

### Product Marketing

Marketing of products will be done on the "Portals" launched by banks. More and more product specific portals (viz., portals for car loan, housing finance, consumer loans, education loans, etc.) will become the need of the hour. Salient features of the scheme along with specific facilities being offered on the product will be flashed on the Net. The key information available on the portal could be application form, a list of the banks' retail boutiques where the loans would be disbursed, an automatic monthly instalment calculator, a colour choice indicator and link-ups for technical specifications on various models of cars.

### Special Banking Facilities

Banks will be forced to provide special banking facilities on various products to their customers. Some of such facilities could be:

1. Allowing customers to access their accounts anytime they like
2. Making relation managers at branches the main point of contact for high net worth customers
3. Providing investment advices on mutual fund products
4. Making available broking services to buy and sell shares
5. Offering ATM cards with the facility of withdrawing cash from any ATM of the bank in the country
6. Offering preferential rates and discounts on the bank's loan and overdraft products to high net worth clients
7. Providing emerging services including lost/stolen card reporting, emergency card replacement, emergency cash advances, medical and legal references and help in replacing lost or stolen pass ports, documents or cards.

### Internet Banking Facilities

Banks will start providing many facilities under the Internet banking. Such facilities may include inquiring transactions (both bank accounts and depository accounts), giving instructions for funds transfer between accounts, making requests for demand drafts, opening and renewing term deposits, exchanging e-mail with the bank, making inquiry on loans, guarantees and letters of credits, requesting bank for opening letters of credit, etc., paying electricity, telephone, other utility bills and credit card bills on the Net.

**Branch Networking**

Networking of branches by banks will be more pronounced in the days to come. Foreign banks and new breed of private sector bank along with the PSBs are in the process of formulating/ finalizing their plans for networking their branches countrywide. Some banks have already networked some of their branches on the test basis. This service will not only provide multi-branch banking facilities to customers but also make the task of inter-branch reconciliation, connectivity of ATMs, funds management, cash management, etc., more easier. Management Information System in the process will also become more effective, which will ultimately support the decision-making system in the bank.

**Risk and Issues**

Though Electronic and Internet banking do offer comforts to customers by delivering services at their doorsteps, there are some risk factors also which need attention of concerned banks today. The likely challenges the tech-savvy banks may face in the new millennium are summarized below:

- Electronic fraud is a scourge in the Western countries. In our country also banks may face this problem in near future.
- Unless electronic message is safeguarded from unauthorized access by hackers, people will continue to hesitate to use electronic banking.
- Adequacy of telecommunication infrastructure is also necessary. The electronic banking needs large-scale wide area network connectivity. India does not have that yet. In fact, according to NASSCOM, the huge disparity between national and the international bandwidth is primarily responsible for poor Internet spread and reliability in the country.
- The key factors for Internet banking are the faith of the people and regulations. How the faith of customers will have to be gained?

## FUTURE SHAPE OF BANKING

Indian banking stands at the threshold of a mega change in the next five years. Many new situations as compared to the present scenario are predicted to emerge. However, the banking industry too sees the opportunities and failures in distinctively different ways (Ninan, 2005). Three substantial reports have been released in the last few weeks: 'India Top 20 Banks' by Crisil, 'Indian Banking 2010: Towards a High Performing Sector' by McKinsey, and the 'Interim Report of the Independent Commission on Banking and Financial Policy' set up by the All-India Bank Officers Confederation.

In the interesting futuristic study, Mckinsey uncovers 'three potential scenarios' that could emerge in the banking sector by 2010; after the entry of large number of foreign banks based on the interplay between and regulating interventions and management strategies. The first is "highlighting" scenario, where the policy makers to intervene to the extent of ensuring system stability and protecting the consumers' interest. In the second is "evolving" scenario, policy makers adopt a pro-market stance but are cautious on pushing reform for more value addition by the banking sector. The third scenario is "stagnating" where the policy makers intervene to set restrictive conditions and management is unable to execute changes to deliver value to shareholders or customers.

The evidences from many emerging market economies shows that a greater reliance on banking FDI has given rise to conditions of stalled overall growth in credit with domestic banks, far greater financial instability to domestic economy during depression, and uncertainty and slow economic growth due to attack from foreign banks by imposing strategic decisions from parent banks into developing markets. These consequences are an expression of loss of economic sovereignty – states Independent Commission.

On consolidation of banks, especially public sector banks, the Commission says that the gains from consolidations are expected along greater economies of scale, and scope available to bigger banks. The evidences do not support an automatic association between large size and profitability. On the other hand, bigger banks tend to rely more on large transactions and, standardise balance sheets. They focus more on fee-based income to seek to avert credit and interest risk, and on trading risk at the securities market. These tendencies give rise to the phenomenon of financial exclusion (whereby a large section of population remains unbanked) at the same time that it endangers financial fragility via a greater exposure to financial markets.

While stressing the need to create a market – driven banking sector with adequate focus on social development, Mckinsey proposes a strong focus on 'social development' by leveraging technology to innovate and profitably provide banking services to lower income and rural markets. S and Perception also makes a reference to rural banking by public sector banks. The most urgent need is to increase credit provision to the rural areas for both agricultural and non-agricultural purposes–states the Commission. Given a chance, the PSBs will close down their rural operations where the incur losses which were made good by urban branches. It is necessary to modify the nature of expectations of profitability of rural branches. What India needs today is a proper banking structure to ensure that these funds reach the end users.

**BANKING IN ORISSA**

The economic development of particular region coincides with the development of banking in that area. The role of well developed financial infrastructure in stimulating and sustaining economic growth is well recognised. In Orissa, the first modern bank namely, Puri Joint Stock Bank came into existence in 1904. Afterwards, the Cuttack Joint Stock Bank and the Jagannath Bank were set up in 1913 and 1919 respectively. The Puri Joint Stock Bank and the Jagannath Bank were liquidated during the mid-thirties and the Cutttack Joint Stock Bank was merged with United Bank of India in the year 1954. On the eve of World War II, a fresh attempt was made to promote commercial banking in State through private initiative. The Maharaja of erstwhile Mayurbhanj State had established Mayurbhanj State Bank in 1938, which was merged with State Bank of India in 1961. Few more non-scheduled banks operated in Orissa and were forced to liquidate their business in late forties (Mishra, 1985).

The first branch of Imperial Bank of India in Orissa was opened at Berhampur (Ganjam) in 1921 and subsequently the second branch at Cuttack in the same year. There were only 14 bank branches in Orissa in 1949, serving 9.91 lakh populations per branch on an average where as 1.19 lakh at the national level. The concentration of bank offices were in larger towns rather than smaller towns and rural areas further highlighted the lopsided and haphazard spread of banking facilities in Orissa. Till the formation of State Bank of India in 1955, hardly any steps were taken by the banks to expand the branch network in Orissa.

**Table 2.5: Banking Activities in Orissa**

| Year | No. of Branches | Deposits (in Rs. Crore) | Advances (in Rs. Crore) | C-D Ratio | Population per Branch ('000) |
|---|---|---|---|---|---|
| 1969 | 100 | 31.13 | 16.61 | 53.4 | 212 |
| 1979 | 714 | 283.51 | 181.90 | 64.2 | 36.0 |
| 1989 | 1896 | 2197.84 | 1757.25 | 83.4 | 16.0 |
| 1999 | 2209 | 10,239.54 | 4,352.59 | 42.51 | 16.2 |
| 2000 | 2213 | 12,653.12 | 5,539.81 | 43.78 | 16.3 |
| 2001 | 2214 | 14,629.02 | 6,745.39 | 46.00 | 16.6 |
| 2002 | 2224 | 18,689.18 | 8,527.15 | 45.63 | 16.6 |
| 2003 | 2232 | 20,347.87 | 10,430.71 | 51.26 | 16.8 |
| 2004 | 2242 | 23,359.86 | 13,390.53 | 57.32 | 17.0 |
| 2005 | 2261 | 27,372.64 | 17,587.83 | 64.25 | 17.1 |

*Sources:* 1. Economic Survey of Orissa, various issues.
2. S.L.B.C. Reports.

The nationalisation of commercial banks in 1969 has provided banking services to the unbanked areas. The number of branches of different commercial banks in Orissa was 100, which has been raised to 1896 by the end of June 1989. During the post-nationalisation period, banks in Orissa have spectacular progress in mobilisation of deposit through various schemes and a wide network of branches. At the nationalisation, aggregate deposits were Rs. 31.13 crore, which went up to Rs. 1884.92 crore by the end of June 1989. The share of aggregate deposit of Orissa to the

National deposit was 0.67 per cent at end of June 1969, has been increased to 1.28 per cent at the end of June 1989. The aggregate credit of the banks were Rs. 16.63 crore against a deposit of Rs. 31.13 crore as on 1969 giving the credit-deposit (C-D) ratio of 53.4 per cent as against the All-India average of 77 per cent. At the end of June 1989, the C-D ratio stood at 83.4 per cent as against the national average of 60 per cent, clearly indicating a better utilisation rate and need for bank credit. The details of banking facilities available in Orissa in the post-nationalisation period are given Table 2.5 (*See on page No. 81*).

It is evident from the Table 2.5 that there were 34 scheduled commercial banks (SCBs) with 1410 branches and 9 regional rural banks (RRBs) with 832 branches are operating in the State as on March 2004 as against 1427 branches of SCBs and 834 RRBs on 31st March 2005. There were 10 commercial banks with 16 branches in private sector operating in Orissa during 2003-04, which has grown to 19 branches by end of March 2005. Recently, a new private bank (named Siran Catholic Bank) and a foreign Bank (named Citi Bank) has opened their offices in Bhubaneswar. At present, the number of branches of private banks has gone up to 29 in Orissa, of which 16 are operating in Bhubaneswar (Bihari, 2005).

The deposits has risen from Rs. 31.13 crore to Rs. 2197.84 crore during 1969 to 1989 period, showing an increase of about 70 times. During the same period, the advances have risen by more than 100 times. During the period (i.e. 1969-2005), the deposits and advances have shown consistently growth trend. The total deposits of the public sector commercial banks stood at Rs. 23, 041.08 crore at the end of March 2005, as against the figure of 1,089.61 crore for private banks and Rs. 27,372.64 crore for all commercial banks (including the RRBs). Similarly, the total advances of the commercial banks in the state was Rs. 17,587.83 crore, out of which the share of public sector banks were Rs. 14,874.98 crore and private sector banks were Rs. 623.72 crore at the end of March 2005. The population served per branch has gone down from 212 thousands in 1969 to 16 thousand in 1989. After that slow progress has been witnessed during the post-liberalisation period (1999-2005). This development was spectacular in the history of development of banking in Orissa.

The trends in credit utilisation in Orissa (indicated by C-D ratio) was also encouraging during that period (1969-89), but in the post-liberalisation period it has become low due to the conservative approaches of the banks and the NPA problems. The C-D ratio is much less than the national average. Out of the total advances, Rs. 10061 crore has gone towards the priority sector registering a growth of 30.55 per cent over the previous year. Similarly, the advances to agriculture, small-scale industries (SSI), and weaker section have gone up by 64 per cent, 21 per cent, and 22 per cent respectively. This trend is visible because of the presence of RRBs and public sector banks; those are committed to the social cause and carry out the policies of the Governments. The private sector banks more focus on commercial advances, more particularly to the service sector.

## REFERENCES


Balachandran, M (2005); "Strategic Model for Re-positioning of PSBs", *IBA Bulletin*, Vol. XXVII, No. 8, (August), pp. 5-8.

Gopalkrishnan, S (2005); "Customer Service and Grievance Redressal Mechanism", *The ICFAI Journal of Banking Law*, October, pp. 29-39.

Govt. of India (1950); "Rural Banking Enquiry Committee Report", New Delhi, p. 1.

Govt.of Orissa (2004-05); "Economic Survey of Orissa", P&C Dept., pp. 13/1-13/3.

Govt. of Orissa (1979); *Statistical Abstracts of Orissa*, pp. 45-50.

IBA Bulletin (August 2005); "Performance Highlights of Public Sector Banks 2004-05", pp. 26-34.

Jain, (1986); *Indigenous Banking in India*, pp. 20-23.

Jalan, Dr. Bimal (2002); "Strengthening Indian Banking and Finance: Progress and Prospectus" *Indian Banking: Managing Transformation*, BECON 2002, Bangalore, pp. 19-21.

Kamesam, Vepa (2002); "Reengineering Operations in Banking System", *Indian Banking: Managing Transformation*, BECON 2002, Bangalore, pp. 28-32.

Macdonnell and Keith (1977); *Vedic Index of Names and Subjects*, Vol. I, p.109.

Mishra, S.N. (1984 ); *Growth of Commercial Banking in India*, Anu Books, Meerut, pp. 20-29.

Mohan, Rakesh (2002); "Transforming Indian Banking: In Search of a Better Tomorrow", *Indian Banking: Managing Transformation*, BECON 2002, Bangalore, pp. 33-40.

Muniappan, G.P (2002); "Reorienting Structure", *Indian Banking: Managing Transformation*, BECON 2002, Bangalore, pp. 24-25.

Panadikar, S.G. (1998); *Banking in India*, Orient Longman, New Delhi, pp. 1-19.

Panda, Jagannath and Dash, R.K. (1991); *Development Banking in India*; Discovery Publishing House, New Delhi, pp. 53-55.

Rao, K.N (2005); "India's Universal Banks – ICICI Bank", *Professional Banker*, August, pp. 17-22.

Rao, K.N (2005); "India's Universal Banks – State Bank Group", *Professional Banker*, August, pp. 23-24.

Rao, K.N (2005); "Universal Banking", *Professional Banker*, August, pp. 13-16.

Reserve Bank of India (1954); "Banking and Monetary Statistics"; Bombay, p. 275.

Reserve Bank of India (2003-04); *Report on Banking Trends and Progress*, Mumbai, pp. 221-253.

Sharma, H.C. (1969); *Growth of Banking in a Developing Economy—A Case Study of Rajasthan*, p. 25.

SLBC 102nd Meeting Agenda & Notes (2005), UCO Bank, Regional Office, Bhubaneswar, p. 5.

Ninan, Oommen A. (2005); "Future shape of Banking", *The Hindu*, October 24, p. 17.

*CHAPTER–3*

# ROLE OF MARKETING IN BANKING

## INTRODUCTION

"The future is not ahead of us. It has already happened. Unfortunately, it is unequally distributed among companies, industries, and nations"– Kotler (2003). Today it is fashionable to talk about marketing in a globalise era. The last decade of 20th century has seen four distinct faces of change in the banking and financial sector in India – globalisation, deregulation, technological change and innovation. In a rapidly changing and expanding competitive environment, banks are no longer confined to their traditional activities but are venturing into unknown territories like bank assurance, value-added services, etc. Moreover, due to the rise in literacy level and increasing awareness, the customers of today have become more learned about the risks, returns and costs associated with various financial services and have gained the power of choosing his banker. As a result, the banks faced the burnt of intense competition both from their counterparts and upcoming specialised financial institutions. Therefore, to combat with the volatility and risks associated with financial market; a specialised marketing function has emerged in the banking sector focusing on the customer. The new generation private banks and the foreign banks have already realised that they cannot compete with the public sector banks for their natural advantages of reach and customer base. They have adopted non-price strategy to create new markets. At this backdrop, this chapter provides a theoretical perspective concerning marketing and its application to banking based on review of relevant literatures and marketing research studies both from India and abroad.

Banking sector is probably the most important financial sector not just in terms of turnover, profit and employment, but also in its paramount impact on all spheres of the economy. The five-year plans in India, always call for tremendous efforts for resources mobilisation by all concerned. Since the banks are the major repositories of public savings and purveyors of credit, they have been increasingly called upon to mobilise and channel their resources for meeting plan objectives. In order to meet the ever increasing expectations of the society from the banking system, it is utmost important that the banking industry should keep pace with changing needs of the society. During the last two decades, more particularly after liberalisation of Indian economy, Indian banks have undergone unprecedented qualitative and quantitative changes. After nationalisation of commercial banks in India (1969 and 1980), the emphasis of the banks have changed from 'class-baking' to 'mass-banking'. Now the question before the Indian public sector banks to face the competition and survive between the twin contrasting objectives of profit making and social-banking.

The recent years have witnessed significant developments in international banking. Competition, disintermediation, new services and unique promotion schemes are some of the emerging features of changing international banking scenario. The globalisation of financial markets has been facilitated by the progressive removal of controls and barriers to movement capital across the borders (unification of currency and trade pacts among the European economy). This process has been further accelerated by the development of technology particularly in the field of telecommunication, information technology and electronic banking system. India is not far behind in this regard. It has made its laws flexible and liberal, allowed foreign banks to operate and progressively loosen the hackles in the path of smooth functioning of the banking sector. Now commercial banks in India are provided operational freedom and will be held accountable for their own results. The major problem before the commercial banks, more particularly the public sector banks in India, is their long-run survival by retaining their valued customers.

## THE MARKETING CONCEPT

Marketing is a very common word in the dictionary of managers and planners. But it has been defined by various authors differently focusing on its role and functions. Kotler (2003), the marketing *guru* has defined marketing as 'a social and managerial process by which individual and groups obtain what they need and want through creating and exchanging products and value with others'. For a managerial definition, marketing has often been described as 'the art of selling' but the important part of marketing is not selling, rather it is the 'tip of marketing iceberg'. Peter F. Drucker (1973), a leading management thinker, puts marketing as "there will always, one can assume, be need for some selling. But the aim of marketing is to make selling superfluous. The aim of marketing is to know and understand the customer so well that the product or service fits him and sells itself. Ideally, marketing should result in a customer who is ready to buy. All that should be needed then is to make the product or service available."

The American Marketing Association (AMA) offers the following definition: "Marketing is the process of planning and executing the conception, pricing, promotion, and distribution of ideas, goods and services to create exchanges that satisfy individual and organisational goals." Coping with the exchange processes calls for considerable amount of work and skill. A potential exchange thinks about the means of achieving desired responses from the other parties. Thus, marketing management is the art and science of choosing target markets and getting, keeping, and growing customers through creating, delivering, and communicating superior customer value.

People do not purchase a product or use a service *per se*. Instead they are seeking ways of satisfying a need. Thus, marketing is concerned with identifying 'consumer needs' and determining ways in which the organisation is able to meet these needs in a profitable manner (Laurent, 1982). Understanding customer needs is essential to marketing. This will enable the organisation to design and offer product and services to satisfy the customers' needs.

The marketing concept (Fig. 3.1) is a basis for decision-making and a guide for effectively managing resources (Stanton, 1987). This concept recognises that the objectives of the company are customer satisfaction at profitable volume through co-ordination of marketing objectives.

**Marketing Concept**

| SUCCESSFUL BUSINESS | | |
|---|---|---|
| MARKETING CONCEPT | | |
| CUSTOMER ORIENTATION | PROFITABLE SALES VOLUME | CO-ORDINATION OF MARKETING ACTIVITIES |

**Fig. 3.1**

**Customer Orientation**

The planning and operations of the Organisation should be directed at enhancing customer satisfaction. Customer orientation is the firm's orientation towards larger customer interest. The satisfied customers often become effective sales people for the bank through word-of-mouth advertising and communications with the acquaintances (Pezzullo, 1982). What is required for an organisation is to be marketing oriented and not sales orientated. Sales orientation focuses the business on making a product or delivering a service and then working at getting it sold. In this approach, the emphasis is on getting the customer to do what the firm desires. A marketing orientation, on the other hand, makes the organisation to find what the customer wants and then working at getting the business to provide it. Here, the emphasis is on getting the firm to do what the customer desires. In the former case, the company is bending upon customer demand to fit the company's supply. In the later case, it is bending its supply to the will of customer demand (Stanton, 1987).

**Profitable Operation**

The marketing concept places a stress on the use of management tools to pursue the profit objective. It is concerned with creating a profitable volume, not just volume. Here, the marketing problem is, however, not to offer products/services to satisfy the customer needs, but to satisfy the customers' need at a price profitable to the organisation (Bal, 1992). For marketing oriented organisations, the pursuit of profit is often characterised by the use of operations research and computer aided techniques, sophisticated cost accounting and profit centre analysis (Pezzullo, 1982). The management must be aware of the relative profit earning potential of different products or services needed by the target customers. Hence, this will satisfy those needs of the customers and still earn a profit. This does not mean that the firm should never sell a product or service at a loss; however, when it does so, it should (1) recognise that it is doing so, and (2) be sure to have a very good reason.

Companies address the needs by putting forth a value proposition, a set of benefits they offer to satisfy their needs (Kotler, 2003). The intangible value proposition is made physical by an offering, which can be a combination of products, services, information, and experiences. The offering will be successful, if it delivers value and satisfaction to the target buyer. The buyer chooses between different offerings on the basis of which is perceived to deliver the most value. Value can be primarily be seen as a combination of quality, service and price (QSP), called the customer value triad. Value increases with quality and service and decreases with price. The marketer can increase the value of the customer offering in several ways:

- Raise benefits
- Reduce costs
- Raise benefits and Reduce costs
- Raise benefits by more than the rise in costs
- Lower benefits by less than the reduction in costs

**Co-Ordination of Marketing Activities**

All marketing activities in a firm should be organisationally co-ordinated (Stanton, 1987). The company's activities should be devoted to determining customer wants and then satisfying those wants, while still making a profit over a long run. It becomes very important that the people in an organisation work together toward common goals. Through common commitment to the organisational marketing activities, they will help the organisation to be successful. When all the departments of the organisation work together to serve the customer's interests, the result is integrated marketing (Kotler, 2003). Unfortunately, not all the employees are trained and motivated to work for the customer. Integrated marketing takes place on two levels. First, various marketing functions – sales forces, advertising, customer service, product management, marketing research – must work together. Second, marketing must be embraced by other departments; as they must also "think customers". To foster teamwork among all departments, the company carries out internal as well as external marketing. External marketing is marketing directed towards people outside the organisation, while internal marketing is task of hiring, training, and motivating able employees who want to serve customers well. In fact, internal marketing must precede external marketing. It makes no sense to promise excellent service before the company's staffs are ready to provide it.

## THE MARKETING PROCESS

For effective marketing, it is essential to know the marketing process. The marketing process involves five major steps, which are shown in Fig. 3.2.

### THE MARKETING PROCESS

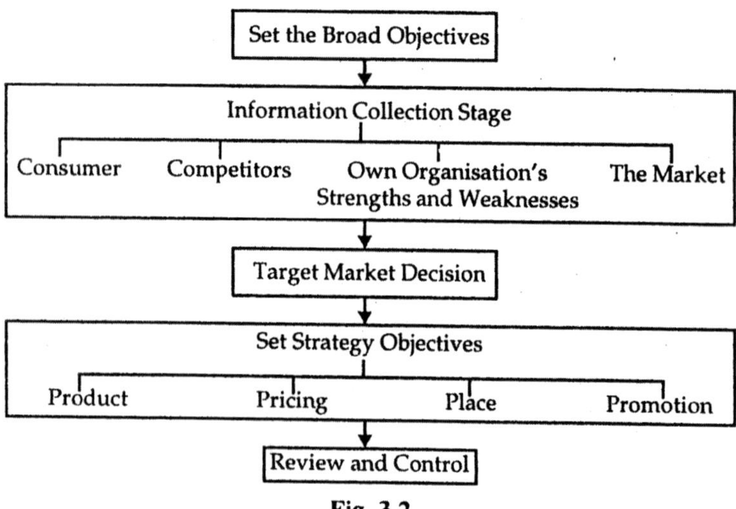


**Fig. 3.2**

*Source:* Adopted from C.R. Laurent (1982); "Marketing role in Banking", *The Bankers Magazine.*

**Setting the Marketing Objectives**

The first step in the marketing process is to define the objectives in clear and specific terms, which are to be achieved during a defined time period. Marketing objectives are composed of the basic objectives, goals and targets (Gandhi, 1985). The formulation of the basic marketing objectives requires close interaction between the Company's top management and the marketing manager, because those are shaped and influenced by the organisation's basic objectives. Out of all the objectives; the one which is more precise (quantifiable), achievable, and communicable; it will be more effective as a motivator and organiser (Laurent, 1982). If a particular organisation is very diverse in its operations, a number of objectives have to be developed, giving consideration to their relative consistency. The objectives set by the organisation may be consumer orientated, may sales oriented, may be profit oriented, etc.

**Information Collection Stage**

Given the broad marketing objectives of consumer orientation, the next step is to collect information about the present and potential consumers in the target market in order to identify their specific needs. As the markets of today are very complex, the marketing manager requires the right information to assist him in making the best decisions concerning the nature of the marketing strategy to be adopted. To measure the attractiveness of any given market, it requires estimating the market's over all size, growth, and profitability. Modern marketing practices call for dividing the market into major segments, evaluating them, selecting and targeting to certain ones, and deciding the company's positioning in each market (Kotler, 2003).

The overall market information regarding the size, growth, market opportunities, and threats will give a good indication of competitive stance that should be adopted. The information, relative strengths and weaknesses of the products and services, and the market of the organisation will help a company to take necessary steps to turn its weaknesses into strengths. Information regarding other competitors will help the company to formulae competitive strategies to achieve its objectives. Information regarding the awareness, attitude, motives, and perceptions of a target market segment will help to design the right product and develop the right promotional strategy.

**Target Market Decision**

The days of standardised products and mass marketing strategy have already been over. Marketers must speak differently to different demographic groups with particular emphasis on benefits to specific demographic groups (Davis and Cohn, 1989). Once the marketers have detailed information about their customers, they can easily segment the market. Here any segment may conceivably be selected as a target market to be reached with a distinct marketing mix. Under competitive conditions, it is seldom possible for any firm to acquire control over the total market. After identifying the distinct market segments, the next step is to evaluate and prioritise each segment. This prioritisation holds the key to ensure effective market penetration. The marketing manager should find out, for each segment, the likely volume of business, likely cost of reaching that business, likely long-term prospects, and likely parameters of the marketing strategy. In order to ensure the best utilisation of the limited resources, the organisation has to decide the target markets that can best help them to achieve the profit objectives.

**Developing the Marketing Strategy**

Strategy is the connecting link between planning and action. Marketing strategy is essentially the firm's product-market choice, which is guided by environmental necessities and firm's objectives and capabilities. Formulation of effective marketing strategy should guide the philosophy of customer's need satisfaction in the target segment. This involves setting objectives for each of the marketing variables; viz., product, price, place, and promotion. The specific nature of the products and services to be offered, the specific level and nature of market awareness and sales to be achieved and the particular promotional method to be used, the number points at which the services are to be made available, and if flexibility exists in terms of pricing, then at range that should vary are the decisions which are required for developing a marketing strategy.

### Review and Control

Having defined the parameters of the marketing strategy to be developed, the last step is to implement them and at regular intervals, monitor the progress and achievements. Where variances exist, they should be examined to determine why they have occurred and identify whether the problem lies in the strategy or its implementation. If required, care should be taken to modify the market plan, as no market plan is perfect. The individual components of the market plan should work as a synergistic unit.

Customer feedback should form the basis for bringing about improvement in quality of service and product deigns. Intimate knowledge about different segments of customers requires investment of time, money, and expertise. But results of marketing efforts driven by real knowledge can provide a handsome return.

## EFFECTIVE MARKETING STRATEGY

Marketing strategies and tactics are concerned with taking decisions on a number of variables to influence mutually-satisfying exchange transactions and relationships. Typically, marketers have a number of tools they can use, and these include mega-marketing (Kotler, 2003) and the so-called 4ps of marketing (McCarthy, 1999), among others. This section examines certain relevant dimensions of marketing strategy and effectiveness.

### Marketing Research

Researching the market for any product or service is undertaken to gather relevant information and data that aid a number of marketing management decisions, which include the development of a new product, modification of an existing product, the content of advertising, pricing level, distribution channels, customer and client behaviour, among others. The effectiveness of marketing research is often studied in relation to specific marketing decisions. Its importance as a marketing variable has been recognized over time (Rothwell et al, 1974; British Institute of Management, 1975; Baker and Abou-Zeid, 1982; Connell, 1979; Takeuchi and Quelch, 1983; Alexander, 1985; Walsh and Roy, 1983; among others). It seems logical, therefore, to hypothesize that market research has a positive influence on organisational performance/effectiveness. Given the dictate of the marketing concept that the customer/client is, or should be, the focus of the organization, it is axiomatic that marketing and market research be included in an organization's operations that result into managerial effectiveness. However, investigations of the existence and effectiveness of marketing and market research have been called into some question. Criticism by Ames (1970), Wilson (1984) and King (1985), among others, has emphasised that counting the number of heads in marketing research departments, or estimating marketing research budgets, focuses on the trappings of marketing, not its substance. While much research exists which can help companies implement marketing research strategies and policies, relatively little work has been done which suggests how these marketing research variables relate to organisational performance and effectiveness, either in absolute terms or in relation to other marketing factors (Baker and Hart, 1989).

**Product Strategy**

Some normative and empirical researchers have posited that, ultimately, organizational effectiveness is a function of its product or service policy (Baker, 1985; Majaro, 1977; Borden, 1963; Aluko, 1983). For example, "Price" is the price of the product or service, "advertising" is the advertising of the product or service, "distribution" is the distribution of the product or service, and "promotion" is the promotion of the product or service. All of these are product considerations (Kent, 1984). NEDO (1977) published a study on non-price factors influencing export performance or effectiveness, and one of the major aspects of the research was defined as product, including design, reliability, specification, delivery, and after-sales service.

The necessity of product innovation is widely recognised as being of critical importance, not only to organizational and strategic effectiveness, but also to a nation (Baker, 1985; Kotler, 2003). It is to be noted, however, that many factors which comprise product or service policy, (such as product differentiation, design, performance, reliability, technological advancement, superior manufacturing, new product development, product modifications, diversification, etc.) are organic ways of gaining competitive advantage and achieving organizational success and effectiveness. King (1985), in an assessment of marketing, makes the point that "Real" marketing's take-off point is designing a product or service to meet the needs and wants of a group of customers or clients. It embraces suitability for purpose, quality, design, availability, after sales service, and other aspects of a customer's/client's relationship with a product brand.

**Promotional Strategy**

The quality of a product/service can be enhanced by what Piercy (1982) calls 'marketing intangibles'. A number of studies have included 'service' on the list of factors distinguishing product success from failure. For example, in the list of strengths displayed by Japanese industry, Baranson (1980) included 'financial support' and 'after-sales service'. The sales team can be a source of competitive advantage and effectiveness for a company. Piercy (1985) has noted that aggressive selling was the Critical Success Factor (CSF) in the sample companies. Similarly, Baker and Abou-Zeid (1982) have shown that in award-winning British companies, personal selling was the most widely used method of promotion. A great deal has been written regarding the comparative success of various selling styles and a various sales attributes. Complex models have been developed to aid the decisions central to the management of sales forces in the field, namely; allocating selling effort and setting sales force size; territorial design; sales forecasting; evaluation and control (Bestwick and Cravens, 1977). Sales volume is also seen to be a function of environmental factors, company marketing strategy and tactics, sales-force organisation, and policies and procedures such as organisation, deployment of resources, recruiting and selection, training, rewards and incentives, evaluation and control (Walker, Churchill and Ford, 1979; Ryans and Weinberg, 1981; Avlonitis, Boyle and Kouremenos, 1985). Personal selling is an important marketing tool, which depends for its success/effectiveness on a number of factors such as organisation, training, remuneration and motivation, supervision, and evaluation (Baker and Hart, 1989).

Contemporary strategic marketing practice calls for more than developing a good product or service, pricing it adequately, and making it available to target customers or clients. Organizations should also promote their products and services to present and potential customers and clients. Udel (1968) identified marketing promotions as the most important facet of marketing strategy leading to effectiveness. Advertising, an aspect of promotional strategy, has both an informative and persuasive role, and in this respect can alter customers'/clients' perceptions of a product or service. As Pickering (1976) suggests, advertising can increase brand loyalty, thereby decreasing price elasticity through increased differentiation. Bain (1956) posited that advertising can have a cumulative and long lasting effect on organisational and strategic performance.

### Pricing Strategy

Some studies have included price on the list of critical factors, which determine success and effectiveness. Atkin and Skinner (1975), for example, reveal that companies regard pricing policy/ strategy as being either vital or most important to their business performance and effectiveness. Also, Mikesell and Farah (1980) posit that the decline of the USA share of markets in developing countries was mainly due to price factors. By contrast, a number of writers maintain that price is the least important determinant of demand. Posner and Steel (1979), for example, contend that non-price factors are paramount in advanced countries. Such a view is upheld by the studies of Kavis and Lipsey (1971), Udell (1964) and Patchford and Ford (1976). Evidently, there is great diversity of perspective with regard to the relative importance of price and non-price factors in determining the success and effectiveness of strategies and companies.

### Mega-Marketing Strategy

In addition to the traditional marketing mix elements (i.e., the so-called 4Ps of marketing) of product, price, place, and promotion, marketing executives can use the tool of mega-marketing to achieve marketing objectives (Kotler, 2003). Mega-marketing is the strategically coordinated use of economic, psychological, political, and public relations skills to gain the co-operation and understanding of some relevant parties in order to enter and/or operate in a given market efficiently and effectively.

Marketing is concerned with the management of mutually-satisfying exchange transactions and relationships between and among the relevant parties. However, it is sometimes desirable to create additional incentives, services, and pressures for non-customers/clients. Mega-marketing, thus, takes an enlarged perspective of the skills and resources needed to enter and operate in certain markets or segments. In addition to preparing attractive product or offers for customers or clients, mega-marketing may use connections with powerful people in positions of authority to corner marketing jobs. Also, situations exist where markets in which the established participants or approvers have made it difficult for companies with similar or even better marketing offers to enter or operate. The difficulties or barriers can be in form of discriminatory legal requirements, political favouritism, cartel agreements, social or cultural biases, unfriendly distribution channels, and refusals to cooperate, among others. These challenges and difficulties can be handled via mega-marketing strategy. Marketers have traditionally defined marketing environment as those external factors, which cannot be controlled by an organisation. But mega-marketing posits that environmental factors can be handled through lobbying, legal action, negotiation, public relations, among others (Zeithaml and Berry, 1984). Also, traditionally, it is assumed and posited, through Say's Law of economics, that demand creates its own supply. But some markets can be blocked sometimes, thereby creating supply shortages, and this may necessitate the use of mega-marketing strategy.

**Distribution Strategy**

An important proposition in marketing and economics is that consumption depends on availability/distribution (Baker, 1980/81). But despite its obvious importance, distribution remains a largely neglected topic in marketing (Baker, 1992; Drucker, 1962). The marketing manager has two fundamental alternatives with respect to distribution strategy: he can either seek to work closely with intermediaries, or else assume their functions and push his products or services through the distribution channel; or he can seek to establish a franchise with ultimate consumers or clients and therefore pull his product or service through. Push strategies usually emphasize personal selling, while pull strategies tend to emphasize advertising and sales promotion (Baker, 1992). When selecting a channel of distribution for corporate effectiveness, a marketing manager should pay special attention to environmental factors, product and market characteristics, and company's strengths and weaknesses, among others.

When considering distribution policy and strategy, corporate marketing managers might try to gain competitive advantage by seeking a higher level of customer/client service. In this context, customer/client service is seen to mean all aspects of the distribution process, which add value to the exchange transaction from the customer/client perspective (Wilson, Gilligan and Pearson, 1992). However, higher levels of customer/client service can mean higher costs of distribution, and this might; therefore, reduce a company's price competitiveness and effectiveness. Wilson (1979) highlights the necessity to see costs as a whole since a reduction in one area can generate a disproportionate increase in another area. For example, it might be cheaper and more efficient to use an expensive means of transportation (e.g. air) than to maintain a number of local warehouses.

The distribution strategy is possibly more difficult to manage than the other elements of the marketing mix because its operational decisions involve other functions to a greater extent (Osuagwu, 2001). It is perhaps because of this organizational fragmentation of responsibility in distribution strategy activities that the idea of distribution as an integrative activity in business has only relative and recently developed (Wilson, Gilligan and Pearson, 1992). The need for auditing all the marketing-mix elements stems from change, and the distribution element of the marketing mix has, perhaps, been subject to more changes than any other element of the marketing mix in some countries. For example, in the UK, substantial changes have been observed in containerisation, computerisation, and distribution channels (Wilson, Gilligan and Pearson, 1992).

According to Chen (1999), in an industry, which is as complicated as the financial industry, there is no simple formula, which can predict successful and unsuccessful organizations from the surrounding environment. Critical Success Factors (CSFs) and a company's competitive ability and capability are the salient ingredients for competitive advantage (Bamberger, 1989). Therefore, an appropriate identification of a bank's CSFs can provide an avenue for assessing and building up its effectiveness and competitive advantage (Sheng, 1999). Corporate business strategy (in marketing, operations/production, finance, and personnel, among others) has been identified as an effective strategy that influences resource allocation, competitive advantage, and consequently, corporate efficiency and effectiveness (Hofer and Schendel, 1978).

## MARKETING OF SERVICES

The post-World War has witnessed rapid growth in the service sector, and more so the USA has become the World's first 'service economy', where in terms of output and employment, services has become the largest sector in the economy. The shift towards service economy has been a feature of many economically developed countries in recent years (Cowell, 1984). The growth of service industries can be traced to the economic development of a society and the socio-cultural change has accompanied it. The contribution of service sector to Indian economy was just 35 per cent in the 1980s, which has grown substantially in the last two decades. Today, it is the number one contributor to Indian economy with more than 49 per cent contribution and employs around 18 per cent of the workforce, clearly illustrating the growth and importance of this sector. This sector has fuelled worldwide economic growth, and it now accounts for 58 per cent of world GNP. However, along with this tremendous growth, comes the challenge to the service industry to live up to the customers, who are continuously benchmarking one experience against another, and are expecting improved services in every area (Dhananjayan, 2005). They are also becoming least tolerant to delays and failures in services, and expect every service provider to deliver world-class performance in every interaction. The growing demand for service excellence also gives an opportunity to service providers to emerge as leaders in their chosen field. ICICI bank has emerged as the leader in new-age banking, despite competition from the old and established banks, foreign banks, and the emerging new banks in the private sector. This is due to their standard in banking service along with a large distribution network achieved in short time, and impeccable delivery at all their touch points (Dhananjayan, 2005).

The dramatic growth of service industry has enabled the Indians to reach anyone in the world, from any corner of the country. Few years ago, banking was restricted to a handful of people, has spread to spread to every to street, with a private or public sector bank offering convenience and innumerable facilities. Increase affluence combined with increasing complexities of life and increasing insecurities have led to the phenomenal growth in the banking and insurance sector. The credit/debit cards with the ATM networks have proved to be a perfect substitute for cash. Recently, we have also noticed significant changes in the service sector in India, more so in the banking and insurance sector. During the last decade, many multi-national banks and insurance companies have entered India and have already established themselves in this sector. The entry of new private sector banks has poised a greater threat to the public sector banks, which altogether operates under sheltered regimes. At this juncture, the importance of service marketing assumes significant height. The following paragraphs discuss the service marketing strategies adopted by banks.

**Characteristics of Services**

Services have a number of unique characteristics that make them different from products. Some of the most commonly accepted characteristics those affect the designing of a marketing strategy are discussed below with their marketing implications.

*Intangibility:* Unlike physical products, services are not tangible. They can not be seen, touched, tasted, heard or smelled, but can be felt when experienced. This make the task of marketing services more complicated and stressed the marketers. The customers' expectations and perception about different services plays a vital role in designing the organisation's marketing plan. The sales force and the advertising department concentrate on the benefits to be derived from the service, rather than emphasising the service itself (Stanton and Futrell, 1987). Almost all the services are a mixture of tangibility and intangibility and fall on a continuum starting with pure tangibles (products) to pure intangibles (services). In order to convey the idea that it provides quick and efficient services, banks can tangibilise its positioning strategy through a number of tools like site and layout of the bank, efficient and responsive manpower, modern equipments and work technologies.

*Inseparability:* In most cases the service provider has to be present to perform the service and it can not be separated from him. Services are provided by a person who possesses a particular skill. This is in direct contrast to tangible products, which can be produced in a factory today, put into inventory tomorrow, sold latter on, and consumed in a still latter date. From a marketing stand point, inseparability frequently means that direct sale is the only possible channel of distribution and this limits the firm's scale of operation.

*Heterogeneity:* Services are highly variable, as the human element is involved in providing and rendering services. Services depend on who provides them and where they are provided. This makes standardisation a very difficult task to achieve. The newly joined bank clerk may not be as efficient as their experienced counterpart in processing a cheque. This is despite the fact the rules and procedures have been developed to reduce the role of human element and ensure maximum efficiency. Service companies should therefore pay particular attention to the product – planning stage of their marketing programmes. From the beginning, management has to do all to ensure consistency of quality.

*Perishability:* Services cannot be stored and perishes if not consumed. A service not availed is a total loss and no salvages can be made out of that. Very often the service providers face a fluctuating demand, which aggravates the marketing scenario. The combination of perishability and fluctuating demand offers challenges of product planning, pricing, and promotion to the managers of a service company. From marketing point of view, the same technique can be applied to both product and services. Successful marketing of both requires marketing research, designing the product/services and adopting a marketing strategy to market them. However, for marketing of services, the marketing manager must understand the nature and characteristics of services and the manner in which they impinge upon the marketing strategy.

**Change in Marketing Focus — The Service Triangle**

With the service industry becoming more and more dominant in the world today, a whole new paradigm of marketing is evolving. A shift focus from the conventional 4 Ps of marketing to a more evolved structure, involving all the elements in the buy-and-sell and touch-and-feel process, has become necessary.

The service-marketing triangle is built with employees, technology, and the service strategy as the corner points and customers at the heart of that triangle. To serve the customers better, the organisation should focus on employees, who provide the service to the customers, and make them an integral part of the service strategy. Combining this with technological advancements, which enable quicker and better service, with which a service organisation can arrive at the right formula for success in the service industry.

**Services Marketing Triangle**

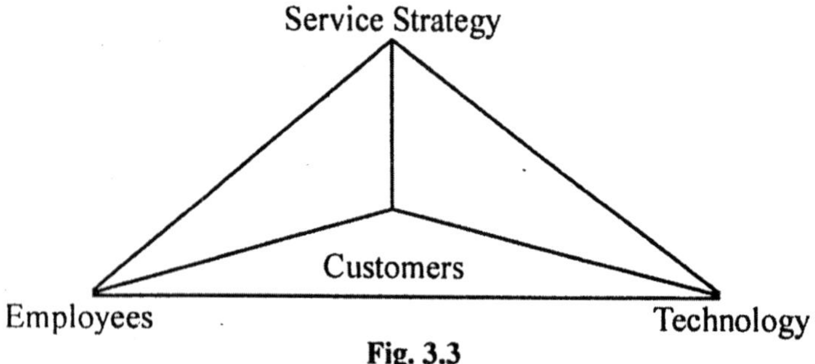


**Fig. 3.3**

(Adopted from Dhananjayan; Marketing Mastermind, February 2005)

**The Services Marketing Mix**

One of the most basic concepts in marketing is the marketing mix, defined as the elements of an organisation controls that can be used to satisfy the customers (Zeithaml and Bitner, 2003). Unlike marketing of products, the services also have four elements in the marketing mix; viz. product, price, place, and promotion. Apart from that, there are three more elements, like people, process, and physical evidence are there in the marketing mix for service marketing. A combination of these seven Ps makes marketing offers of the service provider. The first 4 Ps appear as core decision variables in a marketing plan. The notion of mix implies that all of these variables are interrelated and depend on each other to some extent. Further, the marketing mix philosophy implies that there is an optimal mix of the seven factors for a given market segment at a given point of time.

Careful management of *product, price, place, and promotion* will also be essential to the successful marketing of services. However, it needs certain modifications when applied to services. For example, traditionally promotion is thought of as involving decisions related to sales, advertising, etc. In services, these factors are also important, but as the services are to be produced and consumed simultaneously, service delivery people are involved in 'real time' promotion of the service even if their jobs are typically defined in terms of the operational function they perform (Zeithaml and Bitner, 2002).

A customer sees a company through its employees. Therefore, people as the performers of services are very important. The behaviour and attitude of personnel providing the service has great influence on the customers' overall perception of the service. The experiences of the customers are quite important, as they are the potential source of influence on other customers. Thus, the competence and commitment of service people is responsible for creation of services, which is quite important from marketing point of view.

In service organisations, the system by which customers receives delivery of services, constitute the process. In a service firm, there is no clear-cut inputs or outputs, rather it is a value addition process for the customers. The simplicity and operational ease of the process and procedures relating to the delivery system are also quite important.

## SERVICE QUALITY

Customer service is the primary end of any bank. A customer always wants something and expects that the bank should come up to the level to fulfil those needs. Again, the more you provide, still more the consumer needs. Service quality is about meeting customers' needs and requirements, and how well the service level delivered matches customer expectations. Service quality in banking implies consistently anticipating and satisfying the needs and expectations of customers (Howcroft, 1991). Raddon (1987) while emphasizing the importance of service quality in banks. Berry and Parasuraman (1991) also hold the view that high quality service gives credibility to the field sales force and advertising, stimulates favourable word-of-mouth communications, enhances customers' perception of value, and boosts the morale and loyalty of employees and customers alike.

Increased competition, slower growth, and mature markets are also forcing many businesses to review their customer service strategy. Many businesses are channelling more efforts to retain existing customers rather than to acquire new ones. There is enough evidence that demonstrates the strategic benefits of quality in contributing to market share and returns on investment (Adrian, 1995; Bateson, 1995; Berry and Parasuraman, 1991; Buzzel and Wiersema, 1981; Reichheld and Sasser, 1990) and lowering manufacturing cost and improving productivity (Garvin, 1983; Kotlar, 1999; Leonard and Sasser, 1982). Maximizing customer satisfaction through quality customer service has been described as the 'the ultimate weapon in all industries, when competitors are roughly matched, those that stress customer service will win." (Davidow and Uttal, 1989).

### Customer Expectations

Customer expectations are beliefs about service delivery that function as standards or reference points against which performance is judged. Because customers compare their perceptions of performance with these reference points when evaluating service quality, thorough knowledge about customer expectations is critical to service marketers (Zeithaml and Bitner, 2003). Knowing what the customer expects is the first and possibly most critical step in delivering quality service. Being wrong about what customers want can mean losing a customer's business when another company hits the target exactly. Being wrong also can mean not surviving in a fiercely competitive market. The level of expectation can vary widely depending on the reference point the customer holds. Although most of the customers has an intuitive sense of what expectations are; service marketers need a far more thorough and clear definition of expectations in order to comprehend, measure, and manage them. Expectations play a crucial role in customer evaluation of services. The marketers need to understand and would like to have control over those factors/forces which may influences customer expectations but most of such factors are uncontrollable. The two largest influences on desired service level are personal needs and philosophies about service (Zeithaml and Bitner, 2003). Personal needs; those states or conditions essential to physical or psychological well-being of the customer, are pivotal factors that shape what the consumer desired in a service. Another enduring service intensifier is personal service philosophy – the customer's underline generic attitude about the meaning of service and the proper conduct of service providers.

**Customer Perceptions**

How the customers perceive services, how they assess their experiences in terms of services and whether they are satisfied are the main concerns of customer perception. Figure 3.4 graphically illustrates the relationship between satisfaction and service quality. Zeithaml and Bitner (2003) have used the terms satisfaction and quality interchangeably. Consensus is growing that the two concepts are fundamentally different in terms of their underlying causes and outcomes (Parasuraman et al, 1988; Oliver, 1988; Brady and Cronin, 2001). Although they have something in common, satisfaction is generally viewed as a broader concept, whereas service quality focuses specifically on dimensions of service. Based on this view, perceived service quality is a component of customer satisfaction as illustrated in the diagram.

### Customer Perceptions of Quality and Customer Satisfaction

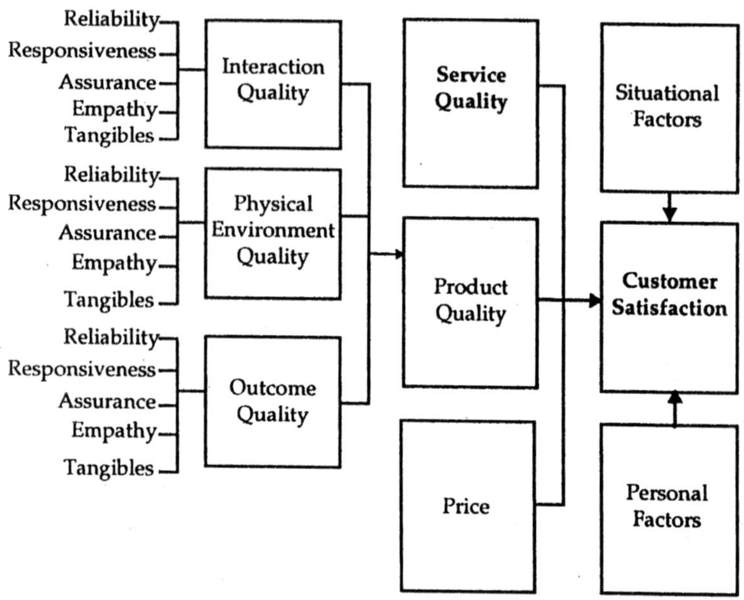


**Fig. 3.4**

*Source:* Zeithaml, V A and Bitner, M.J. (2003). *Services Marketing: Integrating Customer Focus Across the Firms*, 3rd Edition, Tata-McGraw Hill, New Delhi. p. 85

Service quality is a focused evaluation that reflects the customer's perception of elements of service such as interaction quality, physical environment quality, and outcome quality (Brady and Cronin, 2000). These elements are in turn evaluated based on specific service quality dimension: reliability, assurance, responsiveness, empathy and tangibles (Parasuraman et al, 1988). Satisfaction on the other hand, is more inclusive: it is influenced by perceptions of service quality, product quality and price as well as situational factor and personal factors. Customer satisfaction is a broader concept that will be influenced by perceptions of service quality but that will include perceptions of product quality, price, personal factors such as consumer's emotional state, and even uncontrollable situational factors (Oliver, 1988).

## Customer Satisfaction

Satisfaction is the customer's fulfilment response. It is a judgement that a product or a service feature, or the product or service itself, provides a pleasurable level of consumption related fulfilment (Oliver, 1993). Thus satisfaction means the customer's evaluation of a product or service in terms of whether that product or service has met their needs and expectations. Failure to meet needs and expectations is assumed to result in dissatisfaction with the product or service. This is governed by a set of theories explaining the post purchase evaluation (theories of disconfirmation). Numerous theoretical structures have been proposed to examine the antecedents of satisfaction and develop meaningful measures of the construct (Ravichandran and Thyagarajan, 1998). Four psychological theories may be considered as important while predicting the effects of product evaluation and consumer satisfaction. They are: cognitive dissonance (assimilation), contrast, generalised negativity and assimilation contrast (Anderson, 1973).

Dissonance or assimilation theory signifies that any discrepancy between expectation and product performance will be minimised or assimilated by consumers adjusting his perception of the product to be more consistent with his expectations (Loudon and Dela Bita, 2000). Leon Festinger (1957) suggests that an individual has cognitive elements (knowledge) about his past behaviour, beliefs and attitudes in his environment. These pieces of information are cognition, which consumer likes to have consistent with one another. Jonathan Freedman (1964) suggests that a slight under statement of the products' qualities in advertising might lead to higher consumer satisfaction with the company's product. The generalised negativity theory is that any discrepancy between expectation and reality results in a generalised negative state, causing the product to receive a more unfavourable rating than if it had matched with expectations. Finally, the assimilation-contrast approach maintains that there are zones or latitudes of acceptance and rejection in consumer perception. If the disparity between expectation and product performance is sufficiently small to fall into the consumer's latitude of acceptance, he will tend to assimilate the difference. However if the discrepancy is larger than the zone of tolerance, the contrast effect will come into play and the consumer magnifies the perceived disparity between product and his expectations for it. The theory assumes that the individual have ranges or latitudes of acceptance, rejection and neutrality (Hoveland et al, 1948).

**The Gap in Service Quality**

Despite the best efforts by the service provider, gaps exist in the services offered to the customers, and the same is reflected in several complaints voiced by customers' everyday through different media. The following reasons can be attributed to this:

- Word of mouth, past experiences, and the brand promise through communication lead to certain level of service expectation among the customers.
- This expectation is continuously being benchmarked against what the consumer gets in reality, during his interaction with the service provider.
- The gap between what was expected and what is perceived/ experienced in reality decides the satisfaction that the consumer finally gets out of the product/service.

**BANK MARKETING**

Bank marketing is the creation and delivery of financial services suitable to meet the customers' needs at a profit to the bank. Two important functions of bank marketing are to mobilise deposits on one hand and to attract the borrowers and the users of financial services on the other (Meidan, 1984). The importance of bank marketing stems from intense competition not only from other banks, but also from host of financial institutions operating for different specialised purposes. The need for bank marketing also arises due to increasing sophistication of bank customers, improvement in technology, and increased cost of meeting the customers' needs. A way of thinking along marketing lines is essential in all areas of banking to enable the banks to match the banks' resources with the customers' needs in a more profitable manner.

The concept of bank marketing is significant for the reasons that customers are changing in terms of their wants, needs, desires, expectation and problems (Joshi, 1988). As social institution, banks need to evaluate their offerings in customer terms, i.e., satisfying customer needs at a profit to the bank (Bal, 1992). Deryk Weyer of Barclays Bank has come out with a comprehensive definition of bank marketing. He had explained it as identifying the most profitable markets now and in future, assessing the present and future needs of the customers, setting the business development goals and marketing plans to meet them, and managing the services and promoting them to achieve the plans – all in the context of changing environment in the market (Bhatt, 1988).

The following model has been developed by Arthur Meidan to show the marketing approach to Banking services.

**Marketing Approach to Banking Services**

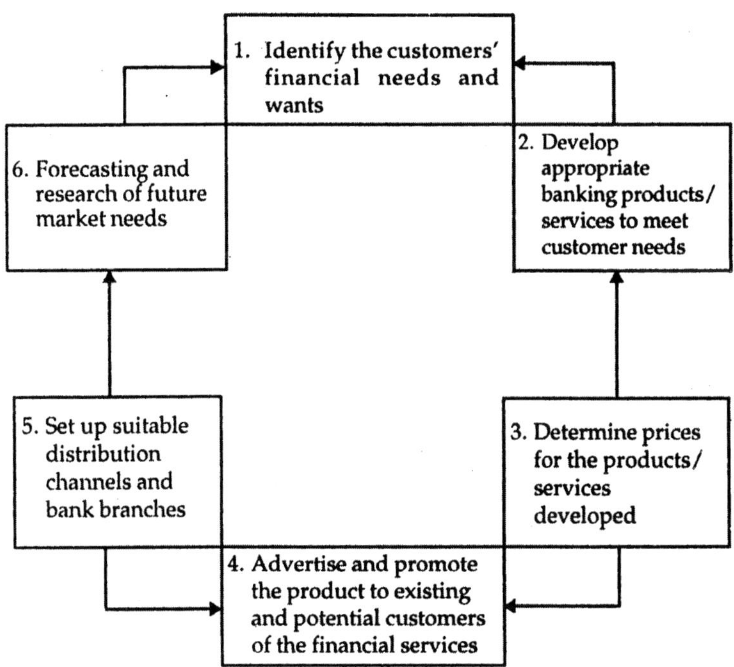


**Fig. 3.5**

*Source:* Adopted from *Arthur Meidan (1984)*, Bank Marketing Management, Macmillan, Hong Kong, p. 16.

**Relevance of Marketing in Banking**

Marketing is concerned with identifying customers' needs and determining ways to meet these needs in a profitable manner. There was a general misconception that marketing is more relevant in product marketing, but not valid for services industries like banking. In today's competitive world, bank marketing is becoming increasingly necessary. Banking sector is probably the most important financial sector not just in terms of turnover, profit and employment, but also in its paramount impact on other spheres of economy. For these reasons, in the last few years, there has been growing interest in applying marketing techniques and tools in the field of banking (Meidan, 1984).

The rising importance of marketing in banking sector is underlined by four major factors: (i) increased competition for customers; (ii) increased sophistication of these customers; (iii) increased use of technology; and (iv) increased cost of meeting customer needs at a profit (Meidan, 1984). Marketing is also relevant in banks as the customers are changing in terms of their wants, needs, desires and expectations. Mr. M.N. Goiporia (1987) has said in the Annual General Body Meeting (AGM) of Indian Bankers Association that the relevance of aggressive marketing in banks has come to the forefront as never before. With a string of incentive packed non-banking saving instruments entering the market in a big way, increasing our market share apart, even retention of the varied market segments call for innovative and aggressive marketing strategies" (Madhukar, 1990). Growing competition, emergence of new range of banking services, need for innovative product development, compulsions in the area of profitability of business, coverage of new spatial areas, ensuring optimum use of vast banking infrastructure, need for ensuring a better focus on customer satisfaction, improving the extent of professionalisation in banking, and a better appreciation of long-term perspectives are some of the valid reasons that can be cited to bring home the need for total marketing orientation in the banks (Bal, 1992). Banking has swiftly moved from the concept of being a place to hold money to that of a place that provides complete solution to the financial needs of the customers. This increased consumer orientation can be traced to the increased competitiveness of the overall financial markets.

**Evolution of Bank Marketing in the West**

Marketing came into banks in the late 1950s, not in the form of marketing concept, but in the form of advertising and promotion (Kotler, 2003). Bankers' attitudes and conception of marketing changed in the 1960s. This has changed dramatically in 1970s. The 1970s was the great era of transition in bank marketing field. During this period things – first, people – second culture reasserted itself into people – first and things – second. The level of knowledge among bank customers and their expectation of quality, variety, convenience and value have risen significantly. The development of information technology (IT) and computerisation, and its popularisation brought a new era for banks. Automation has played an important role in the delivery of retail services via automated teller machines and terminals. The death of traditional banking, adoption of marketing strategy coupled with the changing and more varied goals of the banking industry, have made the banks a far more exciting place than ever before. The American Bankers Association (ABA) has extended commendable support to its member banks in developing their marketing functions. The following facts reveal that even within the ABA, the marketing function has shifted from one department to other till marketing itself became a separate department (Madhukar, 1990).

**Indian Bank Marketing Scene**

In India, the banks began to realise the importance of marketing concepts in as early as 1970s. The first major step in the field of marketing was initiated by the State Bank of India in 1972, when it reorganised itself on the basis of major market segments. It has created four major segments, such as; small industries and business, agricultural, commercial and institutional, and personal services banking (Saxena, 1988). The organisational structure of the bank has been redesigned to best accommodate the market segmentation approach. In early 1980s, banks in India started thinking in terms of product development, market penetration, and market development. With nationalisation of major commercial banks in India (1969 and 1980), there was a steady increase in the number of branches of different banks and a wide coverage to provide banking services at every doorstep. Banks also accelerated the process of equipping their staff with marketing capabilities in terms of both skills and attitudes through different training programmes (Saxena, 1988). At present, banks in India provide more than 50 different types of services to various customers ranging from deposit and credit accounts to various ancillary and consultancy services in addition to international trade facilities. If we will compare these services with services rendered by banks in developed countries, we are far lagging behind them (Singh, 1996). Even foreign banks operating in India offer many innovative financial services.

In mid-1990s, the newly created private banks and the foreign banks expanded their banking operations in India in a big way because of the liberalisation policies of the Government. But the public sector banks lagged behind due to the rigid regulatory framework imposed upon the banking system. The regulatory measures of Reserve Bank of India and the Government reduce the lendable resources for innovative and creative banking (Bhattacharya, 1989). There is also dearth for appropriate incentives for successful marketing activities.

**Marketing Research in Indian Banks**

Marketing research (MR) is the process by which a bank attempts to obtain information about its present and potential customers and competitors, which forms an integral part of the decision making process. Information about MR activities undertaken by Indian banks is hardly available. Some banks, particularly by the larger ones, have been making a limited number of studies in the areas of scanning the economic environment and long-range planning. Some banks also have undertaken exercises to forecasting and also collecting information relating to their market share vis-à-vis those of their main competitors, on ongoing basis (Madhukar, 1990). Prof. Bhatt (1991) in his study found that most of the market research studies by Indian banks were conducted for internal use and no formal reports were prepared. The most important subject for market research in terms of number of studies conducted is the customer service/customer profile/ opinion studies. He also found that only Canara Bank has conducted a research in the area of new services development and that also in the early 1990. During that period hardly any studies was conducted to know the needs of the customers. Most of the banks did not have full fledged 'Research and Development Cell' and it was suggested to have one in their respective head-offices (Datta, 1991). The period after 1995 was much different from the earlier ones, due to the entry of new private banks and foreign banks in a big way.

## REFERENCES


Adewunmi, W. (1985); *Twenty-five Years of Merchant Banking in Nigeria,* Lagos: Lagos University Press.

Agu, C.C. (1988); Nigerian *Banking Structure and Performance,* Onitsha: Africana-Fep Publishers Limited.

Alder, L. (1967); Systems Approach to Marketing, *Harvard Business Review, 38*(3), May/June, pp. 105-118.

Alexander, L. (1985); Successfully Implementing Strategic Decisions, *Long Range Planning,* 18(3), pp. 91-97.

Aluko, M.A. (1983); Determinants of Leadership in the Channels of Distribution, *Nigerian Journal of Business Management,* pp. 77-81.

Alvonitis, G.J., Boyle, K.A. and Kouremenos, A.G. (1985); The Relationship Between Selling Styles and Sales Management Practices: Some Evidence, Proceedings of the Joint Annual Conference of the Marketing Education Group and the Academy of Marketing Science, Held at the University of Sterling.

Ames, B.C. (1970); Trapping Versus Substance in Industrial Marketing, *Harvard Business Review,48,* July / August, 33-46.

Anderson, Rolphe E. (1973); "Consumer Dissatisfaction: The Effect of Disconfirmed Expectancy on Perceived Product Performance", *Journal of Marketing Research,* Vol. 10 (February), pp. 38-44.

Andrew, Kenneth (1986); *Bank Marketing Handbook,* England: Woodhead-Faulkner Ltd.

Aristobulo, J. (1991); From Good Bankers to Bad Bankers: Ineffective Supervision and Management Deterioration As Major Elements in Banking Crises, *EDI Working Papers,* World Bank Washington.

Atkin, B. and Skinner, R.N. (1975); *How is British Industry?,* London: Industrial Market Research Association.

Bain, J.S. (1956); *Price Theory,* New York: John Wiley & Sons.

Baker J.A. (1987); The Role of Environment in Marketing Services: The Consumer Perspective. In Czepiel J.A., Congram C.A. Shanahan, J. (Eds.), *The Services Challenges: Integrating for Competitive Advantage,* Chicago: American Association, pp. 79-84.

Baker, M.J. and Abou-Zeid, E.D. (1982); *Successful Exporting*, London: Westbunn.

Baker, M.J. and Hart, S.J. (1989); *Marketing and Competitive Success*, London: Philip Allan.

Baker, M.J. (1980); Maxims for Marketing in the Eighties, *Advertising, 66*, Winter.

Baker, M.J. (1992); *Marketing Strategy and Management*, London: Macmillan Press Ltd.

Bal, R.K. (1992); *Promotion of Services and Deposit Mobilisation in Indian Banking Industry: A Marketing Approach*, Unpublished Thesis Submitted to Utkal University, pp. 21-48.

Bamberger, I. (1995); Developing Competitive Advantage, *Long Range Planning*, 22(5), 27-35.

Baranson, J. (1980); *The Japanese Challenge to US Industry*, New York: Lexington Books, D.C. Health & Co.

Beswick, C.A. and Cravens, D.W. (1977); A Multi-Stage Decision Model for Sales Force Management, *Journal of Marketing Research*, May.

Bhatt, Atul (1991); "Bank Marketing, Market Research and Indian Banks", *Prajnan*, (January-March,), pp. 45-55.

Bhattacharya, B.N (1989); "Marketing Approach to Promoting Banking Services", Vikalpa, (April-June), pp. 35-38.

Bitner, M.J. and Hubbert, A.R. (1993); "Encounter Satisfaction vs. Overall Satisfaction vs. Quality: The Customer's Voice," in Service Quality: New Directions in Theory and Practice, ed. R.T. Rust and R.L. Oliver (Newbury Park, CA: Sage), pp. 71-93.

Borden, N.H. (1963); The Growing Problem of Product Line Planning in C.J. Dirksen, C.J.

Brady Jr., M.K. and J.J. Cronin (2001); "Some New Thoughts on Conceptualizing Perceived Service Quality: A Hierarchical Approach," *Journal of Marketing* 65 (July), pp. 34-49.

British Institute of Management (BIM). Managing the Export Function: Policies and Practices in the Small and Medium Company, *Survey Report*, No. 26.

Bush, R.F. and Brobst, B. (1979); *Marketing Simulation: Analysis for Decision-Making*, New York: Harper and Row Publishers.

Carman, J.M (1990); "Consumer Perceptions of Service Quality: An Assessment of the SERVQUAL Dimensions," *Journal of Retailing*, 66(1), 33-35.

Chen, T. (1999); Critical Success Factors for Various Strategies in the Banking Industry, *The International Journal of Bank Marketing*, 17(2).

Churchill, G.A (1979); "A Paradigm for Developing Better Measures of Marketing Constructs," *Journal of Marketing Research*, 16 (February), 64-71

Connell, D. (1979); The UK's Performance in Export Markets: Some Evidence from International Trade Data, *NEDO Discussion Paper 6.*

Cravens, W., Hills, G.E. and Woodruff, R.B. (1980). *Marketing Decision-Making: Concepts and Strategy*, Illinois: Richard D. Irwin Inc.

Cronin, J.J., Brady Jr., M.K. and Hult, G.T.M. (2000); "Assessing the Effects of Quality, Value, and Customer Satisfaction on Consumer Behavioural Intentions in Service Environments," *Journal of Retailing* 7(2), Summer, pp. 193-218.

Dabholkar, P.A., Shepherd, C.D. and Thorpe, D.I. (2000); "A Comprehensive Framework for Service Quality: An Investigation of Critical Conceptual and Measurement Issues Through a Longitudinal Study," *Journal of Retailing* 7(2), Summer, pp. 139-73.

Davis, E., Gouzouli, C., Spence, M. and Star, J. (1993); Measuring the Performance of Banks, *Business Strategy Review*, 4(3), 1-14.

Davis, Jan L. and Cohn, Jonathan (1989); "Marketing Financial Services in a Fragmented Market", *Bank Marketing*, (January), 25-27.

Day, G.L. and Reibstein, D.J. (1997); *Wharton on Dynamic Competitive Strategy*, New York: Wiley and Sons.

Dhananjayan, G. (2005); "Services Marketing: Integrating People, Technology and Strategy", *Marketing Mastermind*, February, pp. 17-23.

Dutta, S.K. (1991); "Customer Service of Banks", SBI Monthly Review, January, pp.15-22.

Ekpo-Ufot, A. (1992); The state-of the-art of Finance-Accounting Management in Some Lagos Organisations in the Chemical Industry: An Exploratory Study In Ojo, A.T. (ed.), *Business Performance Improvement Through Cost Management*, Lagos: University of Lagos Press.

Festinger, Leon (1957); *Theory of Cognitive Dissonance*, Harper and Row, New York, p. 120.

Freedman, Jonathan, L. (1964); "Involvement, Discrepancy and Change", *Journal of Abnormal and Social Psychology*, Vol. 69 (Sept.) pp. 290-295.

Gandhi, J.C. (1993); *Marketing: A Managerial Introduction*, Tata McGraw-Hill Publishing Co. Ltd, New Delhi.

Garvin, D.A. (1983); "Quality on the Line," *Harvard Business Review*, 61(September-October), 65-73.

Gavini, Augustine. L. and Athma Prasanta (1997), "Customer Service in Commercial Banks—Expectation and Reality", *Indian Journal of Marketing*, Volume XXVII, Nos. 5, 6, 7 (May-July).

Goode, W.J. and Hatt, P.K. (1952); *Methods in Social Research*, Singapore: McGraw-Hill Book Co.

Hoveland, C.L., Lumsdain, A.A. and Sheffield, F.D. (1948); *Experiments on Mass Communication* (Vol. 3), Princeton University Press, New Jersey. p. 8.

Howard, John, A. and Sheth, J.N. (1969); *The Theory of Buyer Behaviour*, Wiley and Sons, New York, p. 145.

Jain, S. (1983); Evolution of Strategic Marketing, *Journal of Business Research*, 11( 4), 407-425.

John, F.A. (1999); Successful Market Innovation, *European Journal of Innovation Management*, 2, 6-11.

Johne, A. (1999); Innovation in Medium-sized Insurance Companies: How Marketing Adds Value, *The International Journal of Bank Marketing*, 18(1).

Kaptan, Sanjay and Nilkanth V. Sagane (1995); "Customer Service in Bank: Some Points to Ponder", *Business Analyst*, Volume 15, Number 1.

Kent, R. (1984); Marketing Faith and Marketing Practice: A Study of Product Range in the Scottish Food Processing Industry, Unpublished M.Sc. Thesis, Department of Marketing, University of Strathclyde.

Kim, L. and Lim, Y. (1988); Environment, Generic Strategies, and Performance in a Rapidly Developing Country: A Taxonomic Approach, *Academy of Management Journal*, 31( 4), 802-827.

Kim, W.C. & Mauborgne, R. (1997); Value Innovation: The Strategic Logic of High Growth, *Harvard Business Review*, Jan-Feb., 102-112.

King, S. (1985); "Has Marketing Failed or was it Never Really Tried?" *Journal of Marketing Management*, 1(1), Summer.

Kinnear, T.C. and Taylor, J.R. (1983); *Marketing Research*, New Delhi: Prentice Hall of India Private Limited.

Kotler, P. (1980); *Marketing Management: Analysis, Planning and Control*, Englewood Cliffs, New Jersey: Practice Hall.

Kotler, P. (1986); Megamarketing", *Harvard Business Review*, March/April, 117-124.

Kotler, P. (2003); *Marketing Management*, Prentice Hall of India, New Delhi, pp. 8-26.

Krishnaveni, R. and Divya Prava, D. (2004); "Measuring Service Quality in Banking Sector", *Prajnan: Journal of Social and Management Sciences*, XXXIII (1), pp. 47-55.

Kronger, A., and Lockley, L.C. (eds.), *Readings in Marketing*, New York: R.D. Irvin.

Lassitz, R.W. and Green, S.B. (1975); Effects of the Number of Scale Points on Reliability: A. Monte Carlo Study, *Journal of Applied Psychology*, 60, pp. 10-13.

Laurent, C.R. (1982); "Marketing's Role in Banking", *The Bankers Magazine*, July-Aug., p. 28.

Leithmann, D.R. and Hulbert, J. (1972); Are Three-point Scales Always Good, *Journal of Marketing Research*, 19, pp. 444-446.

Levine, G. (1981); *Introductory Statistics for Psychology: The Logic and the Methods*, New York: Academic Press.

Madhukar, R.K. (1990); "Indian Banking—The Next Phase", *The Journal of Institute of Bankers*, Bombay.

Majaro, S. (1977); *International Marketing: A Strategic Approach to World Markets*, New Jersey: George Allen and Unwin.

Mamman, H. and Oluyemi, S.A. (1994); Bank management Issues and Restoring the Health of Nigerian Banks Through Improving the Quality of Management/Employees, *NDIC Quarterly*, 4(4), 56-70.

Mann, J. (1980); (ed.), *European Journal of Marketing*, 14( 9), 21.

Mathews, J.B., Buzzell, R.D., Levitt, T. and Frank, R. E. (1964); *Marketing: An Introductory Analysis*, New York: McGraw-Hill Book Company.

McCarthy, E. J. (1975); *Basic Marketing*, New York: D. Irwin.

Meidan, Arthur (1984); *Bank Marketing Management*, Macmillan, Hong Kong, p. 16.

Mikesell, R.F. and Farah, M.G. (1980); US Export Competitiveness in Manufactures in the Third World Markets, The Centre for Strategic and Information Studies, George Town University.

Mitchell, I.S. and Agenmonmen, A.I. (1984); Marketers' Attitudes Towards the Marketing Concept in Nigerian Business and Non-business Operations, *Columbia Journal of World Business*, 19, pp. 62-71.

Ndekwu, E.C. (1994); *First Bank of Nigeria: A Century of Banking*, Ibadan: Spectrum Books Limited.

NEDO, (1977); *The U.K. Printing and Book Binding Machinery Industry's Market Prospect to 1980*, London: Printing and Book Binding Machinery.

Nwachukwu, D.O. (1993); New Products in a Competitive Banking Environment, *First Bank Business and Economic Report*, July, 11-17.

Okoroafo, S.C. (1993); Firm Performance in a Liberalized Environment: Empirical Evidence from a Developing Country, *Journal of Business Research*, 28, 173-187.

Oliver, R.L. (1994); "A Conceptual Model of Service Quality and Service Satisfaction: Compatible Goals, Different Concepts' in *Advances in Services Marketing and Management*, Vol. 2, ed. T.A. Swartz, D.E. Bowen, and S.W. Brown (Greenwich, CT: JAI Press), pp. 65-85.

Oluyemi, S.A. (1995); Deregulation and the Performance of Insured Banks in Nigeria: An Overview, *NDIC Quarterly*, 5( 1), 49-67.

Osuagwu, L. (2001); "Marketing Strategy Effectiveness in Nigerian Banks", *Academy of Marketing Studies Journal*, Vol. 5, No. 1, pp. 95-115.

Osuagwu, L. (1997); Marketing Strategies, Environmental Factors, and Performance Measures in the Nigerian Banking Industry, Ph.D Thesis, School of Postgraduate Studies, University of Lagos.

Parasuraman, A., Zeithaml, V.A. and Berry, L.L. (1994); "Reassessment of Expectations as a Comparison Standard in Measuring Service Quality: Implications for Future Research," *Journal of Marketing* 58, No. 1 (January), pp. 111-24.

Parasuraman, A., Zeithaml, V.A. and Berry, L.L. (1988); "SERVQUAL: A Multiple-Item Scale for Measuring Consumer Perceptions of Service Quality," *Journal of Retailing* 64 (Spring), pp. 12-40.

Patchford, B.T. Ford, G.T. (1976); A Study of Prices and Market Share in the Computer Mainframe Industry, *Journal of Business*, April.

Pezzullo, M.A. ( 1982); Marketing for Bankers. American Bankers Association, Washington.

Pickering, J.F. (1976); *Industrial Structure and Market Conduct*, NJ: Robertson & Co.

Piercy, N.F. (1982); Cost and Profit Myopia in Marketing, *Quarterly Review of Marketing*, 7(4), 1-12.

Piercy, N.F. (1985); *Marketing Organisation: An Analysis of Information Processing, Power and Politics*, London: Allen & Unwin.

Posner, M. & Steel, A. (1979); Price Competitiveness and Performance of Manufacturing Industry, In Blackaby, F. (ed.), *De Industrialization*, New York: Heinemann Educational Books.

Ravichandran, M. and Thyagarajan, V. (1998); "Consumer Satisfaction—Determinants and Measurement", *The Journal of NMIMS* (July-December), pp. 42-55.

Reisz, P. (1980); Managing Our Way to Economic Decline, *Harvard Business Review*, July-August.

Rothwell, R. (1974); SAPPHO Updated-Project SAPPHO Phase II, *Research Policy*, 3, 258-91.

Rust, R.T. and Oliver, R L (1994); *Service Quality — New Directions in Theory and Practice*, Sage Publications, New York.

Ryans, A.B. and Weinberg, G.B. (1981); Sales Force Management: Integrating Research Advances, *California Management Review*, *XXIV*(1), Fall.

Saxena, K.K. (1988); *Bank Marketing: Concepts and Applications*, Skylark Publications, New Delhi.

Sheng, A. (1991); The Role of the Central Bank in Banking Crisis: An Overview, In Patrick and Vaez- Zadeh (eds.), *The Evolving Role of Central Banks*, Washington DC: IMF.

Singh, O.N. (2001); "Indian Banking—Emerging Challenges and Strategies", *IBA Bulletin;* Vol. XXIII, No. 3, March.

Srinivason, A. (1994); Alternative Measures of System Effectiveness: Associations and Implications, *MIS Quarterly*, 9(3), 817-832.

Stanton, William J. (1987); and Futrell, Charles, Fundamentals of Marketing, 8th Edn: McGraw-Hill Book Company, New York.

Takeuchi, H. & Nonaka, I. (1986); The New Product Development Game, *Harvard Business Review*, January/February.

Udell, C.J. (1972); *Successful Marketing Strategies in American Industries*, Wisconsin: MIMIR.

Udell, J.G. (1964); How Important is Pricing in Competitive Strategy, *Journal of Marketing*, 28(1), 44-48.

Umoh, P.N. (1992); Strategies for Survival and Growth of Insured Banks, *NDIC Quarterly*, 2(2), 19-24.

Umunnaehila, A. (1996); *Bank Failures in Nigeria: History, Causes, and Remedies*, Lagos: Foundations Publishers.

Walker, Michael C. *An Introduction to Bank Marketing Research*, BRMA Research Publication.

Walsh, V. and Roy, R. (1985); The Designer As Gate Keeper in Manufacturing Industry, *Design Studies*, 6(3).

Wilson, R.M.S. (1979); *Management Controls and Marketing Planning*, London: Heinemann Press.

Wilson, R.M.S. (1984); Financial Control of the Marketing Function, In Hart, N.A. (ed.), *The Marketing of Industrial Products*, London: McGraw-Hill.

Wilson, R.S., Gilligan, C. and Pearson, D.J. (1992); *Strategic Marketing Management: Planning, Implementation, and Control*, Oxford: Butterworth-Heinemann Ltd.

Zeithaml, C.P. and Zeithaml, V.A. (1984); Environmental Management: Revising the Marketing Perspective, *Journal of Marketing*, Spring, 47.

Zeithaml, V.A. and Bitner, Mary Jo (2003); "Services Marketing: Integrating Customer Focus Across the Firm"; Tata McGraw-Hill (3ed), New Delhi, pp. 59-114.

# CHAPTER–4

# SURVEY OF CUSTOMERS

## INTRODUCTION

The banking sector is facing enormous challenges of attracting the new customers and retaining the existing ones. The problems commonly encountered by the bankers are shifting of customer loyalty, inability to inventory, difficulty in synchronizing demand and supply, controlling the performance quality of human interaction, etc. – need to be articulated and tackled by managers. The attraction, retention, and building strong customer relationships through quality services are at the heart of the modern marketing (Zeithaml and Bitner, 2003). A sound marketing strategy is required to be adopted by the banker to build customer trust and retain them in the business and for competitive advantage across the industry. The strategy should focus on service quality rather than existing marketing mix, understanding of the customer expectations and perceptions and what they imply for the marketer, use of technology, planning for service recovery, customer-defined service standards, value pricing, etc. (Dhananjayan, 2005). At this backdrop, the main objective of this chapter is to analyse the data collected from the customers to understand their banking behaviour; with particular emphasis on the following factors:

(a) Reasons for opening accounts with a bank;

(b) Expectation and perceptions of the customers regarding banking services; and

(c) Perception of customers on different banking parameters; viz. transactions in deposit account, loans and advances, other services like ATMs, phone-banking, premises and administration, pension account, etc. for measuring their satisfaction and dissatisfaction.

## STUDY DESIGN AND METHODOLOGY

The data for the study were collected through a structured questionnaire from 337 customers. Initially 600 samples were planned covering 300 customers of both private and public sector banks. Because of the small number of branches of private banks and their urban concentration, unwillingness of the customers to provide data, time and budgetary constraints restricted the sample size to 337, out of which 242 from public banks and 95 from private banks. A questionnaire for customer survey was designed keeping the broad parameters in mind, which was pre-tested before finalisation. The data regarding perceptions and expectations of customers were collected in interval scales (in a 4-point scale), and for measuring the importance they attach to different factors for selection of a bank, a 7-point scale was used. Apart from this, some qualitative data like demographic background, reasons for opening an account, views regarding staff, etc. are collected. The forthcoming sections, analyse the data so collected from the customers keeping the broad objectives in view.

## CUSTOMER PROFILE

The demographic backgrounds of the sample respondents in six parameters are presented in Table 4.1 to understand the customer profiles i.e., age, education, gender, occupation, income and type of banks they operate.

Table 4.1: **Customer Profile**

| | Parameters | Frequency | Percentage |
|---|---|---|---|
| Age | Below 30 years | 163 | 48.37 |
| | 30-40 years | 89 | 26.41 |
| | 40-60 years | 57 | 16.91 |
| | 60 years and above | 28 | 8.31 |
| Education | Up to HSC | 33 | 9.79 |
| | Graduate | 93 | 27.60 |
| | Postgraduate | 106 | 31.45 |
| | Professional | 105 | 31.16 |
| Gender | Male | 259 | 76.85 |
| | Female | 78 | 23.15 |
| Occupation | Salaried | 196 | 58.16 |
| | Self-employed | 7 | 2.08 |
| | Professional | 22 | 6.53 |
| | Business | 21 | 6.23 |
| | Student | 47 | 13.95 |
| | Retired | 26 | 7.72 |
| | Housewife | 18 | 5.34 |
| Income | Less than Rs. 1 lakh | 126 | 37.39 |
| | Rs. 1-2 lakh | 148 | 43.92 |
| | Rs. 2-3 lakh | 37 | 10.98 |
| | Rs. 3-4 lakh | 17 | 5.04 |
| | Rs. 4 lakh and above | 9 | 2.67 |
| Type of Bank | Public | 242 | 71.81 |
| | Private | 95 | 28.19 |
| Total | | 337 | 100.00 |

It is observed from the Table 4.1 that young customers (below the age of 30 years) constitute the majority of sample (48.37%). The proportion of senior citizens is the lowest (8.31%) in the sample. This behaviour corroborates the general trend in the industry. Similarly, the post-graduates and professionally educated respondents dominate the sample (31.45% and 31.16% respectively). This observed behaviour may be due to urban biasness of the sample and increased willingness of educated people to participate in the survey. Again, the representation of the females (23.15%) is smaller in the sample as less number of women in Orissa are working and having bank account. So far, the financial matters are male dominated. Occupation-wise analysis revealed that salaried class (58.16%) dominates the sample compared to others. In the recent years, banks are giving educational loans for higher studies; inducing more and more students to avail the facility. As a result, student respondents constitute the second largest group in the sample. Similarly, the lower income groups having income less than Rs. one lakh dominate the sample (37.39% of sample respondents) and 43.92 per cent are between Rs. 1-2 lakh; combined together they constituted about 81.31 per cent of the sample. This sample behaviour corresponds to the socio-economic profile of the State. As explained earlier, customers of public sector banks (71.81%) dominate the sample.

Table 4.2 describes the customer profile and the type of banks they have chosen for their transactions. It is evident from Table 4.2 that 67.48 per cent of the young respondents transacts with public sector banks, while, 32.5 per cent with private banks. All the respondents in different age groups have shown similar behaviour, except 40-60 years age group; where the dominance of public sector banks (91.23%) is visible. This may be due to the fact that they have an account with public sector banks before the entry of private banks into Orissa in mid-1990s. The $\chi^2$ value is significant at 1 per cent level of significance indicating age-groups of the respondents and their choices of the bank are dependent on each other.

It is observed from the same table that less educated customers (93.94%) have a choice for public banks and the post-graduates more inclined to private banks. This trend is observed may be due to the large presence of public banks with wide ranges products more suitable for lower income groups, while private banks are offering value-added services for special group of customers (mass-banking vs. class-banking approaches). The $\chi^2$-value is significant at 1 per cent level of significance indicating the dependence between type of education and choice of a bank. More or less the behaviour in gender is similar, and the $\chi^2$ value for gender variation is not significant.

**Table 4.2: Customer Profile by Type of Banks**

| | Parameters | Public | | Private | | Total | | Chi Square |
|---|---|---|---|---|---|---|---|---|
| | | f | % | f | % | f | % | |
| Age | Below 30 years | 110 | 67.48 | 53 | 32.52 | 163 | 100.00 | 12.81* |
| | 30-40 years | 61 | 68.54 | 28 | 31.46 | 89 | 100.00 | |
| | 40-60 years | 52 | 91.23 | 5 | 8.77 | 57 | 100.00 | |
| | 60 years and above | 19 | 67.86 | 9 | 32.14 | 28 | 100.00 | |
| Education | Up to HSC | 31 | 93.94 | 2 | 6.06 | 33 | 100.00 | 13.08* |
| | Graduate | 67 | 72.04 | 26 | 27.96 | 93 | 100.00 | |
| | Postgraduate | 66 | 62.26 | 40 | 37.74 | 106 | 100.00 | |
| | Professional | 78 | 74.29 | 27 | 25.71 | 105 | 100.00 | |
| Gender | Male | 191 | 73.75 | 68 | 26.25 | 259 | 100.00 | 2.07 |
| | Female | 51 | 65.38 | 27 | 34.62 | 78 | 100.00 | |
| Occupation | Salaried | 134 | 68.37 | 62 | 31.63 | 196 | 100.00 | 23.33* |
| | Self-employed | 6 | 85.71 | 1 | 14.29 | 7 | 100.00 | |
| | Professional | 12 | 54.55 | 10 | 45.45 | 22 | 100.00 | |
| | Business | 21 | 100.00 | 0 | 0.00 | 21 | 100.00 | |
| | Student | 42 | 89.36 | 5 | 10.64 | 47 | 100.00 | |
| | Retired | 17 | 65.38 | 9 | 34.62 | 26 | 100.00 | |
| | Housewife | 10 | 55.56 | 8 | 44.44 | 18 | 100.00 | |

*(Contd...)*

| | Parameters | Public | | Private | | Total | | Chi Square |
|---|---|---|---|---|---|---|---|---|
| | | f | % | f | % | f | % | |
| Income | Less than Rs. 1 lakh | 97 | 75.78 | 31 | 24.22 | 128 | 100.00 | 15.27* |
| | Rs. 1-2 lakh | 92 | 62.16 | 56 | 37.84 | 148 | 100.00 | |
| | Rs. 2-3 lakh | 31 | 83.78 | 6 | 16.22 | 37 | 100.00 | |
| | Rs. 3-4 lakh | 16 | 94.12 | 1 | 5.88 | 17 | 100.00 | |
| | Rs. 4 lakh and above | 6 | 85.71 | 1 | 14.29 | 7 | 100.00 | |
| | All Samples | 242 | 71.81 | 95 | 28.29 | 337 | 100.00 | * 1% level of significance |

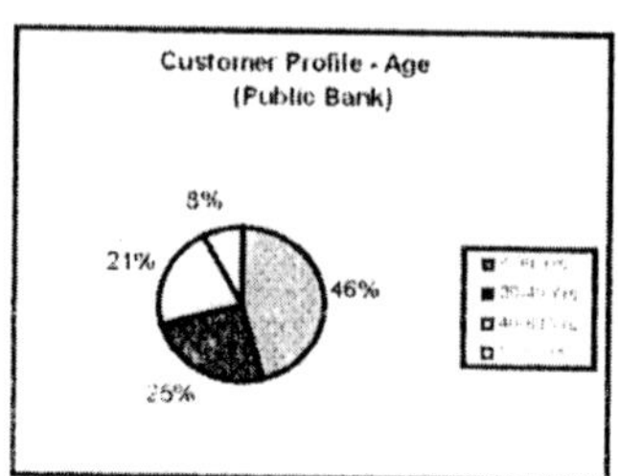
Customer Profile - Age
(Public Bank)
8%
21%
46%
25%

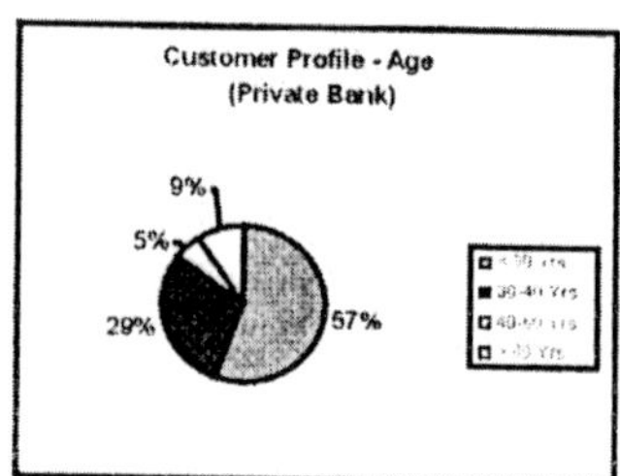
Customer Profile - Age
(Private Bank)
9%
5%
29%
57%

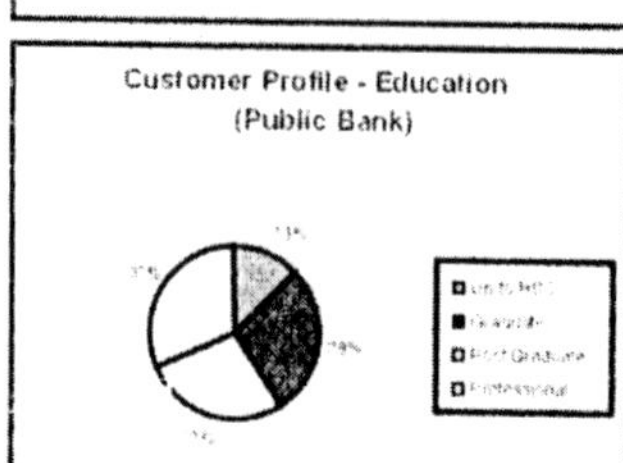
Customer Profile - Education
(Public Bank)

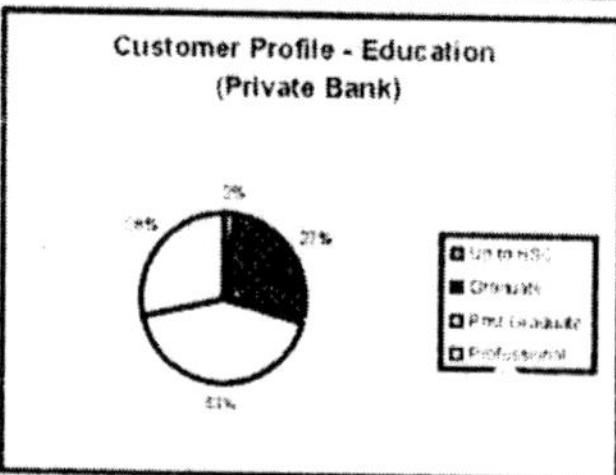
Customer Profile - Education
(Private Bank)

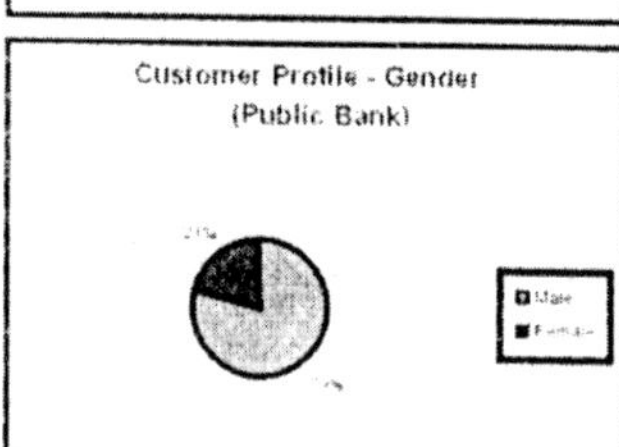
Customer Profile - Gender
(Public Bank)

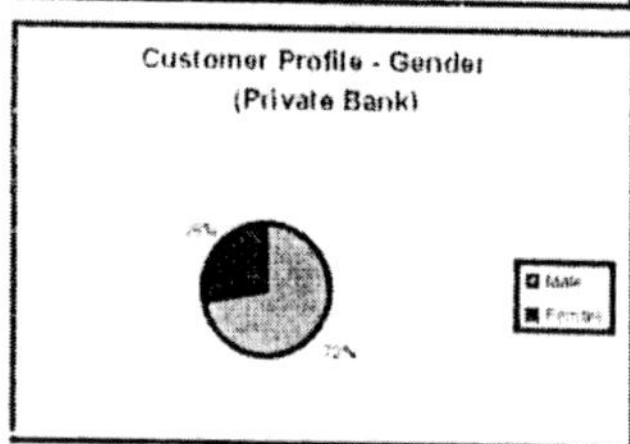
Customer Profile - Gender
(Private Bank)

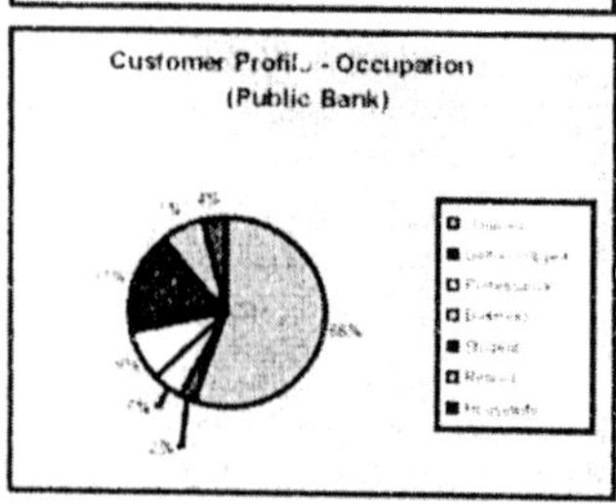
Customer Profile - Occupation
(Public Bank)

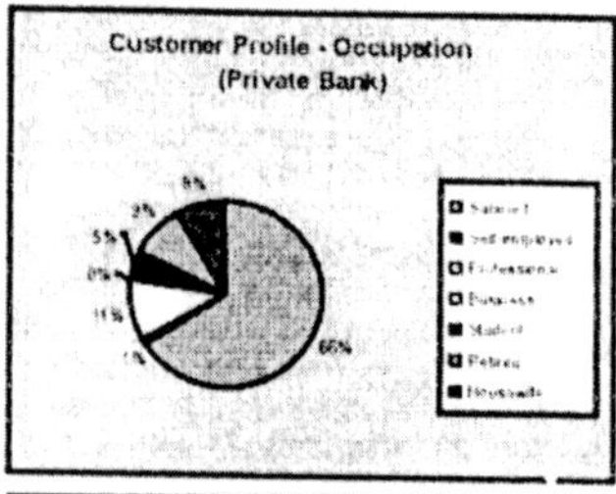
Customer Profile - Occupation
(Private Bank)
66%

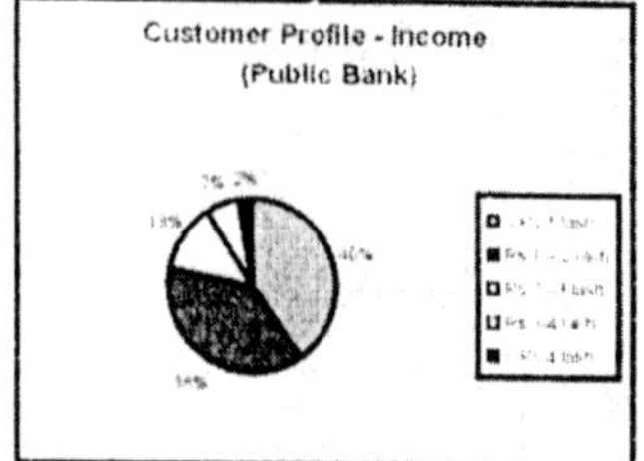
Customer Profile - Income
(Public Bank)

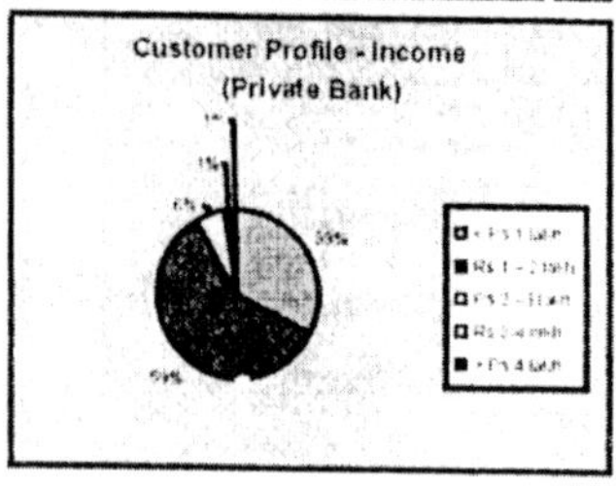
Customer Profile - Income
(Private Bank)

Taking into account the occupation of the customers, salaried persons dominate the sample. The professionals and housewives have shown more preference for private banks compared to the other groups (45.45% and 44.44% respectively); while all the businessmen have chosen to transact with public sector banks. Students and self-employed persons have a clear preference for public sector banks. The $\chi^2$ value is significant at 1 per cent level of significance, implying that customers with occupational variations have a preference for a bank. Similarly, for different income groups public sector banks are more preferred except the income group of Rs. 1- 2 lakhs. The $\chi^2$ value is significant at 1 per cent level, indicating the influence of levels of income for choice of a bank.

**Table 4.3: Type of Bank Accounts**

(Figures are in percentage)

| | Parameters | Type of Accounts | | | | | |
|---|---|---|---|---|---|---|---|
| | | S | C | S/C | S/FD | C/FD | S/C/FD |
| Age | Below 30 years | 84.66 | 4.91 | 2.45 | 7.36 | 0.00 | 0.61 |
| | 30-40 years | 73.03 | 0.00 | 1.12 | 25.84 | 0.00 | 0.00 |
| | 40-60 years | 68.42 | 7.02 | 0.00 | 17.54 | 1.75 | 5.26 |
| | 60 years and above | 71.43 | 0.00 | 0.00 | 28.57 | 0.00 | 0.00 |
| Education | Up to HSC | 81.82 | 0.00 | 3.03 | 15.15 | 0.00 | 0.00 |
| | Graduate | 69.89 | 5.38 | 4.30 | 16.13 | 0.00 | 4.30 |
| | Postgraduate | 80.19 | 2.83 | 0.00 | 16.04 | 0.94 | 0.00 |
| | Professional | 80.95 | 3.81 | 0.00 | 15.24 | 0.00 | 0.00 |
| Gender | Male | 79.54 | 3.47 | 1.54 | 14.67 | 0.39 | 0.39 |
| | Female | 71.79 | 3.85 | 1.28 | 19.23 | 0.00 | 3.85 |
| Occupation | Salaried | 75.00 | 4.59 | 2.55 | 16.84 | 0.51 | 0.51 |
| | Self-employed | 14.29 | 42.86 | 0.00 | 42.86 | 0.00 | 0.00 |
| | Professional | 90.91 | 0.00 | 0.00 | 9.09 | 0.00 | 0.00 |
| | Business | 71.43 | 0.00 | 0.00 | 28.57 | 0.00 | 0.00 |
| | Student | 97.87 | 0.00 | 0.00 | 2.13 | 0.00 | 0.00 |
| | Retired | 73.08 | 0.00 | 0.00 | 26.92 | 0.00 | 0.00 |
| | Housewife | 77.78 | 0.00 | 0.00 | 5.56 | 0.00 | 16.67 |

*(Contd...)*

| | Parameters | Type of Accounts | | | | | |
|---|---|---|---|---|---|---|---|
| | | S | C | S/C | S/FD | C/FD | S/C/FD |
| Income | Less than Rs. 1 lakh | 82.81 | 3.91 | 2.34 | 8.59 | 0.00 | 2.34 |
| | Rs. 1-2 lakh | 76.35 | 4.05 | 1.35 | 17.57 | 0.00 | 0.68 |
| | Rs. 2-3 lakh | 67.57 | 0.00 | 0.00 | 29.73 | 2.70 | 0.00 |
| | Rs. 3-4 lakh | 70.59 | 5.88 | 0.00 | 23.53 | 0.00 | 0.00 |
| | Rs. 4 lakh and above | 85.71 | 0.00 | 0.00 | 14.29 | 0.00 | 0.00 |
| Type of Bank | Public | 74.79 | 3.31 | 0.00 | 20.25 | 0.41 | 1.24 |
| | Private | 85.26 | 4.21 | 5.26 | 4.21 | 0.00 | 1.05 |

S- Savings C-Current FD- Fixed Deposit

Table 4.3 discusses the type of accounts maintained by the sample respondents. As reported, most of the respondents also maintain more than one account. By combining them, six groups of account holders emerge. Savings bank account dominates the type of account in all categories of respondents. Next to savings bank account, customers go for different types of fixed-deposits. Some of the account holders maintain both savings bank and fixed deposits. Similarly, some of the respondents maintain savings bank account, current account and fixed account. Current accounts are not very popular among the sample respondents; as no interest is paid in this account. The tendency to put money into fixed accounts rises with increase in age. More than one-forth of the customers in the age group more than 30 years have some kind of fixed deposits. In educational back ground, all the respondents maintain similar type of accounts. No specific trend is observed in gender variations, except females have little more numbers of fixed deposits. In occupational variation, all the current account holders are either a self-employed person or a salaried person. No businessman is operating a current account in the sample. Housewives and retired persons have more fixed deposit accounts. People in the higher income group have more fixed deposit accounts. Further, it is noticed that these respondents prefer public sector banks fixed-deposit accounts. This indicates that with regard to the financial products, particularly in the context of deposits, public sector banks are not lagging behind.

Table 4.4: Customer Profile by Years of Transaction

| | Parameters | Up to 5 Years | | 5-10 Years | | Above 10 Years | | Total | |
|---|---|---|---|---|---|---|---|---|---|
| | | f | % | f | % | f | % | f | % |
| Age | Below 30 years | 112 | 68.77 | 51 | 31.23 | 0 | 0.00 | 163 | 100.00 |
| | 30-40 years | 56 | 62.92 | 31 | 34.83 | 2 | 2.25 | 89 | 100.00 |
| | 40-60 years | 29 | 50.88 | 24 | 42.11 | 4 | 7.02 | 57 | 100.00 |
| | 60 years and above | 19 | 67.86 | 7 | 25.00 | 2 | 7.14 | 28 | 100.00 |
| Education | Up to HSC | 23 | 69.70 | 9 | 27.27 | 1 | 3.03 | 33 | 100.00 |
| | Graduate | 50 | 53.76 | 33 | 35.48 | 10 | 10.75 | 93 | 100.00 |
| | Postgraduate | 72 | 67.92 | 32 | 30.19 | 2 | 1.89 | 106 | 100.00 |
| | Professional | 61 | 58.10 | 31 | 29.52 | 13 | 12.38 | 105 | 100.00 |
| Gender | Male | 142 | 54.83 | 93 | 35.91 | 24 | 9.27 | 259 | 100.00 |
| | Female | 64 | 82.05 | 12 | 15.38 | 2 | 2.56 | 78 | 100.00 |
| Occupation | Salaried | 124 | 63.27 | 63 | 32.14 | 9 | 4.59 | 196 | 100.00 |
| | Self-employed | 0 | 0.00 | 1 | 14.29 | 6 | 85.71 | 7 | 100.00 |
| | Professional | 15 | 68.18 | 7 | 31.82 | 0 | 0.00 | 22 | 100.00 |
| | Business | 14 | 66.67 | 5 | 23.81 | 2 | 9.52 | 21 | 100.00 |
| | Student | 29 | 61.70 | 18 | 38.30 | 0 | 0.00 | 47 | 100.00 |
| | Retired | 17 | 65.38 | 7 | 26.92 | 2 | 7.69 | 26 | 100.00 |
| | Housewife | 14 | 77.78 | 4 | 22.22 | 0 | 0.00 | 18 | 100.00 |

*(Contd...)*

| | Parameters | Up to 5 Years | | 5-10 Years | | Above 10 Years | | Total | |
|---|---|---|---|---|---|---|---|---|---|
| | | f | % | f | % | f | % | f | % |
| Income | Less than Rs. 1 lakh | 82 | 64.06 | 36 | 28.13 | 10 | 7.81 | 128 | 100.00 |
| | Rs. 1-2 lakh | 92 | 62.16 | 50 | 33.78 | 6 | 4.05 | 148 | 100.00 |
| | Rs. 2-3 lakh | 23 | 62.16 | 12 | 32.43 | 2 | 5.41 | 37 | 100.00 |
| | Rs. 3-4 lakh | 8 | 47.06 | 4 | 23.53 | 5 | 29.41 | 17 | 100.00 |
| | Rs. 4 lakh and above | 1 | 14.28 | 3 | 42.86 | 3 | 42.86 | 7 | 100.00 |
| Type of Bank | Public | 136 | 56.20 | 80 | 33.06 | 26 | 10.74 | 242 | 100.00 |
| | Private | 70 | 73.68 | 25 | 26.32 | 0 | 0.00 | 95 | 100.00 |
| Total | | 206 | 61.13 | 105 | 31.16 | 26 | 7.72 | 337 | 100.00 |

It is evident from the Table 4.4 that 61.13 per cent of the accounts are in operation for less than 5 years. Across all categories of respondents, comparison among the age-groups indicate that the number of years of operation of an account correspond to the age of the customer. No one of the respondent below the age of 30 years has operated an account for more than 10 years. No specific trend is observed in educational background differences. Females have relatively new account s operated for less than five years (82.05%) compared to the males (54.83%). In occupational variations, students do not have accounts of more than 10 years old, while self-employed person do not have a new account (less than 5 years). Similarly, in the given sample, year of operation of an account has correspondence to the income level. Private Banks are relatively new; hence do not have accounts beyond 10 years.

## BANKING BEHAVIOUR OF CUSTOMERS

### Reasons for Opening a Deposit Account

There are several reasons/motives to select a bank for opening an account for transaction by a customer. The customers considered host of factors like service quality, convenient location, working hours, ATM network, overall reputation, etc. for choosing a particular bank (Outlook Money Survey, 2004). In another study, Venkatesan (2004) observed that company operates salary accounts, pre-existing relationship, and a force of habit are quite important. Further analysis of these factors across customers revealed that proximity is the principal determinant of choice of public sector banks, while service quality for private banks. The responses of the sample respondents are presented in the Table 4.5.

## Table 4.5: Reasons for Opening Account

(Figures are in percentage)

| | Parameters | Reasons | | | | | | | | | |
|---|---|---|---|---|---|---|---|---|---|---|---|
| | | a | b | c | d | e | f | g | h | i | j |
| Age | Below 30 years | 26.99 | 30.06 | 0.61 | 32.52 | 62.58 | 31.29 | 9.20 | 11.66 | 36.81 | 3.07 |
| | 30-40 years | 22.47 | 41.57 | 1.12 | 31.46 | 68.54 | 7.87 | 1.12 | 8.99 | 25.84 | 0.00 |
| | 40-60 years | 14.04 | 36.84 | 0.00 | 26.32 | 26.32 | 12.28 | 5.26 | 14.04 | 40.35 | 5.26 |
| | 60 years and above | 3.57 | 21.43 | 0.00 | 39.29 | 25.00 | 3.57 | 0.00 | 0.00 | 46.43 | 0.00 |
| Education | Up to HSC | 24.24 | 33.33 | 33.33 | 63.64 | 21.21 | 9.09 | 12.12 | 30.30 | 0.00 | 0.00 |
| | Graduate | 24.73 | 22.58 | 2.15 | 26.88 | 58.06 | 19.35 | 7.53 | 13.98 | 37.63 | 1.08 |
| | Postgraduate | 28.30 | 36.79 | 0.00 | 40.57 | 54.72 | 24.53 | 4.72 | 4.72 | 33.02 | 6.60 |
| | Professional | 11.43 | 40.00 | 0.00 | 26.67 | 49.52 | 14.29 | 3.81 | 12.38 | 37.14 | 0.00 |
| Gender | Male | 18.53 | 31.66 | 0.77 | 32.05 | 55.60 | 21.24 | 4.63 | 9.65 | 40.54 | 2.70 |
| | Female | 32.05 | 39.74 | 0.00 | 30.77 | 52.56 | 14.10 | 8.97 | 12.82 | 17.95 | 1.28 |
| Occupation | Salaried | 16.84 | 43.37 | 0.51 | 31.63 | 48.47 | 10.71 | 3.57 | 10.20 | 29.08 | 2.55 |
| | Self-employed | 0.00 | 57.14 | 14.29 | 42.86 | 85.71 | 42.86 | 14.29 | 42.86 | 14.29 | 0.00 |
| | Professional | 68.18 | 13.64 | 0.00 | 59.09 | 81.82 | 50.00 | 4.55 | 18.18 | 77.27 | 0.00 |
| | Business | 23.81 | 19.05 | 0.00 | 57.14 | 57.14 | 23.81 | 4.76 | 9.52 | 52.38 | 0.00 |
| | Student | 27.66 | 17.02 | 0.00 | 4.26 | 72.34 | 44.68 | 14.89 | 4.26 | 34.04 | 6.38 |
| | Retired | 3.85 | 23.08 | 0.00 | 38.46 | 30.77 | 3.85 | 0.00 | 0.00 | 50.00 | 0.00 |
| | Housewife | 33.33 | 16.67 | 0.00 | 27.78 | 66.67 | 22.22 | 11.11 | 22.22 | 22.22 | 0.00 |

*(Contd...)*

| | Parameters | Reasons | | | | | | | | | |
|---|---|---|---|---|---|---|---|---|---|---|---|
| | | a | b | c | d | e | f | g | h | i | j |
| Income | Less than Rs. 1 lakh | 25.00 | 28.91 | 0.78 | 21.88 | 66.41 | 34.38 | 12.50 | 9.38 | 35.94 | 3.91 |
| | Rs. 1-2 lakh | 20.95 | 32.43 | 0.68 | 39.86 | 42.57 | 8.11 | 1.35 | 13.51 | 36.49 | 2.03 |
| | Rs. 2-3 lakh | 16.22 | 54.05 | 0.00 | 24.32 | 64.86 | 8.11 | 2.70 | 2.70 | 32.43 | 0.00 |
| | Rs. 3-4 lakh | 17.65 | 35.29 | 0.00 | 47.06 | 47.06 | 41.18 | 0.00 | 11.76 | 29.41 | 0.00 |
| | Rs. 4 lakh and above | 14.29 | 28.57 | 0.00 | 42.86 | 71.43 | 0.00 | 0.00 | 0.00 | 28.57 | 0.00 |
| Type of Bank | Public | 20.25 | 37.19 | 0.00 | 23.14 | 52.89 | 19.83 | 6.20 | 12.40 | 38.02 | 2.89 |
| | Private | 25.26 | 24.21 | 2.11 | 53.68 | 60.00 | 18.95 | 4.21 | 5.26 | 28.42 | 1.05 |
| | All Customers | 21.66 | 33.53 | 0.59 | 31.75 | 54.90 | 19.58 | 5.64 | 10.39 | 35.31 | 2.37 |

a- Convenient Working Hours b- Proximity to Office/Home c- Attractive Financial Products
d- Company Salary Accounts e- Availability of ATMs f- Excellent Customer Service
g- Recommended by Friends h- No Other Banks Nearby i - Overall Excellent Reputation
j- Others

It is evident from Table 4.5 that availability of ATMs/ATM networks (54.90%) is the single most important factor across all categories of respondent. The next important factors are overall reputation of the bank (35.31%), where the company maintains salary account (31.75%), proximity of location (33.53%) and convenient working hours (21.66%). Though customer service is an important parameter for choosing the bank, a relatively low score is given to it by the sample respondents. The probable reasons for this may be due to the factors like the expectations of customers for services may be low and they have been made tangible and automated, more dependent on machines than man, speed and accuracy has become dominant, etc. The dehumanization of banking premises reduces the importance of factors like friendly staff, overall representation, etc.; even today customer do not go to the bank and do not recognize the face of the bankers.

The reasons attributed by customers in their background indicated that older and retired people, self-employed and professionals put more emphasis on reputation of the bank. Usually this group of people have maintained the account for a longer period. The myth that private banks are better could not be established with the present sample except the factor like ATMs and company salary accounts. The private banks have successfully roped small and medium-sized companies, on whose behalf they maintain the salary accounts. Factors like convenient location, and overall reputation, the public banks are ahead of the private banks. Females attribute reasons like convenient working hours, and proximity to home as more important compared to that of males; who in turn indicate overall reputation of the bank as more important. In rest of the cases, the trend is quite similar to the observations made earlier.

### Accounts with Other Banks

Most of the customers in the sample have more than one bank account. The reasons for operating second account with another bank are many. The prominent among them are convenient working hours, proximity to home, ATM network, financial products, etc. Table 4.6 describes the type of accounts maintained by the sample respondents with other banks.

**Table 4.6: Accounts in Other Banks**

(Figures are in percentage)

| | Parameters | No Account | Account in | | |
|---|---|---|---|---|---|
| | | | Pub. | Pvt. | Pub/Pvt. |
| Age | Below 30 years | 34.36 | 34.97 | 23.31 | 7.36 |
| | 30-40 years | 23.60 | 29.21 | 26.97 | 20.22 |
| | 40-60 years | 35.09 | 35.09 | 19.30 | 10.53 |
| | 60 years and above | 7.14 | 71.43 | 14.29 | 7.14 |
| Education | Up to HSC | 18.18 | 42.42 | 12.12 | 12.12 |
| | Graduate | 38.71 | 30.11 | 21.51 | 9.68 |
| | Postgraduate | 27.36 | 44.34 | 20.75 | 7.55 |
| | Professional | 26.67 | 32.38 | 24.76 | 16.19 |
| Gender | Male | 27.41 | 41.31 | 22.01 | 9.27 |
| | Female | 35.90 | 20.51 | 25.64 | 17.95 |
| Occupation | Salaried | 26.02 | 33.67 | 26.53 | 13.78 |
| | Self-employed | 0.00 | 42.86 | 42.86 | 14.29 |
| | Professional | 4.55 | 72.73 | 18.18 | 4.55 |
| | Business | 19.05 | 47.62 | 23.81 | 9.52 |
| | Student | 72.34 | 12.77 | 8.51 | 6.38 |
| | Retired | 7.69 | 73.08 | 15.38 | 3.85 |
| | Housewife | 38.89 | 16.67 | 27.78 | 16.67 |
| Income | Less than Rs. 1 lakh | 38.28 | 32.81 | 21.88 | 7.03 |
| | Rs. 1-2 lakh | 26.35 | 40.54 | 24.32 | 8.78 |
| | Rs. 2-3 lakh | 18.92 | 24.32 | 24.32 | 32.43 |
| | Rs. 3-4 lakh | 17.65 | 47.06 | 17.65 | 17.65 |
| | Rs. 4 lakh and above | 14.29 | 57.14 | 14.29 | 14.29 |
| | All Customers | 29.38 | 36.50 | 22.85 | 11.28 |

It is observed from the above table that 99 respondents (29.38% to the total) do not have second bank account. Similarly, 11.28 per cent of respondents have second bank account in both private and public sector banks. 36.5 per cent of the respondents have second account with a public sector bank and rest

22.85 per cent with private banks. When these figures are compared with the main accounts, the share of private banks has increased. It is also observed from the table that respondents in higher age (particularly the senior citizens) have a clear preference for public sector banks. The female respondents have shown their preference to have the second account with private banks compared to that of male counter parts. More number of females also maintains the second account with both public and private banks. The respondents with regard to occupation variations indicated that professionals and retired persons have a preference for public sector banks. The overall scenario is almost same for public and private banks.

**Table 4.7: Type of Bank Accounts in Other Banks**

**(Figures are in percentage)**

| | Parameters | Type of Accounts | | | |
|---|---|---|---|---|---|
| | | S | C | S/C | S/FD |
| Age | Below 30 years | 86.92 | 1.87 | 11.21 | 0.00 |
| | 30-40 years | 94.12 | 0.00 | 4.41 | 1.47 |
| | 40-60 years | 89.19 | 8.11 | 0.00 | 2.70 |
| | 60 years and above | 100.00 | 0.00 | 0.00 | 0.00 |
| Education | Up to HSC | 85.19 | 3.70 | 11.11 | 0.00 |
| | Graduate | 91.23 | 5.26 | 3.51 | 0.00 |
| | Postgraduate | 83.12 | 1.30 | 12.99 | 2.60 |
| | Professional | 100.00 | 0.00 | 0.00 | 0.00 |
| Gender | Male | 89.36 | 2.66 | 7.45 | 0.53 |
| | Female | 96.00 | 0.00 | 2.00 | 2.00 |
| Occupation | Salaried | 96.55 | 2.76 | 0.00 | 0.69 |
| | Self-employed | 100.00 | 0.00 | 0.00 | 0.00 |
| | Professional | 52.38 | 0.00 | 47.62 | 0.00 |
| | Business | 70.59 | 5.88 | 23.53 | 0.00 |
| | Student | 100.00 | 0.00 | 0.00 | 0.00 |
| | Retired | 100.00 | 0.00 | 0.00 | 0.00 |
| | Housewife | 81.82 | 0.00 | 9.09 | 9.09 |

*(Contd...)*

| | Parameters | Type of Accounts | | | |
|---|---|---|---|---|---|
| | | S | C | S/C | S/FD |
| Income | Less than Rs. 1 lakh | 89.87 | 1.27 | 7.59 | 1.27 |
| | Rs. 1-2 lakh | 90.83 | 2.75 | 5.50 | 0.92 |
| | Rs. 2-3 lakh | 93.33 | 3.33 | 3.33 | 0.00 |
| | Rs. 3-4 lakh | 85.71 | 0.00 | 14.29 | 0.00 |
| | Rs. 4 lakh and above | 100.00 | 0.00 | 0.00 | 0.00 |
| | All Customers | 90.76 | 2.10 | 6.30 | 0.84 |

S- Savings C- Current FD- Fixed Deposit

Table 4.7 discusses the type of accounts with other banks by demographic profile of the respondents. Customers mainly maintain three types of accounts – savings banks, current and fixed deposit accounts. It is observed that about 90 per cent of the respondents have savings accounts only, while 6.3 per cent have savings and current accounts and 0.84 per cent have fixed deposit accounts with the second bank. All the respondents above 60 years and retired persons have their accounts with public banks. In terms of occupational variations, businessmen and professionals maintain their current accounts with the second bank. The rest of the cases correspond to overall scenario of the sample.

Table 4.8 discusses the years of transaction with the second bank by demographic profiles of the sample respondents. It is observed that 81.09 per cent of the respondents have the accounts with the second bank for less than 5 years, while only 4.28 per cent of the customers have accounts beyond 10 years. Like the earlier situation for main banks, the number of years of operation commensurate with age of the sample respondents. Similarly, respondents with higher income also have maintained the account beyond 10 years. In different demographic variations, the trend is not significant.

Table 4.8: Customer Profile by Years of Transaction in Other Banks

| | Parameters | Up to 5 Years | | 5-10 Years | | Above 10 Years | | Total | |
|---|---|---|---|---|---|---|---|---|---|
| | | f | % | f | % | f | % | f | % |
| Age | Below 30 years | 90 | 84.11 | 17 | 15.89 | 0 | 0.00 | 107 | 100.00 |
| | 30-40 years | 56 | 82.35 | 10 | 14.71 | 2 | 2.94 | 68 | 100.00 |
| | 40-60 years | 28 | 75.68 | 5 | 13.51 | 4 | 10.81 | 37 | 100.00 |
| | 60 years and above | 15 | 57.70 | 7 | 26.92 | 4 | 15.38 | 26 | 100.00 |
| Education | Up to HSC | 22 | 81.48 | 5 | 18.52 | 0 | 0.00 | 27 | 100.00 |
| | Graduate | 47 | 82.46 | 6 | 10.53 | 4 | 7.02 | 57 | 100.00 |
| | Postgraduate | 59 | 76.62 | 16 | 20.78 | 2 | 2.60 | 77 | 100.00 |
| | Professional | 65 | 84.42 | 8 | 10.39 | 4 | 5.19 | 77 | 100.00 |
| Gender | Male | 152 | 80.85 | 27 | 14.36 | 9 | 4.79 | 188 | 100.00 |
| | Female | 41 | 82.00 | 8 | 16.00 | 1 | 2.00 | 50 | 100.00 |
| Occupation | Salaried | 116 | 80.00 | 19 | 13.10 | 10 | 6.90 | 145 | 100.00 |
| | Self-employed | 4 | 57.14 | 3 | 42.86 | 0 | 0.00 | 7 | 100.00 |
| | Professional | 18 | 85.71 | 3 | 14.29 | 0 | 0.00 | 21 | 100.00 |
| | Business | 16 | 94.12 | 1 | 5.88 | 0 | 0.00 | 17 | 100.00 |
| | Student | 12 | 92.31 | 1 | 7.69 | 0 | 0.00 | 13 | 100.00 |
| | Retired | 17 | 70.83 | 7 | 29.17 | 0 | 0.00 | 24 | 100.00 |
| | Housewife | 10 | 90.91 | 1 | 9.09 | 0 | 0.00 | 11 | 100.00 |

*(Contd...)*

| | Parameters | Up to 5 Years | | 5-10 Years | | Above 10 Years | | Total | |
|---|---|---|---|---|---|---|---|---|---|
| | | f | % | f | % | f | % | f | % |
| Income | Less than Rs. 1 lakh | 67 | 84.81 | 12 | 15.19 | 0 | 0.00 | 79 | 100.00 |
| | Rs. 1-2 lakh | 89 | 81.65 | 16 | 14.68 | 4 | 3.67 | 109 | 100.00 |
| | Rs. 2-3 lakh | 24 | 80.00 | 3 | 10.00 | 3 | 10.00 | 30 | 100.00 |
| | Rs. 3-4 lakh | 12 | 85.71 | 2 | 14.29 | 0 | 0.00 | 14 | 100.00 |
| | Rs. 4 lakh and above | 1 | 17.67 | 2 | 33.33 | 3 | 50.00 | 6 | 100.00 |
| | All Customers | 193 | 81.09 | 35 | 14.71 | 10 | 4.20 | 238 | 100.00 |

Table 4.9: Reasons for Opening Account in Other Banks

| | Parameters | Reasons | | | | | | | | | |
|---|---|---|---|---|---|---|---|---|---|---|---|
| | | a | b | c | d | e | f | g | h | i | j |
| Age | Below 30 years | 17.67 | 9.77 | 2.79 | 13.49 | 14.88 | 12.56 | 3.72 | 0.47 | 19.53 | 5.12 |
| | 30-40 years | 21.88 | 22.66 | 2.34 | 7.81 | 7.03 | 13.28 | 2.34 | 0.00 | 20.31 | 2.34 |
| | 40-60 years | 15.38 | 18.46 | 9.23 | 4.62 | 1.54 | 16.92 | 7.69 | 7.69 | 16.92 | 1.54 |
| | 60 years and above | 11.11 | 25.00 | 0.00 | 8.33 | 27.78 | 2.78 | 0.00 | 0.00 | 0.00 | 25.00 |
| Education | Up to HSC | 17.86 | 21.43 | 8.93 | 12.50 | 8.93 | 1.79 | 0.00 | 21.43 | 5.36 | 5.36 |
| | Graduate | 16.04 | 14.15 | 4.72 | 6.60 | 10.38 | 12.26 | 4.72 | 4.72 | 18.87 | 7.55 |
| | Postgraduate | 16.97 | 12.73 | 1.21 | 14.55 | 13.94 | 17.58 | 1.82 | 0.61 | 13.33 | 7.27 |
| | Professional | 21.37 | 19.66 | 5.98 | 7.69 | 9.40 | 7.69 | 5.98 | 0.00 | 21.37 | 0.85 |
| Gender | Male | 16.95 | 15.52 | 3.74 | 9.20 | 12.93 | 10.92 | 4.02 | 1.72 | 18.39 | 6.61 |
| | Female | 21.88 | 17.71 | 2.08 | 13.54 | 7.29 | 18.75 | 2.08 | 0.00 | 15.63 | 1.04 |
| Occupation | Salaried | 15.81 | 21.79 | 4.27 | 11.11 | 6.41 | 9.40 | 3.85 | 2.56 | 19.66 | 5.13 |
| | Self-employed | 21.43 | 21.43 | 7.14 | 0.00 | 0.00 | 7.14 | 21.43 | 0.00 | 21.43 | 0.00 |
| | Professional | 17.33 | 4.00 | 4.00 | 13.33 | 17.33 | 18.67 | 4.00 | 0.00 | 20.00 | 1.33 |
| | Business | 22.50 | 10.00 | 0.00 | 10.00 | 22.50 | 12.50 | 0.00 | 0.00 | 17.50 | 5.00 |
| | Student | 41.67 | 0.00 | 0.00 | 0.00 | 12.50 | 29.17 | 0.00 | 0.00 | 16.67 | 0.00 |
| | Retired | 11.76 | 23.53 | 0.00 | 8.82 | 26.47 | 2.94 | 0.00 | 0.00 | 0.00 | 26.47 |
| | Housewife | 17.39 | 8.70 | 4.35 | 8.70 | 13.04 | 26.09 | 4.35 | 0.00 | 17.39 | 0.00 |

*(Contd...)*

| | Parameters | Reasons | | | | | | | | | |
|---|---|---|---|---|---|---|---|---|---|---|---|
| | | a | b | c | d | e | f | g | h | i | j |
| Income | Less than Rs. 1 lakh | 19.74 | 15.13 | 1.32 | 11.18 | 12.50 | 13.82 | 1.97 | 0.00 | 18.42 | 5.92 |
| | Rs. 1-2 lakh | 14.80 | 12.76 | 4.59 | 11.73 | 12.76 | 12.76 | 5.10 | 2.55 | 16.33 | 6.63 |
| | Rs. 2-3 lakh | 25.00 | 26.79 | 3.57 | 5.36 | 3.57 | 8.93 | 1.79 | 1.79 | 21.43 | 1.79 |
| | Rs. 3-4 lakh | 16.13 | 19.35 | 6.45 | 6.45 | 12.90 | 16.13 | 6.45 | 0.00 | 16.13 | 0.00 |
| | Rs. 4 lakh and above | 22.22 | 22.22 | 0.00 | 0.00 | 22.22 | 0.00 | 0.00 | 0.00 | 22.22 | 11.11 |
| | All Customers | 18.02 | 15.99 | 3.38 | 10.14 | 11.71 | 12.61 | 3.60 | 1.35 | 17.79 | 5.41 |

a- Convenient Working Hours b- Proximity to Office/Home c- Attractive Financial Products
d- Company Salary Accounts e- Overall Excellent Reputation f- Excellent Customer Service
g- Recommended by Friends h- No Other banks Nearby i- Availability of ATMs
j- Others

Table 4.9 discusses the reasons for opening the second account with some other bank. It is observed from the above table that convenient working hour, ATM network and proximity to home are the important reasons for opening an account with other banks. This trend is similar to the reasons attributed by the respondents for the main bank. Respondents belonging to higher age group, retired, businessmen and higher income group people choose a bank because of overall reputation of the bank. Housewives and students have indicated that their choice is governed by the levels of the customer services offered by the bank. No significant variation is evident among the respondents in demographic variations. Further, it is inferred from the foregoing analysis that the banks should concentrate on the first three factors to attract more and more customers. Attractive financial products or recommendations of friends or the non-availability of other banks is not the powerful factors to influence the customers to open the second account.

The Table 4.10 depicts the number of visits by the customer to the bank. The numbers of visits are substantially reduced due to the availability of the ATMs. It is observed from Table 4.10 that only 2.10 per cent of the customers visit the branch more than five times in a month, while 86.91 per cent has less than two visits in a month. Again 50 per cent of them reported that hardly they have any visit to the branch. The frequent visitors to the bank are customers in their 40-60 years age group, post-graduate, males, salaried persons and are in the income group of Rs. 1-2 lakh. With the increase in ATM networks, the number of visits will further reduce. This saves the time of the customer.

### Type of Banking Services Availed

The prime motives for opening an account with a bank are to avail some services. The opinions about different services availed by sample respondents are presented in Table 4.11.

## Customer Visits to the Bank

### Table 4.10: Customer Visits Per Month to Other Banks

| | Parameters | Up to 2 Visits | | 3-5 Visits | | Above 5 Visits | |
|---|---|---|---|---|---|---|---|
| | | f | % | f | % | f | % |
| Age | Below 30 years | 78 | 72.90 | 27 | 25.23 | 2 | 1.87 |
| | 30-40 years | 44 | 64.71 | 24 | 35.29 | 0 | 0.00 |
| | 40-60 years | 20 | 54.05 | 14 | 37.84 | 3 | 8.11 |
| | 60 years and above | 22 | 84.62 | 4 | 15.38 | 0 | 0.00 |
| Education | Up to HSC | 20 | 76.92 | 6 | 23.08 | | 0.00 |
| | Graduate | 32 | 58.18 | 22 | 40.00 | 1 | 1.82 |
| | Postgraduate | 62 | 78.48 | 14 | 17.72 | 3 | 3.80 |
| | Professional | 50 | 64.10 | 27 | 34.62 | 1 | 1.28 |
| Gender | Male | 122 | 64.89 | 61 | 32.45 | 5 | 2.66 |
| | Female | 42 | 84.00 | 8 | 16.00 | 0 | 0.00 |
| Occupation | Salaried | 97 | 66.90 | 44 | 30.34 | 4 | 2.76 |
| | Self-employed | 0 | 0.00 | 7 | 100.00 | 0 | 0.00 |
| | Professional | 16 | 76.19 | 5 | 23.81 | 0 | 0.00 |
| | Business | 13 | 76.47 | 3 | 17.65 | 1 | 5.88 |
| | Student | 10 | 76.92 | 3 | 23.08 | 0 | 0.00 |
| | Retired | 20 | 83.33 | 4 | 16.67 | 0 | 0.00 |
| | Housewife | 8 | 72.73 | 3 | 27.27 | 0 | 0.00 |
| Income | Less than Rs. 1 lakh | 61 | 77.22 | 17 | 21.52 | 1 | 1.27 |
| | Rs. 1-2 lakh | 71 | 65.14 | 35 | 32.11 | 3 | 2.75 |
| | Rs. 2-3 lakh | 21 | 70.00 | 8 | 26.67 | 1 | 3.33 |
| | Rs. 3-4 lakh | 7 | 50.00 | 7 | 50.00 | 0 | 0.00 |
| | Rs. 4 lakh and above | 4 | 66.67 | 2 | 33.33 | 0 | 0.00 |
| | Total | 164 | 68.91 | 69 | 28.99 | 5 | 2.10 |

Table 4.11: Type of Banking Services Availed

| | Parameters | Type of Services | | | | | | | |
|---|---|---|---|---|---|---|---|---|---|
| | | a | b | c | d | e | f | g | h |
| Age | Below 30 years | 11.19 | 20.48 | 3.81 | 4.52 | 10.48 | 4.76 | 26.90 | 17.86 |
| | 30-40 years | 10.53 | 18.62 | 7.29 | 5.26 | 9.72 | 4.45 | 28.74 | 15.38 |
| | 40-60 years | 17.89 | 13.01 | 13.01 | 6.50 | 13.01 | 8.13 | 15.45 | 13.01 |
| | 60 years and above | 20.75 | 16.98 | 13.21 | 7.55 | 0.00 | 0.00 | 32.08 | 9.43 |
| Education | Up to HSC | 11.63 | 17.44 | 5.81 | 10.47 | 6.98 | 24.42 | 15.12 | 15.12 |
| | Graduate | 8.73 | 14.85 | 12.23 | 3.93 | 11.79 | 7.86 | 23.58 | 17.03 |
| | Postgraduate | 14.34 | 19.49 | 4.04 | 7.72 | 11.03 | 3.31 | 25.00 | 15.07 |
| | Professional | 14.45 | 21.48 | 4.30 | 3.52 | 7.03 | 3.13 | 30.08 | 16.02 |
| Gender | Male | 12.79 | 20.12 | 6.40 | 4.99 | 8.11 | 5.46 | 26.52 | 15.60 |
| | Female | 11.88 | 13.86 | 7.92 | 5.94 | 15.84 | 2.97 | 24.75 | 16.83 |
| Occupation | Salaried | 13.87 | 18.28 | 9.24 | 3.78 | 9.45 | 5.46 | 24.58 | 15.34 |
| | Self-employed | 0.00 | 20.00 | 0.00 | 0.00 | 5.00 | 20.00 | 35.00 | 20.00 |
| | Professional | 3.70 | 18.52 | 2.47 | 14.81 | 12.35 | 3.70 | 23.46 | 20.99 |
| | Business | 13.85 | 23.08 | 3.08 | 9.23 | 10.77 | 3.08 | 26.15 | 10.77 |
| | Student | 12.39 | 20.35 | 0.88 | 0.00 | 10.62 | 3.54 | 30.97 | 21.24 |
| | Retired | 19.57 | 15.22 | 8.70 | 15.22 | 0.00 | 0.00 | 32.61 | 8.70 |
| | Housewife | 11.90 | 14.29 | 9.52 | 2.38 | 21.43 | 4.76 | 23.81 | 11.90 |

*(Contd...)*

| | Parameters | Type of Services | | | | | | | |
|---|---|---|---|---|---|---|---|---|---|
| | | a | b | c | d | e | f | g | h |
| Income | Less than Rs. 1 lakh | 10.56 | 20.19 | 6.52 | 2.80 | 11.80 | 4.66 | 25.78 | 17.70 |
| | Rs. 1-2 lakh | 14.41 | 16.10 | 7.63 | 6.50 | 10.17 | 4.80 | 25.71 | 14.69 |
| | Rs. 2-3 lakh | 10.68 | 21.36 | 4.85 | 7.77 | 7.77 | 4.85 | 28.16 | 14.56 |
| | Rs. 3-4 lakh | 16.67 | 18.75 | 6.25 | 8.33 | 4.17 | 8.33 | 22.92 | 14.58 |
| | Rs. 4 lakh and above | 12.50 | 25.00 | 6.25 | 0.00 | 0.00 | 0.00 | 37.50 | 18.75 |
| | All Customers | 12.57 | 18.62 | 6.76 | 5.22 | 9.96 | 4.86 | 26.10 | 15.90 |

a- Realisation of Instruments
b- Remittances like DD/MT
c- Consumer/Auto/Housing Loan
d- Safe Deposit Locker
e- Term Deposit/Recurring Deposit
f- Payment of Various Bills/Taxes
g- ATM & Phone Booking
h- Credit/Debit Card

Table 4.11 presents the banking services availed by the customers in demographic variations. The most often used/ availed services as evident from the table are ATM and phone banking; followed by remittances and debit/credit cards. Respondents in the higher age-groups (above 40 years) are searching for more loan facilities compared to the younger ones. The younger people have shown their interest only in vehicle loans/educational loans; while the elder ones searched for housing and other loans. The locker facilities and availing other value-added services are still not very popular among the respondents. The respondents in all demographic groups have not shown any significant variations in availing different types of services. Hence, it can be concluded that for availing different types of services no significant influence of demographic variables is observed.

**Analysis of Loan Accounts**

Giving loans to the consumers is another important function of a bank. But the purposes and the portfolio of loans have undergone sea changes during the last decade. Loans are no more called loans, rather referred as financial products to be marketed by banks like any other physical products. This indicates how the marketing strategy of the banks also has changed. New generation private banks like ICICI Bank is quite aggressive in introducing different financial products like car loan, home loan, etc., which are sold by marketing agents even by opening stalls in the road-sides. Table 4.13 presents the major types of loans availed by respondents are vehicle loan, housing loan, educational loans, personal loans, etc.

Table 4.13 describes the loan behaviour of the respondents in demographic variation. Highest number of respondents has opted for vehicle loan, followed by education loan. Out of the total 337 respondents, 72 persons have availed a vehicle loan, constituting 21.36 per cent of the total. Further analysis revealed that out of the 72 persons only four are female (5.56%). Again, in terms of their age, the respondents in the upper age group have availed the vehicle loan most (42.86%). Only 12.27 per cent of people below the age of 30 years have availed the vehicle loan. Similarly, about 47 per cent of the respondents availing the vehicle loan have technical and professional education. Out of the Service-holders, about 22.96 per cent of them and only one student has availed the vehicle loan. The trend is quite obvious, as banks have a preference for service-holders as the source of income is stable and perennial and risk of the loan is also less. Again, most of the respondents in the middle income group (Rs. 2-3 lakhs) have opted for a vehicle loan (more than 50%).

Another important type of loan is housing loan, where only 32 respondents (9.50%) have availed the loan. As housing loans are mainly big loans, hence both the banks and the customers have played the safe. The backgrounds of the respondents for housing loan are salaried people with lower middle income (Rs. 1-2 lakhs) and belong to middle-age group. Gender and educational variation seems to have little influence in availing a housing loan.

Now the banks are promoting educational loan in a big way, which has been evident from the Table 4.12. The students are the single most important group with 19.5 per cent of sample students have availed the educational loan for themselves to purşue their higher education such as graduation (technical), post-graduation and professional education. The demographic backgrounds of such groups are: they are young, are students and mostly belong to the lower and lower-middle income groups.

Similarly, another important type of loan is personal loan, which was availed mostly by the salaried people followed by professionals. They typically belongs to lower or lower-middle income group, indicating the need pattern and financial constraints. This type of loans is not very much preferred among the retired person. A few respondents have gone for other types of loans, which have not been covered here. Again, here the younger people belonging to lower group dominate, indicating their need dominancy. As evident from the data, nobody has opted for consumer durable loans. The overall profile of loan customers are more tilted towards the young service-holders belonging to the lower/lower-middle income group. The $\chi^2$ value indicates that loan profile and customer profile are dependent on each other.

**Table 4.12: Types of Loans Availed by the Respondents**

| Demo. Parameters | | No. of Respondents | Types of loans | | | | | | | | | | | |
|---|---|---|---|---|---|---|---|---|---|---|---|---|---|---|
| | | | 1 | % | 2 | % | 3 | % | 5 | % | 6 | % | No Loans | % |
| Gender | Female | 78 | 4 | 5.56 | 10 | 13.89 | 13 | 18.06 | 8 | 11.11 | 0 | 0.00 | 43 | 55.13 |
| | Male | 259 | 68 | 26.25 | 22 | 8.49 | 53 | 20.46 | 43 | 16.60 | 10 | 3.86 | 73 | 28.19 |
| Age | <30 yrs. | 163 | 20 | 12.27 | 12 | 7.36 | 53 | 32.52 | 20 | 12.27 | 5 | 3.07 | 57 | 34.97 |
| | 30-40 yrs. | 89 | 24 | 26.97 | 3 | 3.37 | 11 | 12.36 | 16 | 17.98 | 2 | 2.25 | 35 | 39.33 |
| | 40-60 yrs. | 57 | 16 | 28.07 | 14 | 24.56 | 1 | 1.75 | 13 | 22.81 | 0 | 0.00 | 13 | 22.81 |
| | Above 60 yrs. | 28 | 12 | 42.86 | 2 | 7.14 | 1 | 3.57 | 2 | 7.14 | 3 | 10.71 | 11 | 39.29 |
| Education | Up to HSC | 33 | 10 | 30.30 | 3 | 9.09 | 0 | 0.00 | 4 | 12.12 | 1 | 3.03 | 16 | 48.48 |
| | Grad. | 93 | 11 | 11.83 | 15 | 16.13 | 20 | 21.51 | 14 | 15.05 | 4 | 4.30 | 33 | 35.48 |
| | P.Grad. | 106 | 16 | 15.09 | 10 | 9.43 | 28 | 26.42 | 13 | 12.26 | 4 | 3.77 | 39 | 36.79 |
| | Prof. | 105 | 35 | 33.33 | 4 | 3.81 | 18 | 17.14 | 20 | 19.05 | 1 | 0.95 | 28 | 26.67 |

*(Contd...)*

| Demo. Parameters | | No. of Respondents | Types of loans | | | | | | | | | | | |
|---|---|---|---|---|---|---|---|---|---|---|---|---|---|---|
| | | | 1 | % | 2 | % | 3 | % | 5 | % | 6 | % | No Loans | % |
| Occupation | Business | 21 | 6 | 28.57 | 1 | 4.76 | 5 | 23.81 | 6 | 28.57 | 1 | 4.76 | 3 | 14.29 |
| | H Wife | 18 | 0 | 0.00 | 4 | 22.22 | 3 | 16.67 | 4 | 22.22 | 0 | 0.00 | 7 | 38.89 |
| | Profess | 22 | 5 | 22.73 | 1 | 4.55 | 11 | 50.00 | 4 | 18.18 | 0 | 0.00 | 1 | 4.55 |
| | Retired | 26 | 11 | 42.31 | 3 | 11.54 | 1 | 3.85 | 1 | 3.85 | 3 | 11.54 | 8 | 30.77 |
| | Salaried | 196 | 45 | 22.96 | 21 | 10.71 | 15 | 7.65 | 29 | 14.80 | 2 | 1.02 | 81 | 41.33 |
| | Self Employed | 7 | 4 | 57.14 | 2 | 28.57 | 0 | 0.00 | 0 | 0.00 | 3 | 42.86 | 1 | 14.29 |
| | Students | 47 | 1 | 2.13 | 0 | 0.00 | 31 | 65.96 | 0 | 0.00 | 0 | 0.00 | 15 | 31.91 |
| Income | <Rs. 1 lakh | 128 | 16 | 12.50 | 13 | 10.16 | 47 | 36.72 | 13 | 10.16 | 3 | 2.34 | 39 | 30.47 |
| | 1-2 lakh | 148 | 28 | 18.92 | 17 | 11.49 | 13 | 8.78 | 19 | 12.84 | 5 | 3.38 | 71 | 47.97 |
| | 2-3 lakh | 37 | 18 | 48.65 | 2 | 5.41 | 3 | 8.11 | 11 | 29.73 | 1 | 2.70 | 3 | 8.11 |
| | 3-4 lakh | 17 | 7 | 41.18 | 0 | 0.00 | 2 | 11.76 | 7 | 41.18 | 1 | 5.88 | 1 | 5.88 |
| | > 4 lakh | 7 | 3 | 42.86 | 0 | 0.00 | 1 | 14.29 | 1 | 14.29 | 0 | 0.00 | 2 | 28.57 |
| | Total | 337 | 72 | 21.36 | 32 | 9.50 | 66 | 19.58 | 51 | 15.13 | 10 | 2.97 | 116 | 34.42 |

1. Vehicle Loan 2. Housing Loan 3. Education Loan

4. Consumer Durable loan 5. Personal Loan 6. Other Loans

## CUSTOMER'S PERCEPTION AND EXPECTATIONS

In availing a particular type of services, the customer searches for his past experiences—what he got for what he had searched? This gives a unique situation called customer experiences. This has been explained by two behavioural constructs-expectation and perception. Finding out what customers expect is essential to providing service quality. Research holds the key for understanding customer's expectations and perceptions of services. Not knowing what customers expect is one of the root causes of not delivering up to the customers' expectations. *Provider gap* is the difference between customer expectations of service and the organizations understanding of these expectations (Zeithaml and Bitner, 2003). The term organization is represented through the person responsible to create or change service policies, procedures and standards. In today's organizations, the authority to make adjustments in service delivery is delegated to empowered teams and front-line people.

Why does this provider gap occur? Many reasons may be attributed for the same, such as: no direct interaction with the customers, unwillingness to ask about expectations and unpreparedness in addressing them. When the people with the authority and responsibility for setting priorities do not fully understand customer's service expectations, they may trigger a chain of poor decisions and suboptimal resource allocations that result in perception of poor service quality. In accurate understanding of the customers ultimately end up with heavy expenditures in undesirable areas—the end result is no gains but only pains. An inaccurate understanding of what customers expect and what really matters to them leads to service performances that falls short of customer expectations. The first step necessary in improving service quality is for management to acquire accurate information about customer expectations. At this backdrop, in the following sections, an attempt has been made to understand the customer expectations and perceptions for different types of banking parameters like deposit account, loan account, value-added services and the administration and promises. The expectations and perceptions of customers between private and public banks for different parameters like customer deposit accounts, loan accounts, value-added services, and premises and administration are measured in a 4–point scale (ranging from 'not at all' (1) to 'most important' (4) for expectations and from 'unsatisfactory' (1) to 'excellent' (4) for perceptions). The differences between the mean values of different parameters are termed as quality gap. Positive gaps indicate satisfaction and negative gaps as dissatisfaction of the customers with that particular parameter.

**Savings and Time Deposit Services**

The relationship of a customer starts with a bank either by opening an account for deposit or for an advance/loan. While opening a pure deposit account (viz. savings and term deposit) the customer is considering a host of parameters. The following tables discuss the expectations and perceptions of customers by type of banks in different parameters measured in a 4-point scale.

Table 4.13 depicts the summery of customer expectations and perceptions on deposit accounts of the total respondents (overall). It is evident from the table that both the expectations and perceptions are higher than the mid-point (2.5). This indicates that the consumers attach more importance to both the expectations and perceptions in respect to all the parameters. The levels of expectations of customers are highest for quick cash transactions like deposit and withdrawal (3.72), while the lowest is for renewal or modification of nominations. Similarly, for perceptions, the highest score (3.53) is for quick account opening and the lowest is for renewal or modification of nomination. When the gap is calculated highest gap is observed in pass-book updation (0.48) and lowest for renewal of nominations. Positive gaps (satisfaction) is observed with six variables, while negative gaps (dissatisfaction) with four ones. Positive gap is observed with variables like quick opening of accounts, updation of pass-book, issue of cheque book, standing instructions, nomination facility and renewal of nomination. This indicates that the customers are satisfied with the above mentioned services rendered by the banks. The customers are not satisfied with their banks in relation to factors like quick transaction of cash, clearance of outstation cheques, intimation of maturity and settlement of death claims.

Table 4.13: Customers' Expectations and Perceptions on Deposit Accounts—All Banks

| Parameters | Mean Score | | | Correlation | t-value |
|---|---|---|---|---|---|
| | Perception | Expectation | Gap (P-E) | | |
| Quick A/C Opening | 3.53 | 3.37 | 0.16 | 0.039 | -3.077* |
| Updation of Pass Book | 3.30 | 2.82 | 0.48 | -0.075 | -6.918* |
| Issue of Cheque Book | 3.12 | 2.87 | 0.25 | -0.061 | -3.773* |
| Standing Instructions | 2.81 | 2.60 | 0.21 | 0.191* | -3.534* |
| Nomination Facility | 2.91 | 2.88 | 0.03 | 0.202* | -0.497 |
| Quick Transactions of Cash | 3.37 | 3.72 | -0.35 | -0.022 | 6.239* |
| Clearance of Outstation Cheque | 3.10 | 3.43 | -0.33 | 0.232* | 5.52* |
| Intimation of Maturity | 2.83 | 3.00 | -0.17 | 0.138** | 2.609* |
| Renewal of Nomination | 2.68 | 2.53 | 0.15 | 0.400* | -2.393* |
| Settlement of Death Claims | 2.76 | 2.90 | -0.14 | 0.600* | 2.118** |

* 1% Level of Significance ** 5% Level of Significance

The difference of means for perceptions and expectations were tested for significance by applying 2-tail paired t-test. The differences in the mean values of expectation and perceptions in all parameters except nomination facility are statistically significant, indicating the existence of differences between perceptions and expectations of the customers. Further, it is noticed that all the variables except settlement of death claims are significant at 1 per cent level of significance. Higher gaps are indicated by significant t-values. It can be inferred that the management has to take sufficient care to see that such gaps do not exist; and if at all exists it should be a sufficiently small one. Hence, to improve quality of service for better satisfactions of customers, both the technical and functional quality should be taken care of.

The correlation coefficients (r) between the expectations and perceptions of customers relating to parameters, it is observed that r is significant at 1per cent level of significance for parameters like standing instructions, nomination facility, clearance of out station cheques, renewal of nominations and statement of birth claims; and at 5 per cent levels of significance for intimation of maturity of FD Rs. Inverse relationships (-r) is also observed for factors like updation of pass-books, issue of cheque books and cash transactions indicating bigger gaps in these variables. Significant 'r' is observed with smaller gaps, indicating both are closely related to each other.

Customers' perceptions and expectations with respect to ten parameters of deposit services are also studied for public and private sector banks separately. The summary results of that are presented in Tables 4.13(A) and 4.13(B). It is observed from Table 4.13(A) that the customers of public sector banks have given sufficient importance to all the parameters for both expectations and performance except expectations of renewal of nomination (2.42). When the gap is calculated, six factors have positive gaps indicating satisfaction and the highest gap is observed in respect of updation of pass-book (0.38). Similarly, in four other factors, negative gaps are observed indicating dissatisfaction of the customers and the highest is quick deposit and withdrawal of cash (-0.32).

Table 4.13 (A): Customers' Expectations and Perceptions on Deposit Accounts—Public Banks

| Parameters | Mean Score | | | Correlation | t-value |
|---|---|---|---|---|---|
| | Perception | Expectation | Gap (P-E) | | |
| Quick A/C Opening | 3.51 | 3.42 | 0.09 | 0.074 | -1.462 |
| Updation of Pass Book | 3.24 | 2.86 | 0.38 | 0.061 | -5.196* |
| Issue of Cheque Book | 3.07 | 2.83 | 0.24 | -0.029 | -3.086* |
| Standing Instructions | 2.77 | 2.64 | 0.13 | 0.301* | -1.972 |
| Nomination Facility | 2.95 | 2.81 | 0.14 | 0.284* | -1.909 |
| Quick Transactions of Cash | 3.38 | 3.70 | -0.32 | 0.077 | 5.234* |
| Clearance of Outstation Cheque | 3.11 | 3.37 | -0.26 | 0.381* | 4.099* |
| Intimation of Maturity | 2.84 | 2.93 | -0.09 | 0.252* | 1.162 |
| Renewal of Nomination | 2.74 | 2.45 | 0.29 | 0.397* | -4.058* |
| Settlement of Death Claims | 2.81 | 2.85 | -0.04 | 0.618* | 0.546 |

1% Level of Significance.

Table 4.13 (B): Customers' Expectations and Perceptions on Deposit Accounts—Private Banks

| Parameters | Mean Score | | | Correlation | t-Value |
|---|---|---|---|---|---|
| | Perception | Expectation | Gap (P-E) | | |
| Quick A/C Opening | 3.61 | 3.21 | 0.40 | -0.040 | -3.678* |
| Updation of Pass Book | 3.44 | 2.73 | 0.71 | -0.414* | -4.661* |
| Issue of Cheque Book | 3.26 | 2.96 | 0.30 | -0.186 | -2.169** |
| Standing Instructions | 2.94 | 2.46 | 0.48 | -0.081 | -3.352* |
| Nomination Facility | 2.82 | 3.06 | -0.24 | 0.017 | 1.848 |
| Quick Transactions of Cash | 3.34 | 3.76 | -0.42 | -0.294 | 3.415* |
| Clearance of Outstation Cheque | 3.07 | 3.56 | -0.49 | -0.190* | 3.737* |
| Intimation of Maturity | 2.78 | 3.22 | -0.44 | -0.247 | 2.982* |
| Renewal of Nomination | 2.51 | 2.76 | -0.25 | 0.533* | 2.263** |
| Settlement of Death Claims | 2.62 | 3.04 | -0.42 | 0.590* | 3.122* |

* 1% Level of Significance  ** 5% Level of Significance

The analysis of private banks (Table 4.13(B)) indicates that the positive gaps are witnessed for four parameters and negative gaps for the rest six parameters. The highest score of satisfaction is 0.71 for updation of pass-book and dissatisfaction is -0.49 for clearance of out station cheques. A comparison of public and private banks indicates that though the pattern of expectations and perceptions are similar; both the banks are lagging behind to match the customer's expectations. Pass book updation is much faster than expected in both the banks, while withdrawal or deposit of cash is slower and collection of out-station cheques are delayed indicating customer dissatisfaction for both the banks.

The coefficient of correlation (r) between perception and expectations for public sector banks are significant for six factors like standing instruction, nomination facility, clearance of out station cheques, like intimation of maturity, renewal of nomination, while four parameters are significant for private banks (viz. updation of pass-book, clearance of out station cheques, renewal of nominations and settlement of death claims). Significant 'r' is visible with smaller gaps indicating close association between the expectation and perception of those factors. The results of t-test indicate that t-values for five factors like updation of pass-book, issue of cheque books, etc. are statistically significant at 1per cent level of significance; while seven factors for private banks are significant at 1 per cent level and two more factors at 5 per cent levels of significance. Hence, it can be summed up that both the types of banks are not able to match to the expectations of the customers perfectly; and the more number of significant t-values indicate bigger gaps exists between the expectations and perceptions of customers for the private banks.

**Loan Account Services**

The consumer expectations and perceptions of different loans availed by the customers in bank variations are presented in Table 4.14. For this purpose data were collected in a 4-point scale ranging from '*not at all important* ' to ' *most important* ' for measuring expectations; and ' *unsatisfactory* ' to ' *excellent* ' for performance ratings.

Table 4.14: Customers' Expectations and Perceptions on Loan Accounts—All Banks

| Parameters | Mean Score | | | Correlation | t-value |
|---|---|---|---|---|---|
| | Perception | Expectation | Gap (P-E) | | |
| Guidance and Counselling | 3.41 | 3.42 | -0.01 | 0.244* | 0.085 |
| Sanction of Loan in Time | 3.07 | 3.66 | -0.59 | -0.102 | 6.389* |
| Easy Documentation | 3.30 | 3.44 | -0.14 | 0.077 | 2.048** |
| Procedure and Paper Work | 3.05 | 3.15 | -0.10 | 0.369* | 1.502 |
| Adequate Amount of Loan | 3.22 | 3.45 | -0.23 | 0.349* | 3.522* |
| Competitive Rate of Interest | 2.98 | 3.48 | -0.50 | 0.239* | 5.986* |
| Easy Payment Schedule | 3.17 | 3.52 | -0.35 | 0.161** | 4.786* |
| Calculation of Interest | 3.16 | 3.31 | -0.15 | 0.070 | 1.716 |
| Issuance of Statement of A/Cs | 3.03 | 2.93 | 0.10 | -0.183** | -1.029 |
| Transparency of Terms and Conditions | 3.08 | 3.40 | -0.32 | 0.379* | 3.983* |

* 1% Level of Significance ** 5% Level of Significance

Table 4.14 discusses the data collected from the sample respondents in 10 different parameters measuring the perceptions and expectations of customers with regard to loan accounts. The existence of differences between perceptions and expectations are tested through t-test for all the banks combined. It is observed from the table that the mean scores of expectation and perceptions are higher than the mid-value (i.e. 2.5) indicating more importance is attached to all the parameters by the respondents. The highest score is observed in guidance and counselling for performance; while sanction of loans in time for expectation. The gap is negative in all parameters except issue of statement of accounts, implied that the performance of the banks falls short of expectations of the customers.

The difference among the means for expectations and perceptions are tested through t-values. It is evident from the data, that parameters like sanction of loan in time, adequate amount of loan, competitive interest rates, easy payment schedule and transparency of terms and conditions are statistically significant at 1 per cent level, while easy documentation at 5 per cent level. The correlation coefficients (r) are statistically significant for factors like counselling and guidance, procedures and proper work, adequacy of loan amount, competitive interest rate, payment schedules, issuance of statement of accounts, and transparency of terms and conditions.

Tables 4.14 (A) and 4.14 (B) describe the loan behaviours of customers in public and private sector banks with respect to above mentioned 10 parameters. The perception of sample respondents ranges from "3.02 to 3.35"; which is "2.92 to 3.62" for expectations for public sector banks. The higher scopes indicate customers are giving more importance to all the parameters. In eight different parameters negative gap is observed, indicating dissatisfaction of the customers. The correlation coefficient (r) is significant for seven parameters except sanction of loan in time, easy documentations and payment schedules indicating close association among parameters of sample behaviour.

Table 4.14 (A): Customers' Expectations and Perceptions on Loan Accounts—Public Banks

| Parameters | Mean Score | | | Correlation | t-value |
|---|---|---|---|---|---|
| | Perception | Expectation | Gap (P-E) | | |
| Guidance and Counselling | 3.35 | 3.38 | -0.03 | 0.193** | 0.364 |
| Sanction of Loan in Time | 3.09 | 3.62 | -0.53 | -0.041 | 4.971* |
| Easy Documentation | 3.37 | 3.39 | -0.02 | 0.097 | 0.270 |
| Procedure and Paper Work | 3.16 | 3.09 | 0.07 | 0.444* | -0.988 |
| Adequate Amount of Loan | 3.33 | 3.47 | -0.14 | 0.394* | 1.962 |
| Competitive Rate of Interest | 3.02 | 3.46 | -0.44 | 0.207** | 4.407* |
| Easy Payment Schedule | 3.25 | 3.46 | -0.21 | 0.264* | 2.757* |
| Calculation of Interest | 3.28 | 3.35 | -0.07 | 0.105 | 0.757 |
| Issuance if Statement of A/Cs | 3.08 | 2.92 | 0.16 | -0.194** | -1.425 |
| Transparency of Terms and Conditions | 3.18 | 3.40 | -0.22 | 0.476* | 2.738* |

* 1% Level of Significance ** 5% Level of Significance

Table 4.14 (B): Customers' Expectations and Perceptions on Loan Accounts—Private Banks

| Parameters | Mean Score | | | Correlation | t-value |
|---|---|---|---|---|---|
| | Perception | Expectation | Gap (P-E) | | |
| Guidance and Counselling | 3.61 | 3.53 | 0.08 | 0.424* | -0.683 |
| Sanction of Loan in Time | 3.00 | 3.79 | -0.79 | -0.487* | 4.551* |
| Easy Documentation | 3.03 | 3.62 | -0.59 | 0.155 | 4.334* |
| Procedure and Paper Work | 2.68 | 3.38 | -0.70 | 0.386** | 4.870* |
| Adequate Amount of Loan | 2.84 | 3.39 | -0.55 | 0.188 | 3.586* |
| Competitive Rate of Interest | 2.81 | 3.54 | -0.73 | 0.442* | 5.097* |
| Easy Payment Schedule | 2.89 | 3.70 | -0.81 | -0.079 | 4.954* |
| Calculation of Interest | 2.76 | 3.16 | -0.40 | -0.163 | 2.073** |
| Issuance if Statement of A/Cs | 2.84 | 2.95 | -0.11 | -0.143 | 0.539 |
| Transparency of Terms and Conditions | 2.76 | 3.38 | -0.62 | 0.054 | 3.067* |

* 1% Level of Significance ** 5% Level of Significance

Similarly, for private banks the mean score range for exceptions and perceptions are 2.95 to 3.70 and 2.68 to 3.61 respectively, indicating a wide gap. Nine out of ten gaps are negative indicating dissatisfaction of the sample customers. The major reasons for dissatisfaction are payment schedule (–0.81), sanction time (–0.79), and rate of interest (–0.73), which are higher than the public sector banks. The correlation coefficients are significant for factors like counselling and guidance, sanction of loan in time, procedure, and interest rates for private banks. The expectations of sample customers of public sector banks in respect of the 10 parameters behave in the same line as that of private banks. The mean score of expectations for all parameters except issue of statements of the accounts is above 3.00 for both public and private banks. But as regards to perceptions, the respondents weigh public sector banks higher in comparison to private banks for all parameters except guidance and counselling.

The gap in the perception and expectations of the respondents are computed to judge the level of satisfaction of the customers in the given parameters. It is observed that customers of both public and private banks are not satisfied taking into account the parameters under study except procedure and paper work, and issue of statement of accounts for public sector banks and guidance and counselling for private banks. The t-values for factors like sanction time of loans, interest rates, payment schedule and issue of account statements are significant for public sector banks; which are as many as eight factors for private banks. Thus, it can be inferred that there lies a significant difference in expectations and performances of different parameters of loan behaviour of customers for both the banks, and differences are more for private banks. Hence, both the banks should look into the matter and take appropriate steps to reduce the gaps.

### Value-Added Services

Today the expectations of consumers have changed a lot and they expect anything and every thing on the earth. The banking sector is not an exception to it. But the advent of high speed technology like Information Technology (IT) has helped the banks to promote more and more new value added services. The most prominent among them are ATMs, Credit Cards and Phone Banking. With these advanced services, the life styles of the customers also have changed. Credit Cards have reduced the importance of cash in the market and ATMs and Phone Banking has made the banking premises dehumanized. The behaviour of sample respondents for these three services is represented in Tables 4.15, 4.15 (A) and 4.15 (B) for all banks, public banks and private banks respectively. The quality gap is measured and the significance of results was tested through t-tests. The different parameters of banking behaviour are measured in a 4-point scales (i.e. not at all important to most important for expectation and unsatisfactory to excellent for performances).

The customer expectations and perceptions for different value-added services in respect of all banks are presented in the Tables 4.15. The mean scores of perceptions and exceptions ranging from 3.06 to 3.72 and 2.72 to 3.60 respectively indicate a smaller gap. Thirteen out of the fifteen gaps are positive indicating customer satisfaction for these parameters. Similarly, 12 correlation coefficients are significant. And ten t-values are significant indicating substantial differences exist between expectations and performance of different services for the sample respondents.

The behaviour of customers for public and private banks are presented in Tables 4.15 (A) and 4.15 (B) respectively. The range of mean values for perception and exception of public bank customers are 3.06 to 3.77 and 2.63 to 3.59 respectively indicating higher perception and lower expectations. High scores in both the parameters indicate that all the factors are quite important for the respondents. Out of the fifteen gaps only one factor (i.e. transparency in service charges) is negative and rest fourteen factors are positive indicating higher satisfaction for customers. This trend is also conferred by t-values, where 11 out of 15 are statistically significant indicating the difference among sample means. Ten r-values are statistically significant indicating similarity of sample behaviour.

For private banks, the range of mean values for expectations is 2.79 to 3.63 and for perceptions it is 2.86 to 3.67 indicating a smaller positive gap. Out of the 15 gaps, 7 are negative and rest are positive and again the r-values are significant for five factors indicating a mixed trend. To test the mean differences through t-values, only three out of fifteen factors are statistically significant. Hence, it can be concluded that the customers of private bank experience a mixed trend (satisfaction and dissatisfaction) for the value added services and the smaller gaps indicate matching of performance to customer expectations.

Table 4.15: Customers' Expectations and Perceptions on ATM, Phone Banking and Credit Cards—All Banks

| Parameters | Mean Score | | | Correlation | t-value |
|---|---|---|---|---|---|
| | Perception | Expectation | Gap (P-E) | | |
| Network, Spread & No. of ATMs | 3.70 | 3.60 | 0.10 | 0.032 | -1.972** |
| Service Enabled through ATMs | 3.65 | 3.41 | 0.24 | 0.237* | -4.418* |
| Location of ATMs | 3.63 | 3.55 | 0.08 | 0.197* | -1.802 |
| Safety and Security | 3.58 | 3.60 | -0.02 | 0.126** | 0.413 |
| Easy Access to ATMs | 3.72 | 3.34 | 0.38 | 0.077 | -6.317* |
| Availability of Stationery | 3.06 | 2.72 | 0.34 | 0.132** | -4.838* |
| Adequate Cheque Drop Boxes | 3.21 | 2.91 | 0.30 | 0.303* | -4.723* |
| Prompt Issue of Credit/ATM Cards | 3.34 | 3.21 | 0.13 | 0.236* | -2.046** |
| Timely Renewal of Credit Card | 3.32 | 3.14 | 0.18 | 0.294* | -2.400** |
| Accuracy of Monthly Statements | 3.47 | 3.36 | 0.11 | 0.133** | -1.790 |
| Receipt of Monthly Statement in Time | 3.18 | 3.16 | 0.02 | 0.165** | -0.261 |
| Transparency in Service Charges | 3.09 | 3.24 | -0.15 | 0.070 | 2.050** |
| Wide Acceptability of Card | 3.45 | 3.43 | 0.02 | 0.501* | -0.450 |
| Phone Banking Facility on Demand | 3.06 | 2.83 | 0.23 | 0.248* | -3.254* |
| Proper Service on Phone Banking | 3.24 | 2.95 | 0.29 | 0.283* | -4.804* |

* 1% Level of Significance ** 5% Level of Significance

Table 4.15 (A): Customers' Expectations and Perceptions on ATM, Phone Banking and Credit Cards—Public Banks

| Parameters | Mean Score | | | Correlation | t-value |
|---|---|---|---|---|---|
| | Perception | Expectation | Gap (P-E) | | |
| Network, Spread & No. of ATMs | 3.72 | 3.59 | 0.13 | -0.054 | -1.930 |
| Service Enabled through ATMs | 3.72 | 3.41 | 0.31 | 0.168** | -4.814* |
| Location of ATMs | 3.65 | 3.54 | 0.11 | 0.226* | -2.017** |
| Safety and Security | 3.63 | 3.59 | 0.04 | 0.157** | -0.576 |
| Easy Access to ATMs | 3.77 | 3.33 | 0.44 | 0.140 | -6.617* |
| Availability of Stationery | 3.06 | 2.63 | 0.43 | 0.120 | -5.137* |
| Adequate Cheque Drop Boxes | 3.29 | 2.90 | 0.39 | 0.342* | -5.272* |
| Prompt Issue of Credit/ATM Cards | 3.39 | 3.20 | 0.19 | 0.220* | -2.579** |
| Timely Renewal of Credit Card | 3.40 | 3.15 | 0.25 | 0.301* | -3.041* |
| Accuracy of Monthly Statements | 3.50 | 3.30 | 0.20 | 0.122 | -2.738* |
| Receipt of Monthly Statement in Time | 3.29 | 3.09 | 0.20 | 0.261* | -2.664* |
| Transparency in Service Charges | 3.10 | 3.20 | -0.10 | 0.047 | 1.144 |
| Wide Acceptability of Card | 3.49 | 3.44 | 0.05 | 0.480* | -0.799 |
| Phone Banking Facility on Demand | 3.10 | 2.84 | 0.26 | 0.293* | -3.197* |
| Proper Service on Phone Banking | 3.22 | 2.92 | 0.30 | 0.306* | -4.408* |

* 1% Level of Significance    ** 5% Level of Significance

Table 4.15 (B): Customers' Expectations and Perceptions on ATM, Phone Banking and Credit Cards—Private Banks

| Parameters | Mean Score | | | Correlation | t-value |
|---|---|---|---|---|---|
| | Perception | Expectation | Gap (P-E) | | |
| Network, Spread & No. of ATMs | 3.67 | 3.63 | 0.04 | 0.388* | -0.468 |
| Service Enabled through ATMs | 3.44 | 3.40 | 0.04 | 0.433* | -0.362 |
| Location of ATMs | 3.58 | 3.57 | 0.01 | 0.117 | -0.163 |
| Safety and Security | 3.46 | 3.64 | -0.18 | 0.062 | 1.658 |
| Easy Access to ATMs | 3.58 | 3.38 | 0.20 | -0.049 | 1.710 |
| Availability of Stationery | 3.07 | 2.96 | 0.11 | 0.170 | -0.917 |
| Adequate Cheque Drop Boxes | 2.97 | 2.95 | 0.02 | 0.175 | -0.163 |
| Prompt Issue of Credit/ATM Cards | 3.22 | 3.27 | -0.05 | 0.305** | 0.426 |
| Timely Renewal of Credit Card | 3.07 | 3.12 | -0.05 | 0.279** | 0.369 |
| Accuracy of Monthly Statements | 3.39 | 3.53 | -0.14 | 0.217 | 1.184 |
| Receipt of Monthly Statement in Time | 2.86 | 3.36 | -0.50 | 0.031 | 3.696* |
| Transparency in Service Charges | 3.05 | 3.34 | -0.29 | 0.152 | 2.140** |
| Wide Acceptability of Card | 3.34 | 3.39 | -0.05 | 0.574* | 0.622 |
| Phone Banking Facility on Demand | 2.95 | 2.79 | 0.16 | 0.134 | 1.069 |
| Proper Service on Phone Banking | 3.31 | 3.03 | 0.28 | 0.226 | 2.090** |

* 1% Level of Significance ** 5% Level of Significance

To sum up; the customers of the public sector bank experiences more satisfaction compared to the private bank customers in the given sample. The results support the theories of disconfirmation; when expectations are low consumers perceive better benefits out of the performance, what is true for public sector banks. Again, the myths that public sector banks are far behind the private banks in technology adoption and in providing modern services are not true, rather they have surpassed the private banks. This may be, due to heavy investment by public sector banks in technology, more particularly State Bank of India.

**Administration and Premises of the Banks**

In marketing of services, physical factors like ambiances, technology, etc. play a vital role. From a service, what a consumer expects? The more important is the consumer experiences which means how the services are delivered. The cosy environment will attract more number of customers, than a congested unfriendly atmosphere. Another important trend in the last decade which posses maximum threat to the service sector is technology – more specifically information technology (IT) – which is currently shaping the field and influencing the practice of service marketing. These physical facilities with the aid of technology are profoundly changing how services are delivered, enabling both customers and bankers to get and provide better, and more efficient and customized services with global reach and tied with their home locations.

The views of the respondents regarding their expectations and perceptions on administration and permission of the banks are presented in Tables 4.16, 4.16 (A) and 4.16 (B). The views of the respondents under eight parameters are collected in a 4-point scale ranging from 'not at all important' to 'most important' for expectations and 'unsatisfactory' to 'excellent' for performance ratings. The difference of mean values for performance and expectations give provider gap indicating positive gap as satisfaction and negative as dissatisfaction. Further the t-values are calculated to test the significance of difference of performance and expectations.

Table 4.16: Customers' Expectations and Perceptions on Administration and Premises of Banks—All Banks

| Parameters | Mean Score | | | Correlation | t-value |
|---|---|---|---|---|---|
| | Perception | Expectation | Gap (P-E) | | |
| Adequacy of Premises | 3.14 | 3.29 | -0.15 | 0.038 | 2.267** |
| Proper Sitting Place to Customers | 3.19 | 3.28 | -0.09 | -0.110 | 1.296 |
| Location of the Branch | 3.42 | 3.51 | -0.09 | 0.082 | 1.551 |
| Overall Ambience and Getup | 3.20 | 3.14 | 0.06 | -0.038 | -1.018 |
| Suitable Sign Boards | 3.12 | 2.95 | 0.17 | 0.093 | -2.250** |
| Enquiry Counter | 2.99 | 3.56 | -0.57 | 0.031 | 8.810* |
| Availability of Stationery | 2.93 | 2.94 | -0.01 | 0.254* | -0.129 |
| Adequate Lighting and Parking Facility | 2.86 | 3.14 | -0.28 | -0.067 | 3.359* |

* 1% Level of Significance ** 5% Level of Significance

Table 4.16 (A): Customers' Expectations and Perceptions on Administration and Premises of Banks—Public Banks

| Parameters | Mean Score | | | Correlation | t-value |
|---|---|---|---|---|---|
| | Perception | Expectation | Gap (P-E) | | |
| Adequacy of Premises | 3.07 | 3.28 | -0.21 | 0.001 | 2.648** |
| Proper Sitting Place to Customers | 3.14 | 3.27 | -0.13 | -0.103 | 1.428 |
| Location of the Branch | 3.44 | 3.54 | -0.10 | 0.068 | 1.409 |
| Overall Ambience and Getup | 3.14 | 3.14 | 0.00 | -0.100 | -0.069 |
| Suitable Sign Boards | 3.05 | 2.87 | 0.18 | -0.013 | -1.949 |
| Enquiry Counter | 2.79 | 3.53 | -0.74 | -0.065 | 9.115* |
| Availability of Stationery | 2.83 | 2.80 | 0.03 | 0.121 | -0.365 |
| Adequate Lighting and Parking Facility | 2.82 | 3.09 | -0.27 | -0.224* | 2.466** |

* 1% Level of Significance ** 5% Level of Significance

Table 4.16 (B): Customers' Expectations and Perceptions on Administration and Premises of Banks—Private Banks

| Parameters | Mean Score | | | Correlation | t-value |
|---|---|---|---|---|---|
| | Perception | Expectation | Gap (P-E) | | |
| Adequacy of Premises | 3.32 | 3.30 | 0.02 | 0.144 | -0.120 |
| Proper Sitting Place to Customers | 3.30 | 3.31 | -0.01 | -0.151 | 0.105 |
| Location of the Branch | 3.38 | 3.45 | -0.07 | 0.110 | 0.660 |
| Overall Ambience and Getup | 3.35 | 3.14 | 0.21 | 0.120 | -1.948 |
| Suitable Sign Boards | 3.28 | 3.16 | 0.12 | 0.339* | -1.136 |
| Enquiry Counter | 3.50 | 3.66 | -0.16 | 0.218 | 1.796 |
| Availability of Stationery | 3.18 | 3.27 | -0.09 | 0.432* | 0.961 |
| Adequate Lighting and Parking Facility | 2.95 | 3.28 | -0.33 | 0.348* | 2.700* |

* 1% Level of Significance ** 5% Level of Significance

Table 4.16 discusses the mean scores of performance, and expectations of sample respondents for all banks along with the correlation and t-values. It is evident from the data that the range of mean scores for perceptions is 2.86 to 3.42 and for expectations is 2.94 to 3.51. This indicates all the values are in the upper side (mid-value is 2.50) and expectations are higher than perceptions. The consumers attach sufficient importance to all the parameters to describe the administration and premises of the banks. Six out of eight gaps are negative and the highest gap is indicated by the factor 'enquiry counters' (–0.57) implying more dissatisfaction. The coefficient of correlation (r) is significant only for availability of stationary. Similarly, the t-values for factors like premises, sign boards, enquiry counters, and lighting and parking facilities are significant indicating substantial differences among the mean values confirming the gap between exceptions and perceptions.

Tables 4.16(A) and 4.16(B) discuss the mean scores and t-values for expectations and perceptions of different factors of administration and premises by the sample respondents in bank variation. It is evident from the data that five gaps are negative for public sector banks and highest gap is observed for the factor like enquiry counter (–0.74) indicating dissatisfaction of the customers regarding premises. The r is significant for the factor like lighting and parking facilities. The t-values for factors like enquiry counter, premises, and lighting and parking facilities are significant indicating substantial difference exists between perception and expectations. The gap analysis for private banks indicates that five out of eight are negative indicating dissatisfaction of the customers, highest being for adequacy of lighting and parking facilities (–0.33). The r–values for three factors like sign boards; availability of stationary and parking facilities are significant. Hence, it can be concluded that the private banks are able to match to the customers expectations; thereby reducing dissatisfaction, with regard to administration and premises of the bank.

To sum up, as is evident from the data, private banks are better off than the counter part public banks. The major factors of dissatisfaction for public banks are enquiry counter; while parking space for private banks. However, both the banks are not lagging far behind to match the customer's expectations.

## ANALYSIS OF STAFF BEHAVIOUR

In the foregoing sections, a discrepancy between the customer expectations and actual services delivered is observed for different parameters. For performing services well and treating customers correctly, high quality of service performance is not a certainty. Standards must be designed, which is backed by appropriate resources (people, systems, and technology) and also must get adequate support to be effective; that is employees must be trained, motivated, measured, and compensated on the basis of performance along these standards (Zeithaml and Bitner, 2003). Thus, even when standards accurately reflects customers expectations, if the company fails to provide support for them – if it does not facilitate, encourage, and require their achievements – standards may not improve. Any good standard must focus on service employee and HR practices that facilitates delivery of quality services. The assumption is that when customer expectations are well understood and services have been designed and specified to confirm to those expectations, the customer will derive satisfaction.

When the sample respondents are asked to rate the employees (staff) of the bank regarding their behaviour towards the customers, the views so generated are presented in Table 4.17 on different parameters by customer profile.

It is observed from Table 4.17 that 80.12 per cent of the respondents are of the view that the staffs are available in their seats during working hours in general, which is 75.79 per cent for private banks and 81.82 per cent for public banks. In the second parameter, i.e. customer friendly approach of the staffs, the private banks (90.53%) is far ahead of public sector banks (68.60%) and the overall being 74.78 per cent. Similarly, the views of respondents regarding feeling of the staff for customer care the overall responses (69.73) are quite low and private banks are little ahead of public banks with regard to courteous and polite language of the staff. The overall response is 75.67 per cent, where the private banks are ahead of their public counterparts. But in the fifth factor, i.e., attention to customer needs, both types of banks are miserable and the overall response is as low as 55.49 per cent and the public sector banks are lagging behind.

Table 4.17: Customers' Views on Staff Behaviour

| Parameters | | Staff Behaviour | | | | | | | |
|---|---|---|---|---|---|---|---|---|---|
| | | a | b | c | d | e | f | g | h |
| Age | <30 years | 80.37 | 77.91 | 66.87 | 78.53 | 60.12 | 85.28 | 64.42 | 60.12 |
| | 30-40 years | 78.65 | 69.66 | 71.91 | 69.66 | 49.44 | 95.51 | 65.17 | 55.06 |
| | 40-60 years | 77.19 | 68.42 | 64.91 | 66.67 | 38.60 | 78.95 | 43.86 | 24.56 |
| | 60 yrs. and above | 89.29 | 85.71 | 89.29 | 96.43 | 82.14 | 57.14 | 53.57 | 42.86 |
| Education | Up to HSC | 75.76 | 75.76 | 78.79 | 60.61 | 78.79 | 60.61 | 48.48 | 48.48 |
| | Graduate | 78.49 | 72.04 | 60.22 | 64.52 | 44.09 | 74.19 | 52.69 | 41.94 |
| | Postgraduate | 79.25 | 80.19 | 65.09 | 88.68 | 62.26 | 93.40 | 72.64 | 64.15 |
| | Professional | 83.81 | 71.43 | 82.86 | 71.43 | 57.14 | 86.67 | 54.29 | 47.62 |
| Gender | Male | 77.61 | 70.66 | 72.59 | 71.81 | 54.05 | 83.01 | 54.83 | 46.72 |
| | Female | 88.46 | 88.46 | 60.26 | 88.46 | 60.26 | 89.74 | 78.21 | 66.67 |
| Occupation | Salaried | 78.06 | 72.96 | 66.33 | 73.98 | 50.51 | 88.78 | 63.27 | 45.41 |
| | Self-employed | 100.00 | 100.00 | 85.71 | 100.00 | 100.00 | 85.71 | 42.86 | 57.14 |
| | Professional | 90.91 | 68.18 | 77.27 | 72.73 | 63.64 | 81.82 | 63.64 | 68.18 |
| | Business | 85.71 | 76.19 | 90.48 | 80.95 | 66.67 | 90.48 | 61.90 | 61.90 |
| | Student | 72.34 | 63.83 | 57.45 | 59.57 | 44.68 | 80.85 | 48.94 | 59.57 |
| | Retired | 88.46 | 88.46 | 88.46 | 100.00 | 84.62 | 53.85 | 53.85 | 42.31 |
| | Housewife | 83.33 | 100.00 | 72.22 | 88.89 | 55.56 | 88.89 | 66.67 | 72.22 |

*(Contd...)*

| Parameters | | Staff Behaviour | | | | | | | |
|---|---|---|---|---|---|---|---|---|---|
| | | a | b | c | d | e | f | g | h |
| Income | < Rs. 1 lakh | 80.95 | 77.78 | 66.67 | 78.57 | 60.32 | 84.92 | 63.49 | 63.49 |
| | Rs. 1-2 lakh | 79.05 | 78.38 | 65.54 | 79.05 | 55.41 | 82.43 | 61.49 | 43.92 |
| | Rs. 2-3 lakh | 81.08 | 56.76 | 89.19 | 59.46 | 40.54 | 97.30 | 48.65 | 40.54 |
| | Rs. 3-4 lakh | 94.12 | 76.47 | 88.24 | 76.47 | 58.82 | 76.47 | 58.82 | 47.06 |
| | Rs. 4 lakh and above | 55.56 | 44.44 | 66.67 | 44.44 | 44.44 | 77.78 | 44.44 | 55.56 |
| Type of Bank | Public | 81.82 | 68.60 | 68.60 | 70.25 | 52.89 | 82.64 | 52.48 | 47.11 |
| | Private | 75.79 | 90.53 | 72.63 | 89.47 | 62.11 | 89.47 | 80.00 | 62.11 |
| | All Customers | 80.12 | 74.78 | 69.73 | 75.67 | 55.49 | 84.57 | 60.24 | 51.34 |

a- Availability of Staff
b- Customer Friendly Approach
c- Feeling of Customer Care
d- Courteous and Polite Language
e- Attention to Customer Needs
f- Working Knowledge on banking Products
g- Overall Discipline
h- Customer Counselling

Further it is observed from the table that the knowledge of the staff regarding banking products is reasonably good for both the banks, and employees of private banks have little edge over their counterparts. But on the last two factors, i.e., overall discipline, and customer counselling; the overall views of the respondents are not good. In rest of the parameters, similar trend is observed for both the banks.

To sum up, in all eight dimensions the views of the respondents for private banks is better than the public sector banks, except availability of staff factor. This trend is observed because of two probable reasons:

(i) Being the government banks, the public sector bank employees have a typical mind set and may not be appreciated by the customer; and

(ii) Ageing is one of the major problems of public sector banks that are why most of the employees have lost their dynamism and vigour. Hence, it is advisable to induct fresh blood into public banks to regain vitality, and to be more customer friendly.

## CUSTOMER SATISFACTION

The thrust on efficient customer service has increased manifold with the on set of competition from private players since the day of liberalisation, use of improved information technology (IT) has led to low cost, instantaneous communication and lot more facilities. Today, the concept of banking is not merely confined to accepting deposits, giving loans, or transferring money; rather banks have diversified into insurance, brokering, advisory services, merchant banking, and so on, added to this is the idea of customer satisfaction – providing the customer with what he wants, when he wants, and where he wants. The levels of customer service are one of the major strategies in the hands of the banks to increase their market share. The present section attempts to analyse the levels of customer satisfaction with customer demographic profiles. Table 4.18 presents the data relating to the levels of satisfaction by the customers.

Table 4.18: Satisfaction of Services Rendered by Customer Profile

| Parameters | | Yes-fully | | Yes-partially | | Not satisfied | | Total | |
|---|---|---|---|---|---|---|---|---|---|
| | | f | % | f | % | f | % | f | % |
| Age | Below 30 | 55 | 33.74 | 98 | 60.12 | 10 | 6.13 | 163 | 100.00 |
| | 30-40 | 24 | 26.97 | 49 | 55.06 | 16 | 17.98 | 89 | 100.00 |
| | 40-60 | 26 | 45.61 | 21 | 36.84 | 10 | 17.54 | 57 | 100.00 |
| | 60 and above | 2 | 7.14 | 26 | 92.86 | 0 | 0.00 | 28 | 100.00 |
| Education | Up to HSC | 7 | 21.21 | 22 | 66.67 | 4 | 12.12 | 33 | 100.00 |
| | Graduate | 39 | 41.94 | 51 | 54.84 | 3 | 3.23 | 93 | 100.00 |
| | Post Graduate | 27 | 25.47 | 64 | 60.38 | 15 | 14.15 | 106 | 100.00 |
| | Professional | 34 | 32.38 | 57 | 54.29 | 14 | 13.33 | 105 | 100.00 |
| Gender | Male | 79 | 30.50 | 150 | 57.92 | 30 | 11.58 | 259 | 100.00 |
| | Female | 28 | 35.90 | 44 | 56.41 | 6 | 7.69 | 78 | 100.00 |
| Occupation | Salaried | 70 | 35.72 | 100 | 51.02 | 26 | 13.26 | 196 | 100.00 |
| | Self-employed | 6 | 85.71 | 1 | 14.29 | 0 | 0.00 | 7 | 100.00 |
| | Professional | 1 | 4.55 | 19 | 86.36 | 2 | 9.09 | 22 | 100.00 |
| | Business | 4 | 19.05 | 14 | 66.67 | 3 | 14.28 | 21 | 100.00 |
| | Student | 17 | 36.17 | 27 | 57.45 | 3 | 6.38 | 47 | 100.00 |
| | Retired | 2 | 7.69 | 24 | 92.31 | 0 | 0.00 | 26 | 100.00 |
| | Housewife | 7 | 38.89 | 9 | 50.00 | 2 | 11.11 | 18 | 100.00 |

*(Contd...)*

| Parameters | | Yes-fully | | Yes-partially | | Not satisfied | | Total | |
|---|---|---|---|---|---|---|---|---|---|
| | | f | % | f | % | f | % | f | % |
| Income | < Rs. 1 lakh | 40 | 31.25 | 78 | 60.94 | 10 | 7.81 | 128 | 100.00 |
| | Rs. 1-2 lakh | 47 | 31.76 | 85 | 57.43 | 16 | 10.81 | 148 | 100.00 |
| | Rs. 2-3 lakh | 11 | 29.73 | 19 | 51.35 | 7 | 18.92 | 37 | 100.00 |
| | Rs. 3-4 lakh | 8 | 47.06 | 8 | 47.06 | 1 | 5.88 | 17 | 100.00 |
| | > Rs. 4lakh | 1 | 14.29 | 4 | 57.14 | 2 | 28.57 | 7 | 100.00 |
| Bank type | Public | 81 | 33.47 | 136 | 56.20 | 25 | 10.33 | 242 | 100.00 |
| | Private | 26 | 27.37 | 58 | 61.05 | 11 | 11.58 | 95 | 100.00 |
| | All Customers | 107 | 31.75 | 194 | 57.57 | 36 | 10.68 | 337 | 100.00 |

It is observed from the table given below that most of the customers are partially satisfied (57.57%) with the services rendered by their banks. The levels of dissatisfaction is more in the age-groups of 30-40 years and 40-60 years (17.98% and 17.54% respectively); compared to the other groups. Senior citizens have no dissatisfaction with their bankers. The graduates are happier with their bankers compared to other groups. In gender variations females are more satisfied. In occupational differences, the salaried persons, and businessmen were unhappy compared to others. Respondents in the income group of 3-4 lakhs are more satisfied compared to others. Customers of different banks also have shown no significance differences in the levels of satisfaction.

To sum up, the sample customers have shown more or less similar levels of satisfaction in their demographic variations. Further analysis of the reasons for dissatisfaction attributed by the respondents are indicated as lack of adequate number of ATMs, unfriendly attitude of the bank staff, delay in transaction (time), etc. The major reasons for dissatisfaction of the public sector banks in ATM network, while delay in transaction processing is for private banks. Both the types of banks suffer from staff attitude to provide service to the customers.

Table 4.19 discusses the data relating to complaints lodged by the customers and resolution in time. It is evident from the table 67.36 per cent of the respondents have not lodged any complaint. The rest (32.64%) have some occasions to lodge complain but 48.18 per cent of them have got in time solution to their problems. The middle-aged professionals have lodged complaints more than other groups. The highest of unresolved complaints are by the professional.

The students have the lowest complaints. People with higher level of incomes have lodged more complaints are evidenced from the table. 62.16 per cent respondents in the income group of Rs. 2-3 lakhs, and 52.94 per cent in the group of Rs. 3-4 lakhs have lodged complaints; out of which more than 50 per cent were not resolved in time. Similarly, slightly more number of complaints was lodged against private banks compared to public banks. In both the cases, more than 50 per cent of the cases were not resolved in time. Hence, it could be summed up that the bankers have to gear up themselves to handle the grievances more quickly and efficiently.

Table 4.19: Customer Complaint by Customer Profile

| Parameters | | Yes-Resolved | | Yes-Not resolved | | No Complaint | | Total | |
|---|---|---|---|---|---|---|---|---|---|
| | | f | % | f | % | f | % | f | % |
| Age | Below 30 | 17 | 10.43 | 28 | 17.18 | 118 | 72.39 | 163 | 100.00 |
| | 30-40 | 24 | 26.97 | 17 | 19.10 | 48 | 53.93 | 89 | 100.00 |
| | 40-60 | 8 | 14.04 | 9 | 15.79 | 40 | 70.18 | 57 | 100.00 |
| | 60 and above | 4 | 14.29 | 3 | 10.71 | 21 | 75.00 | 28 | 100.00 |
| Education | Up to HSC | 5 | 15.15 | 8 | 24.24 | 20 | 60.61 | 33 | 100.00 |
| | Graduate | 6 | 6.45 | 10 | 10.75 | 77 | 82.80 | 93 | 100.00 |
| | Postgraduate | 21 | 19.81 | 18 | 16.98 | 67 | 63.21 | 106 | 100.00 |
| | Professional | 21 | 20.00 | 21 | 20.00 | 63 | 60.00 | 105 | 100.00 |
| Gender | Male | 41 | 15.83 | 48 | 18.53 | 170 | 65.64 | 259 | 100.00 |
| | Female | 12 | 15.38 | 9 | 11.54 | 57 | 73.08 | 78 | 100.00 |
| Occupation | Salaried | 38 | 19.39 | 34 | 17.35 | 124 | 63.27 | 196 | 100.00 |
| | Self-employed | 3 | 42.86 | 0 | 0.00 | 4 | 57.14 | 7 | 100.00 |
| | Professional | 3 | 13.64 | 11 | 50.00 | 8 | 36.36 | 22 | 100.00 |
| | Business | 2 | 9.52 | 7 | 33.33 | 12 | 57.14 | 21 | 100.00 |
| | Student | 0 | 0.00 | 1 | 2.13 | 46 | 97.87 | 47 | 100.00 |
| | Retired | 3 | 11.54 | 3 | 11.54 | 20 | 76.92 | 26 | 100.00 |
| | Housewife | 4 | 22.22 | 1 | 5.56 | 13 | 72.22 | 18 | 100.00 |

*(Contd...)*

| Parameters | | Yes-Resolved | | Yes-Not resolved | | No Complaint | | Total | |
|---|---|---|---|---|---|---|---|---|---|
| | | f | % | f | % | f | % | f | % |
| Income | < Rs. 1 lakh | 13 | 10.16 | 15 | 11.72 | 100 | 78.13 | 128 | 100.00 |
| | Rs. 1-2 lakh | 25 | 16.89 | 22 | 14.86 | 101 | 68.24 | 148 | 100.00 |
| | Rs. 2-3 lakh | 10 | 27.03 | 13 | 35.14 | 14 | 37.84 | 37 | 100.00 |
| | Rs. 3-4 lakh | 3 | 17.65 | 6 | 35.29 | 8 | 47.06 | 17 | 100.00 |
| | > Rs. 4 lakh | 2 | 28.57 | 1 | 14.29 | 4 | 57.14 | 7 | 100.00 |
| Bank type | Public | 37 | 15.29 | 38 | 15.70 | 167 | 69.01 | 242 | 100.00 |
| | Private | 16 | 16.84 | 19 | 20.00 | 60 | 63.16 | 95 | 100.00 |
| | All Customers | 53 | 15.73 | 57 | 16.91 | 227 | 67.36 | 337 | 100.00 |

Table 4.20: Defining the Bank by Customer Profile

| Parameters | | Dynamic | | Progressive | | Friendly | | Methodical | | Not up-to Expectation | | Total | |
|---|---|---|---|---|---|---|---|---|---|---|---|---|---|
| | | f | % | f | % | f | % | f | % | f | % | f | % |
| Age | Below 30 | 19 | 11.66 | 51 | 31.29 | 36 | 22.09 | 38 | 23.31 | 19 | 11.66 | 163 | 100.00 |
| | 30-40 | 6 | 6.74 | 32 | 35.96 | 13 | 14.61 | 23 | 25.84 | 15 | 16.85 | 89 | 100.00 |
| | 40-60 | 1 | 1.75 | 14 | 24.56 | 14 | 24.56 | 20 | 35.09 | 8 | 14.04 | 57 | 100.00 |
| | 60 and above | 4 | 14.29 | 14 | 50.00 | 2 | 7.14 | 5 | 17.86 | 3 | 10.71 | 28 | 100.00 |
| Education | Up to HSC | 2 | 6.06 | 11 | 33.33 | 8 | 12.00 | 7 | 21.21 | 5 | 15.15 | 33 | 87.76 |
| | Graduate | 10 | 10.75 | 36 | 38.71 | 14 | 15.05 | 23 | 24.73 | 10 | 10.75 | 93 | 100.00 |
| | Postgraduate | 7 | 6.60 | 38 | 35.85 | 22 | 20.75 | 23 | 21.70 | 16 | 15.09 | 106 | 100.00 |
| | Professional | 11 | 10.48 | 26 | 24.76 | 21 | 20.00 | 33 | 31.43 | 14 | 13.33 | 105 | 100.00 |
| Gender | Male | 27 | 10.42 | 76 | 29.34 | 47 | 18.15 | 67 | 25.87 | 42 | 16.22 | 259 | 100.00 |
| | Female | 3 | 3.85 | 35 | 44.87 | 18 | 23.08 | 19 | 24.36 | 3 | 3.85 | 78 | 100.00 |
| Occupation | Salaried | 12 | 6.12 | 54 | 27.55 | 38 | 19.39 | 62 | 31.63 | 30 | 15.31 | 196 | 100.00 |
| | Self-employed | 0 | 0.00 | 4 | 57.14 | 3 | 42.86 | 0 | 0.00 | 0 | 0.00 | 7 | 100.00 |
| | Professional | 3 | 13.64 | 9 | 40.91 | 3 | 13.64 | 4 | 18.18 | 3 | 13.64 | 22 | 100.00 |
| | Business | 2 | 9.52 | 3 | 14.29 | 4 | 19.05 | 10 | 47.62 | 2 | 9.52 | 21 | 100.00 |
| | Student | 8 | 17.02 | 20 | 42.55 | 10 | 21.28 | 3 | 6.38 | 6 | 12.77 | 47 | 100.00 |
| | Retired | 4 | 15.38 | 14 | 53.85 | 2 | 7.69 | 3 | 11.54 | 3 | 11.54 | 26 | 100.00 |
| | Housewife | 1 | 5.56 | 7 | 38.89 | 5 | 27.78 | 4 | 22.22 | 1 | 5.56 | 18 | 100.00 |

(Contd...)

| Parameters | | Dynamic | | Progressive | | Friendly | | Methodical | | Not up-to Expectation | | Total | |
|---|---|---|---|---|---|---|---|---|---|---|---|---|---|
| | | f | % | f | % | f | % | f | % | f | % | f | % |
| Income | <Rs. 1 lakh | 13 | 11.02 | 41 | 34.75 | 26 | 22.03 | 18 | 15.25 | 20 | 16.95 | 118 | 100.00 |
| | Rs.1-2 lakh | 12 | 7.59 | 58 | 36.71 | 27 | 17.09 | 46 | 29.11 | 15 | 9.49 | 158 | 100.00 |
| | Rs. 2-3 lakh | 4 | 10.81 | 7 | 18.92 | 7 | 18.92 | 12 | 32.43 | 7 | 18.92 | 37 | 100.00 |
| | Rs. 3-4 lakh | 1 | 5.88 | 3 | 17.65 | 5 | 29.41 | 7 | 41.18 | 1 | 5.88 | 17 | 100.00 |
| | Rs. 4 lakh and above | 0 | 0.00 | 2 | 28.57 | 0 | 0.00 | 3 | 42.86 | 2 | 28.57 | 7 | 100.00 |
| Bank type | Public | 23 | 9.50 | 68 | 28.10 | 48 | 19.83 | 67 | 27.69 | 36 | 14.88 | 242 | 100.00 |
| | Private | 7 | 7.37 | 43 | 45.26 | 17 | 17.89 | 19 | 20.00 | 9 | 9.47 | 95 | 100.00 |
| | All Customers | 30 | 8.90 | 111 | 32.94 | 65 | 19.29 | 86 | 25.52 | 45 | 13.35 | 337 | 100.00 |

Table 4.20 presents the view of the respondents regarding how they define their own banks. It is evident from the responses that majority of the customers have defined their bank as progressive (32.94%), while 13.35 per cent of the sample rejected the bank by responding as *"yet to come up to expectations"*. Similarly, 25.52 per cent have described their banks as systematic and methodical, indicating rigid and fixed procedures and 19.29 per cent described it as customer friendly. Further analysis revealed that about 15 per cent of the respondents attributed public sector banks are not up to mark; which is about 9 per cent for private banks. Again, private banks are termed as progressive (45.26%), while public sector banks as systematic and methodical. The single largest group of respondents belonging to the income group of less than Rs. 1 lakh have defined the bank is not up to the mark. The male respondents have higher expectations than the females. Similarly, customers in the higher age group (40-60 years) and the service holders have expressed their dissatisfactions with the banks.

## CUSTOMERS' EXPECTATION OF NEW SERVICES

In a changing world, the customers always expect something new. This is also applicable to the banking services, where the customers expect some thing more from their banks. In the past, the bankers have also provided a lot new services, which also fuels customers' expectations. The expectations of the customers regarding new services are presented in Table 4.21.

It is observed from the table that only 36.20 per cent of the respondents have expressed their desires for new services from the bank. More or less all the respondent groups have the similar type of behaviour in this regard. In bank variations, customers of private bank (37.89%) are expecting more new services then their counterparts in private banks. In terms of age differences, the younger respondents (below 30 years) expect more new services compared to others. Similarly, the graduates and post-graduates expect more new services than others. In occupational variations the students (80.85%) are expecting more new services compared to others, while the salaried class (21.43%) have the lowest expectations. In income variations the income group below Rs. 1 lakh (57.81%) has the highest level of expectation compared to others. To sum up, the customers expect a large number of new services which varies across customer profile, but more or less similar in banks variations.

Table 4.21: Customers' Expectation of New Services

| Parameters | | Yes | | No | | No Response | |
|---|---|---|---|---|---|---|---|
| | | f | % | f | % | f | % |
| Age | Below 30 | 80 | 49.08 | 69 | 42.33 | 14 | 8.59 |
| | 30-40 | 21 | 23.60 | 60 | 67.42 | 8 | 8.99 |
| | 40-60 | 11 | 19.30 | 34 | 59.65 | 12 | 21.05 |
| | 60 and above | 10 | 35.71 | 15 | 53.57 | 3 | 10.71 |
| Education | Up to HSC | 10 | 30.30 | 17 | 51.52 | 6 | 18.18 |
| | Graduate | 36 | 38.71 | 42 | 45.16 | 15 | 16.13 |
| | Postgraduate | 43 | 40.57 | 62 | 58.49 | 1 | 0.94 |
| | Professional | 33 | 31.43 | 57 | 54.29 | 15 | 14.29 |
| Gender | Male | 98 | 37.84 | 133 | 51.35 | 28 | 10.81 |
| | Female | 24 | 30.77 | 45 | 57.69 | 9 | 11.54 |
| Occupation | Salaried | 42 | 21.43 | 124 | 63.27 | 30 | 15.31 |
| | Self-employed | 3 | 42.86 | 4 | 57.14 | 0 | 0.00 |
| | Professional | 13 | 59.09 | 6 | 27.27 | 3 | 13.64 |
| | Business | 7 | 33.33 | 14 | 66.67 | 0 | 0.00 |
| | Student | 38 | 80.85 | 9 | 19.15 | 0 | 0.00 |
| | Retired | 10 | 38.46 | 13 | 50.00 | 3 | 11.54 |
| | Housewife | 9 | 50.00 | 8 | 44.44 | 1 | 5.56 |

*(Contd...)*

| Parameters | | Yes | | No | | No Response | |
|---|---|---|---|---|---|---|---|
| | | f | % | f | % | f | % |
| Income | Less than 1 lakh | 74 | 57.81 | 44 | 34.38 | 10 | 7.81 |
| | 1-2 lakh | 32 | 21.62 | 95 | 64.19 | 21 | 14.19 |
| | 2-3 lakh | 9 | 24.32 | 25 | 67.57 | 3 | 8.11 |
| | 3-4 lakh | 6 | 35.29 | 8 | 47.06 | 3 | 17.65 |
| | 4 lakh and above | 1 | 14.29 | 6 | 85.71 | 0 | 0.00 |
| Type of Bank | Public | 86 | 35.54 | 124 | 51.24 | 32 | 13.22 |
| | Private | 36 | 37.89 | 54 | 56.84 | 5 | 5.26 |
| | All Customers | 122 | 36.20 | 178 | 52.82 | 37 | 10.98 |

When the customers feel happy with the bank they act as advertisers. They spread good words-of-mouth about the bank and recommend the same to others. This is how the bank gets new business by using the goodwill of existing customers. The views of the sample respondents regarding recommending the bank to friends and relatives are given in Table 4.22.

**Table 4.22: Customers' Views on Recommending the Bank to Friends and Relatives**

| Parameters | | Yes | | No | |
|---|---|---|---|---|---|
| | | f | % | f | % |
| Age | Below 30 | 145 | 88.96 | 18 | 11.04 |
| | 30-40 | 77 | 86.52 | 12 | 13.48 |
| | 40-60 | 42 | 73.68 | 15 | 26.32 |
| | 60 and above | 14 | 50.00 | 14 | 50.00 |
| Education | Up to HSC | 28 | 84.85 | 5 | 15.15 |
| | Graduate | 72 | 77.42 | 21 | 22.58 |
| | Post Graduate | 95 | 89.62 | 11 | 10.38 |
| | Professional | 83 | 79.05 | 22 | 20.95 |
| Gender | Male | 204 | 78.76 | 55 | 21.24 |
| | Female | 74 | 94.87 | 4 | 5.13 |
| Occupation | Salaried | 161 | 82.14 | 35 | 17.86 |
| | Self-employed | 7 | 100.00 | 0 | 0.00 |
| | Professional | 20 | 90.91 | 2 | 9.09 |
| | Business | 16 | 76.19 | 5 | 23.81 |
| | Student | 44 | 93.62 | 3 | 6.38 |
| | Retired | 12 | 46.15 | 14 | 53.85 |
| | Housewife | 18 | 100.00 | 0 | 0.00 |
| Income | Less than 1 lakh | 113 | 88.28 | 15 | 11.72 |
| | 1-2 lakh | 119 | 80.41 | 29 | 19.59 |
| | 2-3 lakh | 29 | 78.38 | 8 | 21.62 |
| | 3-4 lakh | 12 | 70.59 | 5 | 29.41 |
| | 4 lakh and above | 5 | 71.43 | 2 | 28.57 |
| Type of Bank | Public | 199 | 82.23 | 43 | 17.77 |
| | Private | 79 | 83.16 | 16 | 16.84 |
| | All Customers | 278 | 82.49 | 59 | 17.51 |

It is observed from the above table that majority of the respondents (82.49%) are happy with their banks and they will recommend the bank to others. But the rest 17.51 per cent are not going to recommend the bank to others. In terms of bank variations, the levels of satisfaction of customers of private banks are slightly better than the public banks. The view of the customers sharply falls with rise in income as evident from the table. Respondents with lower income recommend the bank more than their counterparts with higher income. The females in general and house-wives in particular are happy with their banks and are going to recommend it to their relatives. But in contrast to that retired persons above the age of 60 years are more unhappy (53.85%) and majority of them are not going to recommend for the same. Varied trend is observed in difference of educational backgrounds. Cent per cent of the self-employed are going to recommend their banks to their friends and relatives.

Further probing on the reasons for not recommending their banks to others are described in Table 4.23.

**Table 4.23: Reasons for not Recommending the Bank**

| Reasons | Public | | Private | |
|---|---|---|---|---|
| | f | % | f* | % |
| All Friends and Relatives have A/Cs | 4 | 9.30 | 0 | 0.00 |
| Attitude of Staff is not good | 7 | 16.28 | 3 | 18.75 |
| Poor Service Quality | 1 | 2.33 | 3 | 18.75 |
| Management is not good | 0 | 0.00 | 1 | 6.25 |
| No such special Attraction | 3 | 6.98 | 1 | 6.25 |
| Too much time-taking | 11 | 25.58 | 2 | 12.50 |
| Other banks are better | 3 | 6.98 | 2 | 12.50 |
| Lack of Cooperation | 0 | 0.00 | 2 | 12.50 |
| No need to recommend | 5 | 11.63 | 3 | 18.75 |
| Not happy with the bank | 3 | 6.98 | 1 | 6.25 |
| Not up to date | 2 | 4.65 | 1 | 6.25 |
| Rigid policies | 3 | 6.98 | 0 | 0.00 |
| Stereotyped | 1 | 2.33 | 1 | 6.25 |
| Comparatively costly | 0 | 0.00 | 1 | 6.25 |
| Total Respondents | 43 | 100.00 | 16 | 100.00 |

Percentages are to the Total *Multiple responses

It is evident from the table that the major reasons for not recommending by the respondents of public sector banks is too much delay in processing the transactions (25.58%); followed by the attitudes of the staff (16.28%). Similarly, the customers of private banks rejected their banks on the ground that the bank is not too good to be recommended to others and lack of cooperation from the staffs. Further, the attitude of the staffs and poor service quality are common reasons for rejection by the respondents in general. Hence, it is important for the banks to improve the service attitude of the staff and reduce the transaction time to improve customer satisfaction and stop the negative feelings of the customers; which may spread as words-of-mouth of the disappointed customers.

## SUGGESTIONS FOR IMPROVEMENTS IN CUSTOMER SERVICE

When the respondents are asked for suggestions to improve in customer services, both the satisfied and dissatisfied customers of public and private banks have given a long list of suggestions. The suggestions of the sample respondents in bank variations are presented in Table 4.24.

It is observed from the Table 4.24 that most of the suggestions from the customers are relating to staff factors. Out of that the most important one given by the respondents from public sector banks is customer care and services (35.06%). It is followed by quick disposal of customers (11.69%) and polite behaviour of the staff (11.04%); while for the private banks the major suggestions are e-services (17.81%), behaviour of the staff (16.44%), and customer friendly staffs (13.70%) are given by the respondents. Some other suggestions like better physical facilities (4.55%) and more number of ATMs (5.19%) for the public sector banks; while quick disposal of customers are highlighted by the respondents. This implies that the private banks are better equipped in physical facilities compared to public banks and improvement in the staff factor is common requirement of the banks in general to improve business performance.

**Table 4.24: Suggestions for Improvement in Customer Service**

| Suggestions | Public | | Private | |
|---|---|---|---|---|
| | f | % | f | % |
| More ATMs/Network | 8 | 5.19 | 1 | 1.37 |
| Action oriented Staff | 4 | 2.60 | 0 | 0.00 |
| Banker-Customer Meet | 1 | 0.65 | 0 | 0.00 |
| Customer Caring and Services | 54 | 35.06 | 5 | 6.85 |
| Customer Friendly Staff | 9 | 5.84 | 10 | 13.70 |
| Cooperation among the Staff | 3 | 1.95 | 1 | 1.37 |
| Quick disposal of Customers | 18 | 11.69 | 7 | 9.59 |
| Professional and Dynamic Staff | 5 | 3.25 | 5 | 6.85 |
| E-services | 6 | 3.90 | 13 | 17.81 |
| Lower interest rates | 1 | 0.65 | 0 | 0.00 |
| Better Physical Facilities | 1 | 0.65 | 0 | 0.00 |
| Customer Loyalty Programmes | 7 | 4.55 | 1 | 1.37 |
| Proper guidance | 1 | 0.65 | 3 | 4.11 |
| Punctuality of Staff | 5 | 3.25 | 3 | 4.11 |
| Polite Behaviour of Staff | 17 | 11.04 | 12 | 16.44 |
| Due respect to Customers | 4 | 2.60 | 0 | 0.00 |
| Training for Better Customer service | 3 | 1.95 | 1 | 1.37 |
| Customer Counselling | 0 | 0.00 | 5 | 6.85 |
| Systematic Procedures | 2 | 1.30 | 3 | 4.11 |
| Total Respondents | 154 | 100.00 | 73 | 100.00 |

Percentages are to the Total *109 did not respond

## CUSTOMERS' CHOICE OF A BANK

Most often the customers face a problem of selecting a bank to operate. In the densely banked urban areas, lot of alternatives are available for customer and he is also very particular in choosing specific attributes for selecting a bank. The factors for selection of a bank are presented in Table 4.25.

## Table 4.25: Factors for Selection of a Bank

| Factors | Mean Score | | | |
|---|---|---|---|---|
| | Pub | Pvt. | Gap | t-value |
| No of ATMs /Network | 6.69 | 6.72 | -0.03 | -0.431 |
| Prompt Service | 6.56 | 6.55 | 0.01 | 0.143 |
| Appearance of the Bank | 5.77 | 5.65 | 0.12 | 0.783 |
| Company Salary A/C | 4.81 | 5.24 | -0.43 | -2.065** |
| Smart front-office Staff | 5.60 | 5.49 | 0.11 | 0.661 |
| Gifts offered by Bank | 4.71 | 4.79 | -0.08 | -0.386 |
| Facilities for payment of Bills | 5.53 | 5.82 | -0.29 | -1.484 |
| Customized Service | 6.61 | 5.63 | 0.98 | 3.105* |
| No of Branches /Network | 5.82 | 5.92 | -0.10 | 0.686 |
| Specialized Staff for Financial Services | 6.14 | 6.01 | 0.13 | 1.092 |
| On-line computer services | 5.96 | 5.85 | 0.11 | 0.716 |
| Employees willing to Help | 6.31 | 6.14 | 0.17 | 1.433 |
| Merchant Banking Facilities | 5.21 | 4.92 | 0.29 | 1.500 |
| Bank's Image | 6.26 | 6.13 | 0.13 | 0.984 |
| Availability of parking space | 5.97 | 5.78 | 0.19 | 1.275 |
| Distance from Home/Office | 6.11 | 5.86 | 0.25 | 2.083** |
| Individual attention to Customers | 6.32 | 6.34 | -0.02 | -0.117 |
| Credit/Debit Card facilities | 6.19 | 6.18 | 0.01 | 0.046 |
| Bank's Power & Influence | 5.36 | 5.46 | -0.10 | -0.614 |
| Availability of News papers | 6.16 | 4.97 | 1.19 | 0.939 |
| Bank is an One-stop-Vendor | 6.61 | 5.60 | 1.01 | 0.044 |
| Computerization of Operations | 6.44 | 6.29 | 0.15 | 1.153 |
| Facility for loans | 6.30 | 6.20 | 0.10 | 0.697 |
| Minimum deposit amount | 5.87 | 6.21 | -0.34 | -2.518* |
| Evening/Off hour services | 5.92 | 6.36 | -0.44 | -3.052* |
| Locker facilities | 6.01 | 6.01 | 0.00 | 0.012 |
| Ethical conduct of Bank | 6.01 | 5.91 | 0.10 | 0.751 |
| Foreign Exchange Transaction | 5.59 | 5.26 | 0.33 | 1.689 |
| Competitive pricing | 6.13 | 6.06 | 0.07 | 0.559 |
| Communication with Customers | 5.80 | 5.66 | 0.14 | 0.959 |
| Total Respondents | 242 | 95 | | |

* 1% Level of Significance ** 5% Level of Significance

Table 4.25 discusses the mean values of different parameters in bank variation. Thirty different factors are chosen for study of reasons for selecting a bank by private and public sector bank customers. It is evident from the table that customers of both the types of banks have given sufficient weightage to all the likely factors while choosing a bank. Highest gap in the mean scores between private and public banks is observed in the factors customised and unique services of the bank. Similarly, the t-values between the bank variations are significant for factors like unique and customised services, minimum deposit amount, and off-hour services at 1 per cent level of significance; while company transacts with a particular bank and distance from home and (or) office at 5 per cent levels of significance. In rest of the factors, the gaps are not sufficient, indicating no significant difference lies among those factors in the eyes of the customers. Further probing indicates that the positive gaps for the factors like company transacts with bank, customised services and distance from home/office means customers view public banks better than the private ones, the probable reasons for such trend is that public banks are widely located indicating its convenient locations, while private banks offer specialised services like '*zero balance*' with salary accounts and usually more transactions through ATMs.

Tables 4.26 to 4.29 describes the results of factor analysis. For grouping the factors, initial eigen of more than 1 is selected and by using principal component analysis (PCA) method through varimax rotation of factors. As indicated in Table 4.26, the total number of factors were reduced to nine explaining 70.634 per cent of the variations in the sample through PCA method selecting the factors having more than '1' as eigen-value and calculating rotated sum of squares of the loadings. The first factor having 7.752 eigen-value, reduced to 3.063 explains 10.209 per cent of the variance. The details are shown in the Table 4.26.

Table 4.26: Total Variance Explained

| Component | Initial Eigen-values | | | Extraction Sums of Squared Loadings | | | Rotation Sums of Squared Loadings | | |
|---|---|---|---|---|---|---|---|---|---|
| | Total | % of Variance | Cumulative % | Total | % of Variance | Cumulative % | Total | % of Variance | Cumulative % |
| 1. | 7.752 | 25.839 | 25.839 | 7.752 | 25.839 | 25.839 | 3.063 | 10.209 | 10.209 |
| 2. | 2.400 | 8.001 | 33.841 | 2.400 | 8.001 | 33.841 | 2.900 | 9.667 | 19.875 |
| 3. | 2.204 | 7.345 | 41.186 | 2.204 | 7.345 | 41.186 | 2.596 | 8.654 | 28.529 |
| 4. | 1.952 | 6.505 | 47.691 | 1.952 | 6.505 | 47.691 | 2.393 | 7.977 | 36.506 |
| 5. | 1.666 | 5.553 | 53.244 | 1.666 | 5.553 | 53.244 | 2.372 | 7.908 | 44.414 |
| 6. | 1.618 | 5.393 | 58.637 | 1.618 | 5.393 | 58.637 | 2.241 | 7.470 | 51.884 |
| 7. | 1.434 | 4.781 | 63.419 | 1.434 | 4.781 | 63.419 | 2.070 | 6.899 | 58.782 |
| 8. | 1.146 | 3.821 | 67.239 | 1.146 | 3.821 | 67.239 | 1.779 | 5.930 | 64.712 |
| 9. | 1.019 | 3.395 | 70.634 | 1.019 | 3.395 | 70.634 | 1.777 | 5.922 | 70.634 |
| 10. | .938 | 3.128 | 73.762 | | | | | | |
| 11. | .890 | 2.967 | 76.728 | | | | | | |
| 12. | .729 | 2.431 | 79.160 | | | | | | |

*(Contd...)*

| | Initial Eigen-values | | | Extraction Sums of Squared Loadings | | | Rotation Sums of Squared Loadings | | |
|---|---|---|---|---|---|---|---|---|---|
| Component | Total | % of Variance | Cumulative % | Total | % of Variance | Cumulative % | Total | % of Variance | Cumulative % |
| 13. | .702 | 2.341 | 81.501 | | | | | | |
| 14. | .635 | 2.115 | 83.616 | | | | | | |
| 15. | .570 | 1.899 | 85.515 | | | | | | |
| 16. | .531 | 1.771 | 87.287 | | | | | | |
| 17. | .481 | 1.603 | 88.890 | | | | | | |
| 18. | .437 | 1.457 | 90.347 | | | | | | |
| 19. | .414 | 1.381 | 91.728 | | | | | | |
| 20. | .370 | 1.235 | 92.962 | | | | | | |
| 21. | .338 | 1.126 | 94.088 | | | | | | |
| 22. | .328 | 1.093 | 95.181 | | | | | | |
| 23. | .282 | .939 | 96.120 | | | | | | |
| 24. | .243 | .810 | 96.930 | | | | | | |
| 25. | .209 | .696 | 97.625 | | | | | | |

*(Contd...)*

| Component | Initial Eigen-values | | | Extraction Sums of Squared Loadings | | | Rotation Sums of Squared Loadings | | |
|---|---|---|---|---|---|---|---|---|---|
| | Total | % of Variance | Cumulative % | Total | % of Variance | Cumulative % | Total | % of Variance | Cumulative % |
| 26. | .184 | .614 | 98.239 | | | | | | |
| 27. | .165 | .551 | 98.790 | | | | | | |
| 28. | .136 | .454 | 99.244 | | | | | | |
| 29. | .125 | .417 | 99.661 | | | | | | |
| 30. | .102 | .339 | 100.000 | | | | | | |

Extraction Method: Principal Component Analysis.

Table 4.27: Rotated Component Matrix (a)

| | Component | | | | | | | | |
|---|---|---|---|---|---|---|---|---|---|
| | 1 | 2 | 3 | 4 | 5 | 6 | 7 | 8 | 9 |
| 1. | .228 | -.104 | 3.500E-02 | -.111 | -.127 | .620 | .254 | .389 | -2.720E-02 |
| 2. | .317 | .282 | .493 | -1.929E-02 | .286 | -8.845E-02 | .147 | .200 | .338 |
| 3. | .121 | .819 | 7.323E-02 | -.170 | .104 | 4.737E-02 | .124 | .101 | -6.850E-02 |
| 4. | .176 | .197 | 3.289E-02 | .544 | -.187 | .129 | 8.323E-02 | .123 | .351 |
| 5. | .124 | .785 | 3.977E-02 | 7.065E-02 | 5.952E-02 | .148 | 7.406E-02 | -8.715E-02 | .107 |
| 6. | 5.253E-02 | .126 | -1.721E-02 | .274 | -1.619E-02 | .781 | 9.141E-02 | -3.482E-02 | -.108 |
| 7. | 7.213E-02 | 7.300E-02 | .765 | 8.418E-02 | 6.597E-02 | .196 | -3.396E-02 | 1.743E-02 | .151 |
| 8. | .172 | 6.860E-02 | .728 | .302 | 6.328E-02 | -.161 | .289 | .112 | -2.622E-02 |
| 9. | 6.629E-02 | .215 | 3.715E-02 | -.132 | 9.362E-04 | 2.537E-02 | .748 | .136 | -8.110E-02 |
| 10. | .534 | .330 | 2.685E-02 | 6.731E-02 | -2.278E-02 | 9.959E-02 | .558 | .120 | 6.024E-02 |
| 11. | 7.724E-02 | 6.745E-02 | .352 | .440 | .174 | .194 | .612 | .114 | .135 |
| 12. | .786 | 9.085E-02 | .110 | .327 | 9.865E-02 | 2.620E-02 | 9.716E-02 | 7.746E-03 | -.117 |
| 13. | .125 | .541 | .130 | .510 | 7.895E-02 | 3.075E-02 | .223 | .355 | -.114 |

*(Contd...)*

| | Component | | | | | | | | |
|---|---|---|---|---|---|---|---|---|---|
| | 1 | 2 | 3 | 4 | 5 | 6 | 7 | 8 | 9 |
| 14. | .651 | .204 | .294 | -6.673E-02 | -3.100E-02 | 4.254E-02 | -.283 | .127 | -.257 |
| 15. | .225 | .567 | .394 | .283 | .114 | -.209 | 2.013E-02 | 5.711E-02 | -1.555E-02 |
| 16. | 6.857E-02 | -7.076E-03 | .190 | .716 | -3.153E-02 | 8.028E-03 | -.229 | 7.891E-02 | -7.570E-04 |
| 17. | .384 | .176 | .432 | 9.519E-02 | 8.587E-02 | 2.988E-02 | -.480 | .168 | 9.752E-02 |
| 18. | .302 | 8.254E-02 | .274 | -.136 | .480 | .186 | -8.633E-03 | .462 | -.289 |
| 19. | .299 | .315 | .162 | -1.984E-02 | .283 | .224 | .105 | .221 | -.485 |
| 20. | .104 | .524 | .111 | .240 | .252 | .510 | 5.696E-02 | 8.008E-03 | -.167 |
| 21. | -5.405E-02 | -.187 | .139 | .580 | .463 | .276 | .158 | 1.435E-02 | -.189 |
| 22. | .111 | 7.621E-02 | .213 | -.125 | .733 | 7.247E-02 | -2.132E-02 | .111 | -4.308E-02 |
| 23. | .665 | 3.100E-02 | .297 | -.128 | .266 | .128 | .126 | .221 | 6.172E-02 |
| 24. | -6.091E-02 | 9.662E-02 | .124 | -9.180E-02 | .127 | .740 | -.164 | -5.540E-02 | .409 |
| 25. | 7.770E-03 | -2.150E-02 | .264 | 1.746E-02 | 7.146E-02 | 8.252E-02 | -2.849E-02 | .152 | .784 |
| 26. | 5.667E-02 | 1.712E-02 | .134 | .210 | .127 | 2.143E-03 | 8.771E-02 | .837 | .120 |
| 27. | .667 | .211 | 2.548E-03 | 9.744E-02 | .371 | -6.473E-03 | .129 | -.166 | .192 |
| 28. | -4.370E-02 | .266 | -5.681E-02 | .381 | .294 | 2.786E-02 | .262 | .478 | .338 |
| 29. | .326 | .120 | .486 | 9.047E-02 | .369 | .156 | -.134 | 5.422E-02 | 2.689E-02 |
| 30. | .218 | .209 | -1.905E-02 | .171 | .745 | -.123 | 3.434E-02 | 7.500E-02 | .142 |

Table 4.28: Factor Analysis Results

| Factor 1 | Factor 2 | Factor 3 |
|---|---|---|
| * Specialised staff<br>* Willing to help<br>* Bank's image<br>* Facility for loans<br>* Ethical conduct | * Appearance of the bank<br>* Smart front-office staff<br>* Merchant banking facilities<br>* Availability of parking space<br>* Availability of Newspaper | * Prompt service<br>* Facility for payment of bills<br>* Customised services<br>* Individual attention<br>* Competitive pricing |
| **Factor 4** | **Factor 5** | **Factor 6** |
| * Company salary A/C<br>* Distance from home/office<br>* One-stop-vendor | * Credit/Debit card facility<br>* Computerisation<br>* Communication with customers | * No. of ATMs<br>* Gifts offered to customers<br>* Minimum deposit amount |
| **Factor 7** | **Factor 8** | **Factor 9** |
| * No. of branches<br>* Online computer services | * Locker facilities<br>* Forex Transactions | * Banks' power and influence<br>* Off-hour services |

**Table 4.29: Comparison of Means of Factors by Bank Type**

| Factors | Mean Score | | | |
|---|---|---|---|---|
| | Public | Private | Gap | t-value |
| Factor-1 | 6.20 | 6.08 | 0.12 | 1.324 |
| Factor-2 | 5.54 | 5.36 | 0.18 | 1.402 |
| Factor-3 | 6.13 | 6.08 | 0.05 | 0.510 |
| Factor-4 | 5.51 | 5.57 | - 0.06 | - 0.505 |
| Factor-5 | 6.14 | 6.05 | 0.09 | 0.864 |
| Factor-6 | 5.75 | 5.91 | - 0.16 | - 1.358 |
| Factor-7 | 5.89 | 5.88 | 0.01 | 0.054 |
| Factor-8 | 5.80 | 5.64 | 0.16 | 1.101 |
| Factor-9 | 5.64 | 5.91 | - 0.27 | - 2.604* |
| Respondents | 242 | 95 | | |

Table 4.27 depicts the Rotated component matrix indicating the factor loadings of nine different factors. In the table, the factors having highest loadings ignoring the signs is grouped under that component. Thus, the thirty factors are clubbed in nine components as given in Table 4.28 along with the number of that component. Further, the factors so extracted are taken as the base for comparing the public and private sector banks. The mean scores of these factors in bank variations are presented in Table 4.28. The naming of a component is done considering the common properties/ similar meanings of the factors clubbed into that particular group. Factors with higher loading are considered more important for interpretation purpose.

Table 4.29 discusses the gap between the public and private banks regarding the weightage the respondents attach to various parameters for selecting a bank. Factor-9 comprising of parameters like power of the bank to influence and off-hour transaction facilities has the highest gap, which is also statistically significant at 1 per cent level of significance. For rest of the factors, t-values are not significant indicating differences among the means are not significant implying both the types of banks as similar in the eyes of the respondents.

**SUMMARY**

After opening up the financial sector to the global players, Indian banking sector faces enormous challenges of attracting and retaining customers. For the present study, data were collected from 337 respondents, out of which 242 from public sector banks and rest 95 from private banks. The study revealed that the public banks are ahead of the private banks in attracting and retaining customers because of good personal relationship with the customers. Reasons for opening accounts with a bank by the customers are factors like convenient location, overall reputation, etc. It is evident from the study that 67.48 per cent of the young respondents transacts with public sector banks, while 32.5 per cent with private banks. Further, it is observed that less educated customers (93.94%) have a choice for public banks compared to post-graduates more inclined to private banks. Private Banks are offering more value-added services for special group of customers (class-banking approaches). Customers mainly maintain three types of accounts – savings banks, current and fixed deposit accounts. Savings bank accounts are the most preferred one and next to it customers go for different types of fixed-deposits. Most of the customers have more than one bank accounts. 36.5 per cent of the respondents have second account with a public sector bank and rest 22.85 per cent with private banks, while 11.28 per cent of respondents have second bank account in both private and public sector banks.

The demographic profile of the respondents indicates that all the respondents above 60 years and retired persons have their accounts with public banks. People with higher age group, retired, businessmen and higher income group people want to operate with a bank because of overall reputation of the bank. The number of visits by the customer to the bank has substantially gone down due to availability of ATMs. The overall scenario for banking behaviour of customers is almost similar for public and private banks.

Developing a product for the customers without knowing what customer expects is futile. As regards to the expectations and perceptions of the customers regarding service quality with respect to four different types of services, it is observed that customers of the public sector bank experiences more satisfaction compared to the private bank customers in the given sample. Further, it is evident from the data, private banks are better off than the public sector banks regarding premises and administrations. The major factors of dissatisfaction for public banks are enquiry counter; while parking space for private banks. However, both the banks are not lagging far behind to match the customer's expectations.

The availability of the staffs in counter is quite important to deliver different types pf services. It is observed that 75.79 per cent of the respondents are of the view that staffs are available in their seats for private banks, which is 81.82 per cent for public banks. Again in bank variations, private banks are little ahead of public banks in terms of feelings of staff towards the customers. Both the types of banks suffer from staff attitude to provide service to the customers. Similarly, slightly more number of complaints was lodged against private banks compared to public banks. Again, private banks are termed as progressive (45.26%), while public sector banks as systematic and methodical. Similarly, customers in the higher age group (40-60 years) and the service holders have expressed their dissatisfactions with the banks.

The customers of private bank (37.89%) are expecting more new services then their counterparts in private banks. When the customers feel happy with the bank they act as advertisers. The levels of satisfaction of customers of private banks are slightly better than the public banks. Respondents with lower income recommend the bank more than their counterparts with higher income. Customers have given many suggestions for improvement in quality of services, the most important one as suggested by the respondents for the public sector banks is customer care and services (35.06%). Thirty different factors are chosen for understanding the reasons for selecting a bank by the sample customers. The customers of both the bank groups have given more weightage to different factors for choosing a bank. Highest gap in the mean scores between private and public banks is observed in the factors customised and unique services of the bank, which are also statistically significant.

## REFERENCES

Anthanassoponlous, Antresa. D. (1997); "Service Quality and Operating Efficiency Synergies for Management Control in the Provision of Financial Services: Evidence from Greek Bank Branches", *European Journal of Operational Research*, 98, pp. 300-313.

Dhanajayan, G. (2005); "Service Marketing: Integrating People, Technology and Strategy", *Marketing Mastermind*, February, pp. 17-23.

Gavini, A. L. and Athma P. (1997); "Customer Service in Commercial Banks — Expectation and Reality", *Indian Journal of Marketing*, Vol. XXVII, No. 5, 6, 7, (May, June, July).

Gronros, C. (1984a); "A Service Quality Model and its Marketing Implications", European *Journal of Marketing*, Volume 18, November 4, pp. 36-44.

Kaptan, Sanjay and Nilkanth V. Sagane (1995); "Customer Service in Bank: Some Points to Ponder", *Business Analyst*, Volume 15, Number 1.

Lewis, B. and Smith, A.M. (1984); "Customer Care in Financial Service Organisations", *International Journal of Bank Marketing*, Volume 7, Number 5, pp. 13-22.

Lewis, B. and Smith, A.M. (1984); "Customer Care in Financial Service Organisations", *International Journal of Bank Marketing*, Volume 7, Number 5, pp. 13-22.

Olsen, M. (1992); "Quality in Banking Services", Department of Business Studies, Stockholm University.

Parasuraman, A., Zeithaml. V.A. and Berru, L.L. (1985); "A Conceptual Model of Service Quality and its Implications for Future Research", *Journal of Marketing*, Volume 49, Fall, pp. 41-50.

Parasuraman, A., Zeithaml, V.A. and Berry, L.L. (1985); "Service Quality in Financial Institutions", *Journal of Marketing*, Volume 39, pp. 31-45.

Paul, E. Plesk, "Defining Quality at the Marketing/Development Interface", *Quality Progress*, June 1987.

Rao, Nageshwar (1987); "Customer Service in Banks Must Improve, *Yojna*, Volume 31, Number 31, July 16-31, p. 2022.

Singh, Balraj, et. al. (1979); "Perceived Advantage of Taking Loan from Bank and Suggestions for Improvements", *The Banker*, Volume XXVI, Number 10, December. pp. 24-27.

Venkatesan, V. (2004); "Banks that Care", *Outlook Money*, 15 September, pp. 24-28.

Zeithaml, V.A. and Bitner, Mary Jo (2003); "Services Marketing: Integrating Customer Focus Across the Firm"; Tata McGraw-Hill (3 ed.), New Delhi, pp. 59-114.

# CHAPTER–5

# SURVEY OF BANKERS

## INTRODUCTION

Survival of the fittest is the order of the day. Customer service has become quite important in the present day situation as competition is increasing among the banks. Every one is trying to woe the same customer. Retaining the existing customers and attracting new ones has become very difficult; more so for the public sector banks (Bhatt, 1990). Public sector banks have their own limitations as they have to achieve twin objectives of profitability and social objectives. Again, the large number of branches; more so in non-banking areas, may fulfil the social objectives. But they may not be a viable proposition for running business. Similarly, the new generation private sector banks with limited branches and heavy focus on urban markets may face a limited area to operate.

Bankers are an integral part of the banking system. They are the bridge between the organisation and the customers. They came in contact with the customer regularly and are in a better position to understand the expectations of the customers. As a service provider, their roles are quite important in changing the perception of customers. As indicated in different studies, the perception of quality of services and customer satisfaction depends on the banker (Adrian, 1995; Bateson, 1995 and Parasuraman et al, 1991). Service quality is meeting customers' needs matching to their expectations (Howcroft, 1991). The bankers are also responsible for lowering the cost of services and improving productivity (Garvin, 1983; Kotler, 1999). Customer service has been described as 'the ultimate' tool to counter competition (Davidow and Uttal, 1989). Poor quality places the bank in a disadvantages position and customers may shift to competing banks.

At this backdrop, the study of bankers and their views about the customers are quite important for formulating sound policies for the future. An analysis of services provided by the banks and the customers' point of view might sound interesting at this juncture. Such analysis will provide the banks with a quantitative and qualitative estimate of their services as perceived by the bankers. Again from interactive marketing point of view, the banks should motivate their staffs to provide better deal to the customers as interactive marketing calls for involvement of all employees to satisfy the customers.

Keeping these broad issues in mind, the present chapter analyses the views and perception of bankers on understanding the customers, the reasons for their satisfaction/dissatisfaction at business potentiality vis-à-vis competitors in forging a marketing strategy to combat competitor and to be the winner. The bankers through their daily interactions are in a better position to understand the customer. The views expressed by the bankers are qualitative in nature hence tend to be subjective.

## DESIGN OF STUDY

The study is based on primary data collected through a structured questionnaire from executives/officers and staff of both public and private sector banks operating in Orissa. The questionnaire was designed after making a pilot survey soliciting the views of the bankers regarding these issues. The questionnaires were sent through professional investigators to collect the data from pre-determined samples covering both public and private sector banks operating in rural and urban areas in different sizes. Then, follow-up interviews were made either telephonically or personally to solicit further views in this matter. Ultimate, data from 157 bankers were collected, which were analysed in the subsequent sections. The data are processed through SPSS (statistical package for social sciences) and analysis was made by drawing cross-tables, calculating percentage, and by applying factor analysis whereever reduction of factors are required. '$\chi^2$' and 't' test, are applied to test the significance of the results wherever it is considered to be necessary.

## DATA ANALYSIS

### Profile of Bankers

The data collected from the respondents were classified mainly by three parameters; namely type of bank, size of bank, and the location of the bank. Table 5.1 describes the profile of the sample 157 bankers. The size of the banks is defined on the volume of business of the concerned branch of the bank. However, the respondents in most of the cases mentioned about the size of the branch. For simplicity the size of the bank is defined as: a branch having business up to Rs. 25 crore is small, between Rs. 25-75 crore is medium, and above Rs. 75 crore is large.

**Table 5.1: Profile of Bankers**

| Parameters | Variables | Frequency | % to Total |
|---|---|---|---|
| Type of Bank | Public | 118 | 75.16 |
| | Private | 39 | 24.84 |
| Size of Bank | Large | 48 | 30.57 |
| | Medium | 90 | 57.32 |
| | Small | 19 | 12.11 |
| Location of Bank | Rural | 33 | 21.02 |
| | Urban | 124 | 78.98 |
| | **Total** | **157** | **100.00** |

Out of the total sample, 75.16 per cent of the bankers belong to public sector banks and rest 24.84 per cent are from private sector banks including one foreign bank. The higher percentage of public sector banker is quite evident from the larger number of public sector banks correspond to private banks operating in Orissa. Similarly size-wise; middle-sized branches (57.32%) dominate the sample. Again more number of urban branches explains the inherent limitations of data collection. More number of branches concentrates in urban areas and accessing them is easier compared to widely dispersed rural branches. All the private banks are operating only in seven cities of the state.

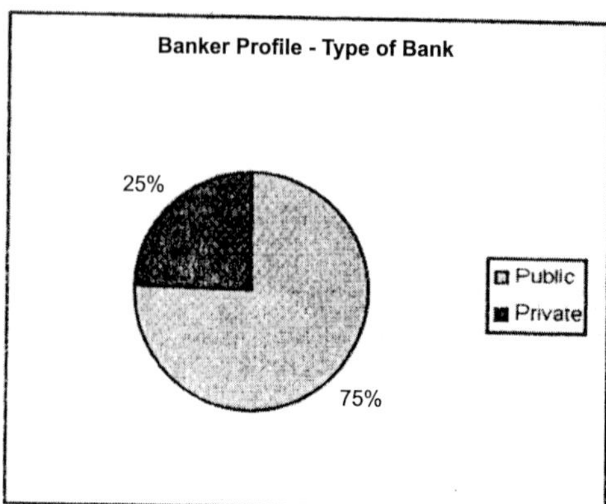


Fig. 5.1

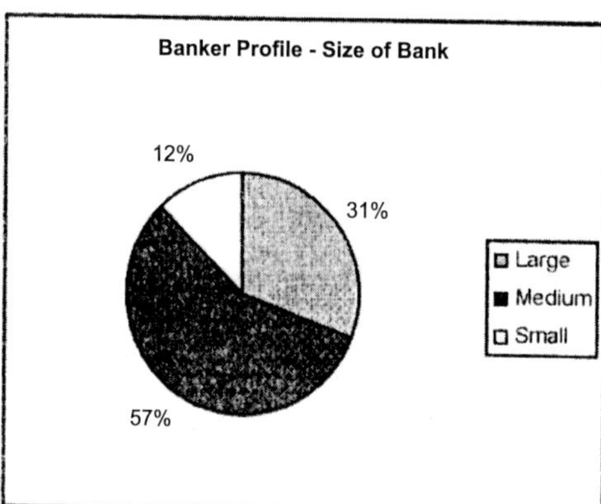


Fig. 5.2

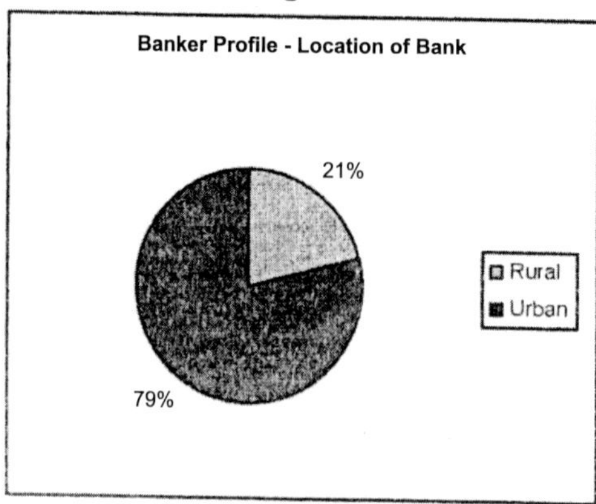


Fig. 5.3

## Perception of Branch Location

Suitable location of the branch helps in bringing more business. Location of the branch is within the discretion of the management and proper location should be chosen while opening a branch of a bank. The market place is the most suitable location, while a remote concern may be considered as unsuitable from business point of view.

**Table 5.2: Perception of Branch Location**

| Parameters | | Unsuitable | Satisfactory | Good | Very Good | Excellent | Total | Chi-Square |
|---|---|---|---|---|---|---|---|---|
| Type of Bank | Public | 3 | 3 | 30 | 40 | 42 | 118 | 5.79 |
| | | (2.54) | (2.54) | (25.42) | (33.90) | (35.59) | (100.00) | |
| | Private | 0 | 0 | 6 | 12 | 21 | 39 | |
| | | (0.00) | (0.00) | (15.38) | (30.77) | (53.85) | (100.00) | |
| Size of Bank | Large | 0 | 0 | 10 | 9 | 29 | 48 | 42.33* |
| | | (0.00) | (0.00) | (20.83) | (18.75) | (60.42) | (100.00) | |
| | Medium | 0 | 3 | 24 | 39 | 24 | 90 | |
| | | (0.00) | (3.33) | (26.67) | (43.33) | (26.67) | (100.00) | |
| | Small | 3 | 0 | 2 | 4 | 10 | 19 | |
| | | (15.79) | (0.00) | (10.53) | (21.05) | (52.63) | (100.00) | |

*(Contd...)*

| Parameters | | Unsuitable | Satisfactory | Good | Very Good | Excellent | Total | Chi -Square |
|---|---|---|---|---|---|---|---|---|
| Location of Branch | Rural | 3 | 0 | 5 | 19 | 6 | 33 | 25.73** |
| | | (9.09) | (0.00) | (15.15) | (57.58) | (18.18) | (100.00) | |
| | Urban | 0 | 3 | 31 | 33 | 57 | 124 | |
| | | (0.00) | (2.42) | (25.00) | (26.61) | (45.97) | (100.00) | |
| | Total | 3 | 3 | 36 | 52 | 63 | 157 | |
| | | (1.91) | (1.91) | (22.93) | (33.12) | (40.13) | (100.00) | |

* Significant at 1% ** Significant at 5% Figure in parentheses refer percentages

Table 5.2 describes the present location of the branch from business point of view as perceived by the bankers. Five different ratings were used to study different banking parameters like type, size and location of the branch to perceive its locational advantage.

The table indicates that very small percentage of public sector banks face locational disadvantage, while all of the locations of the private banks are suitable from business point of view and 53.85 per cent are reported to be excellent. When the same is compared with public sector banks, 35.59 per cent have excellent location. The $\chi^2$ values are not significant, indicating no significant difference in perception of branch location. When the views of the bankers are compared in respect of their size variations, $\chi^2$ values is significant at 1 per cent level, indicating significant in perception of branch locations by the bankers. This indicates advantage of location for larger branches. Similarly, when perceptions of bankers are studied in locational variations, $\chi^2$ values are also significant. This indicates significant difference lies in terms of perception of branch location in urban and rural areas. This implies smaller branches in rural areas face the unsuitability of branch locations from business point of view.

### The Premises

Good premises for bank branches are essential for smooth operation of banking business. A congenial environment inside the bank improves efficiency and willingness of employees to provide better customer service; so also the customer will derive more pleasure and satisfaction from the services delivered by the bankers. Tables 5.3 (A), 5.3 (B), and 5.3 (C) discuss the availability of physical facilities (described in seven variables) in five different ratings across three banking profiles.

The physical facilities available inside the bank premises are presented in Table 5.3 (A). Most of the bankers are of the opinion that the branches under study have adequate floor space. About 71 per cent of public sector banks and 76 per cent of private banks have adequate floor space, while less than 8 per cent of the banks have inadequate floor space. The respondents of public banks have opined that 12.71 per cent banks have inadequate number of staffs, which is not there in private banks. Similarly, more than 30 per cent of public sector banks and about 15 per cent in private banks have just sufficient staff. Further, the numbers of computers available in the banks are mostly adequate and in bank variations the difference is not significant. Similarly, half of the public sector banks have reported to be either inadequate or just sufficient counters or ATMs, which is about 40 per cent in private banks. Considering different amenities available inside the bank, private banks reported to be much ahead of public banks. Similar trend is observed in air cooling factors, where more than 92 per cent reported to be comfortable in private banks, which is 62 per cent for public sector banks.

The analysis of differences among variables (Table 5.3 (A)) relating to physical facilities available between private and public sector banks indicate that factors like number of employees (factor-b), number of counters/ATMs (factor-d), bank amenities (factor-f), and air cooling (factor-g) are statistically significant at 1 per cent level of significance, while for rest of the variables $\chi^2$ values are not significant. This indicates existence of substantial difference between the two types of banks in terms of physical facilities available in their premises. Further probing indicates that the public sector banks have to improve a lot to match with private banks in this regard.

The size-wise analysis also indicates that a big gap (statistically significant) exists among the large, medium and small sized branches for variables like '*floor* space', 'number of ATMs/ counters', and 'air cooling'. This particular behaviour is quite obvious as the larger sized branches can afford to have more physical facilities than the smaller ones. As regards to the location of branches, urban and rural branches enjoy distinct advantages of physical facilities like 'number of employees' and 'number of computers' (significant at 1% level) and 'waiting space' at 5 per cent level of significance. Thus, it can be inferred that smaller rural branches are in a disadvantageous position compared to their urban counter parts, more particularly the private banks in urban areas.

Table 5.3 (A): Physical Facilities by Type of Bank

| Parameters | | a | b | c | d | e | f | g |
|---|---|---|---|---|---|---|---|---|
| Public | More than Adequate | 18 | 6 | 9 | 9 | 15 | 12 | 0 |
| | | (15.25) | (5.08) | (7.63) | (8.74) | (12.71) | (10.17) | (0.00) |
| | Adequate | 66 | 40 | 55 | 27 | 24 | 43 | 39 |
| | | (55.93) | (33.90) | (46.61) | (26.21) | (20.34) | (36.44) | (33.05) |
| | Comfortable | 16 | 21 | 27 | 19 | 36 | 30 | 33 |
| | | (13.56) | (17.80) | (22.88) | (18.45) | (30.51) | (25.42) | (27.97) |
| | Just Sufficient | 9 | 36 | 21 | 24 | 30 | 15 | 24 |
| | | (7.63) | (30.51) | (17.80) | (23.30) | (25.42) | (12.71) | (20.34) |
| | Inadequate | 9 | 15 | 6 | 24 | 13 | 18 | 22 |
| | | (7.63) | (12.71) | (5.08) | (23.30) | (11.02) | (15.25) | (18.64) |
| | **Total** | 118 | 118 | 118 | 103 | 118 | 118 | 118 |
| | | 100.00) | (100.00) | (100.00) | (100.00) | (100.00) | (100.00) | (100.00) |

*(Contd...)*

| Parameters | | a | b | c | d | e | f | g |
|---|---|---|---|---|---|---|---|---|
| Private | More than Adequate | 6 | 3 | 6 | 0 | 6 | 12 | 12 |
| | | (15.38) | (7.69) | (15.38) | (0.00) | (15.38) | (30.77) | (30.77) |
| | Adequate | 24 | 27 | 21 | 21 | 9 | 18 | 12 |
| | | (61.54) | (69.23) | (53.85) | (53.85) | (23.08) | (46.15) | (30.77) |
| | Comfortable | 3 | 3 | 6 | 3 | 15 | 6 | 12 |
| | | (7.69) | (7.69) | (15.38) | (7.69) | (38.46) | (15.38) | (30.77) |
| | Just Sufficient | 3 | 6 | 3 | 6 | 3 | 3 | 3 |
| | | (7.69) | (15.38) | (7.69) | (15.38) | (7.69) | (7.69) | (7.69) |
| | Inadequate | 3 | 0 | 3 | 9 | 6 | 0 | 0 |
| | | (7.69) | (0.00) | (7.69) | (23.08) | (15.38) | (0.00) | (0.00) |
| | **Total** | 39 | 39 | 39 | 39 | 39 | 39 | 39 |
| | | (100.00) | (100.00) | (100.00) | (100.00) | (100.00) | (100.00) | (100.00) |
| **Grand Total** | | 157 | 157 | 157 | 142 | 157 | 157 | 157 |
| Chi-Square | | 0.99 | 18.34* | 5.25 | 19.08* | 5.68 | 16.73* | 46.43* |

a- Floor Space  b- No. of Employees  c- No. of Computers  d- No. of Counters/ATMs
e- Waiting Space  f- Bank Amenities  g- Air Cooling/Conditioning

*Figure in parentheses refer percentages*

Table 5.3 (B): Physical Facilities by Size of Bank

| Parameters | | a | b | c | d | e | f | g |
|---|---|---|---|---|---|---|---|---|
| Large | More than Adequate | 13 | 5 | 5 | 8 | 7 | 2 | 0 |
| | | 27.08 | 10.42 | 10.42 | 16.67 | 14.58 | 4.17 | 0.00 |
| | Adequate | 30 | 22 | 26 | 10 | 15 | 18 | 17 |
| | | 62.50 | 45.83 | 54.17 | 20.83 | 31.25 | 37.50 | 35.42 |
| | Comfortable | 0 | 10 | 11 | 15 | 8 | 14 | 11 |
| | | 0.00 | 20.83 | 22.92 | 31.25 | 16.67 | 29.17 | 22.92 |
| | Just Sufficient | 0 | 8 | 6 | 4 | 12 | 9 | 14 |
| | | 0.00 | 16.67 | 12.50 | 8.33 | 25.00 | 18.75 | 29.17 |
| | Inadequate | 5 | 3 | 0 | 11 | 6 | 5 | 6 |
| | | 10.42 | 6.25 | 0.00 | 22.92 | 12.50 | 10.42 | 12.50 |
| | **Total** | 48 | 48 | 48 | 48 | 48 | 48 | 48 |
| | | 100.00 | 100.00 | 100.00 | 100.00 | 100.00 | 100.00 | 100.00 |

*(Contd...)*

| Parameters | | a | b | c | d | e | f | g |
|---|---|---|---|---|---|---|---|---|
| Medium | More than Adequate | 9 | 3 | 6 | 0 | 12 | 18 | 9 |
| | | 10.00 | 3.33 | 6.67 | 0.00 | 13.33 | 20.00 | 10.00 |
| | Adequate | 48 | 36 | 42 | 33 | 15 | 36 | 27 |
| | | 53.33 | 40.00 | 46.67 | 42.31 | 16.67 | 40.00 | 30.00 |
| | Comfortable | 18 | 9 | 21 | 3 | 33 | 21 | 33 |
| | | 20.00 | 10.00 | 23.33 | 3.85 | 36.67 | 23.33 | 36.67 |
| | Just Sufficient | 12 | 30 | 15 | 21 | 18 | 6 | 12 |
| | | 13.33 | 33.33 | 16.67 | 26.92 | 20.00 | 6.67 | 13.33 |
| | Inadequate | 3 | 12 | 6 | 21 | 12 | 9 | 9 |
| | | 3.33 | 13.33 | 6.67 | 26.92 | 13.33 | 10.00 | 10.00 |
| | **Total** | 90 | 90 | 90 | 78 | 90 | 90 | 90 |
| | | 100.00 | 100.00 | 100.00 | 100.00 | 100.00 | 100.00 | 100.00 |

*(Contd...)*

| Parameters | | a | b | c | d | e | f | g |
|---|---|---|---|---|---|---|---|---|
| Small | More than Adequate | 2 | 1 | 4 | 1 | 2 | 4 | 3 |
| | | 10.53 | 5.26 | 21.05 | 6.25 | 10.53 | 21.05 | 15.79 |
| | Adequate | 12 | 9 | 8 | 5 | 3 | 7 | 7 |
| | | 63.16 | 47.37 | 42.11 | 31.25 | 15.79 | 36.84 | 36.84 |
| | Comfortable | 1 | 5 | 1 | 4 | 10 | 1 | 1 |
| | | 5.26 | 26.32 | 5.26 | 25.00 | 52.63 | 5.26 | 5.26 |
| | Just Sufficient | 0 | 4 | 3 | 5 | 3 | 3 | 1 |
| | | 0.00 | 21.05 | 15.79 | 31.25 | 15.79 | 15.79 | 5.26 |
| | Inadequate | 4 | 0 | 3 | 1 | 1 | 4 | 7 |
| | | 21.05 | 0.00 | 15.79 | 6.25 | 5.26 | 21.05 | 36.84 |
| | **Total** | 19 | 19 | 19 | 16 | 19 | 19 | 19 |
| | | 100.00 | 100.00 | 100.00 | 100.00 | 100.00 | 100.00 | 100.00 |
| **Grand Total** | | 157 | 157 | 157 | 142 | 157 | 157 | 157 |
| Chi-Square | | 34.14* | 14.56 | 13.15 | 49.58* | 11.68 | 15.16 | 27.11* |

a- Floor Space  b- No. of Employees  c- No. of Computers  d- No. of Counters/ATMs
e- Waiting Space  f- Bank Amenities  g- Air Cooling/Conditioning

*Figure in percentages to total.*

Table 5.3 (C): Physical Facilities by Location of Bank

| Parameters | | a | b | c | d | e | f | g |
|---|---|---|---|---|---|---|---|---|
| Rural | More than Adequate | 4 | 0 | 3 | 0 | 0 | 6 | 0 |
| | | (12.12) | (0.00) | (9.09) | 0.00 | 0.00 | 18.18 | 0.00 |
| | Adequate | 16 | 1 | 8 | 13 | 4 | 8 | 4 |
| | | 48.48 | 3.03 | 24.24 | 48.15 | 12.12 | 24.24 | 12.12 |
| | Comfortable | 7 | 4 | 6 | 1 | 12 | 6 | 6 |
| | | 21.21 | 12.12 | 18.18 | 3.70 | 36.36 | 18.18 | 18.18 |
| | Just Sufficient | 3 | 22 | 10 | 6 | 12 | 6 | 7 |
| | | 9.09 | 66.67 | 30.30 | 22.22 | 36.36 | 18.18 | 21.21 |
| | Inadequate | 3 | 6 | 6 | 7 | 5 | 7 | 16 |
| | | 9.09 | 18.18 | 18.18 | 25.93 | 15.15 | 21.21 | 48.48 |
| | **Total** | 33 | 33 | 33 | 27 | 33 | 33 | 33 |
| | | 100.00 | 100.00 | 100.00 | 100.00 | 100.00 | 100.00 | 100.00 |

*(Contd...)*

| Parameters | | a | b | c | d | e | f | g |
|---|---|---|---|---|---|---|---|---|
| Urban | More than Adequate | 20 | 9 | 12 | 9 | 21 | 18 | 12 |
| | | 16.13 | 7.26 | 9.68 | 7.83 | 16.94 | 14.52 | 9.68 |
| | Adequate | 74 | 66 | 68 | 35 | 29 | 53 | 47 |
| | | 59.68 | 53.23 | 54.84 | 30.43 | 23.39 | 42.74 | 37.90 |
| | Comfortable | 12 | 20 | 27 | 21 | 39 | 30 | 39 |
| | | 9.68 | 16.13 | 21.77 | 18.26 | 31.45 | 24.19 | 31.45 |
| | Just Sufficient | 9 | 20 | 14 | 24 | 21 | 12 | 20 |
| | | 7.26 | 16.13 | 11.29 | 20.87 | 16.94 | 9.68 | 16.13 |
| | Inadequate | 9 | 9 | 3 | 26 | 14 | 11 | 6 |
| | | 7.26 | 7.26 | 2.42 | 22.61 | 11.29 | 8.87 | 4.84 |
| | **Total** | 124 | 124 | 124 | 115 | 124 | 124 | 124 |
| | | 100.00 | 100.00 | 100.00 | 100.00 | 100.00 | 100.00 | 100.00 |
| **Grand Total** | | 157 | 157 | 157 | 142 | 157 | 157 | 157 |
| Chi-Square | | 3.94 | 46.20* | 22.67* | 10.33 | 12.3.6** | 8.04 | 45.95 |

a- Floor Space b- No. of Employees c- No. of Computers d- No. of Counters/ATMs
e- Waiting Space f- Bank Amenities g- Air Cooling/Conditioning

*Figure in percentages to total*

## Banker's Attitude and Levels of Customer Service

Customer service focuses on satisfying the needs of customer at the right time and in a right manner. This involves the staffs—the service delivers, for delivering better satisfaction to the customers. All this indicates right kind of attitude of bank personnel in delivering the services. Similarly, customer quality is quite important, as the bank will focus on high value customers for better business and higher profitability. Tables 5.4 (A), 5.4 (B), and 5.4 (C) discuss the views of the bankers relating to five different factors indicating the service levels in three banking profile variations.

Table 5.4 (A) describes the service factors in types of bank variation. The Table reveals that the variations among the private and public sector banks are statistically significant in all the parameters except customer retention. This implies that the private banks have a cutting edge over their counter parts in terms of standards of services rendered, attitude of staff and types of customers. About 20 per cent of the public sector banks in all the five parameters are either poor or satisfactory as rated by themselves, while none of the private banks rated them in these categories except a small percentage of customer retention. Most of the private banks rated themselves as excellent in those parameters. (a = 53.85 5, b = 61.54%, c = 46.15%, d = 46.15%, and e = 30.77%), as compared to a very low score for public sector banks.

Tables 5.4 (B) and 5.4 (C) indicate that the variation among sizes and locations in all variables are statistically significant. The attitude of bankers in providing customer services differs in a big way among the three sizes and two locations. Further probing indicates that the attitude of service personnel of middle size bank is better than large and small size categories. Similarly, urban branches are able to provide better services and better employee's attitude compared to the rural branches. This behaviour may be due to existence of large gap in terms of employee satisfaction with their jobs (both qualitatively and quantitatively).

Table 5.4 (A): Attitude of Bankers by Type of Bank

| Parameters | | a | | b | | c | | d | | e | |
|---|---|---|---|---|---|---|---|---|---|---|---|
| | | f | % | f | % | f | % | f | % | f | % |
| Public | Poor | 0 | 0.00 | 6 | 5.08 | 9 | 7.63 | 12 | 10.17 | 13 | 11.02 |
| | Satisfactory | 19 | 16.10 | 13 | 11.02 | 19 | 16.10 | 12 | 10.17 | 15 | 12.71 |
| | Good | 30 | 25.42 | 30 | 25.42 | 36 | 30.51 | 40 | 33.90 | 27 | 22.88 |
| | Very Good | 33 | 27.97 | 36 | 30.51 | 27 | 22.88 | 27 | 22.88 | 36 | 30.51 |
| | Excellent | 36 | 30.51 | 33 | 27.97 | 27 | 22.88 | 27 | 22.88 | 27 | 22.88 |
| | Total | 118 | 100.00 | 118 | 100.00 | 118 | 100.00 | 118 | 100.00 | 118 | 100.00 |
| Private | Poor | 0 | 0.00 | 0 | 0.00 | 0 | 0.00 | 0 | 0.00 | 0 | 0.00 |
| | Satisfactory | 0 | 0.00 | 0 | 0.00 | 0 | 0.00 | 3 | 7.69 | 6 | 15.38 |
| | Good | 3 | 7.69 | 6 | 15.38 | 15 | 38.46 | 9 | 23.08 | 10 | 25.64 |
| | Very Good | 15 | 38.46 | 9 | 23.08 | 6 | 15.38 | 9 | 23.08 | 11 | 28.21 |
| | Excellent | 21 | 53.85 | 24 | 61.54 | 18 | 46.15 | 18 | 46.15 | 12 | 30.77 |
| | Total | 39 | 100.00 | 39 | 100.00 | 39 | 100.00 | 39 | 100.00 | 39 | 100.00 |
| Chi-Square | | | 16.12* | | 17.23* | | 16.15* | | 10.79** | | 5.33 |

a- Services Rendered b- Attitude of Officers c- Attitude of Other Staffs d- Level of Customers
e- Customer Retention * 1% Level of Significance ** 5% Level of Significance

Table 5.4 (B): Attitudes of Bankers by Size of Bank

| Parameters | | a | | b | | c | | d | | e | |
|---|---|---|---|---|---|---|---|---|---|---|---|
| | | f | % | f | % | f | % | f | % | f | % |
| Large | Poor | 0 | 0.00 | 2 | 4.17 | 3 | 6.25 | 3 | 6.25 | 6 | 12.50 |
| | Satisfactory | 10 | 20.83 | 6 | 12.50 | 11 | 22.92 | 7 | 14.58 | 10 | 20.83 |
| | Good | 16 | 33.33 | 17 | 35.42 | 19 | 39.58 | 19 | 39.58 | 10 | 20.83 |
| | Very Good | 18 | 37.50 | 13 | 27.08 | 9 | 18.75 | 11 | 22.92 | 14 | 29.17 |
| | Excellent | 4 | 8.33 | 10 | 20.83 | 6 | 12.50 | 8 | 16.67 | 8 | 16.67 |
| | Total | 48 | 100.00 | 48 | 100.00 | 48 | 100.00 | 48 | 100.00 | 48 | 100.00 |
| Medium | Poor | 0 | 0.00 | 0 | 0.00 | 3 | 3.33 | 6 | 6.67 | 6 | 6.67 |
| | Satisfactory | 3 | 3.33 | 6 | 6.67 | 3 | 3.33 | 6 | 6.67 | 9 | 10.00 |
| | Good | 12 | 13.33 | 18 | 20.00 | 27 | 30.00 | 24 | 26.67 | 13 | 14.44 |
| | Very Good | 27 | 30.00 | 24 | 26.67 | 18 | 20.00 | 21 | 23.33 | 32 | 35.56 |
| | Excellent | 48 | 53.33 | 42 | 46.67 | 39 | 43.33 | 33 | 36.67 | 30 | 33.33 |
| | Total | 90 | 100.00 | 90 | 100.00 | 90 | 100.00 | 90 | 100.00 | 90 | 100.00 |

*(Contd...)*

| Parameters | | a | | b | | c | | d | | e | |
|---|---|---|---|---|---|---|---|---|---|---|---|
| | | f | % | f | % | f | % | f | % | f | % |
| Small | Poor | 0 | 0.00 | 4 | 21.05 | 3 | 15.79 | 3 | 15.79 | 1 | 5.26 |
| | Satisfactory | 6 | 31.58 | 1 | 5.26 | 5 | 26.32 | 2 | 10.53 | 2 | 10.53 |
| | Good | 5 | 26.32 | 1 | 5.26 | 5 | 26.32 | 6 | 31.58 | 14 | 73.68 |
| | Very Good | 3 | 15.79 | 8 | 42.11 | 6 | 31.58 | 4 | 21.05 | 1 | 5.26 |
| | Excellent | 5 | 26.32 | 5 | 26.32 | 0 | 0.00 | 4 | 21.05 | 1 | 5.26 |
| | Total | 19 | 100.00 | 19 | 100.00 | 19 | 100.00 | 19 | 100.00 | 19 | 100.00 |
| Chi-Square $\chi^2$ | | | 9.22** | | 25.02* | | 15.90* | | 28.01** | | 13.38* |

a - Services Rendered b- Attitude of Officers c- Attitude of Other Staffs d- Level of Customers

e - Customer Retention * 1% Level of Significance ** 5% Level of Significance

Table 5.4 (C): Attitudes of Bankers by Location of Bank

| Parameters | | a | | b | | c | | d | | e | |
|---|---|---|---|---|---|---|---|---|---|---|---|
| | | f | % | f | % | f | % | f | % | f | % |
| Rural | Poor | 0 | 0.00 | 3 | 9.09 | 3 | 9.09 | 9 | 27.27 | 7 | 21.21 |
| | Satisfactory | 4 | 12.12 | 7 | 21.21 | 4 | 12.12 | 4 | 12.12 | 3 | 9.09 |
| | Good | 13 | 39.39 | 6 | 18.18 | 14 | 42.42 | 11 | 33.33 | 11 | 33.33 |
| | Very Good | 6 | 18.18 | 11 | 33.33 | 6 | 18.18 | 3 | 9.09 | 6 | 18.18 |
| | Excellent | 10 | 30.30 | 6 | 18.18 | 6 | 18.18 | 6 | 18.18 | 6 | 18.18 |
| | Total | 33 | 100.00 | 33 | 100.00 | 33 | 100.00 | 33 | 100.00 | 33 | 100.00 |
| Urban | Poor | 0 | 0.00 | 3 | 2.42 | 6 | 4.84 | 3 | 2.42 | 6 | 4.84 |
| | Satisfactory | 15 | 12.10 | 6 | 4.84 | 15 | 12.10 | 11 | 8.87 | 18 | 14.52 |
| | Good | 20 | 16.13 | 30 | 24.19 | 37 | 29.84 | 38 | 30.65 | 26 | 20.97 |
| | Very Good | 42 | 33.87 | 34 | 27.42 | 27 | 21.77 | 33 | 26.61 | 41 | 33.06 |
| | Excellent | 47 | 37.90 | 51 | 41.13 | 39 | 31.45 | 39 | 31.45 | 33 | 26.61 |
| | Total | 124 | 100.00 | 124 | 100.00 | 124 | 100.00 | 124 | 100.00 | 124 | 100.00 |
| Chi-Square $\chi^2$ | | | 9.22** | | 25.02* | | 15.90* | | 28.01** | | 13.38* |

a- Services Rendered b- Attitude of Officers c- Attitude of Other Staffs d- Level of Customers

e- Customer Retention * 1% Level of Significance ** 5% Level of Significance

**Banker's Perception for Improvement in Service Quality**

Quality of service is one of the important dimensions of providing satisfaction to the customers and also retaining them in business. When the sample bankers are contacted they have attributed several strategies to improve the service quality, which are shown in Table 5.5.

**Table 5.5: Analysis of Perception of Bankers for Improvement in Service Quality**

**(Figures in Percentages)**

| Factors | Type of Bank | | Size of Bank | | | Location of Bank | |
|---|---|---|---|---|---|---|---|
| | Public | Private | Large | Medium | Small | Rural | Urban |
| Attitude to Service of Employees | 8.47 | 15.38 | 16.67 | 6.67 | 10.53 | 3.03 | 12.10 |
| Care and Concern fro the Customer | 16.10 | 15.38 | 35.42 | 6.67 | 10.53 | 0.00 | 20.16 |
| Attracting and Retaining Customers | 0.00 | 7.69 | 0.00 | 3.33 | 0.00 | 0.00 | 2.42 |
| Customise Product and Services | 3.39 | 15.38 | 6.25 | 7.78 | 0.00 | 0.00 | 8.06 |
| Physical Facilities | 32.20 | 15.38 | 31.25 | 24.44 | 36.84 | 21.21 | 29.84 |
| Relationship Banking | 7.63 | 23.08 | 16.67 | 10.00 | 5.26 | 3.03 | 13.71 |
| Prompt Attention to Customer Needs | 10.17 | 7.69 | 14.58 | 6.67 | 10.53 | 0.00 | 12.10 |
| Competitive/Flexible Prices | 7.63 | 0.00 | 4.17 | 6.67 | 5.26 | 9.09 | 4.84 |
| Information Technology | 21.19 | 15.38 | 18.75 | 20.00 | 21.05 | 18.18 | 20.16 |

*(Contd...)*

| Factors | Type of Bank | | Size of Bank | | | Location of Bank | |
|---|---|---|---|---|---|---|---|
| | Public | Private | Large | Medium | Small | Rural | Urban |
| Employee Development | 2.54 | 7.69 | 0.00 | 0.00 | 31.58 | 9.09 | 2.42 |
| Appointing More Service Personnel | 15.25 | 7.69 | 4.17 | 16.67 | 21.05 | 39.39 | 6.45 |
| Qualitative and Productive Customers | 0.00 | 7.69 | 0.00 | 3.33 | 0.00 | 0.00 | 2.42 |
| Branch Head/Controlling Office | 0.00 | 7.69 | 0.00 | 3.33 | 0.00 | 0.00 | 2.42 |
| Promotion of Products | 2.54 | 0.00 | 0.00 | 3.33 | 0.00 | 9.09 | 0.00 |
| Job Redistribution | 2.54 | 0.00 | 0.00 | 3.33 | 0.00 | 9.09 | 0.00 |
| Employee Behaviour | 5.08 | 0.00 | 6.25 | 3.33 | 0.00 | 9.09 | 2.42 |
| Understanding Customer Needs | 2.54 | 0.00 | 0.00 | 3.33 | 0.00 | 9.09 | 0.00 |
| Customer Choice | 2.54 | 0.00 | 4.17 | 0.00 | 5.26 | 0.00 | 2.42 |
| Changing Branch Location | 2.54 | 0.00 | 0.00 | 0.00 | 15.79 | 9.09 | 0.00 |
| Customer Counselling | 2.54 | 0.00 | 0.00 | 3.33 | 0.00 | 9.09 | 0.00 |
| Respondents (Number) | 118 | 39 | 48 | 90 | 19 | 33 | 124 |

Table 5.5 indicates that the strategies suggested by the bankers in order of their performances are physical facilities, use of information technology, concern for customers and appointing more service personnel (staff). Again, remarkable difference exists in the perception of bankers with regard to the size and location variations. For example, the perceptions of bankers regarding concern for customers indicate noticeable differences between large and medium branches (35.42% and 6.67%), and between rural and urban branches (0.00% and 20.16%). Similarly, the perceptions regarding appointing more staff indicate substantial difference between public (15.25) and private (7.69), large (4.17%) and small (21.05%), and rural (39.39%) and urban (6.45%). But the factor like physical facilities and use of information technology, consistently been rated as important by all the groups of bankers. Similarly, two other factors like prompt attention to customer needs and attitude of employees to serve receives varied response.

To sum up, in the changing environment the bankers are depending more on physical and technological factors on one hand and the functional (staff) factors on the other. This trend is in hand-to-hand with any service industry, as they represent the functional quality and human touch to make the service better satisfying. Hence, by giving attention to the above cited factors, the present level of service delivered can be improved.

## Service Quality and Improvement in Business

It has been well understood that the satisfied customers are the biggest advertisers. Quality of service has a positive influence on customer satisfaction. This in turn has an amplified effect. Hence, many studies have concluded that improvement in service quality will bring more business. The views of the sample bankers in this regard are given in Table 5.6.

Table 5.6: Analysis of Service Quality and Improvement in Business

(Figures in Percentages)

| Factors | Type of Bank | | Size of Bank | | | Location of Bank | |
|---|---|---|---|---|---|---|---|
| | Public | Private | Large | Medium | Small | Rural | Urban |
| Attracting and Retaining Customers | 33.05 | 23.08 | 29.17 | 36.67 | 5.26 | 36.36 | 29.03 |
| Satisfied Customers as Advisers | 12.71 | 7.69 | 22.92 | 6.67 | 5.26 | 12.12 | 11.29 |
| Product Addition and Innovation | 8.47 | 7.69 | 18.75 | 3.33 | 5.26 | 3.03 | 9.68 |
| Personalised Service | 2.54 | 7.69 | 0.00 | 3.33 | 15.79 | 9.09 | 2.42 |
| Creating Goodwill | 5.08 | 15.38 | 25.00 | 10.00 | 5.26 | 9.09 | 7.26 |
| Customer Satisfaction | 30.51 | 30.77 | 27.08 | 33.33 | 26.32 | 39.39 | 28.23 |
| Searching for New Segment | 5.08 | 0.00 | 10.42 | 0.00 | 5.26 | 0.00 | 4.84 |
| Cost Reduction | 2.54 | 0.00 | 4.17 | 0.00 | 5.26 | 0.00 | 2.42 |
| Business through Referral | 2.54 | 7.69 | 4.17 | 0.00 | 21.05 | 0.00 | 4.84 |
| Market Rapport | 0.00 | 7.69 | 0.00 | 0.00 | 15.79 | 0.00 | 2.42 |
| Physical Facilities | 10.17 | 0.00 | 6.25 | 6.67 | 15.79 | 18.18 | 4.84 |
| Information Technology | 7.63 | 0.00 | 4.17 | 6.67 | 5.26 | 9.09 | 4.84 |
| Appointing More Service Agents | 5.08 | 0.00 | 4.17 | 3.33 | 5.26 | 9.09 | 2.42 |
| Opening of Franchise | 5.08 | 0.00 | 12.50 | 0.00 | 0.00 | 0.00 | 4.84 |
| Developed Customer Relationship | 2.54 | 0.00 | 0.00 | 0.00 | 15.79 | 9.09 | 0.00 |
| Respondents (Number) | 118 | 39 | 48 | 90 | 19 | 33 | 124 |

Two important factors, i.e., customer satisfaction, attracting and retaining customers (as evident from the study) are the direct results of improvement of service quality. All the sample respondents are unanimous on these two factors and had given highest ratings. The next important factors are satisfied customers as the advertisers and creating goodwill, which in turns bring more business. The private banks (15.38%) emphasised creating goodwill more and the public banks (12.71%) on satisfied customers as advertisers. But no conclusion can be derived in respect of improvement in physical facilities bringing more business in bank variations. There is no response of the private banker in this regard compared to 10.17 per cent of the public sector bankers.

Similarly, the rural branches emphasized more on physical facilities (18.18%) compared to a smaller portion of urban counterparts. Similarly, lot of differences exist in the responses of public and private bankers for factors like market rapport, entering into new segments, etc. Apart from the two important factors mentioned earlier, the rural bankers emphasise more on developing customer relationship and improving technology for better customer satisfaction, while the urban counterparts on product innovation. When the views were compared in terms of sizes of the branches, a clear difference is indicated in factors like business through referral and market rapport. The small branches focus on these two factors to get more business. Personalised service, developing customer relationship and physical facilities are further emphasised by the smaller banks. Large banks put forth creating goodwill, product innovations and operating through franchises for cost-effectiveness as other important factors. The medium sized banks emphasised heavily on retaining customers (36.67%) and proving customer satisfaction (33.33%) as the most important output of improving service quality.

The views of the bankers on bringing more business through improvement in service quality support the general hypothesis. More business can be achieved by creating a large group of satisfied customers.

### Opinion of Bankers About Problems of the Bank

Due to the increased competition and changing customer attitude, the banks are exposed to various types of risks. The marketing environment is also changing in a big way, providing lot of opportunities for the banks. Now the banks are not confined themselves to traditional activities, rather they moved into unknown territories providing lot of value added services. With the changing environment, the banks are facing lot of problems which hinds them from grabbing the new business opportunities. The problems or weakness as perceived by the bankers are given in Table 5.7 below:

**Table 5.7: Analysis of Problems Faced by Banks**

(Figures in Percentages)

| Factors | Type of Bank | | Size of Bank | | | Location of Bank | |
|---|---|---|---|---|---|---|---|
| | Public | Private | Large | Medium | Small | Rural | Urban |
| Technology Integration | 3.39 | 0.00 | 6.25 | 0.00 | 5.26 | 3.03 | 2.42 |
| Poor Quality of Staff | 22.88 | 0.00 | 14.58 | 13.33 | 42.11 | 60.61 | 5.65 |
| Modernisation/Mechanisation | 16.10 | 7.69 | 8.33 | 16.67 | 15.79 | 9.09 | 15.32 |
| Insufficient Staff | 18.64 | 0.00 | 12.50 | 16.67 | 5.26 | 39.39 | 7.26 |
| Inadequate Physical Facilities | 17.80 | 0.00 | 16.67 | 13.33 | 5.26 | 9.09 | 14.52 |
| Matching Technology | 7.63 | 0.00 | 10.42 | 3.33 | 5.26 | 0.00 | 7.26 |
| Poor Maintenance | 5.08 | 0.00 | 4.17 | 3.33 | 5.26 | 9.09 | 2.42 |

*(Contd...)*

| Factors | Type of Bank | | Size of Bank | | | Location of Bank | |
|---|---|---|---|---|---|---|---|
| | Public | Private | Large | Medium | Small | Rural | Urban |
| Staff Attitude | 12.71 | 7.69 | 14.58 | 6.67 | 26.32 | 18.18 | 9.68 |
| Stress on Class Banking | 0.00 | 7.69 | 0.00 | 0.00 | 15.79 | 0.00 | 2.42 |
| Stress on Procedure | 10.17 | 7.69 | 16.67 | 6.67 | 5.26 | 12.12 | 8.87 |
| Rural Concentration | 2.54 | 0.00 | 6.25 | 0.00 | 0.00 | 0.00 | 2.42 |
| Inadequate Training | 0.00 | 7.69 | 0.00 | 3.33 | 0.00 | 0.00 | 2.42 |
| Lack of Local promotion | 5.08 | 0.00 | 0.00 | 6.67 | 0.00 | 9.09 | 2.42 |
| Increased Competition | 0.00 | 15.38 | 0.00 | 6.67 | 0.00 | 0.00 | 4.84 |
| Poor Customer Relationship | 0.00 | 7.69 | 0.00 | 3.33 | 0.00 | 0.00 | 2.42 |
| Locational Disadvantages | 2.54 | 0.00 | 4.17 | 0.00 | 5.26 | 0.00 | 2.42 |
| Frequent Absence of Staffs | 2.54 | 0.00 | 0.00 | 0.00 | 15.79 | 9.09 | 0.00 |
| Average Age of Employees | 2.54 | 0.00 | 6.25 | 0.00 | 0.00 | 0.00 | 2.42 |
| Saturation in Business | 2.54 | 0.00 | 0.00 | 3.33 | 0.00 | 9.09 | 0.00 |
| Poor Recovery of Loans | 2.54 | 0.00 | 6.25 | 0.00 | 0.00 | 0.00 | 2.42 |
| No Weakness Observed | 10.17 | 23.08 | 10.42 | 16.67 | 5.26 | 0.00 | 16.94 |
| Respondents (Number) | 118 | 39 | 48 | 90 | 19 | 33 | 124 |

It is observed form the Table 5.7 that technology integration is a major problem for the old public sector banks, as they have to integrate the old practices with new technology. But this is not at all a problem with new private banks as they start afresh. Poor quality of the staff has been identified by the bankers as the major weakness by group of bankers except the private banks. This problem is more acute in rural small branches, where 60.61 per cent of the respondent identified it. Medium-sized urban public sector banks have attributed inadequate facilities like floor space, parking space, number of computers, etc. as the major problems. Staff attitude in general is one of the major weaknesses of the sample respondents. The major problem identified by the private bankers is increasing competition. But this has been refuted by public sector bankers. Another interesting observation is that 23.08 per cent of the private banks, and 16.94 per cent of the urban banks have not identified any threat/weakness. But one of the public sector bankers has cautioned that presently there is no threat but one has to remain alert. Similarly, the large banks in public sector operating in urban areas face the problem of ageing, as no young men are joining them and adjusting themselves to the changing environment is difficult. Frequent absence of the staffs without prior intimation is a major weakness with small sized rural branches. Their efficiency is further affected by shortage of staff.

### Support for Improvement of Services

Support from the top is quite essential for success of a business. This is more important in case of a commercial organization like bank. The sample bankers have expressed as many as 23 items/factors of support for improvement of their performance at the micro level. The supports that the sample bankers need are described in the Table 5.8.

It is observed from the Table 5.8 that the expectations of the bankers are substantially different from each other across the categories. The major supports that public sector bankers expect from their organizations are: Adequate facilities, Proper technology, more Support staff, and Cooperation from the controlling office.

Table 5.8: Analysis of Support for Improvement of Services

(Figures in Percentages)

| Factors | Type of Bank | | Size of Bank | | | Location of Bank | |
|---|---|---|---|---|---|---|---|
| | Public | Private | Large | Medium | Small | Rural | Urban |
| Proper Technology | 19.49 | 7.69 | 20.83 | 16.67 | 5.26 | 30.30 | 12.90 |
| Product Redesign | 7.63 | 0.00 | 12.50 | 3.33 | 0.00 | 0.00 | 7.26 |
| Channel Redesign | 5.08 | 7.69 | 10.42 | 3.33 | 5.26 | 0.00 | 7.26 |
| More Support Staff | 16.95 | 0.00 | 16.67 | 10.00 | 15.79 | 24.24 | 9.68 |
| Adequate Facilities | 28.81 | 7.69 | 35.42 | 20.00 | 10.53 | 21.21 | 24.19 |
| Co-operation from Controlling Office | 8.47 | 0.00 | 6.25 | 3.33 | 21.05 | 18.18 | 3.23 |
| Competitive Pricing | 2.54 | 0.00 | 4.17 | 0.00 | 5.26 | 0.00 | 2.42 |
| Appropriate Reward/Punishment System | 2.54 | 7.69 | 6.25 | 3.33 | 0.00 | 0.00 | 4.84 |
| Developing Marketing Team | 2.54 | 7.69 | 6.25 | 3.33 | 0.00 | 0.00 | 4.84 |
| Funds for Marketing and Promotion | 2.54 | 23.08 | 0.00 | 10.00 | 15.79 | 0.00 | 9.68 |
| More Compensation to Employees | 2.54 | 0.00 | 0.00 | 3.33 | 0.00 | 0.00 | 2.42 |
| Quick Disposal | 2.54 | 0.00 | 0.00 | 3.33 | 0.00 | 3.03 | 1.61 |
| Delegation to Lower level | 5.08 | 0.00 | 6.25 | 3.33 | 0.00 | 0.00 | 4.84 |

*(Contd...)*

| Factors | Type of Bank | | Size of Bank | | | Location of Bank | |
|---|---|---|---|---|---|---|---|
| | Public | Private | Large | Medium | Small | Rural | Urban |
| Training to Employees | 5.08 | 7.69 | 6.25 | 3.33 | 15.79 | 9.09 | 4.84 |
| Preparing Daily Work Schedules | 0.00 | 7.69 | 0.00 | 3.33 | 0.00 | 0.00 | 2.42 |
| Improvement in Ambiance | 2.54 | 0.00 | 0.00 | 3.33 | 0.00 | 0.00 | 2.42 |
| Focus on Customers | 2.54 | 0.00 | 4.17 | 0.00 | 5.26 | 0.00 | 2.42 |
| Product Knowledge | 5.08 | 0.00 | 0.00 | 3.33 | 15.79 | 18.18 | 0.00 |
| Mechanisation/Modernisation | 2.54 | 7.69 | 0.00 | 6.67 | 0.00 | 18.18 | 0.00 |
| Arrangement for Customer Support | 2.54 | 0.00 | 0.00 | 3.33 | 0.00 | 9.09 | 0.00 |
| Knowledge about Own Limitations (Staff) | 2.54 | 0.00 | 0.00 | 3.33 | 0.00 | 9.09 | 0.00 |
| Erring Staffs | 2.54 | 0.00 | 6.25 | 0.00 | 0.00 | 0.00 | 2.42 |
| Support from RBI and Government | 2.54 | 0.00 | 6.25 | 0.00 | 0.00 | 0.00 | 2.42 |
| No Support | 0.00 | 23.08 | 0.00 | 10.00 | 0.00 | 0.00 | 7.26 |
| Respondents (Number) | 118 | 39 | 48 | 90 | 19 | 33 | 124 |

But the private banks ask for more funds for marketing and promotion (23.08%). When they are contacted further, the officials of the private banks indicated that more promotion of their product and services should be done in their locality. The large sized banks indicated that adequate facilities (35.42%) as the number one support they need followed by proper technology, adequate staff members and new products. But the smaller banks hinted upon cooperation from controlling office as most important support, followed by funds for marketing and promotion. Similarly, the smaller branches focus on training of employees, adequate staff, and sufficient product knowledge to improve business performance. The rural branches emphasize on supports like proper technology, more support staff, adequate facilities, cooperation, mechanization, and product knowledge as most important. Another interesting observation from the responses is that the private banks (23.08%) do not want any support, as they are self-sufficient and capable enough to withstand competition, while all the public sector banks need support in one form or other from their organization. This indicates that the private banks are operating efficiently, as perceived by them, compared to the public sector ones.

### Steps Taken for Improvement of Services

Once the weaknesses are identified, it is desirable to take corrective steps to overcome the difficulties. When the sample respondents were asked what steps they have taken to improve the customer services at their branches, a variety of responses have been put forth and the results are presented in Table 5.9.

Table 5.9 reveals that mechanization/computerization are the most significant achievement during the last three years across all groups of bankers. This is more significant in smaller rural branches. Apart from that the public sector banks have highlighted introduction of innovative products and extended business hours as significant steps. The private banks highlighted steps like providing services at multi-locations, introduction of personal banking, addressing to the needs of the customers, etc. have been taken by them. Similarly, all the respondents, except those from smaller banks have acclaimed introduction of new products as a significant step they have taken. Rural small branches have adopted aggressive marketing strategy as an important step.

Table 5.9: Analysis of Steps Taken for Improvement of Services

(Figures in Percentages)

| Factors | Type of Bank | | Size of Bank | | | Location of Bank | |
|---|---|---|---|---|---|---|---|
| | Public | Private | Large | Medium | Small | Rural | Urban |
| Personalised Approach | 5.93 | 0.00 | 12.50 | 0.00 | 5.26 | 3.03 | 4.84 |
| Aggressive Marketing | 5.08 | 0.00 | 0.00 | 3.33 | 15.79 | 18.18 | 0.00 |
| Addressing to Needs of Customers | 5.93 | 7.69 | 8.33 | 3.33 | 15.79 | 9.09 | 5.65 |
| Introducing Innovative Products | 15.25 | 7.69 | 12.50 | 16.67 | 0.00 | 9.09 | 14.52 |
| Up-selling/Cross-selling | 5.08 | 0.00 | 6.25 | 3.33 | 0.00 | 0.00 | 4.84 |
| Better Facilities | 10.17 | 7.69 | 12.50 | 10.00 | 0.00 | 0.00 | 12.10 |
| Quick Delivery System | 5.08 | 0.00 | 6.25 | 3.33 | 0.00 | 0.00 | 4.84 |
| Personal Banking | 0.00 | 7.69 | 0.00 | 3.33 | 0.00 | 0.00 | 2.42 |
| Putting Check Drop Boxes | 2.54 | 7.69 | 4.17 | 3.33 | 5.26 | 3.03 | 4.03 |
| Mechanisation | 27.12 | 15.38 | 35.42 | 13.33 | 47.37 | 39.39 | 20.16 |
| Frequent Customer Interaction | 12.71 | 7.69 | 12.50 | 13.33 | 0.00 | 9.09 | 12.10 |
| Extended Business Hours | 7.63 | 0.00 | 0.00 | 10.00 | 0.00 | 12.12 | 4.03 |

*(Contd...)*

| Factors | Type of Bank | | Size of Bank | | | Location of Bank | |
|---|---|---|---|---|---|---|---|
| | Public | Private | Large | Medium | Small | Rural | Urban |
| Penetration into Other Business | 2.54 | 0.00 | 6.25 | 0.00 | 0.00 | 0.00 | 2.42 |
| Services at Multi-location | 0.00 | 7.69 | 0.00 | 3.33 | 0.00 | 0.00 | 2.42 |
| Dissatisfaction taken at HO Level | 0.00 | 7.69 | 0.00 | 3.33 | 0.00 | 0.00 | 2.42 |
| Guiding the Customers | 5.08 | 0.00 | 0.00 | 6.67 | 0.00 | 18.18 | 0.00 |
| Skill Development of Employees | 5.08 | 0.00 | 6.25 | 3.33 | 0.00 | 9.09 | 2.42 |
| Educating the Staffs | 5.08 | 0.00 | 10.42 | 0.00 | 5.26 | 0.00 | 4.84 |
| Maximising Customers' Earning | 2.54 | 0.00 | 4.17 | 0.00 | 5.26 | 0.00 | 2.42 |
| Operation of Single Window Service | 7.63 | 0.00 | 6.25 | 6.67 | 0.00 | 18.18 | 2.42 |
| Opening More Accounts | 2.54 | 0.00 | 0.00 | 0.00 | 15.79 | 9.09 | 0.00 |
| Tie-up with Other Banks/FIs | 0.00 | 7.69 | 0.00 | 0.00 | 15.79 | 0.00 | 2.42 |
| Respondents (Number) | 118 | 39 | 48 | 90 | 19 | 33 | 124 |

To sum up, it is evident from the date (Table 5.9) few significant steps the bankers have adopted during the last three years for improvement in business are: mechanization, providing better facilities, etc. This suggests that the public sector banks have miles to go to match with the private banks in terms of tangible factors like Computers, ATMs, Physical evidences, etc.

**Competition**

Competition is one of the key elements of modern business, which provides customers with better, cheaper and wide variety of services. This is more visible in banking industries because of widespread use of information and communication technology on one hand, and more educated and demanding customers on the other. The days for waiting for a service in the banks are over. Now the banks are severely exposed to competition, which has adversely affected the business of the commercial banks. In many cases the sample respondents opined that the competitors are many and levels of competition are also quite varied. The views of the respondents are presented in Tables 5.10 (A) to 5.10 (E), which analyses the types and levels of competition and the ways to counter it.

The Table 5.10 (A) indicates that the banks face competition from many sources. The major competitors for public sector banks are the private banks (62.24%) as perceived by the sample respondents. Similarly, the private banks feel other private banks as their major competitors. The public sector banks feel other public sector banks (40.68%) and all Banks and Financial Institutions as the next competitors. The private banks are competitors to all sized urban branches, while the rural banks feel other public sector banks as their competitors. This particular trend is observable, as the private banks operate in urban areas only. Similarly, all the rural branches are on public sector, which in turn competes with each other. Though, other Financial Institutions are potential source of competitors, the present sample do not attach so much of importance to it. Only a few public banks (2.54%) operating in rural areas do not experience much competition as they are the virtual monopolists in that area.

Table 5.10: (A): Analysis of Major Competitors

(Figures in Percentages)

| Factors | | Type of Bank | | Size of Bank | | | Location of Bank | |
|---|---|---|---|---|---|---|---|---|
| | | Public | Private | Large | Medium | Small | Rural | Urban |
| Public Sector | f | 15 | 13 | 47 | 32 | 55 | 29 | 34 |
| | % | 40.68 | 15.38 | 12.50 | 46.67 | 31.58 | 54.55 | 29.03 |
| Private Sector | f | 115 | 83 | 67 | 47 | 15 | 84 | 69 |
| | % | 54.24 | 115.38 | 83.33 | 66.67 | 47.37 | 15.15 | 83.87 |
| All Banks | f | 15 | 25 | 27 | 11 | 27 | 23 | 24 |
| | % | 27.12 | 15.38 | 25.00 | 26.67 | 10.53 | 27.27 | 23.39 |
| Other Financial Institutions | f | 8 | 13 | 3 | 21 | 9 | 8 | 8 |
| | % | 8.47 | 7.69 | 12.50 | 3.33 | 21.05 | 9.09 | 8.06 |
| No Threat | f | 0 | 0 | 3 | 0 | 9 | 0 | 2 |
| | % | 2.54 | 0.00 | 0.00 | 3.33 | 0.00 | 9.09 | 0.00 |
| Respondents (Number) | | 118 | 39 | 48 | 90 | 19 | 33 | 124 |

The levels of competition are defined as fierce, moderate and low. The views of sample bankers regarding the levels of competition they are currently facing are presented in Table 5.10 (B), given below.

It is observed from the table presented that all the sample bankers are of opinion that all the banks are facing some kind of competition, but with varying degrees. Majority of the public sector banks describe the levels of competition is moderate (66.10%), while 61.54 per cent of the private banks level it as fierce. In terms of size and location of the branches, majority of the sample respondents described levels of competition is moderate, but smaller banks are more exposed to threat. About 21.21 per cent of the rural branches described competition level as low, as they are the virtual monopolists in their segment. Only they are facing little challenges from the local post-office savings banks.

**Table 5.10 (B): Analysis of Levels of Competition**

| Bank | | Fierce | | Moderate | | Low | | Total | |
|---|---|---|---|---|---|---|---|---|---|
| | | f | % | f | % | f | % | f | % |
| Type of Bank | Public | 25 | 21.19 | 78 | 66.10 | 15 | 12.71 | 118 | 100.00 |
| | Private | 24 | 61.54 | 15 | 38.46 | 0 | 0.00 | 39 | 100.00 |
| Size of Bank | Large | 17 | 35.42 | 31 | 64.58 | 0 | 0.00 | 48 | 100.00 |
| | Medium | 24 | 26.67 | 51 | 56.67 | 15 | 16.67 | 90 | 100.00 |
| | Small | 8 | 42.11 | 11 | 57.89 | 0 | 0.00 | 19 | 100.00 |
| Location of Bank | Rural | 6 | 18.18 | 20 | 60.61 | 7 | 21.21 | 33 | 100.00 |
| | Urban | 43 | 34.68 | 73 | 58.87 | 8 | 6.45 | 124 | 100.00 |
| | Total | 49 | 31.21 | 93 | 59.24 | 15 | 9.55 | 157 | 100.00 |

Because of competition, and availability of alternatives, consumers are constantly in search of better and cheaper service providers. In the process, many bankers face the problems of drop-outs. The views of sample respondents regarding drop-outs/lost business are presented in Table 5.10 (C).

**Table 5.10 (C): Analysis of Customer Drop-outs**

| Bank | | Yes | | No | | Total | |
|---|---|---|---|---|---|---|---|
| | | f | % | f | % | f | % |
| Type of Bank | Public | 28 | 23.73 | 90 | 76.27 | 118 | 100.00 |
| | Private | 6 | 15.38 | 33 | 84.62 | 39 | 100.00 |
| Size of Bank | Large | 14 | 29.17 | 34 | 70.83 | 48 | 100.00 |
| | Medium | 15 | 16.67 | 75 | 83.33 | 90 | 100.00 |
| | Small | 5 | 26.32 | 14 | 73.68 | 19 | 100.00 |
| Location of Bank | Rural | 7 | 21.21 | 26 | 78.79 | 33 | 100.00 |
| | Urban | 27 | 21.77 | 97 | 78.23 | 124 | 100.00 |
| | Total | 34 | 21.66 | 123 | 78.34 | 157 | 100.00 |

It is observed from the Table 5.10 (C) that most of the sample banks did not have the experiences of customer drop-outs and loss of business during the last two years. The loss of business is lowest among the private banks (15.38%) and highest among the large banks (29.17%). Further probing reveals that many customers have preferred to open new accounts with other banks rather than closing the present account. Because of rapid growth in the national economy, almost all the banks have good days and experienced business growth. Even some of the sample branch managers opined that they are quite busy in getting new business, and they don't have time to find the reasons why somebody is leaving them. Analysis of drop-out customers will definitely give more insights into the real problem and developing the right kind of products/ strategy to attract and retain customers.

Competition to certain extent is welcomed, but beyond that it paralyses the business and de-motivates its own employees. In this situation the views of sample respondents about their feelings are presented in Table 5.10 (D).

Majority of the sample respondents do not feel handicapped due to competition. Only a small portion of the public sector banks operating in urban areas (7.63%) feels helpless due to intense competition. Smaller rural branches and the private banks do not feel handicapped due to competition; rather some of them opined that they gained out of competition as they resort to aggressive marketing activities and entering into the fortress of the public sector banks.

**Table 5.10 (D): Analysis of Feeling of Handicapped due to Competition**

| Bank | | Yes | | No | | Total | |
|---|---|---|---|---|---|---|---|
| | | f | % | f | % | f | % |
| Type of Bank | Public | 9 | 7.63 | 109 | 92.37 | 118 | 100.00 |
| | Private | 0 | 0.00 | 39 | 100.00 | 39 | 100.00 |
| Size of Bank | Large | 3 | 6.25 | 45 | 93.75 | 48 | 100.00 |
| | Medium | 6 | 6.67 | 84 | 93.33 | 90 | 100.00 |
| | Small | 0 | 0.00 | 19 | 100.00 | 19 | 100.00 |
| Location of Bank | Rural | 0 | 0.00 | 33 | 100.00 | 33 | 100.00 |
| | Urban | 9 | 7.26 | 115 | 92.74 | 124 | 100.00 |
| | Total | 9 | 5.73 | 148 | 94.27 | 157 | 100.00 |

In a competitive market, all the banks have developed their own strategy to counter competition. The strategies adopted by the sample bankers are given in Table 5.10 (E).

It is evident from the Table 5.10 (E) that the responses of the sample bankers are varied and well dispersed. The major strategies adopted by the banks are improving product range, improving service level, aggressive marketing, better facilities, focus on customers, and appropriate and timely decisions. Further it is observed that the public sector banks focus on improving service level (20.34%) and providing better facilities (17.80%) as important strategies. While the private banks thrust upon improving product range (23.08%). Similarly, the larger banks focus on improving service level, providing better facilities and aggressive marketing as their strategies, while the smaller banks give importance to appropriate and timely decisions, and focus on customers. The rural branches, though small in size, have a big base of loyal customers. Hence, they focus on appropriate and timely decisions, improving service level and focus on customers as their important strategies.

Table 5.10 (E): Analysis of Strategies Adopted to Counter Competition

(Figures in Percentages)

| Factors | Type of Bank | | Size of Bank | | | Location of Bank | |
|---|---|---|---|---|---|---|---|
| | Public | Private | Large | Medium | Small | Rural | Urban |
| Improving Product Range | 10.17 | 23.08 | 18.75 | 10.00 | 15.79 | 9.09 | 14.52 |
| Improving Service Level | 20.34 | 0.00 | 25.00 | 13.33 | 0.00 | 18.18 | 14.52 |
| Aggressive Marketing | 12.71 | 7.69 | 18.75 | 10.00 | 0.00 | 9.09 | 12.10 |
| Need-based Strategy | 0.85 | 15.38 | 2.08 | 6.67 | 0.00 | 0.00 | 5.65 |
| Qualitative Advance | 5.08 | 0.00 | 4.17 | 3.33 | 5.26 | 0.00 | 4.84 |
| Promotion of Products/Services | 5.08 | 7.69 | 6.25 | 6.67 | 0.00 | 9.09 | 4.84 |
| Improving Image | 2.54 | 7.69 | 4.17 | 3.33 | 5.26 | 0.00 | 4.84 |
| Better Facilities | 17.80 | 15.38 | 29.17 | 10.00 | 21.05 | 0.00 | 21.77 |
| Better Ambiances | 0.00 | 0.00 | 0.00 | 0.00 | 0.00 | 0.00 | 0.00 |
| Renovated Credit Portfolio | 2.54 | 0.00 | 4.17 | 0.00 | 5.26 | 0.00 | 2.42 |
| Focus on Customers | 11.02 | 15.38 | 0.00 | 13.33 | 36.84 | 12.12 | 12.10 |
| Appropriate and Timely Decision | 11.02 | 15.38 | 6.25 | 13.33 | 21.05 | 21.21 | 9.68 |
| Reducing the Interest Rate | 7.63 | 0.00 | 10.42 | 3.33 | 5.26 | 3.03 | 6.45 |

*(Contd...)*

| Factors | Type of Bank | | Size of Bank | | | Location of Bank | |
|---|---|---|---|---|---|---|---|
| | Public | Private | Large | Medium | Small | Rural | Urban |
| Extending Business Hours | 2.54 | 0.00 | 0.00 | 3.33 | 0.00 | 9.09 | 0.00 |
| Guiding Customers | 2.54 | 0.00 | 0.00 | 3.33 | 0.00 | 9.09 | 0.00 |
| Visit to Customers' Place | 2.54 | 0.00 | 4.17 | 0.00 | 5.26 | 0.00 | 2.42 |
| Regular Touch with Customers | 2.54 | 0.00 | 4.17 | 0.00 | 5.26 | 0.00 | 2.42 |
| Survival of the Fittest | 2.54 | 0.00 | 0.00 | 3.33 | 0.00 | 9.09 | 0.00 |
| Research and Development Team | 2.54 | 0.00 | 6.25 | 0.00 | 0.00 | 0.00 | 2.42 |
| Expanding Market Area | 2.54 | 0.00 | 6.25 | 0.00 | 0.00 | 0.00 | 2.42 |
| Touch With Government Officials | 2.54 | 0.00 | 0.00 | 0.00 | 15.79 | 9.09 | 0.00 |
| No Present Threat | 2.54 | 0.00 | 0.00 | 3.33 | 0.00 | 9.09 | 0.00 |
| Respondents (Number) | 118 | 39 | 48 | 90 | 19 | 33 | 124 |

To sum up, almost all the sample respondents recognised the treat of competition for their business, and also have designed their strategies to combat it. According to the sample respondents, the major threat to their banks are the new private banks with better ambiences, improved facilities and service quality, who can attract customers better. Hence, it is suggested that the banks; more particularly public sector banks should be given more freedom to decide their own strategies to combat competition by improving their facilities and product range. Rural banks, till date, are relatively free from competition should not feel complacent about it. In the age of internet and universal banking, the rural areas will not be left alone. They may be connected with the urban centres and thus, competition can be implanted.

### Achievement of Target

For growth of business, all the business organizations set their own targets; which is reflected in their annual plans. Though, most of the sample respondents have expressed their views that no such explicit target is given to them for achievement, but most of them set their own targets at the branch levels. The views of the sample bankers and the strategies they have adopted to achieve the targets are given in Tables 5.11(A) and 5.11(B).

**Table 5.11 (A): Analysis of Achievement of Target**

| Bank | | Yes | | No | | Total | |
|---|---|---|---|---|---|---|---|
| | | f | % | f | % | f | % |
| Type of Bank | Public | 102 | 86.44 | 16 | 13.56 | 118 | 100.00 |
| | Private | 39 | 100.00 | 0 | 0.00 | 39 | 100.00 |
| Size of Bank | Large | 41 | 85.42 | 7 | 14.58 | 48 | 100.00 |
| | Medium | 84 | 93.33 | 6 | 6.67 | 90 | 100.00 |
| | Small | 16 | 84.21 | 3 | 15.79 | 19 | 100.00 |
| Location of Bank | Rural | 32 | 96.97 | 1 | 3.03 | 33 | 100.00 |
| | Urban | 109 | 87.90 | 15 | 12.10 | 124 | 100.00 |
| | Total | 141 | 89.81 | 16 | 10.19 | 157 | 100.00 |

It is observed from the Table 5.11(A) that most of the banks have achieved their targets in the reference year (2004-05). The achievement of targets by the private bankers is 100 per cent, which is about 86 per cent in case public sector banks. This may be due to their inherent problems like rigid rules and regulations, staff attitudes, etc. When it is compared across the branch size; no clear cut trend is emerging. Similarly in locational variations the rural branches have distinct advantages over their urban counterpart in achieving the targets. This trend may be due to more personal contact with the clients and less of competition. Further, saturation in rural markets has not arrived as many new customers can created.

Table 5.11(B) depicts the strategies adopted by the sample bankers to achieve the targets. It is observed that getting high-value customers or more business from the existing customers is adapted by public sector banks as the major strategies to achieve their target, which is not true in case of private sector banks. Again, the small banks focus on more business from the existing customers (78.95%). The private banks highlighted that allocating individual targets is the most important strategy, followed by building customer relationships and putting personal effort.

To sum up, it is observed that all categories of banks focus on setting individual targets, building relationship with the customer and putting personal efforts as major strategies to achieve the business targets. Again achievement of targets by the sample bankers is partly linked with the growth of the economy, even if no attempt has been made, they enjoy the benefits.

**Adequacy of Compensation**

The compensation for the job done is one of the most important factors of motivation. It is generally believed that the employees in the public sector are better paid for lesser work, than the private sector employees. In Government organisations, when good pay is associated with less accountability and more freedom leads to laxity. The views of the sample bankers regarding the adequacy of the pay package are given in Table 5.12.

**Table 5.11 (B): Analysis of Strategies Adopted to Achieve Target**

(Figures in Percentages)

| Factors | Type of Bank | | Size of Bank | | | Location of Bank | |
|---|---|---|---|---|---|---|---|
| | Public | Private | Large | Medium | Small | Rural | Urban |
| Getting New High valued Customers | 10.17 | 0.00 | 12.50 | 6.67 | 0.00 | 9.09 | 7.26 |
| Business form Existing Customers | 12.71 | 0.00 | 6.25 | 13.33 | 78.95 | 27.27 | 4.84 |
| Putting Personal Efforts | 17.80 | 15.38 | 16.67 | 20.00 | 5.26 | 30.30 | 13.71 |
| Building Customer Relationship | 12.71 | 23.08 | 0.00 | 23.33 | 15.79 | 36.36 | 9.68 |
| Tough Attitude of Staff | 5.08 | 0.00 | 4.17 | 3.33 | 5.26 | 0.00 | 4.84 |
| Need-based Strategy | 2.54 | 0.00 | 4.17 | 0.00 | 5.26 | 0.00 | 2.42 |
| Expenditure Control | 2.54 | 0.00 | 4.17 | 0.00 | 5.26 | 0.00 | 2.42 |
| Developing Marketing Team | 2.54 | 0.00 | 6.25 | 0.00 | 0.00 | 0.00 | 2.42 |
| Up-selling/Cross-selling | 5.08 | 7.69 | 12.50 | 3.33 | 0.00 | 0.00 | 7.26 |
| Allocation of Individual Targets | 12.71 | 30.77 | 18.75 | 13.33 | 31.58 | 9.09 | 19.35 |
| Better Technology | 2.54 | 0.00 | 6.25 | 0.00 | 0.00 | 0.00 | 2.42 |
| Micro Budgeting | 0.00 | 7.69 | 0.00 | 3.33 | 0.00 | 0.00 | 2.42 |

*(Contd...)*

| Factors | Type of Bank | | Size of Bank | | | Location of Bank | |
|---|---|---|---|---|---|---|---|
| | Public | Private | Large | Medium | Small | Rural | Urban |
| Good Net-working | 2.54 | 7.69 | 0.00 | 6.67 | 0.00 | 9.09 | 2.42 |
| Support of all Staff Members | 2.54 | 0.00 | 6.25 | 0.00 | 0.00 | 0.00 | 2.42 |
| Entering into New Segments | 10.17 | 0.00 | 10.42 | 6.67 | 5.26 | 18.18 | 4.84 |
| Aggressive Marketing Strategy | 5.08 | 0.00 | 4.17 | 3.33 | 5.26 | 9.09 | 2.42 |
| Achieving Short-term Targets | 2.54 | 0.00 | 6.25 | 0.00 | 0.00 | 0.00 | 2.42 |
| Net-working with Business Houses | 5.08 | 0.00 | 4.17 | 0.00 | 21.05 | 12.12 | 1.61 |
| Planning at Beginning of the Year | 2.54 | 0.00 | 6.25 | 0.00 | 0.00 | 0.00 | 2.42 |
| Franchising Agreements | 0.00 | 7.69 | 0.00 | 0.00 | 15.79 | 0.00 | 2.42 |
| Respondents (Number) | 118 | 39 | 48 | 90 | 19 | 33 | 124 |

## Table 5.12: Analysis of Adequacy of Compensation

| Bank | | Yes | | No | | Total | |
|---|---|---|---|---|---|---|---|
| | | f | % | f | % | f | % |
| Type of Bank | Public | 87 | 73.7 | 31 | 26.3 | 118 | 100.0 |
| | Private | 33 | 84.6 | 6 | 15.4 | 39 | 100.0 |
| Size of Bank | Large | 38 | 79.2 | 10 | 20.8 | 48 | 100.0 |
| | Medium | 72 | 80.0 | 18 | 20.0 | 90 | 100.0 |
| | Small | 10 | 52.6 | 9 | 47.4 | 19 | 100.0 |
| Location of Bank | Rural | 21 | 63.6 | 12 | 36.4 | 33 | 100.0 |
| | Urban | 99 | 79.8 | 25 | 20.2 | 124 | 100.0 |
| | Total | 120 | 76.4 | 37 | 23.6 | 157 | 100.0 |

It is observed from the Table 5.12 that levels of dissatisfaction regarding pay is more among the public sector bankers compared to the private ones. Similarly, the smaller banks operating in rural areas have felt mostly the inadequacy of the pay (47.4%). This trend, more particularly, matches to the general tendency of the government employees (more demanding). The overall picture of all categories is not significantly different. The bank management should take into cognizance these factors while deciding the pay package.

### Job Knowledge and Growing Customer Demand

As the market has become competitive, the customer demand will change very frequently. Similarly, banks are also innovating new products and value-added services to meet those demands. The views of the bankers regarding the care taken by the banks to improve their job knowledge are presented in Table 5.13.

Most of the bankers are of view that the banks are taking sufficient care to improve the job knowledge of the employees to meet the growing demands of the customers. The banks made circulars to all branches regarding the introduction of new products, which in turn will help to sell these products to the customers.

**Table 5.13: Analysis of Improvement of Job Knowledge of Bankers**

| Bank | | Yes | | No | | Total | |
|---|---|---|---|---|---|---|---|
| | | f | % | f | % | f | % |
| Type of Bank | Public | 115 | 97.5 | 3 | 2.5 | 118 | 100.0 |
| | Private | 39 | 100.0 | 0 | 0.0 | 39 | 100.0 |
| Size of Bank | Large | 48 | 100.0 | 0 | 0.0 | 48 | 100.0 |
| | Medium | 87 | 96.7 | 3 | 3.3 | 90 | 100.0 |
| | Small | 19 | 100.0 | 0 | 0.0 | 19 | 100.0 |
| Location of Bank | Rural | 33 | 100.0 | 0 | 0.0 | 33 | 100.0 |
| | Urban | 121 | 97.6 | 3 | 2.4 | 124 | 100.0 |
| | Total | 154 | 98.1 | 3 | 1.9 | 157 | 100.0 |

### Adoption to Technological Change

Technology has become the driving force of the modern banking. In an era of universal banking, none of the banks can afford to stay isolated without proper technological adoption. But this creates a lot of problems for the employees, particularly to the aged ones. Frequent updation of technology also brings problems of technological integration, particularly between the old manual processes with that of the total dependence on computer. The local problems may not be addressed in the right perspectives. Table 5.14 analyses the views of the sample bankers relating to technology adoption.

It is observed from the Table 5.14 that adoption to technological changes is not at all a problem for new generation private banks as they have started with a technological platform. But a small percentage of public sector banks (8.5%) found it difficult to adapt to new technology. The major reasons attributed for these trends are: (i) stereotype attitude of the staff (aged one) and (ii) proper training given by the banks. In rest of the cases the problem is of similar nature.

**Table 5.14: Analysis of Adoption to Technological Change**

| Bank | | Yes | | No | | Total | |
|---|---|---|---|---|---|---|---|
| | | f | % | f | % | f | % |
| Type of Bank | Public | 108 | 91.5 | 10 | 8.5 | 118 | 100.0 |
| | Private | 39 | 100.0 | 0 | 0.0 | 39 | 100.0 |
| Size of Bank | Large | 45 | 93.8 | 3 | 6.3 | 48 | 100.0 |
| | Medium | 84 | 93.3 | 6 | 6.7 | 90 | 100.0 |
| | Small | 18 | 94.7 | 1 | 5.3 | 19 | 100.0 |
| Location of Bank | Rural | 32 | 97.0 | 1 | 3.0 | 33 | 100.0 |
| | Urban | 115 | 92.7 | 9 | 7.3 | 124 | 100.0 |
| | Total | 147 | 93.6 | 10 | 6.4 | 157 | 100.0 |

**Vanishing Customers**

Again competition has brought a lot of new opportunities for the banking customers. The market is flooded with alternative products/services, and so also service outlets. Hence, the customers tend to quit one service provider in favour of another. Table 5.15 describes the views of the sample respondent regarding vanishing customers.

**Table 5.15: Analysis of Vanishing Customers**

| Bank | | Yes | | No | | Total | |
|---|---|---|---|---|---|---|---|
| | | f | % | f | % | f | % |
| Type of Bank | Public | 102 | 86.4 | 16 | 13.6 | 118 | 100.0 |
| | Private | 36 | 92.3 | 3 | 7.7 | 39 | 100.0 |
| Size of Bank | Large | 37 | 7701 | 11 | 22.9 | 48 | 100.0 |
| | Medium | 87 | 96.7 | 3 | 3.3 | 90 | 100.0 |
| | Small | 14 | 73.7 | 5 | 26.3 | 19 | 100.0 |
| Location of Bank | Rural | 31 | 93.9 | 2 | 6.1 | 33 | 100.0 |
| | Urban | 107 | 86.3 | 17 | 13.7 | 124 | 100.0 |
| | Total | 138 | 87.9 | 19 | 12.1 | 157 | 100.0 |

It is observed from the Table 5.15 that a large portion of the sample respondents take note of the vanishing customers and have tried to find out reasons thereof. The rate of vanishing customers is higher in case of urban large sized public sector banks (22.9%). The probable reasons for such trend may be: (i) more attractive private banks, (ii) dissatisfactions experienced by the customers, and (iii) the apathetic attitude of the staffs. But the overall situation is not bad enough, and the banks are advised to use this source for their benefits.

**Adequacy of Customer Services**

Most often, it is a question in marketing *'what should the customer's get', which* is always debatable. Somebody answers to that *'what they deserve'*. The views of sample bankers regarding adequacy of services offered to the customers are summarized in Table 5.16.

**Table 5.16: Analysis of Adequacy of Levels of Customer Services**

| Bank | | Yes | | No | | Total | |
|---|---|---|---|---|---|---|---|
| | | f | % | f | % | f | % |
| Type of Bank | Public | 91 | 77.1 | 27 | 22.9 | 118 | 100.0 |
| | Private | 30 | 76.9 | 9 | 23.1 | 39 | 100.0 |
| Size of Bank | Large | 43 | 89.6 | 5 | 10.4 | 48 | 100.0 |
| | Medium | 63 | 70.0 | 27 | 30.0 | 90 | 100.0 |
| | Small | 15 | 78.9 | 4 | 21.1 | 19 | 100.0 |
| Location of Bank | Rural | 21 | 63.6 | 12 | 36.4 | 33 | 100.0 |
| | Urban | 100 | 80.6 | 24 | 19.4 | 124 | 100.0 |
| | Total | 121 | 77.1 | 36 | 22.9 | 157 | 100.0 |

It is evident from the above table that the large pool of views regarding inadequacy of customer services came from the medium sized banks, both in public and private sectors. Similarly the rural bankers are more in favour of providing extra to the customers than the urban counterparts. Further probing indicated that most of the customers are happy with the existing products and the banking still dominates around deposit and withdrawal of money.

## MODES OF ATTRACTING NEW BUSINESS

In a competitive market, every business house thrives on attracting new business and retaining the existing customers. The sample bankers have adopted many strategies to attract new business. Tables 5.17 (A) to 17 (C) discuss the modes/methods of attracting new business in type, size and location variations.

**Table 5.17 (A): Mode of Attracting New Business and Type of Banks**

| Sl. No. | Methods | Public Sector | | Private Sector | | |
|---|---|---|---|---|---|---|
| | | No. | % | No. | % | $\chi^2$ |
| (a) | Personal Contact | 93 | 78.8 | 30 | 76.9 | 0.062 |
| (b) | Personal attention to Customer need | 97 | 82.2 | 33 | 84.6 | 0.120 |
| (c) | Door-to-door campaign | 24 | 20.2 | 18 | 46.2 | 9.969* |
| (d) | Aggressive Sales Promotion | 45 | 38.1 | 33 | 84.6 | 25.331* |
| (e) | Distribution of information bulletin | 45 | 39.0 | 15 | 38.5 | 0.003 |
| (f) | Improving service quality | 94 | 79.7 | 33 | 84.6 | 0.465 |
| (g) | Motivating employees forbetter customer deals | 88 | 74.6 | 24 | 61.5 | 2.437 |
| (h) | Others | 9 | 7.60 | 3 | 7.70 | 0.021 |
| | Total | 118 | 100.0 | 39 | 100.0 | |

Attracting and retaining customers is quite important for business success. The study on different methods adopted by the sample bankers indicate that for public sector banks; personal attention to customer needs (82.2%) is most important followed by improving service quality (79.7%) and personal contact (78.8%); while door-to-door campaign (20.2%) is least preferred method. Personal attention (84.6%), aggressive sales promotion (84.6%), and improving service quality get equal weightage. The $\chi^2$ values indicate that methods like door-to-door campaign and aggressive sales promotions are statistically significant at 1 per cent level of significance, indicating a variation in perception among public sector and private bankers. The methods like personal contact, personal attention to consumer needs and improving service quality are most important methods of attracting new business irrespective of the size of the bank. The $\chi^2$ value for these methods in size variation indicates that door-to-door campaign method is statistically significant, suggesting that the use of this method by different sized bank is different from each other. The methods adopted by different banks in their locational variation indicates that door-to-door campaign, distribution of bulletins, and motivating employees for better customer deals are statistically significant as indicated by the $\chi^2$ values.

To sum up, it can be inferred that private banks are resort to aggressive sales promotion and door-to-door campaign to attract new customers than their public sector counterparts, while rural branches focus more on distributing bulletins, motivating employees and door-to-door campaign as methods to attract new business apart from personal contact, personal attention to customer needs and improving service quality as the core methods of attracting new customers. Apart from that, few bankers perceived that more advertisements, increasing number of employees and improving the ambiences, more particularly for public sector banks is important for attracting new customers.

**Table 5.17 (B): Mode of Attracting New Business and Size of Banks**

| Sl. No. | Factors | Large | | Medium | | Small | | |
|---|---|---|---|---|---|---|---|---|
| | | No. | % | No. | % | No. | % | $\chi^2$ |
| (a) | Personal Contact | 39 | 81.3 | 69 | 76.7 | 15 | 78.9 | 0.392 |
| (b) | Personal attention to Customer needs | 37 | 77.1 | 75 | 83.3 | 18 | 94.7 | 3.021 |
| (c) | Door-to-door campaign | 6 | 12.5 | 30 | 33.3 | 6 | 31.6 | 7.191** |
| (d) | Aggressive Sales Promotion | 21 | 43.8 | 51 | 56.7 | 6 | 31.6 | 4.923 |
| (e) | Distribution of information bulletin | 16 | 33.3 | 39 | 43.3 | 6 | 31.6 | 1.799 |
| (f) | Improving service quality | 40 | 83.3 | 72 | 80.0 | 15 | 78.9 | 0.278 |
| (g) | Motivating employees for better customer deals | 35 | 72.9 | 63 | 70.0 | 14 | 73.7 | 0.188 |
| (h) | Others | 3 | 6.3 | 9 | 10.0 | 0 | 0.00 | |
| | Total | 48 | 100.0 | 90 | 100.0 | 19 | 100.0 | |

**Table 5.17 (C): Mode of Attracting New Business and Location of Banks**

| Sl. No. | Factors | Rural | | Urban | | |
|---|---|---|---|---|---|---|
| | | No. | % | No. | % | $\chi^2$ |
| (a) | Personal Contact | 26 | 78.8 | 97 | 78.2 | 0.005 |
| (b) | Personal attention to Customer needs | 26 | 78.8 | 104 | 83.9 | 0.473 |
| (c) | Door-to-door campaign | 15 | 45.5 | 27 | 21.8 | 7.459** |
| (d) | Aggressive Sales Promotion | 13 | 39.4 | 65 | 52.4 | 1.769 |
| (e) | Distribution of information bulletin | 23 | 69.7 | 38 | 30.6 | 16.731* |
| (f) | Improving service quality | 27 | 81.8 | 100 | 80.6 | 0.023 |
| (g) | Motivating employees for better customer deals | 29 | 87.9 | 83 | 66.9 | 5.591** |
| (h) | Others | 6 | 18.2 | 6 | 4.8 | |
| | Total | 33 | 100.0 | 124 | 100.0 | |

**Promotion for Attracting New Business**

Tables 5.18 (A) and 5.18 (B) discusses the views of bankers for banking services in attracting new business. Table 5.18 (A) indicates that both the private and public sector banks' view regarding advertising for attracting new business is similar. But the small rural branches, more so in public sector have hinted upon advertisement as important in attracting new business. The $\chi^2$ values for all the three categories are not significant, indicating the indifference of perception of bankers relating to advertisements in attracting new business.

Table 5.18 (B) describes the reasons attributed by different bankers in attracting new business by advertisements. The basic functions of advertisements like information dissemination, reaching out people about offerings for building mass awareness, telling people about offerings and attracting and retaining customers are important for attracting new business. Smaller rural branches in public sector have emphasised more on advertising for promotion of business.

**Table 5.18(A): Advertising and Attracting New Business**

| | Description | YES | % | NO | % | TOTAL | $\chi^2$ |
|---|---|---|---|---|---|---|---|
| Type of Banks | Public | 91 | 77.1 | 21 | 17.8 | 118 | 2.411 |
| | Private | 30 | 76.9 | 9 | 23.1 | 39 | |
| Size of Banks | Large | 34 | 70.8 | 11 | 22.9 | 48 | 4.844 |
| | Medium | 69 | 76.7 | 18 | 20.2 | 90 | |
| | Small | 18 | 94.7 | 1 | 5.3 | 19 | |
| Location of Banks | Rural | 30 | 90.9 | 3 | 9.1 | 33 | 4.829 |
| | Urban | 91 | 73.4 | 27 | 21.8 | 124 | |

*Note:* Six of the sample respondents have not responded to this question.

Table 5.18 (B): Advertising and Way of Attracting New Business

| Reasons | Public | Private | Large | Medium | Small | Rural | Urban |
|---|---|---|---|---|---|---|---|
| | % | % | % | % | % | % | % |
| Increasing sales | 5.1 | | 6.3 | | 15.8 | 9.1 | 2.4 |
| Information dissemination | 15.3 | 15.4 | 12.6 | 13.4 | 15.8 | 18.2 | 12.1 |
| Spread the New and Innovative ideas | | 7.7 | | 3.3 | | | 2.4 |
| Reaching out people/ Building mass Awareness | 26.3 | 38.5 | 23.0 | 36.5 | 26.3 | 15.2 | 33.1 |
| Tell people about offerings | 20.4 | 15.4 | 16.8 | 20.1 | 21.1 | 36.4 | 14.5 |
| Competitive parity (as others are doing) | 7.6 | 7.7 | 4.2 | 6.7 | 15.8 | 18.2 | 4.8 |
| Attracting/Retaining customers | 11.0 | 7.7 | 10.4 | 6.7 | 26.3 | 24.3 | 6.5 |
| People are alert to Propaganda | | 7.7 | | 3.3 | | | 2.4 |
| Has direct and positive response | 2.5 | 7.7 | | 6.7 | | 9.1 | 2.4 |
| Better and informed Decisions by Customers | 2.5 | | 6.3 | | | | 2.4 |
| Bring differences from others/ Best services to be highlighted | 5.1 | | 6.3 | 3.3 | | 9.1 | 2.4 |
| Image building | 5.1 | | 4.2 | | 21.1 | 9.1 | 2.4 |
| Total number of Respondents | 118 | 39 | 48 | 90 | 19 | 33 | 124 |

Note: Most of the sample respondents have not assigned any reason.

## Opinion of Bankers about Staffs

Table 5.19 describes the opinion of bankers regarding the front office staffs of a bank branch office. All the sample respondents have opined that they are quite important, as they directly come in contact with the customer. The customer gets first impression about the bank through contact with the front office personnel. In service industries, more particularly in banks, they play an important role in providing customer satisfaction. When they are asked to give the views regarding discharging their duties, the private banks replied affirmatively, while 10.2 per cent of the public bank employees, mostly belonging to the rural areas and either large or small in size are not discharging their duties properly.

The role of the front office people in attracting and retaining the customers as reported by the private and large-sized public sector banks are discussed in Table 5.19. The smaller rural banks are far behind in terms of using the front office personnel in attracting and retaining customers. Sometimes it is observed that front office personnel of public sector banks behave irresponsibly while dealing with customers. The front office people often are not aware of the targets they have supposed to achieve. This is more observed with PSBs in various sizes and locations. Similarly, the opinion of the sample bankers regarding their roles in bringing new business, most of the bankers are of positive views. Smaller rural branches of PSBs have shown more negative views in this regard. When solicited the views of the sample bankers, the result has shown similar trend like the other variables.

## Banker Customer Meets

Regular interaction between the Banker and Customer reduces tension and increases customer satisfaction. Table 5.20 describes the frequency of interaction between the Banker and the Customers. The patterns of interactions were described in six different ways namely: monthly: quarterly, half-yearly, annually, occasionally and not at all.

Table 5.19: **Opinion about Staff**

| | | | A | B | % | C | % | D | % | E | % | F | % |
|---|---|---|---|---|---|---|---|---|---|---|---|---|---|
| Bank | Pub | Y | 118 | 106 | 89.3 | 108 | 91.5 | 91 | 77.1 | 97 | 82.2 | 100 | 84.7 |
| | | N | 0 | 12 | 10.2 | 10 | 8.5 | 27 | 22.9 | 21 | 17.8 | 18 | 15.3 |
| | Pvt | Y | 39 | 39 | | 39 | | 36 | 92.3 | 39 | | 39 | |
| | | N | 0 | | | | | 3 | 7.7 | | | | |
| Size | L | Y | 48 | 43 | 89.6 | 48 | | 37 | 77.1 | 40 | 83.3 | 39 | 83.3 |
| | | N | 0 | 5 | 10.4 | | | 11 | 22.9 | 8 | 16.7 | 9 | 18.8 |
| | M | Y | 90 | 87 | 96.7 | 84 | 93.3 | 72 | 80.0 | 81 | 90.0 | 84 | 93.3 |
| | | N | 0 | 3 | 3.3 | 6 | 6.7 | 18 | 20.0 | 9 | 10.0 | 6 | 6.7 |
| | S | Y | 19 | 15 | 78.9 | 15 | 78.9 | 18 | 94.7 | 15 | 78.9 | 16 | 84.2 |
| | | N | 0 | 4 | 21.1 | 4 | 21.1 | 1 | 5.3 | 4 | 21.2 | 3 | 15.8 |
| Location | R | Y | 33 | 30 | 90.9 | 29 | 87.9 | 26 | 78.8 | 26 | 78.8 | 27 | 81.8 |
| | | N | 0 | 3 | 9.1 | 4 | 12.1 | 7 | 21.2 | 7 | 21.2 | 6 | 18.2 |
| | U | Y | 124 | 115 | 92.7 | 118 | 95.2 | 101 | 81.5 | 110 | 88.7 | 112 | 90.3 |
| | | N | 0 | 9 | 7.3 | 6 | 4.8 | 23 | 18.5 | 14 | 11.3 | 12 | 9.7 |

A- Importance of Front Office Staff B- Discharging their duties C- Help in attracting Customers

D- Aware of Targets E- Help in bringing new business F- Attention to selective customers

Table 5.20: Frequency of Banker Customer Meet

| | | | Yes-A | Yes-H | Yes-Q | Yes-M | Yes-Occ. | No | Total |
|---|---|---|---|---|---|---|---|---|---|
| Type of Bank | Public | F | 15 | 6 | 39 | 40 | 6 | 12 | 118 |
| | | % | 12.71 | 5.08 | 33.05 | 33.90 | 5.08 | 10.17 | 100.00 |
| | Private | F | | | 15 | 15 | 6 | 3 | 39 |
| | | % | | | 38.46 | 38.46 | 15.38 | 7.69 | 100.00 |
| Size of Bank | Large | F | 11 | 5 | 16 | 8 | 3 | 5 | 48 |
| | | % | 22.92 | 10.42 | 33.33 | 16.67 | 6.25 | 10.42 | 100.00 |
| | Medium | F | 3 | | 30 | 39 | 9 | 9 | 90 |
| | | % | 3.33 | | 33.33 | 43.33 | 10.00 | 10.00 | 100.00 |
| | Small | F | 1 | 1 | 8 | 8 | | 1 | 19 |
| | | % | 5.26 | 5.26 | 42.11 | 42.11 | | 5.26 | 100.00 |
| Location of Branch | Rural | F | | | 16 | 13 | | 4 | 33 |
| | | % | | | 48.48 | 39.39 | | 12.12 | 100.00 |
| | Urban | F | 15 | 6 | 38 | 42 | 12 | 11 | 124 |
| | | % | 12.10 | 4.84 | 30.65 | 33.87 | 9.68 | 8.87 | 100.00 |

A- Annually H- Half-yearly Q- Quarterly M- Monthly O- Occasionally

It is observed from the Table 5.20 that most of the sample banks hold their banker-customer meet regularly either monthly or quarterly basis. The public sector banks have to conduct the same, as it is mandatory. The large banks, mostly in public sector conduct Banker – Customer meets annual basis, as they are too busy in managing the day-to-day matters. Interestingly, some of the respondents from all categories replied that they are not conducting Banker-Customer meet. Some of them replied that they are either too busy or they do not need it.

The banker customer meet can be a good platform to mitigate the differences and solve many problems. This in turn increases customer loyalty and satisfaction. Hence, it is desirable that banks should take necessary steps to increase customer-banker meets. Tables 5.21 (A) and 5.21 (B) describes the steps taken by bankers increase such interaction.

**Table 5.21(A): Banker-Customer Interaction**

| | | Yes | % | No | % | Total |
|---|---|---|---|---|---|---|
| Bank | Pub | 73 | 61.86 | 36 | 30.51 | 118 |
| | Pvt | 33 | 84.62 | 6 | 15.38 | 39 |
| Size | Large | 35 | 72.92 | 13 | 27.08 | 48 |
| | Medium | 54 | 60.00 | 27 | 30.00 | 90 |
| | Small | 17 | 89.47 | 2 | 10.53 | 19 |
| Location | Rural | 25 | 75.76 | 8 | 24.24 | 33 |
| | Urban | 81 | 65.32 | 34 | 27.42 | 124 |

The Table 5.21 describes whether any steps have been taken by the banker to increase banker-customer (B-C) meets. Majority of the sample banks have taken steps to increase B-C meets. The middle-sized urban public sector banks are lagging behind in taking steps to hold B-C meets. When the sample bankers are asked to specify the steps they have taken to increase B-C meets, they have given 16 such steps; which are described in Table 5.21 (B).

**Table 5.21 (B): Steps taken for B-C interaction**

(Figures are in Percentages to Total)

| | | A | B | C | D | E | F | G | H | I | J | K | L | M | N | O | P | Total |
|---|---|---|---|---|---|---|---|---|---|---|---|---|---|---|---|---|---|---|
| Bank | Pub. | 12 | 6 | | 3 | 9 | 3 | 3 | 3 | 3 | 3 | 9 | 3 | 3 | 3 | 3 | 3 | 118 |
| | | 10.17 | 5.08 | 0.00 | 2.54 | 7.63 | 2.54 | 2.54 | 2.54 | 2.54 | 2.54 | 7.63 | 2.54 | 2.54 | 2.54 | 2.54 | 2.54 | 100.0 |
| | Pvt. | 3 | 3 | 3 | | 6 | 3 | 3 | | | | | | | | | | 39 |
| | | 7.69 | 7.69 | 7.69 | 0.00 | 15.38 | 7.69 | 7.69 | 0.00 | 0.00 | 0.00 | 0.00 | 0.00 | 0.00 | 0.00 | 0.00 | 0.00 | 100.0 |
| Size | Large | 8 | 3 | | 2 | | 2 | | | 2 | 3 | 6 | 3 | | 3 | | 3 | 48 |
| | | 16.67 | 6.25 | 0.00 | 4.17 | 0.00 | 4.17 | 0.00 | 0.00 | 4.17 | 6.25 | 12.50 | 6.25 | 0.00 | 6.25 | 0.00 | 6.25 | 100.0 |
| | Medium | 6 | 6 | 3 | | 15 | 3 | 6 | 3 | | | | | 3 | | 3 | | 90 |
| | | 6.67 | 6.67 | 3.33 | 0.00 | 16.67 | 3.33 | 6.67 | 3.33 | 0.00 | 0.00 | 0.00 | 0.00 | 3.33 | 0.00 | 3.33 | 0.00 | 100.0 |
| | Small | 1 | | | 1 | | 1 | | | 1 | | 3 | | | | | | 19 |
| | | 5.26 | 0.00 | 0.00 | 5.26 | 0.00 | 5.26 | 0.00 | 0.00 | 5.26 | 0.00 | 15.79 | 0.00 | 0.00 | 0.00 | 0.00 | 0.00 | 100.0 |

*(Contd...)*

| | | A | B | C | D | E | F | G | H | I | J | K | L | M | N | O | P | Total |
|---|---|---|---|---|---|---|---|---|---|---|---|---|---|---|---|---|---|---|
| Location | Rural | 3 | | | | 6 | | 3 | | | | 3 | | 3 | | 3 | | 33 |
| | | 9.09 | 0.00 | 0.00 | 0.00 | 18.18 | 0.00 | 9.09 | 0.00 | 0.00 | 0.00 | 9.09 | 0.00 | 9.09 | 0.00 | 9.09 | 0.00 | 100.0 |
| | Urban | 12 | 9 | 3 | 3 | 9 | 6 | 3 | 3 | 3 | 3 | 6 | 3 | | 3 | | 3 | 124 |
| | | 9.68 | 7.26 | 2.42 | 2.42 | 7.26 | 4.84 | 2.42 | 2.42 | 2.42 | 2.42 | 4.84 | 2.42 | 0.00 | 2.42 | 0.00 | 2.42 | 100.0 |

A- Free access to Customers

B- Organisational Policy specifications

C- Need-based Approach

D- Invitation on specific Occasions

E- Face-to-Face Interactions

F- Seminars, Quiz, Road Shows, etc.

G- Always in touch with Customers

H- Arranging Health Camps, Farmers Meet, etc.

I- Arranging Customers Meets

J- Better Complaint handling mechanism

K- Meeting Customers at their door-steps

L- Making Customers aware of Govt. Schemes

M- Monthly meet to boost attitude/ attachment

N- Organise meetings to sell different products

O- Writing letters/Inviting them

P- Across the counter, when customers transact

It is observed from the Table 5.21 (B) that almost all categories of sample bankers have given access to customers as a part of frequent B-C meet. Face-to-face interaction is another strategy adopted by few bankers, more particularly by rural branches and middle-sized banks. No specific pattern is observed between the categories of sample bankers.

**Table 5.22: Implementation of Suggestion**

| | | Yes | % | No | % | Total |
|---|---|---|---|---|---|---|
| Bank | Public | 82 | 69.49 | 36 | 30.51 | 118 |
| | Private | 33 | 84.62 | 6 | 15.38 | 39 |
| Size | Large | 29 | 60.42 | 19 | 39.58 | 48 |
| | Medium | 69 | 76.67 | 21 | 23.33 | 90 |
| | Small | 17 | 89.47 | 2 | 10.53 | 19 |
| Location | Rural | 26 | 78.79 | 7 | 21.21 | 33 |
| | Urban | 89 | 71.77 | 35 | 28.23 | 124 |

When the bankers are contacted to know whether they have implemented any such suggestions given by the customers, most of the sample respondents have given an affirmative reply to it. Further analysis revealed that large sized branches mostly in public sector failed to implement the suggestions given by the customers. The reasons for such trends are quite obvious as the public sector banks operate in a controlled region.

**Adequacy of Products to Meet Customers Needs**

The customers have lot of expectations from their bankers and the banker; try to fulfil customer expectations through product innovations. Table 5.23 describes the adequacy of the products.

It is observed from the Table 5.23 that most of the sample respondents felt that the existing products would satisfy the needs of the customer. Those who are little progressive, they keep on changing/introducing new products. The middle-sized public sector banks operating in rural areas realised that the existing products are insufficient to cover the needs and expectations of the customers. Hence, it is advisable for the banks to keep on innovating new product.

### Table 5.23: Adequacy of the Products

| | | Y | % | N | % | Total |
|---|---|---|---|---|---|---|
| Bank | Public | 94 | 79.66 | 21 | 17.80 | 118 |
| | Private | 36 | 92.31 | 3 | 7.69 | 39 |
| Size | Large | 42 | 87.50 | 6 | 12.50 | 48 |
| | Medium | 69 | 76.67 | 18 | 20.00 | 90 |
| | Small | 19 | 100.00 | 0 | 0.00 | 19 |
| Location | Rural | 27 | 81.82 | 6 | 18.18 | 33 |
| | Urban | 103 | 83.06 | 18 | 14.52 | 124 |
| Total | | 130 | | 24 | | 157 |

### Achievement of Social Objectives

After nationalisation of commercial banks in India; the public sector banks are over-shadowed with social responsibilities. Such as priority sector lending, advances to SC and ST and other weaker sections, etc. The views of the sample bankers on achievements of the social objectives are described in Table 5.24.

The Table 5.24 describes the achievements of sample bankers with regard to achievement of social objectives. The public sector banks of different sizes and different locations have opined that they achieved the social objectives as have been entrusted to them from time to time. In this regard the private banks are lagging behind. Further, factors like developing specialised products for the poor and helping for community service have been identified as most important social objectives attained by the sample respondents.

### Future Strategy for Business Improvement

Every organization, be it large or small, looks for a better future. Accordingly the views of the sample respondents regarding their future strategies for improvement of business are shown in Table 5.25.

Table 5.24: Achievement of Social Objectives

(Figures are in percentage to total)

| | Type of Bank | | Size of Bank | | | Location of Branch | |
|---|---|---|---|---|---|---|---|
| | Public | Private | Large | Medium | Small | Rural | Urban |
| A | 17.80 | 7.69 | 12.50 | 16.67 | 15.79 | 18.18 | 14.52 |
| B | 20.34 | 0.00 | 16.67 | 16.67 | 5.26 | 18.18 | 14.52 |
| C | 7.63 | 7.69 | 10.42 | 0.00 | 63.16 | 27.27 | 0.00 |
| D | 0.00 | 7.69 | 0.00 | 3.33 | 0.00 | 0.00 | 2.42 |
| E | 5.08 | 0.00 | 6.25 | 3.33 | 0.00 | 0.00 | 4.84 |
| F | 0.00 | 7.69 | 0.00 | 3.33 | 0.00 | 18.18 | 0.00 |
| G | 2.54 | 0.00 | 0.00 | 3.33 | 0.00 | 0.00 | 2.42 |
| H | 2.54 | 0.00 | 4.17 | 0.00 | 5.26 | 0.00 | 0.00 |
| I | 4.24 | 0.00 | 8.33 | 0.00 | 5.26 | 0.00 | 0.81 |
| J | 4.24 | 0.00 | 8.33 | 0.00 | 5.26 | 0.00 | 0.81 |
| Total | 118 | 39 | 48 | 90 | 19 | 33 | 124 |

A- Development of Product for downtrodden class
B- Community Service/Social/Cultural obligation
C- Concern for Poor and Needy People
D- SME funding
E- Development of awareness in weaker section/non-customers
F- Do things Better, Faster and Cheaper
G- Lower Interest on Advances for Weaker section
H- Assisting for self-employment
I- Small min. balance, poor can afford to open A/c
J- Service charges are less
K- Implementation of priority sector programmes of GOI for weaker section/rural areas

Table 5.25: Suggestion for Business Improvement

| | Type of Bank | | Size of Bank | | | Location of Branch | |
|---|---|---|---|---|---|---|---|
| | Public | Private | Large | Medium | Small | Rural | Urban |
| A | 5.08 | 0.00 | 12.50 | 0.00 | 0.00 | 0.00 | 4.84 |
| B | 7.63 | 0.00 | 6.25 | 3.33 | 15.79 | 9.09 | 4.84 |
| C | 2.54 | 0.00 | 6.25 | 0.00 | 0.00 | 0.00 | 2.42 |
| D | 16.10 | 0.00 | 10.42 | 13.33 | 10.53 | 24.24 | 8.87 |
| E | 0.00 | 0.00 | 0.00 | 0.00 | 0.00 | 0.00 | 0.00 |
| F | 10.17 | 15.38 | 12.50 | 13.33 | 0.00 | 0.00 | 14.52 |
| G | 0.00 | 7.69 | 0.00 | 3.33 | 0.00 | 0.00 | 2.42 |
| H | 7.63 | 0.00 | 12.50 | 3.33 | 0.00 | 9.09 | 4.84 |
| I | 2.54 | 7.69 | 0.00 | 3.33 | 15.79 | 0.00 | 2.42 |
| J | 2.54 | 7.69 | 6.25 | 3.33 | 0.00 | 0.00 | 2.42 |
| K | 2.54 | 0.00 | 6.25 | 0.00 | 0.00 | 0.00 | 2.42 |
| L | 2.54 | 0.00 | 4.17 | 0.00 | 5.26 | 0.00 | 2.42 |
| M | 2.54 | 0.00 | 0.00 | 3.33 | 0.00 | 9.09 | 0.00 |

*(Contd...)*

| | Type of bank | | Size of Bank | | | Location of Branch | |
|---|---|---|---|---|---|---|---|
| | Public | Private | Large | Medium | Small | Rural | Urban |
| N | 2.54 | 0.00 | 0.00 | 3.33 | 0.00 | 9.09 | 0.00 |
| O | 2.54 | 0.00 | 0.00 | 6.67 | 0.00 | 18.18 | 0.00 |
| P | 2.54 | 0.00 | 0.00 | 3.33 | 0.00 | 9.09 | 0.00 |
| Q | 2.54 | 0.00 | 6.25 | 0.00 | 0.00 | 0.00 | 2.42 |
| R | 2.54 | 0.00 | 6.25 | 0.00 | 0.00 | 0.00 | 2.42 |
| S | 0.00 | 0.00 | 0.00 | 0.00 | 0.00 | 0.00 | 0.00 |
| T | 2.54 | 0.00 | 4.17 | 0.00 | 5.26 | 3.03 | 1.61 |
| U | 2.54 | 0.00 | 0.00 | 3.33 | 0.00 | 9.09 | 0.00 |
| V | 2.54 | 0.00 | 6.25 | 0.00 | 0.00 | 0.00 | 2.42 |
| Total | 118 | 39 | 48 | 90 | 19 | 33 | 124 |

A- Going out in search of a new business
B- Create better amenities to reaching people
C- Quicker disposal
D- Large network of ATMs
E- Modernisation
F- Create Relationship
G- Putting Cheque Drop-boxes
H- Advanced Technology, like BPR
I- Making people aware about the Bank
J- Introduction of New Products
K- New range of Services
L- Interactive Marketing
M- Training to Staff on new products
N- Good Staff Relationship
O- Willing and Cooperative Staff
P- More staff appointments
Q- Good Service Facilities
R- Good Organisational Environment
S- Accountability and Target setting
T- Suitable relocation of the Branch
U- Receive Customers with Smile
V- Staff review by Customers

It is evident from Table 5.25 below that the respondents have attributed as many as twenty-two strategies for improvement in business. The public sector banks have largely focus on large network of ATMs and branches to capture more business, followed by better B-C relationship and technological advancement (like introduction of BPR) for faster and appropriate transactions. Similarly, the private banks mostly focus on banker-customer (B-C) relationship, introduction of cheaper and new variety of products, and more promotion is required. The large banks focus more on use of advanced technology, B-C relationship and searching for new business. Similarly, the bankers of all categories focus on large net-work of ATMs/branches to expand business, other than the private banks. B-C relationship is highlighted by all categories of respondents except the small-rural branches. This particular trend indicates that hey might have reached the saturation point in these factors.

## CUSTOMER SATISFACTION

Quality has been recognized as a strategic tool for attaining operational efficiency and improved business performance, and is one of the most important parameter of customer satisfaction (Anderson and Zeithaml, 1984; Babakus and Boller, 1992; Garvin, 1983 etc.). Several authors have discussed the unique importance of quality of service firms (Norman, 1984; Shaw, 1978 etc.) and have demonstrated its positive relationship with customer satisfaction and repeat purchases (Anderson et al, 1994; Boulding et al, 1993; Rust and Oliver, 1994 etc.). One of the obvious conclusions is that firms with superior quality products outperform these marketing inferior quality products (Jain and Gupta, 2004).

Customer satisfaction is a complicated mix of *'hard wares'* (technology, product, price, quality, etc.) and *'soft wares'* (attitude, responsiveness, deliverance, communication, etc.). On one hand, it is a curious mix of facts, and on the other, the perception of customers (Ravichandran and Thyagarajan, 1998). Thus, customer satisfaction means not only giving the customer a good product, but also ensuring customers feel that he can get a genuine product. Therefore, customer satisfaction is a guide; and product and technology are the focus to achieve business objectives. As the customer expectations keep on changing with changing environment, customer satisfaction becomes a dynamic issue and a determined effort is to be continuously made to accesses it (Ravichandran et al, 1998). In a competitive environment, identification of customer needs these are not being addressed properly, will give a wide scope for development. In recent years, consumer satisfaction/dissatisfaction (CS/D) has begun to emerge as a major topic in the field of consumer research (Keith Hunt, 1977).

In a rapidly expanding competitive environment, banks are no longer confined to their traditional activities, but are venturing into unknown financial territories (Mishra and Sarangi, 2000). The fierce competition has compelled all the banks to analyse themselves and to devise suitable strategies based on the concept of customer satisfaction – providing the customer with what he wants, when he wants, and where he wants (Lewis and Smith, 1989; Aurora and Malhotra, 1997; Mishra and Sarangi, 2000). The level of customer satisfaction has becoming one of the major targets in the hands of bankers to increase their future business.

The perception of bankers (the service providers) regarding the reasons of customer satisfaction/dissatisfaction (CS/D) measured with 20 variables have been presented in Tables 5.26, 5.27. These variables have derived from earlier studies done by Parasuraman et al (1989), Lewis and Smith (1989), Kaplan and Sagare (1995), Gaviri and Asthana (1997), etc.

Table 5.26 depicts the banker's perception about customer satisfaction/dissatisfaction measured in a 5-point Likert scale for 20 items. Since the mid-point in the scale is 3, 3-5 is considered as **satisfaction**, while **1-3 as dissatisfaction**. The major reasons for dissatisfaction with public sector banks is the rigid policy, while for the private banks it is mostly service related factors like service charges, interest rates on loans and term deposit and matching to customer's attitude are important. Again factors like Attitude of Staff, Speed of Transactions, Decor of the Bank, Physical Facilities, Computerization and Introduction of new and innovative products; the Private Banks are far ahead of their counterparts. But one factor i.e. Knowledge level of Staffs for public sector banks are higher than the private banks. This trend may be evident, as the Private Banks spends heavily on developing infrastructure, but the investment on staff is more in public sector ones, indicated by better knowledge about banking products/services.

Table 5.26: Factors Representing Satisfaction Level

| Sl. No. | Factors | Public | | Private | |
|---|---|---|---|---|---|
| | | Satisfaction | Dissatisfaction | Satisfaction | Dissatisfaction |
| A | Service Charges | 3.36 | | | 2.89 |
| B | Attitude of Staff | 4.50 | | 4.77 | |
| C | Speed of Transactions | 4.46 | | 4.77 | |
| D | Decor of the Bank | 3.94 | | 4.58 | |
| E | Interest rates on Loans | 3.44 | | | 2.47 |
| F | Interest rates on Deposits | 3.70 | | | 2.94 |
| G | Introduction of new products/ services | 4.49 | | 4.72 | |
| H | Levels of Computerization | 3.95 | | 4.88 | |
| I | Physical Facilities | 3.92 | | 4.80 | |
| J | Inside Atmosphere | 3.78 | | 4.24 | |
| K | B-C Relationship | 3.33 | | 3.11 | |
| L | Quality of Service | 3.90 | | 3.41 | |
| M | Customer Feelings | 3.70 | | 3.94 | |
| N | A/c Opening Time | 3.57 | | 3.75 | |
| O | Bank's Publication | 3.60 | | 3.70 | |
| P | Matching to Customer Attitude | 3.50 | | | 2.91 |
| Q | Bank's Policies | | 2.94 | 3.44 | |
| R | Efficiency of Staff | 3.89 | | 4.00 | |
| S | Knowledge Level of Staff | 4.06 | | 3.37 | |
| T | Communication with Customers | 3.46 | | 3.23 | |

Table 5.27: Total Variance Explained (Rotation Sums of Squared Loadings)

| Components | Public | | | Private | | | Overall | | |
|---|---|---|---|---|---|---|---|---|---|
| | Total | % of Variance | Cumulative % | Total | % of Variance | Cumulative % | Total | % of Variance | Cumulative % |
| 1. | 5.060 | 25.300 | 25.300 | 8.964 | 44.821 | 44.821 | 4.422 | 22.110 | 22.110 |
| 2. | 3.965 | 19.823 | 45.123 | 3.978 | 19.888 | 64.709 | 3.749 | 18.745 | 40.855 |
| 3. | 3.121 | 15.603 | 60.726 | 3.222 | 16.612 | 81.322 | 3.481 | 17.405 | 58.260 |
| 4. | 2.170 | 10.852 | 71.578 | 2.364 | 11.821 | 93.143 | 2.918 | 14.588 | 72.848 |
| 5. | 1.338 | 6.690 | 78.268 | 0.855 | 4.273 | 97.416 | 1.385 | 6.927 | 79.775 |

Table 5.27 describes the rotated sum of squared loadings to explain the variances explained by the 5 components, deduced by using PCA method. The original 20 factors were reduced to 5 components. These 5 components explain around 78 per cent changes for public sector banks, which is as high as 97 per cent for private banks and overall 79 per cent. Again, component 1 explains about 45 per cent variance with the private banks. This suggests that where the bank should invest to increase customer satisfaction.

The 20-variables used for factor analysis are presented in Table 5.27 (A1-A3). The varimax rotated factor loadings against the 20 variables measuring customer satisfaction/dissatisfaction level in private and public banks. By using varimax rotation, five factors were found having eigen-value more than 1. In the rotated factor matrix, those variables having the highest loadings (ignoring signs) are grouped under their respective derived factors [Table 5.28]. Thus, the 20 variables (reasons for satisfaction/ dissatisfaction) were then loaded to five factors.

Factor 1 has an eigen value of 5.060 explaining 25.3 per cent variations for public sector banks, which were 8.964 explaining 44.82 per cent for private banks and 4.422 explaining 22.11 per cent variation for the whole sample. Thus, all the eigen values for 5 factors were considered.

After grouping the factors based on their loadings, that naming has been done based on the size of the factors. Table 5.28 depicts the variables under each group. The factors are named as policy factors, physical factors, customer factors, staff factor, service factor and décor factor.

## Table 5.27 (A1)

**Rotated Component Matrix**

| | Component | | | | |
|---|---|---|---|---|---|
| | 1 | 2 | 3 | 4 | 5 |
| A | .602 | -.369 | -.346 | .167 | 9.262E-02 |
| B | -.295 | .852 | -7.267E-03 | -.180 | 3.908E-02 |
| C | -.312 | .196 | .828 | .114 | .112 |
| D | .190 | 3.156E-02 | .871 | -.307 | -.119 |
| E | .766 | -.171 | -.225 | .426 | -.111 |
| F | .636 | -.183 | -.136 | .576 | -.177 |
| G | -.355 | .814 | -5.445E-03 | -.189 | -1.825E-02 |
| H | -.271 | .703 | .514 | -1.642E-02 | .134 |
| I | .356 | .591 | .608 | -.100 | .146 |
| J | 3.403E-02 | -.251 | .814 | -.148 | .347 |
| K | .830 | -.178 | -.398 | -7.799E-02 | -.104 |
| L | 4.183E-02 | -1.419E-02 | -.251 | .771 | -.180 |
| M | -4.722E-02 | .222 | .156 | 3.744E-02 | .895 |
| N | .743 | -3.551E-03 | .253 | .183 | -.181 |
| O | -4.938E-03 | .521 | .258 | .580 | .295 |
| P | .376 | -.344 | -.292 | .682 | .117 |
| Q | .803 | -.168 | .231 | -.298 | .131 |
| R | 6.012E-02 | .729 | -5.788E-02 | -2.057E-02 | .112 |
| S | .159 | -.431 | 9.974E-02 | .736 | .303 |
| T | .678 | 1.930E-02 | .155 | .318 | .214 |

Extraction Method: Principal Component Analysis.

Rotation Method: Varimax with Kaiser Normalization.

## Table 5.27 (A2)

**Rotated Component Matrix**

| | Component | | | | |
|---|---|---|---|---|---|
| | 1 | 2 | 3 | 4 | 5 |
| A | .643 | -.353 | -.275 | 7.498E-02 | -.171 |
| B | -.258 | .871 | -.116 | -6.043E-02 | .111 |
| C | -.241 | .184 | .781 | .289 | .163 |
| D | .252 | -3.368E-03 | .885 | -.167 | -.106 |
| E | .893 | -.108 | -9.028E-02 | 4.945E-02 | .204 |
| F | .817 | -.141 | 7.119E-02 | 2.354E-02 | .282 |
| G | -.322 | .824 | -.109 | -8.706E-02 | 3.592E-02 |
| H | -.277 | .744 | .417 | .176 | 5.789E-02 |
| I | .346 | .657 | .515 | .174 | 7.639E-02 |
| J | 4.220E-02 | -.283 | .798 | .374 | -.106 |
| K | .834 | -.165 | -.385 | -.160 | -9.976E-02 |
| L | 6.153E-02 | 8.630E-02 | -1.841E-02 | 1.641E-02 | .918 |
| M | -8.052E-02 | .220 | 4.592E-02 | .801 | -.133 |
| N | .723 | -1.039E-02 | .349 | -.117 | -2.567E-02 |
| O | -1.708E-02 | .532 | .238 | .593 | .228 |
| P | .465 | -.438 | -.191 | .481 | .382 |
| Q | .845 | -.185 | .127 | 1.398E-02 | -.102 |
| R | 2.541E-02 | .717 | -7.961E-02 | 8.579E-02 | -8.977E-02 |
| S | .242 | -.397 | .298 | .696 | .169 |
| T | .689 | 9.380E-02 | .246 | .287 | 2.101E-02 |

Extraction Method: Principal Component Analysis.

Rotation Method: Varimax with Kaiser Normalization.

## Table 5.27 (A3)

**Rotated Component Matrix**

| | Component | | | | |
|---|---|---|---|---|---|
| | **1** | **2** | **3** | **4** | **5** |
| A | .776 | 6.432E-03 | -.225 | 7.867E-03 | .464 |
| B | -.867 | -.204 | 7.149E-03 | .306 | -.211 |
| C | -.957 | -.210 | .166 | -.100 | 3.991E-02 |
| D | -.557 | -.271 | .772 | -.122 | 6.854E-02 |
| E | .910 | .198 | -.138 | -7.328E-02 | .209 |
| F | .592 | .707 | -.187 | -.183 | .213 |
| G | -.867 | -.204 | 7.149E-03 | .306 | -.211 |
| H | -.957 | -.210 | .166 | -.100 | 3.991E-02 |
| I | .252 | -.164 | .949 | -6.756E-02 | 5.610E-02 |
| J | -.195 | -.889 | .301 | 5.550E-02 | .256 |
| K | .901 | 6.221E-02 | .371 | 3.971E-02 | -.165 |
| L | .525 | .281 | -.693 | -.189 | .345 |
| M | -1.137E-02 | -4.559E-02 | -6.532E-03 | .997 | -1.738E-02 |
| N | .664 | .612 | .341 | -2.406E-02 | .230 |
| O | .127 | .959 | -.179 | -6.003E-02 | .151 |
| P | .628 | .744 | -.212 | 1.816E-02 | 7.583E-02 |
| Q | .555 | -.564 | .506 | -.133 | .192 |
| R | -1.137E-02 | -4.559E-02 | -6.532E-03 | .997 | -1.738E-02 |
| S | .525 | .281 | -.693 | -.189 | .345 |
| T | .957 | .210 | -.166 | .100 | -3.991E-02 |

Extraction Method: Principal Component Analysis.
Rotation Method: Varimax with Kaiser Normalization.

Table 5.28: **Results of Factor Analysis**

| | Factor I | Factor II | Factor III | Factor IV | Factor V |
|---|---|---|---|---|---|
| PUBLIC | <u>Policy Factors</u><br>– Service Charges<br>– Int. rate (loan)<br>– int. rate (deposit)<br>– B-C Relation<br>– A/C opening time<br>– Bank's Policy<br>– Comm. with Customer | <u>Physical and Functional</u><br>– Attitude of Staff<br>– Introduction of new Prod/Service<br>– Levels of Computerization<br>– Physical Facilities<br>– Efficiency of staff | <u>Décor of Bank</u><br>– Speed of Trans.<br>– Décor of Bank<br>– Inside Atmosphere<br>– Knowledge level of Staff | <u>Customer Factors</u><br>– Customer feelings<br>– Bank's Publication<br>– Matching to Customer Attitude | <u>Service Quality</u><br>– Quality of Service |

*(Contd...)*

| | Factor I | Factor II | Factor III | Factor IV | Factor V |
|---|---|---|---|---|---|
| PRIVATE | **Policy Factors**<br>– Service Charges<br>– Attitude of Staff<br>– Speed of Trans.<br>– Int. rate (loan)<br>– Introduction of new Prod/Serv<br>– Levels of Computerization<br>– B-C Relation<br>– A/C opening time<br>– Bank's Policy<br>– Comm. with customer | **Staff Factors**<br>– int. rate (deposit)<br>– Knowledge level of Staff<br>– Bank's Publication<br>– Matching to Customer Attitude | **Physical Factors**<br>– Décor of Bank<br>– Physical Facilities<br>– Quality of Service<br>– Inside Atmosphere | **Customer Factors**<br>– Customer feelings<br>– Efficiency of Staff | |

*(Contd...)*

| | Factor I | Factor II | Factor III | Factor IV | Factor V |
|---|---|---|---|---|---|
| OVERALL | <u>Policy Factors</u><br>– Service Charges<br>– Int. rate (loan)<br>– int. rate (deposit)<br>– B-C Relation<br>– A/C opening time<br>– Bank's Policy<br>– Comm. with Customer | <u>Functional Factors</u><br>– Attitude of Staff<br>– Introduction of new Prod/Serv<br>– Levels of Computerization<br>– Efficiency of Staff | <u>Physical Factors</u><br>– Speed of Trans.<br>– Décor of Bank<br>– Physical Facilities<br>– Inside Atmosphere | <u>Staff Factors</u><br>– Quality of Service<br>– Bank's Publication<br>– Matching of Customer Attitude<br>– Knowledge level of Staff | <u>Customer Factors</u><br>– Customer feelings |

## SUMMARY

Out of the total sample of 157 bankers, 75.16 per cent of the bankers belong to public sector banks and rest 24.84 per cent are from private sector banks including one foreign bank. The higher percentages of respondents are from public sector banks and it is due to the presence of larger number of public sector banks corresponding to private sector banks operating in Orissa.

Good premises and suitable location of the branch are essential for bank branches for smooth operation of banking business. When the private banks are compared with public sector banks, all the private banks have excellent locations from business point of view compared to 35.59 per cent of public banks. Further probing indicates that the public sector banks are forced to open branches in non-banking areas as a policy of the Government. They have to improve a lot by relocating the premises to match with private banks. Similarly, customer quality in private banks is better and the public banks should focus on high value customers for better business and higher profitability. Now the banks are severely exposed to competition, which has adversely affected the business of the commercial banks.

The major competitors for public sector banks are the private banks (62.24%) as perceived by the sample respondents. Similarly, the private banks also feel other private banks as their major competitors. The public sector banks feel other Banks and Financial Institutions as next important group of competitors. The private banks are competitor to urban branches of all size, while the rural banks feel other public sector banks as their competitors. Majority of the public sector banks describe the levels of competition is moderate (66.10%), while 61.54 per cent of the private banks label it as fierce. The loss of business is lowest among the private banks (15.38%) and highest among the large public sector banks (29.17%). According to the sample respondents, the major threat to their banks are from the new private banks with better ambiences, improved facilities and service quality, who can attract customers better. The sample bankers have adopted many strategies to attract new business. The private banks thrust upon improving product range (23.08%). Both the private and public sector banks suggest advertising for attracting new business.

The roles of the front office people are quite important in attracting and retaining the customers as reported by the respondents of private banks and large-sized public sector banks. Face-to-face interaction is another strategy adopted by few bankers, more particularly by rural branches and middle-sized banks. After nationalisation of commercial banks in India, the public sector banks are over burdened with social responsibilities. The achievement of targets by the private bankers is 100 per cent, which is about 86 per cent in case public sector banks.

Getting high-value customers or more business from the existing customers is being adapted as the major strategies by the public sector banks, which is not true in case of private sector banks. Again, small banks focus on more business from the existing customers (78.95%), which indicates their personal rapport with the customers. For providing better service to customers proper training should be given to the staff by the banks. Again competition has brought lot of new opportunities for the customers of banking sector. The rate of vanishing customers is higher in case of urban large-sized public sector banks (22.9%). The more attractive private banks are able to attract new customers.

The results of factor analysis indicate that rotated factor loadings are used for the 20 variables to measure customer satisfaction/dissatisfaction level in private and public banks. Factor 1 has an eigen-value of 5.060 explaining 25.3 per cent variations for public sector banks, which were 8.964 explaining 44.82 per cent for private banks and 4.422 explaining 22.11 per cent variation for the whole sample. After grouping the factors based on their loadings, that naming has been done based on the size of the factors. The factors are named as policy factors, physical factors, customer factors, staff factor, service factor and décor factor.

## REFERENCES

Anderson, E W., Fornell, C and Lehman, D R (1994); "Customer Satisfaction, Market Share and Profitability: Findings from Sweden," *Journal of Marketing*, 58(3), 53-66.

Anderson, C and Zeithaml, C.P. (1984); "Stage of The Product Life Cycle, Business Strategy and Business Performance", *Academy of Management Journal*, Vol. 27, March, pp. 5-24.

Aurora, S. and Malhotra, M. (1997); "Customer Satisfaction: A Comparative Analysis of Public and Private sector Banks", *Decision*, 24(1-4), (January-December); pp. 109-130.

Babakus, E and Boller, G.W. (1992); "An Empirical Assessment of the Servqual Scale," *Journal of Business Research*, 24(3), 253-68.

Bhatt, A. (1990); *Study of Marketing Research in Banking*, NIBM Pune, p. 5

Boulding, W; Kalra, A, Staelin, R and Zeithaml, V.A. (1993); "A Dynamic Process Model of Service Quality: From Expectations to Behavioural Intentions," *Journal of Marketing Research*, 30 (February), 7-27.

Brown, S.W. and Swartz, T.A. (1989); "A Gap Analysis of Professional Service Quality," *Journal of Marketing*, 53 (April), 92-98.

Dabholkar, P.A., Shepherd, D.C. and Thorpe, D.I (2000); "A Comprehensive Framework for Service Quality: An Investigation of Critical, Conceptual and Measurement Issues through a Longitudinal Study," *Journal of Retailing*, 76(2), 139-173.

Garvin, D.A., (1983); "Quality on the Line," *Harvard Business Review*, 61 (Sept.-October), 65-73.

Gotlieb, J.B., Grewal, D and Brown, S.W. (1994); "Consumer Satisfaction and Perceived Quality: Complementary or Divergent Constructs," *Journal of Applied Psychology*, 79(6), 875-85.

Hunt, K. (ed), (1977); *Conceptualisation and Measurement of Consumer Satisfaction and dissatisfaction*, Marketing Science Institute, Cambridge.

Jain, S.K. and Gupta, G. (2004); "Measuring Service Quality: SERVQUAL vs. SERVPERF Scales" , *VIKALPA*, Vol. 29, No. 2 , April-June, pp. 25-37.

Lewis, B. (1991); "Service Quality: An International Comparison of Bank Customer's Expectations and Perceptions," *Journal of Marketing Management*, 7(1), 47-62.

Mishra, B.B. and Sarangi, M.K. (2000); "Customer needs and Satisfaction: A Comparative Analysis of Public and Private sector Banks in Orissa", *Advantage South Asia*; published by AMDISA, Hyderabad; pp. 386-394.

Norman, R. (1984); *Service Management*. Wiley, New York.

Parasuraman, A., Zeithaml, V.A. and Berry, L.L. (1994); "Reassessment of Expectations As a Comparison Standard in Measuring Service Quality: Implications for Further Research," *Journal of Marketing*, 58 (January), 111-124.

Ravichandran, M. and Thyagarajan, V. (1998); "Consumer Satisfaction-Determinants and Measurement", *The Journal of NMIMS*, (July-December); pp. 42-55.

Rust, R.T. and Oliver, R.L. (1994); *Service Quality-New Directions in Theory and Practice*, Sage Publications, New York.

Shaw, J. (1978); *The Quality-Productivity Connection*, Van Nostrand, New York.

Zeithaml, V.A. and Bitner, Mary Jo (2003); *Services Marketing: Integrating Customer Focus Across the Firms*, 3rd Edition, Tata MçGraw-Hill, New Delhi.

# CHAPTER–6

# MEASURING CUSTOMER SATISFACTION

## INTRODUCTION

Service quality is about meeting customer needs satisfactorily by matching to his expectations. Service quality in banking implies consistently anticipating and satisfying the needs and expectations of customers (Howcrof, 1991). The importance of service quality in Banks has been emphasised in many studies and perceived quality advantage leads them to higher profit (Raddon, 1987; Buzzell and Gale 1987). Parasuraman and Berry (1991) holds the view that high quality service gives credibility to field sales force. Heskett et al. (1990) observed that the longer a company keeps a customer, the more money it stands to make. There is enough evidence that demonstrates the strategic benefits of quality in contributing to profit, market share and returns on investment (Adrian, 1995; Bateson, 1995; Berry et al 1991, Buzzel et al 1981, etc.) and lowering cost and improving productivity (Garvin, 1983; Kotler, 2003; etc.). Maximising customer satisfaction through quality customer service has been described as the 'ultimate weapon' (Davidow and Uttal, 1989).

Quality has come to be recognized as a strategic tool for attaining operational efficiency and improved business performance. This is true for both the goods and services sectors. However, the problem with management of service quality is that it is not easily identifiable and measurable due to inherent characteristics of services which make them different from goods. Notwithstanding the importance of service quality, there have been methodological issues and application problems with regard to its operation. Quality in the context of service industries has been conceptualized differently.

The banking industry as a service industry, directed towards the customer's money and its management. A membership relationship is entailed in this industry due to its continuous nature. Banking is also high in credence quality, meaning that it cannot be evaluated confidently even immediately after receipt of the goods/services. In addition, an extended period of time may be required in this industry for a fully informed evaluation (Devlin, 2001). Hence, customer satisfaction in banking is both difficult to measure and ascertain.

Today, the banking industry has become highly competitive in India. It is not only focusing on providing wide range of products to create competitive advantages; but also emphasises on the importance of services, particularly in maintaining service quality (Sousa, 1999). Using the service quality model (SERVQUAL of Zeithaml et al, 1988), a comparative study of customers of private and public sector banks operating in Orissa is undertaken to identify the differences between the banking attitudes of the respondents toward the service quality management in banks. Further, the study also attempts to identify the customers' expectations of banking services and their respective performances.

In the light of the above research findings, interest in service quality is, thus, unarguably high. Poor quality places a firm at a competitive disadvantage. If customers perceive quality as unsatisfactory, they may be quick to take their businesses elsewhere. Thus, it is clear that service quality offers a way of achieving success among competing services, particularly in the case of firms that offer nearly identical services, such as banks, where establishing service quality may be the only way of differentiating oneself. Such differentiation can yield a higher proportion of consumers' choices and, hence, mean the difference between financial success and failure.

## SERVICE QUALITY: CONCEPTUALIZATION AND OPERATIONALIZATION

Although researchers have studied the concept of service for decades, there is no conceptualisation of service quality (Cronin and Taylor, 1992; Rust and Oliver, 1994). Different researchers focused on different aspects of service quality. The most common definition views quality as the customers' perception of service excellence (Berry et al. 1988; and Parasuraman et al. 1985). The underlying meaning of this definition is that customers form the perception of service quality according to the service performance they experience in the past. Therefore, the service quality is dependent on customer's perceptions of the service.

### Service Quality: The Key Aspect in Satisfying Customers' Needs

Delivering superior service quality appears to be a prerequisite for success of any service firms (Parasuraman et al 1988). As electronic banking becomes more prevalent, nowadays customers are evaluating banks based more on their "high-touch" factors than on their "high-tech" factors in most of the developing economy like India (Angur M.G. et al, 1999). The unique selling proposition (USP) defined by Kotler (1997) of a bank still appears to be personal banking services. Angur M.G. et al, (1999) conducted an empirical study to examine the performance of alternative measures of service quality proposed by Cronin and Taylor (1992), in India and suggested that the service quality concept is not uni-dimensional, rather it appeared to be multidimensional.

In a nutshell, customer perceived service quality is based on five factors, viz. core service/service content, human element of service delivery, non-human element of service delivery (or, systematization), tangibles of service (service spaces), and social responsibility (Sureshchandar et al, 2002). All of these five factors have shown strong evidence of unidimensionality, reliability, convergent, discriminant and criterion-related validities in the study conducted by Sureshchandar et al. The researchers suggested an instrument known as Service Quality Index (SQI) to be used for the measurement of customer perceived service quality levels. Managers of various banks can keep this instrument as a yardstick, on which improvement efforts can be focused.

The quality perceived in a service is a function of the gap between customer's desires or expectations and the perceptions about the service that is actually received (Parasuraman et al, 1985). Gani et al (2003) in their study of Indian banks gave the idea that the service quality of foreign banks figures high comparatively that of Indian banks. To get a high rate in service quality, most of the Indian banks should improve upon service areas. Each bank has to match the expected service and the perceived service to each other so that customer satisfaction is achieved. The promises about the service must not be unrealistic when compared to the customers' perceived service.

Customers generally perceive a difference in the aspects of service quality which are influenced by employee actions. The frontline employee's perceptions of service climate are linked to the customers' perceptions of service quality (Shainesh G. et al, 2003). They defined service climate as the perceptions of employees about the organizational policies and procedures which facilitate a climate that expects and rewards customer service. Again it showed that there exists a little difference in customers' perceptions of service quality across different bank types. But the correlation analysis strongly supports the fact that employee's perception about service climate is related to the customers' perceptions of service quality. The researchers concluded by giving the idea that, private banks have adapted the best practices and used technology to chart their growth.

The internal perspective of service quality measurement is defined as zero defect-doing it right the first time; where as external perspective gives the aspect in terms of customer perception, expectation, satisfaction, attitude and delight (Sachdev S.B. et al, 2004). The researchers found that in case of banking sector, the perceived performance is below "would be" level of performance in respect of reliability, responsiveness, assurance and empathy dimensions of service quality. Banks seem to have performed better in case of tangibility dimension.

Krishnaveni R. and Divya Prabha D. (2004) conducted a survey among corporate customers of banks to know the perceptions of clients about banks' service quality. The six dimensions of the service quality taken for the study are, competence, convenience, customer-orientedness, promptness of service, modernization, and communication. The results revealed that the service qualities still have to be improved and customers expect more monetary concessions in service charges. Customers would feel happier if any improvement in the service is made.

**Assessing Customer Satisfaction: A must for Bankers**

Just as people cannot live without eating, companies can't survive without having satisfied customers (Gould G. 1995). He made a distinction between "making more customers satisfied" and "making specific groups of customers more satisfied". He put more emphasis on the fact that some of the customers can be made much more than just satisfied. Service providers should exceed customers' expectations by considering three selective dimensions, viz. value, service, and dealing with complaints.

Hallowell Roger (1996) measured customer satisfaction through two key elements, one is service and the other one is related to price. The regression results support the inference of a customer satisfaction and the loyalty relationship. However, this is ambiguous regarding the role of price satisfaction in predicting customer loyalty. Again the results indicated that it is wise for any bank to target and serve only those customers whose needs it can meet better than its competitors in a profitable manner. These types of customers will remain for longer periods, consume multiple products; recommend the bank to their friends and relations who may be the source of superior returns to the bank's shareholders.

Aurora and Malhotra (1997) tried to give some idea about factors determining customer satisfaction, the level of customer satisfaction and some marketing strategies in both private and public sector banks in India. They have found six factors of customer satisfaction in public sector banks, viz., routine operations, price, situational, environmental, technology, and interactive. But in private sector banks, there exists seven factors in total, having staff factor as the first ranked and situational factor as the lowest ranked items. Instead of price factor, promotional factor has been explored by researchers in private sector banks.

As compared to public sector, private sector bank customers' level of satisfaction is comparatively more. Proper training and development of bank staff, regular market survey, personalizing the service, efforts to avoid long queues in bank, and attractive environment are key suggested strategies in public sector bank.

A financial firm needs to focus on satisfaction with its offered product line in order to reap maximum gains in overall satisfaction (Krishnan et al, 1999). In order to improve overall customer satisfaction, the bank should prioritise the allocation of resources to increase the perceived quality of their product offerings. The researchers identified four quality attributes as being critical to determining satisfaction with product offerings, viz. product variety which creates customers to consolidate services in one place, ease of opening and closing of accounts, competitive interest rates and fees, and lucid information on all products and services. The research also suggested that the satisfaction with the quality of automated telephone and branch services and financial reporting have a significant impact on overall satisfaction, mainly for different customer segments.

The operationalization of customer satisfaction in banking sector is somewhat hazy, and it should be operationalized along the same dimensions that constitute service quality (Sureshchandar et al, 2002). Studies are conducted by taking two types of hypotheses, one is about the existence of distinctiveness of service quality and customer satisfaction with respect to all the dimensions and the other one is concerned with the correlation between these two. The results showed that these two are different constructs which can be distinguishable from the customers' point of view. It also showed a high correlation between these two constructs. In this context, the service providers should try to continuously improve both service quality and customer satisfaction to be remained in intense competition.

According to Liang et al (2004), the service quality attributes are of two types; one is product related, and the other one non-product related. These two types of attributes may create the perception of functional benefits, symbolic benefits or experiential benefits among customers. The empirical research shows that there is no positive association between experiential benefits and customer satisfaction. But, the results strongly highlighted the fact that customer satisfaction positively affects customers' trust and commitment on service provider, which in turn affects customers' behavioural loyalty. There are many controllable variables can be considered to know other variables' effect on customer satisfaction and repurchase intentions.

In the most of the regional rural banks, customer satisfaction refers to the customer judgment on marketing inclined aspects of bank products and/or services in rural settings by comparing pre-purchase expectations with accumulated experience with the banks having maximum transactions (Sharma et al, 2004). The customers having low income residing in rural areas are showing "just satisfactory" attitude towards all the rural banking services, where as those having higher income show "above average". In both of the cases the level of satisfaction goes in descending order concerning to 4Ps' of marketing mix, viz. product, place, price and promotion respectively. The study suggests 5 steps of strategic action for rural banks, namely identification, measurement, creation, maintenance, and monitoring customer satisfaction by keeping higher level of rating in measurement scale.

## SERVQUAL SCALE

Though initial efforts in defining and measuring service quality emanated largely from the goods sector, a solid foundation for research work in the area was laid down in the mid-eighties by Parasuraman, Zeithaml and Berry (1985). They were amongst the earliest researchers to emphatically point out that the concept of quality prevalent in the goods sector is not extendable to the services sector. Being inherently and essentially intangible, heterogeneous, perishable, and entailing simultaneity and inseparability of production and consumption, services require a distinct framework for quality explication and measurement. As against the goods sector where tangible cues exist to enable consumers to evaluate product quality, quality in the service context is explicated in terms of parameters that largely come under the domain of 'experience' and 'credence' properties and are as such difficult to measure and evaluate (Parasuraman et al 1985; Zeithaml and Bitner, 2003).

One major contribution of Parasuraman et al (1988) was to provide a terse definition of service quality. They defined service quality as 'a global judgment, or attitude, relating to the superiority of the service', and explicated it as involving evaluations of the outcome (i.e., what the customer actually receives from service) and process of service act (i.e., the manner in which service is delivered). In line with the propositions put forward by Gronroos (1982) and Smith and Houston (1982), Parasuraman, Zeithaml and Berry (1985, 1988) posited and operationalized service quality as a difference between consumer expectations of 'what they want' and their perceptions of 'what they get.' Based on this conceptualization and operationalization, they proposed a service quality measurement scale called 'SERVQUAL'. The scale constitutes an important landmark in the service quality literature and has been extensively applied in different service settings. Over a period of time, a few variants of the scale have also been proposed. The 'SERVPERF' scale is one such scale that has been put forward by Cronin and Taylor (1992) in the early nineties. Numerous studies have been undertaken to assess the superiority of two scales, but consensus continues to elude as to which one is a better scale.

The construct of quality measured by SERVQUAL scale involves service quality (as opposed to object quality). Perceived quality is the consumer's judgement of overall excellence or superiority an entity, similar to an overall attitude. Perceived quality is defined as the degree and direction of discrepancy between a consumer's perceptions and expectations (Parasuraman, et al, 1988). Quality is distinguished from satisfaction in that the latter is assumed to involve specific transactions, while expectations are viewed as desire or wants of consumers (not predicted of what will be provided).

The foundation for the SERVQUAL scale is the gap model proposed by Parasuraman, Zeithaml and Berry (1985, 1988). With roots in disconfirmation paradigm, the gap model maintains that satisfaction is related to the size and direction of disconfirmation of a person's experience vis-à-vis his/her initial expectations (Churchill and Surprenant, 1982; Parasuraman, Zeithaml and Berry, 1985; Smith and Houston, 1982). As a gap or difference between customer 'expectations' and 'perceptions,' service quality is viewed as lying along a continuum ranging from 'ideal quality' to 'totally unacceptable quality,' with some points along the continuum representing satisfactory quality. Parasuraman, Zeithaml and Berry (1988) held that when perceived or experienced service is less than expected service, it implies less than satisfactory service quality. But, when perceived service is less than expected service, the obvious inference is that service quality is more than satisfactory. Parasuraman, Zeithaml and Berry (1988) posited that while a negative discrepancy between perceptions and expectations — a 'performance-gap' as they call it — causes dissatisfaction, a positive discrepancy leads to consumer delight.

As the understanding of service quality has emerged, esearchers have developed conceptualizations of the dimensions of service quality. In this direction, much of the programme esearch work in the management domain of services is the onceptual model of 'SERVQUAL' presented by Parasuraman, et l (1985: 1988). They had originally identified ten determinants of ervice quality generic to the service industry. These determinants were Tangibles, Reliability, Responsiveness, Competence, Courtesy, Credibility, Security, Access, Communication, and Understanding the customer. Subsequent research, analysis and esting by Parasuraman et al. (1988) have condensed these into five dimensions of service quality namely: Tangibility, Reliability, Responsiveness, Assurance and Empathy.

The innovators, Parasuraman, Zeithaml and Berry have further developed promulgated and promoted SERVQUAL through a series of publications (Parasuraman et al, 1985, 1988, 1990, 1991, 1994, Parasuraman, 1997; Zeithaml el al,1990, 1993, 1996, Berry and Parasuraman, 1997). Limitations with SERVQUAL are highlighted by the authors themselves (Parasuraman el al, 1991) and in other research studies (Babakhus and Boller 1992; Carman, 1990; Lewis, 1993; Lewis and Mitchell, 1990; Smith, 1992). They relate to respondent's difficulties with negatively worded statements; using two lists of statements for the same items, the number of dimensions of service being assessed; ease of consumer assessment and timing of measurement—before, during or after a service encounter. While there is a healthy and for most part a productive debate regarding the dimensionality of SERVQUAL across industries, and the precise wording of the SERVQUAL items, researchers generally agree that the scale items are good predictors of overall service quality (Babakus and Boller 1992; Bolton and Drew, 1991; Brown and Swartz, 1989; Carman, 1990; Cronin and Taylor, 1992; Parasuraman et al, 1991). The debate underscores the importance of the subject and the significance of the contribution to date. Such interchange will help refine the meaning of service quality.

Based on different conceptualizations, alternative scales have been proposed for service quality measurement (Brady, 2001; Cronin and Brady, 2000; Cronin and Taylor 1992, 1994; Dabholkar et al, 2000; Parasuraman et al, 1985, 1988). Various definitions of the term 'service quality' have been proposed in the past and, based on different definitions; different scales for measuring service quality have been put forward. Despite considerable work undertaken in the area, there is no consensus yet as to which one of the measurement scales is robust enough for measuring and comparing service quality. One major problem with past studies has been their preoccupation with assessing psychometric and methodological soundness of service scales that too in the context of service industries in the developed countries (Jain and Gupta 2004). Virtually no empirical efforts have been made to evaluate the diagnostic ability of the scales in providing managerial insights for corrective actions in the event of quality shortfalls. Furthermore, little work has been done to examine the applicability of these scales to the service industries in developing countries.

Several issues have been raised with regard to use of (P-E) gap scores, i.e., disconfirmation model. Most studies have found a poor fit between service quality as measured through Parasuraman, Zeithaml and Berry's (1988) scale and the overall service quality measured directly through a single-item scale (e.g., Babakus and Boller, 1992; Babakus and Mangold, 1989; Carman, 1990; Finn and Lamb, 1991; Spreng and Singh, 1993). Though the use of gap scores intuitively appealing and conceptually sensible, the ability of these scores to provide additional information beyond that already contained in the perception component of service quality scale is under doubt (Babakus and Boller, 1992; Iacobucci,

Grayson and Ostrom, 1994). Pointing to conceptual, theoretical, and measurement problems associated with the disconfirmation model, Teas (1993, 1994) observed that a (P-E) gap of magnitude '-1' can be produced in six ways: P=1, E=2; P=2, E=3; P=3, E=4; P=4, E=5; P=5, E=6 and P=6, E=7 and these tied gaps cannot be construed as implying equal perceived service quality shortfalls. In a similar vein, the empirical study by Peter, Churchill and Brown (1993) found difference scores being beset with psychometric problems and, therefore, cautioned against the use of (P-E) scores.

Validity of (P-E) measurement framework has also come under attack due to problems with the conceptualization and measurement of expectation component of the SERVQUAL scale, while perception (P) is definable and measurable in a straight forward manner. It is because of the vagueness of the expectation concept, some researchers manner as the consumer's belief about service is experienced, expectation (E) is subject to multiple interpretations and as such has been operationalized differently by different authors/researchers (e.g., Jain and Gupta, 2004; Babakus and Inhofe, 1991; Brown and Swartz, 1989; Dabholkar et al, 2000; Gronroos, 1990; Teas, 1993, 1994). Initially, Parasuraman, Zeithaml and Berry (1985, 1988) defined expectation close in the lines of Miller (1977) as 'desires or wants of consumers,' i.e., what they feel a service provider should offer rather than would offer. This conceptualization was based on the reasoning that the term 'expectation' has been used differently in service quality literature than in the customer satisfaction literature where it is defined as a prediction of future events, i.e., what customers feel a service provider would offer. Parasuraman, Berry and Zeithaml (1990) labelled this 'should be' expectation as 'normative expectation,' and posited it as being similar to 'ideal expectation' (Zeithaml and Parasuraman, 1991). Later, realizing the problem with this interpretation, they themselves proposed a revised expectation (E) measure, i.e., what the customer would expect from 'excellent' service (Parasuraman, Zeithaml and Berry, 1994); like Babakus and Boiler (1992), Bolton and Drew (1991a), Brown, Churchill and Peter (1993), and Carman (1990) stressed the need for developing a methodologically more precise scale. The SERVPERF scale — developed by Cronin and Taylor (1992) — is one of the important variants of the SERVQUAL scale. For, being based on the perception component alone, it has been conceptually and methodologically posited as a better scale than the SERVQUAL scale which has its origin in disconfirmation paradigm.

**Model Description**

**SERVQUAL MODEL**

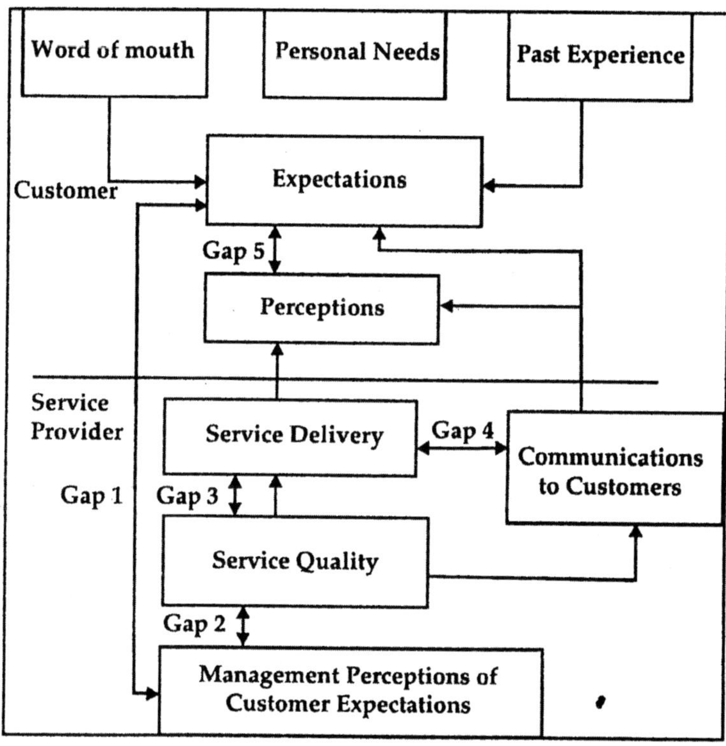


**Fig. 6.1**

The SERVQUAL model has two parts: viz.; customer expectations of the service of service firms before the customer experiences it; and customer perceptions of the service provider after they have received their services. The customer expectations are built by the consumers' personal needs, their past experience and are affected by other consumers' comments — word-of-mouth. Perceptions are created after experiencing the service, however dissatisfaction may occur if expectations are high but the service is not perceived to be the same. Perceptions can be low due to problems created by the service provider when they misinterpret customer expectations; raise customer expectations too high; are unable to control service quality; cause communication breakdowns with customers; and create faults in the service delivery. All these may cause gaps where the service offered does not meet customer expectations. They perceive the service to be poorer than they had expected.

**The Scale Description**

Parasuraman et al (1988) developed a 22-item instrument, called as SERVQUAL for assessing customer perceptions of service quality in service organizations. They gave a distinction between service quality and satisfaction by saying that perceived service quality is a global judgment, or attitude, relating to the superiority of the service, but satisfaction is linked to a specific transaction. Initially, the researchers took ten dimensions of service quality as the input to derive some items for the SERVQUAL scale. The new dimensions of service quality are five in number, viz. tangibles, reliability, responsiveness, assurance and empathy. It has now a variety of applications in banking industry, especially in assessing customer expectations about and perceptions of service quality delivered by different banks. It also helps in identifying the areas of managerial attention for future improvement.

Since they have defined service quality as being a gap between customer's expectations and perceptions of performance on these variables, their service quality measurement scale is comprised of a total of 44 items composed of two matched sets of 22 items (22 for expectations and 22 for perceptions). Customers' responses to their expectations and perceptions are obtained on a 7-point Likert scale and are compared to arrive at (P-E) gap scores. The higher (more positive) the perception minus expectation score, the higher is perceived to be the level of service quality. In an equation form, the measurement of service quality can he expressed as follows:

$SQ_i = P_i - E_i$

Where

$SQ_i$ = perceived service quality of an attribute

$P_i$ = Average perception of individual ' i ' with respect to performance of a service attribute

E = Average expectation of individual ' i ' with respect to performance of a service attribute

A number of other industry specific empirical studies have been conducted using SERVQUAL Model which includes some mostly cited studies carried out in banks are Lewis (1991), Lassar et al (2000), Angur el al (1999) and Blanchard et al (1994). Therefore, SERVQUAL is chosen as an ideal instrument for studying service quality perceptions in banks.

In view of the above-mentioned facts, an analysis of service quality perceptions from providers (banks) and customer's point of view may sound interesting at this juncture. Such an analysis will provide banks a quantitative estimate of their services being perceived with intricate details such as whether banks are meeting, exceeding or are below the perceptions of their respective customers. The present chapter, therefore, attempts to achieve the following objectives:

1. Make a comparative study of service quality perceptions of banks, under study, with service quality perceptions of their respective customers;
2. Know whether the banks are at, above or below the perceptions of their respective customers; and
3. Suggest, on the basis of study results, ways and means for improving service quality in banks with a view to make overall banking service more effective arid efficient.

## RESULTS AND DISCUSSION

In line with the objectives of the study, the main areas of questioning and analysis concerned expectations and perceptions of service quality and its dimensions: tangibility, reliability, responsiveness, assurance and empathy. As already stated, expectations and perceptions were measured on a seven point strongly disagree to strongly agree scale. Mean differences between expectations and perceptions of service quality of banks and their respective customers' were calculated separately for the banks, under study, followed by a t-test to determine the level of significant difference. The results obtained from this computation are presented in Tables 6.1 to 6.7.

## The Service Quality Dimensions

The model suggests five dimensions of service quality. They are tangibility, reliability, responsiveness, assurance and empathy. These dimensions pertaining to different initial variables are presented in Table 6.1.

**Table 6.1: Variables of the SERVQUAL Model**

| Sl. No. | Initial Variables | Service quality dimensions |
|---|---|---|
| 1. | Modern Looking Equipment | Tangibility |
| 2. | Visually Appealing Physical Facilities | |
| 3. | Neat Appearance of Employees | |
| 4. | Visually Appealing Materials | |
| 5. | Keeping Promises | Reliability |
| 6. | Sincere in Solving Customer Problems | |
| 7. | Dependable in Transactions | |
| 8. | Provide Services as Promised | |
| 9. | Keeping Accurate Records | |
| 10. | Inform When Service will be Performed | Responsiveness |
| 11. | Prompt Service from Employees | |
| 12. | Employees' Willingness to Help | |
| 13. | Employees' Response to Requests | |
| 14. | Customers' Confidence on Employees | |
| 15. | Safe Feeling of Customers in Transaction | Assurance |
| 16. | Courteous Employees | |
| 17. | Adequate Support to Employees | |
| 18. | Individual Attention by Bank | Empathy |
| 19. | Personal Attention by Employees | |
| 20. | Understanding Specific Needs of the Customers | |
| 21. | Customers' Best Interests at Heart | |
| 22. | Convenient Operating Hours | |

**Comparison of Sample Means by Type of Banks**

The views of the sample respondents regarding the services offered by the banks under study are presented in Table 6.2.

**Table 6.2: Comparison of Mean and t-Values of Expectations and Performance by Bank Type**

| Component | Public | | | | Private | | | |
|---|---|---|---|---|---|---|---|---|
| | Performance | Expectation | Gap | t Value | Performance | Expectation | Gap | t Value |
| Modern Looking Equipment | 5.182 | 5.595 | -0.413 | -2.447** | 5.274 | 5.568 | -0.295 | -1.188 |
| Visually Appealing Physical Facilities | 5.008 | 4.831 | 0.178 | 1.148 | 4.832 | 4.800 | 0.032 | 0.152 |
| Neat Appearance of Employees | 5.095 | 4.926 | 0.169 | 1.124 | 4.947 | 4.747 | 0.200 | 0.876 |
| Visually Appealing Materials | 5.095 | 4.570 | 0.525 | 4.164* | 4.705 | 4.442 | 0.263 | 1.204 |
| **Tangibility** | **5.095** | **4.980** | **0.115** | **0.995** | **4.939** | **4.889** | **0.050** | **0.282** |
| Keeping Promises | 4.983 | 4.736 | 0.248 | 1.729 | 4.884 | 4.484 | 0.400 | 2.001** |
| Sincere in Solving Customer Problems | 5.087 | 4.364 | 0.723 | 4.763* | 5.137 | 4.232 | 0.905 | 4.115* |
| Dependable | 5.017 | 4.678 | 0.339 | 2.073** | 4.768 | 4.589 | 0.179 | 0.808 |
| Provide Services as Promised | 4.843 | 4.616 | 0.227 | 1.482 | 5.200 | 4.663 | 0.537 | 2.238** |
| Keeping Accurate Records | 5.116 | 5.884 | -0.769 | -5.122* | 5.274 | 5.853 | -0.579 | -2.732* |

*(Contd...)*

| Component | Public | | | | Private | | | |
|---|---|---|---|---|---|---|---|---|
| | Performance | Expectation | Gap | t Value | Performance | Expectation | Gap | t Value |
| **Reliability** | **5.009** | **4.855** | **0.154** | **1.454** | **5.053** | **4.764** | **0.288** | **2.011**** |
| Inform When Service will be Performed | 3.488 | 4.000 | -0.512 | -2.888* | 3.516 | 3.768 | -0.253 | -1.009 |
| Prompt Service from Employees | 3.901 | 4.273 | -0.372 | -2.232** | 3.811 | 4.074 | -0.263 | -1.210 |
| Employees' Willingness to Help | 4.178 | 4.835 | -0.657 | -4.093* | 4.316 | 4.737 | -0.421 | -1.620 |
| Employees' Response to Requests | 4.475 | 4.087 | 0.388 | 2.643* | 4.737 | 4.284 | 0.453 | 2.151** |
| **Responsiveness** | **4.010** | **4.299** | **-0.288** | **2.377**** | **4.095** | **4.216** | **-0.121** | **-0.735** |
| Customers' Confidence on Employees | 4.186 | 4.860 | -0.674 | -4.377* | 4.579 | 4.737 | -0.158 | -0.818 |
| Safe Feeling of Customers in Transaction | 4.388 | 5.545 | -1.157 | -7.708* | 4.800 | 5.453 | -0.653 | -2.922* |
| Courteous Employees | 4.847 | 5.202 | -0.355 | -2.704* | 4.874 | 5.042 | -0.168 | -0.911 |
| Adequate Support to Employees | 5.116 | 5.211 | -0.095 | -0.734 | 4.989 | 5.021 | -0.032 | -0.179 |
| **Assurance** | **4.634** | **5.205** | **-0.570** | **'-5.663*** | **4.811** | **5.063** | **-0.253** | **-2.21**** |
| Individual Attention by Bank | 3.988 | 4.103 | -0.116 | -0.675 | 4.147 | 4.032 | 0.116 | 0.454 |
| Personal Attention by Employees | 4.112 | 4.496 | -0.384 | -2.525** | 3.863 | 4.505 | -0.642 | -2.687* |

*(Contd...)*

| Component | Public | | | | Private | | | |
|---|---|---|---|---|---|---|---|---|
| | Perfor-mance | Expect-ation | Gap | t Value | Perfor-mance | Expect-ation | Gap | t Value |
| Understanding Specific Needs of the Customers | 4.070 | 4.744 | -0.674 | -4.399* | 4.189 | 4.589 | -0.400 | -1.784 |
| Customers' Best Interests at Heart | 3.872 | 4.686 | -0.814 | -5.443* | 3.863 | 4.495 | -0.632 | -2.826* |
| Convenient Operating Hours | 4.851 | 4.616 | 0.236 | 1.591 | 4.800 | 4.716 | 0.084 | 0.397 |
| **Empathy** | **4.179** | **4.529** | **-0.350** | **3.099*** | **4.173** | **4.467** | **-0.295** | **-1.745** |

* 1% Level of Significance.

** 5% Level of Significance.

Referring to Table 6.2; the comparison of customer expectations and perceptions of public banks, it is observed that the sample customers have very similar opinion as indicated from the mean values of different dimensions. The gap (P-E) as shown in Fig. 6.2 and Fig. 6.3, is positive for first two factors (i.e. tangibility and reliability) of public sector bank respondents indicating satisfaction of the customers. In the rest three factors (i.e. responsiveness, assurance and empathy) the gap is negative indicating dissatisfaction of the customers, which are also statistically significant as indicated from the t-values. Further, component-wise analysis indicates that the higher level of dissatisfactions are observed in factors like; (i) keeping accurate and error-free records; (ii) modern looking equipments, (iii) bank informs when the services will be performed, (iv) promptness of employees, (v) willingness of employees to help; in all components of assurance, and empathy except convenient working hours. This indicates the major reasons of dissatisfaction of customers in public banks are staff related. There are only three components where the customer's satisfaction is statistically significant (i.e. visually appealing materials, sincerity in solving customer problems and the bank is dependable.

A comparison between opinion of respondents for perceptions and expectations exhibits that out of the five dimensions of service quality gaps two are positive indicating customers satisfaction and rest three are negative indicating customer dissatisfaction. The levels of satisfaction with private bank are significant for reliability dimension, where as they are dissatisfied with assurance dimension (significant at 5% level). Further component-wise analysis indicates highest level of satisfaction is associated with sincerity in solving customer problems (0.905) while highest level of dissatisfaction with safe feeling of customers in transactions and customer's best interests at heart.

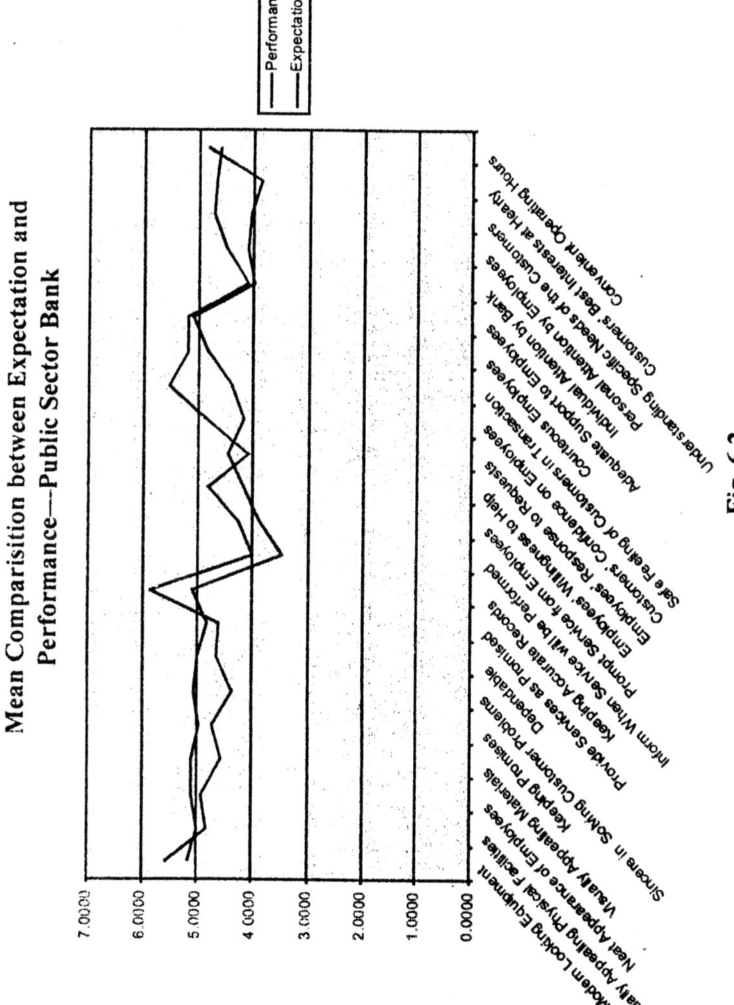
Mean Comparisition between Expectation and Performance—Public Sector Bank
Performance
Expectation
7.0000
6.0000
5.0000
4.0000
3.0000
2.0000
1.0000
0.0000
Modern Looking Equipment
Visually Appealing Physical Facilities
Neat Appearance of Employees
Visually Appealing Materials
Keeping Promises
Sincere in Solving Customer Problems
Dependable
Provide Services as Promised
Keeping Accurate Records
Inform When Service will be Performed
Prompt Service from Employees
Employees' Willingness to Help
Employees' Response to Requests
Customers' Confidence on Employees
Safe Feeling of Customers in Transaction
Courteous Employees
Adequate Support to Employees
Individual Attention by Bank
Personal Attention by Employees
Specific Needs of the Customers
Customers' Best Interests at Heart
Convenient Operating Hours
Understanding

Fig. 6.2

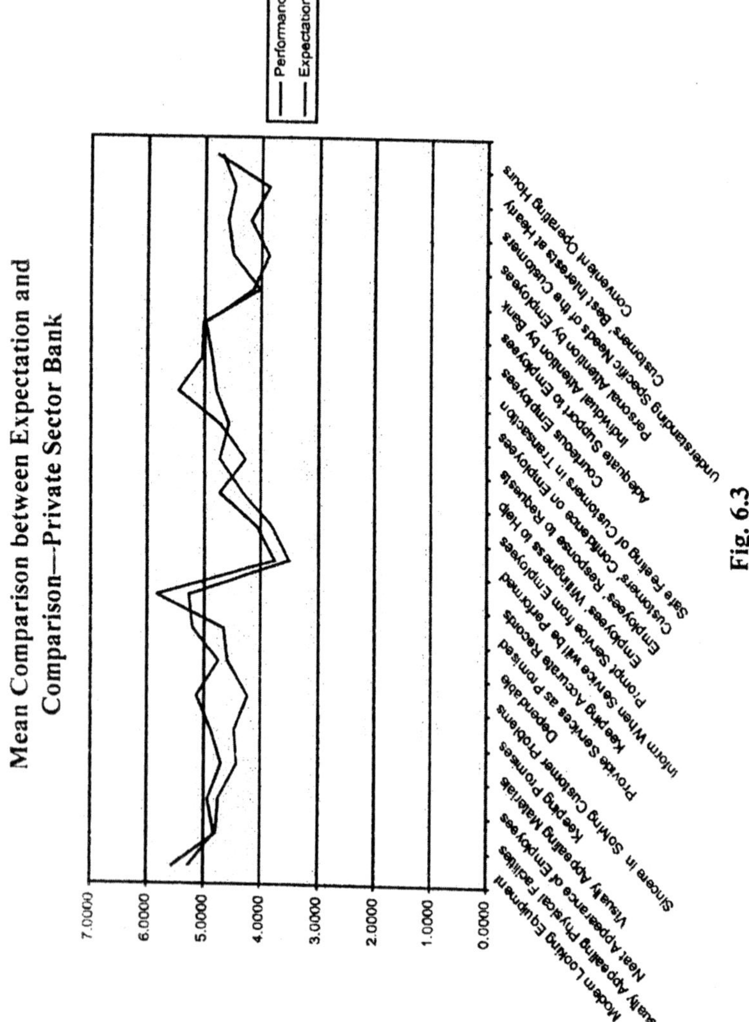
Mean Comparison between Expectation and Comparison—Private Sector Bank
Performance
Expectation
7.0000
6.0000
5.0000
4.0000
3.0000
2.0000
1.0000
0.0000
Modern Looking Equipment
Visually Appealing Physical Facilities
Neat Appearance of Employees
Visually Appealing Materials
Keeping Promises
Sincere in Solving Customer Problems
Dependable
Provide Services as Promised
Keeping Accurate Records
Inform When Service will be Performed
Prompt Service from Employees
Employees' Willingness to Help
Employees' Response to Requests
Customers' Confidence on Employees
Safe Feeling of Customers in Transaction
Courteous Employees
Adequate Support to Employees
Individual Attention by Bank
Personal Attention by Employees
Understanding Specific Needs of the Customers
Customers' Best Interests at Heart
Convenient Operating Hours

Fig. 6.3

The results of SERVQUAL items show similar trend in responses of customers of private and public sector banks. The mean scores for both expectation and perception of banks are in the middle-range indicating not very-high levels of expectations from the banks. Figure 6.2 and 6.3 presents the mean scores of expectations and perceptions of respondents of public and private banks respectively. In bank variations, the quality gap is significant for private banks but not for the public bank is reliability (2.011**); while for public banks but not for private banks is empathy (- 3.099*). Higher differences for mean scores are observed for public banks, compared to that of private banks.

**Results of PCA — Private Banks**

Principal component analysis (PCA) was used to interpret the 22 components of service quality for expectations and perceptions given in Tables 6.3 (A) and 6.3 (B); 6.3 (A) and 6.3 (B) to compare with the initial findings (see Table 6.3 (C). The findings of the initial models were five dimensions, as compared with seven dimensions are extracted for expectations of the respondents from private banks. The results of the factor analysis for private banks are given in the subsequent tables.

Table 6.3 (A) showing KMO measures of sampling adequacy as 0.637 and approximate Chi-Square significant at 1 per cent level, indicating the applicability of factor analysis. Table 6.3 (A) depicts the total variance explained by the first seven factors is 75.106 per cent. Similarly, Table 6.3 (B), given the Rotated component matrix indicating the loadings of different factors. The solutions for 5 – components suggested by Zeithmal et al are compared with the sample results indicating validity of the scales and suggesting the basis in Table 6.3 (C) for expectations.

As indicated from the table, 1[st] factor comprises of seven components covering three dimensions of the original models explaining 18.33 per cent of the variances. Similarly, second factor comprising of six components explain 15.81 per cent of variations in the expectations of the customers. The loadings of different components indicate the importance of those factors in the model.

Table 6.3 (A): Results of Factor Analysis (Private Bank-Expectations)

| Total Variance Explained | | | | | | | | | |
|---|---|---|---|---|---|---|---|---|---|
| | Initial Eigen-values | | | Extraction Sums of Squared Loadings | | | Rotation Sums of Squared Loadings | | |
| Component | Total | % of Variance | Cumulative % | Total | % of Variance | Cumulative % | Total | % of Variance | Cumulative % |
| 1. | 5.414 | 24.609 | 24.609 | 5.414 | 24.609 | 24.609 | 4.033 | 18.330 | 18.330 |
| 2. | 4.015 | 18.251 | 42.860 | 4.015 | 18.251 | 42.860 | 3.478 | 15.809 | 34.138 |
| 3. | 1.927 | 8.761 | 51.620 | 1.927 | 8.761 | 51.620 | 2.132 | 9.691 | 43.829 |
| 4. | 1.576 | 7.165 | 58.786 | 1.576 | 7.165 | 58.786 | 1.828 | 8.309 | 52.138 |
| 5. | 1.324 | 6.016 | 64.802 | 1.324 | 6.016 | 64.802 | 1.802 | 8.191 | 60.328 |
| 6. | 1.185 | 5.386 | 70.187 | 1.185 | 5.386 | 70.187 | 1.748 | 7.945 | 68.273 |
| 7. | 1.082 | 4.919 | 75.106 | 1.082 | 4.919 | 75.106 | 1.503 | 6.832 | 75.106 |
| 8. | .934 | 4.245 | 79.351 | | | | | | |
| 9. | .815 | 3.703 | 83.053 | | | | | | |
| 10. | .662 | 3.008 | 86.061 | | | | | | |

*(Contd...)*

Total Variance Explained

| Component | Initial Eigen-values | | | Extraction Sums of Squared Loadings | | | Rotation Sums of Squared Loadings | | |
|---|---|---|---|---|---|---|---|---|---|
| | Total | % of Variance | Cumulative % | Total | % of Variance | Cumulative % | Total | % of Variance | Cumulative % |
| 11. | .589 | 2.675 | 88.736 | | | | | | |
| 12. | .413 | 1.877 | 90.613 | | | | | | |
| 13. | .394 | 1.790 | 92.404 | | | | | | |
| 14. | .358 | 1.628 | 94.032 | | | | | | |
| 15. | .310 | 1.410 | 95.442 | | | | | | |
| 16. | .242 | 1.102 | 96.543 | | | | | | |
| 17. | .222 | 1.009 | 97.552 | | | | | | |
| 18. | .163 | .742 | 98.295 | | | | | | |
| 19. | .126 | .573 | 98.868 | | | | | | |
| 20. | .108 | .489 | 99.357 | | | | | | |
| 21. | 7.763E-02 | .353 | 99.710 | | | | | | |
| 22. | 6.381E-02 | .290 | 100.000 | | | | | | |

Extraction Method: Principal Component Analysis.
KMO Measures of Sample Adequacy = 0.637
Chi-Square = 1274.86*

Table 6.3 (B): **Results of Factor Analysis (Private Bank-Expectations)**

| Rotated Component Matrix(a) | | | | | | | |
|---|---|---|---|---|---|---|---|
| | Component | | | | | | |
| | 1 | 2 | 3 | 4 | 5 | 6 | 7 |
| E1 | 2.346E-02 | -5.241E-02 | .135 | .856 | .134 | .114 | -4.148E-02 |
| E2 | -.129 | .468 | -1.403E-02 | .417 | .455 | -.331 | 6.277E-02 |
| E3 | -9.416E-02 | .445 | -.138 | .700 | -9.570E-03 | 8.538E-02 | -2.937E-03 |
| E4 | 1.792E-02 | .766 | -2.456E-02 | .142 | 4.886E-03 | -.159 | -.105 |
| E5 | 8.399E-02 | .846 | .187 | 4.508E-03 | 7.998E-02 | .146 | .225 |
| E6 | .131 | .681 | .164 | 5.426E-02 | -.126 | .303 | .354 |
| E7 | .510 | .263 | .289 | .360 | -.213 | -.387 | 2.033E-03 |
| E8 | .147 | .794 | .168 | 2.407E-02 | .120 | -6.925E-02 | -.151 |
| E9 | -.104 | 7.073E-02 | .736 | -.189 | -2.611E-02 | -.240 | -.186 |
| E10 | .689 | .149 | -.143 | -5.301E-02 | .140 | 8.121E-02 | .135 |
| E11 | .631 | .111 | .154 | -9.093E-02 | 4.506E-02 | .596 | 4.115E-02 |
| E12 | .588 | 5.402E-02 | -1.672E-02 | -2.333E-02 | .621 | .382 | 1.154E-02 |

*(Contd...)*

**Rotated Component Matrix(a)**

| | Component | | | | | | |
|---|---|---|---|---|---|---|---|
| | 1 | 2 | 3 | 4 | 5 | 6 | 7 |
| E13 | 9.416E-02 | 1.747E-02 | -.246 | .225 | -4.869E-02 | .808 | 2.199E-02 |
| E14 | 1.826E-02 | .277 | .745 | .221 | .287 | .106 | -3.491E-02 |
| E15 | 2.041E-02 | 7.512E-02 | .497 | .183 | .738 | -.137 | -2.866E-02 |
| E16 | .187 | .609 | .127 | 6.339E-02 | .519 | 5.475E-02 | .190 |
| E17 | -1.902E-02 | .238 | .565 | .138 | .151 | -.104 | .567 |
| E18 | .863 | .128 | 1.764E-02 | 5.113E-02 | -5.864E-02 | 1.321E-02 | 1.675E-02 |
| E19 | .804 | 5.458E-02 | -1.295E-02 | -8.360E-02 | .262 | -3.088E-02 | -6.257E-02 |
| E20 | .721 | -.123 | -.175 | -.102 | -5.847E-02 | 5.389E-02 | .469 |
| E21 | .357 | 5.782E-02 | -.311 | -.116 | 1.035E-02 | 5.666E-02 | .755 |
| E22 | .621 | -9.629E-03 | 9.451E-02 | .206 | -.297 | .237 | .282 |

Extraction Method: Principal Component Analysis.

Rotation Method: Varimax with Kaiser Normalization.

(a) Rotation converged in 20 iterations.

**Table 6.3 (C): Results of Factor Analysis (Private Banks)**

Expectation

| Factors | Variables | Components | Loadings | Variance Explained |
|---|---|---|---|---|
| Factor – 1 | 7. Dependable | Reliability/ Responsibility/ Empathy | 0.510 | 18.330% |
| | 10. Inform when service will be performed | | 0.689 | |
| | 11. Prompt Service from Employees | | 0.631 | |
| | 18. Individual Attention by Bank | | 0.863 | |
| | 19. Personal Attention by Employees | | 0.804 | |
| | 20. Understanding Specific Needs of the Customers | | 0.721 | |
| | 22. Convenient Operating Hours | | 0.621 | |
| Factor – 2 | 2. Visually Appealing Physical Facilities | Tangibility/ Reliability/ Assurance | 0.468 | 15.809% |
| | 4. Visually Appealing Materials | | 0.766 | |
| | 5. Keeping Promises | | 0.846 | |
| | 6. Sincere in Solving Customer Problems | | 0.681 | |
| | 8. Provide Services as Promised | | 0.794 | |
| | 16. Courteous Employees | | 0.609 | |

*(Contd...)*

| Expectation | | | | |
|---|---|---|---|---|
| Factors | Variables | Components | Loadings | Variance Explained |
| Factor – 3 | 9. Keeping Accurate Records<br>14. Customers' Confidence on Employees | Responsiveness/Assurance | 0.736<br>0.745 | 09.691% |
| Factor – 4 | 1. Modern Looking Equipment<br>3. Neat Appearance of Employees | Tangibility | 0.856<br>0.700 | 08.309% |
| Factor – 5 | 12. Employees' Willingness to Help<br>15. Safe Feeling of Customers in Transaction | Responsiveness/Assurance | 0.621<br>0.738 | 08.191% |
| Factor – 6 | 13. Employees' Response to Requests | Responsiveness | 0.808 | 07.945% |
| Factor – 7 | 17. Adequate Support to Employees<br>21. Customers' Best Interests at Heart | Assurance/Empathy | 0.567<br>0.755 | 06.832% |

*(Contd...)*

**Perceptions**

| Factors | Variables | Components | Loadings | Variance Explained |
|---|---|---|---|---|
| | 5. Keeping Promises | | 0.737 | |
| | 6. Sincere in Solving Customer Problems | | 0.555 | |
| | 8. Provide Services as Promised | | 0.593 | |
| Factor – 1 | 9. Keeping Accurate Records | Reliability/Assurance | 0.585 | 17.434% |
| | 14. Customers' Confidence on Employees | | 0.833 | |
| | 15. Safe Feeling of Customers in Transaction | | 0.865 | |
| | 16. Courteous Employees | | 0.718 | |
| | 10. Inform when service will be performed | | 0.715 | |
| | 12. Employees' Willingness to Help | | 0.673 | |
| Factor – 2 | 13. Employees' Response to Requests | Responsiveness/Empathy | 0.522 | 16.009% |
| | 20. Understanding Specific Needs of the Customers | | 0.822 | |
| | 21. Customers' Best Interests at Heart | | 0.766 | |

*(Contd...)*

Perceptions

| Factors | Variables | Components | Loadings | Variance Explained |
|---|---|---|---|---|
| Factor – 3 | 1. Modern Looking Equipment | Tangibility | 0.816 | 12.281% |
| | 2. Visually Appealing Physical Facilities | | 0.773 | |
| Factor – 4 | 18. Individual Attention by Bank | Empathy | 0.824 | 08.244% |
| | 19. Personal Attention by Employees | | 0.766 | |
| Factor – 5 | 3. Neat Appearance of Employees | Tangibility | 0.578 | 07.568% |
| | 4. Visually Appealing Materials | | 0.875 | |
| Factor – 6 | 7. Dependable | Reliability/Responsiveness | 0.774 | 06.622% |
| | 11. Prompt Service from Employees | | 0.505 | |
| Factor – 7 | 17. Adequate Support to Employees | Assurance/Empathy | 0.713 | 06.165% |
| | 22. Convenient Operating Hours | | -0.607 | |

Table 6.4 (A): Results of Factor Analysis (Private Bank-Perceptions)

| Total Variance Explained | | | | | | |
|---|---|---|---|---|---|---|
| | Initial Eigen-values | | | Rotation Sums of Squared Loadings | | |
| Component | Total | % of Variance | Cumulative % | Total | % of Variance | Cumulative % |
| 1. | 5.771 | 26.230 | 26.230 | 3.835 | 17.434 | 17.434 |
| 2. | 4.003 | 18.196 | 44.426 | 3.522 | 16.009 | 33.443 |
| 3. | 1.841 | 8.367 | 52.793 | 2.702 | 12.281 | 45.724 |
| 4. | 1.362 | 6.191 | 58.984 | 1.814 | 8.244 | 53.968 |
| 5. | 1.300 | 5.911 | 64.895 | 1.665 | 7.568 | 61.536 |
| 6. | 1.074 | 4.880 | 69.774 | 1.457 | 6.622 | 68.159 |
| 7. | 1.001 | 4.550 | 74.324 | 1.356 | 6.165 | 74.324 |
| 8. | .757 | 3.439 | 77.763 | | | |
| 9. | .713 | 3.242 | 81.006 | | | |
| 10. | .663 | 3.014 | 84.020 | | | |
| 11. | .603 | 2.739 | 86.759 | | | |
| 12. | .479 | 2.175 | 88.935 | | | |

*(Contd...)*

**Total Variance Explained**

| | Initial Eigen-values | | | Rotation Sums of Squared Loadings | | |
|---|---|---|---|---|---|---|
| **Component** | **Total** | **% of Variance** | **Cumulative %** | **Total** | **% of Variance** | **Cumulative %** |
| 13. | .448 | 2.039 | 90.973 | | | |
| 14. | .410 | 1.862 | 92.835 | | | |
| 15. | .350 | 1.593 | 94.428 | | | |
| 16. | .300 | 1.362 | 95.791 | | | |
| 17. | .216 | .981 | 96.772 | | | |
| 18. | .185 | .842 | 97.614 | | | |
| 19. | .176 | .800 | 98.413 | | | |
| 20. | .142 | .647 | 99.060 | | | |
| 21. | .125 | .569 | 99.630 | | | |
| 22. | 8.148E-02 | .370 | 100.000 | | | |

Extraction Method: Principal Component Analysis.

KMO Measures of Sample Adequacy = 0.698

Chi-Square = 1143.01*

As depicted from the Table 6.4 (A), KMO measures 0.698 and significance level of Bartlett's test of sphericity at 0.000, suggests the need for factor analysis of performance of private banks as viewed by the respondents. By applying PCA method seven factors were extracted explaining 74.321 per cent of the variances. Table 6.4 (B) indicates the compositions and loadings of different components in different factors. Table 6.3 (C) compares the sample results with the initial solutions suggested in the model for different components of customer perceptions.

As indicated in Table 6.4 (c) for rating of performances of private banks, factor 1 derived from the sample results are comprising of seven components covering reliability and assurance dimensions of performance in the original model, factor 2 has five components covering response and empathy dimensions in the model, and explains 16.01 per cent of the variances in the perception of respondents.

A comparison between the perceptions of the respondents for private banks indicate, through the number of extracted factors is seven in both the cases, but there are a lot of differences in their compositions. This suggests that the perceptions and expectations of respondents may not be comparable.

**Results of PCA — Public Sector Banks**

To understand the variations among the perceptions and expectations of public sector banks for service quality, the 22 items were analysed by using Principal Component Analysis (PCA) method. The results of PCA method is compared with the original model suggested by Zeithmal et al (1988) for better introspection into customers' expectations and perception of service quality in the banks.

Table 6.4 (B): Results of Factor Analysis (Private Bank-Perceptions)

| Rotated Component Matrix | | | | | | | |
|---|---|---|---|---|---|---|---|
| | Component | | | | | | |
| | 1 | 2 | 3 | 4 | 5 | 6 | 7 |
| P1 | .111 | .119 | .816 | .147 | 6.142E-02 | .120 | 7.925E-03 |
| P2 | .259 | -.162 | .773 | 3.722E-02 | .256 | -1.082E-02 | .137 |
| P3 | .199 | -.170 | .491 | -1.187E-02 | .578 | -.228 | .209 |
| P4 | 6.496E-02 | -4.114E-02 | .196 | -5.868E-02 | .875 | 9.773E-04 | 3.188E-02 |
| P5 | .737 | -.133 | .450 | -8.622E-02 | 6.920E-02 | .116 | -.120 |
| P6 | .555 | 8.488E-03 | .517 | -.202 | .171 | .171 | -.312 |
| P7 | .186 | -.162 | .149 | -9.257E-02 | -2.361E-02 | .774 | .115 |
| P8 | .593 | .233 | .367 | -1.329E-04 | 3.407E-02 | -.233 | .180 |
| P9 | .585 | .213 | .378 | -.310 | .351 | 7.698E-03 | .109 |
| P10 | 8.542E-02 | .715 | -.264 | .319 | .210 | -2.186E-02 | -7.617E-02 |
| P11 | -3.464E-02 | .481 | -.457 | .162 | -6.233E-02 | .505 | -1.725E-02 |
| P12 | 9.163E-02 | .673 | 1.475E-02 | .203 | -5.789E-02 | -.410 | .242 |
| P13 | -.138 | .522 | 6.580E-02 | 1.514E-02 | -.430 | -.287 | -5.269E-02 |

*(Contd...)*

**Rotated Component Matrix**

| | Component | | | | | | |
|---|---|---|---|---|---|---|---|
| | 1 | 2 | 3 | 4 | 5 | 6 | 7 |
| P14 | .833 | -.106 | -2.993E-02 | 7.175E-02 | 7.725E-02 | .118 | -8.387E-02 |
| P15 | .865 | -8.039E-02 | -3.160E-02 | .154 | -7.116E-02 | -8.008E-02 | .228 |
| P16 | .718 | 9.180E-02 | .190 | -.129 | .154 | .215 | .226 |
| P17 | .299 | 8.723E-03 | .145 | -.278 | .182 | .178 | .713 |
| P18 | 5.512E-02 | .241 | -3.157E-02 | .824 | -4.351E-02 | -.239 | -.185 |
| P19 | -7.240E-02 | .372 | .205 | .766 | -5.148E-02 | .163 | -4.349E-02 |
| P20 | -.191 | .822 | 6.993E-02 | .269 | -.161 | -3.897E-02 | 7.440E-02 |
| P21 | 6.740E-02 | .764 | 1.631E-02 | 7.793E-03 | -4.395E-02 | 6.097E-02 | -.170 |
| P22 | 1.282E-02 | .598 | 1.234E-02 | 6.931E-02 | -2.033E-02 | 3.502E-02 | -.607 |

Extraction Method: Principal Component Analysis.

Rotation Method: Varimax with Kaiser Normalization.

Table 6.5 (A): Results of Factor Analysis (Public Banks-Expectations)

| Total Variance Explained | | | | | | | | | |
|---|---|---|---|---|---|---|---|---|---|
| | Initial Eigenvalues | | | Extraction Sums of Squared Loadings | | | Rotation Sums of Squared Loadings | | |
| Component | Total | % of Variance | Cumulative % | Total | % of Variance | Cumulative % | Total | % of Variance | Cumulative % |
| 1. | 4.889 | 22.224 | 22.224 | 4.889 | 22.224 | 22.224 | 2.802 | 12.738 | 12.738 |
| 2. | 3.891 | 17.686 | 39.910 | 3.891 | 17.686 | 39.910 | 2.761 | 12.549 | 25.286 |
| 3. | 1.863 | 8.469 | 48.379 | 1.863 | 8.469 | 48.379 | 2.215 | 10.070 | 35.356 |
| 4. | 1.566 | 7.119 | 55.498 | 1.566 | 7.119 | 55.498 | 2.173 | 9.878 | 45.234 |
| 5. | 1.449 | 6.587 | 62.085 | 1.449 | 6.587 | 62.085 | 1.950 | 8.864 | 54.098 |
| 6. | 1.193 | 5.425 | 67.510 | 1.193 | 5.425 | 67.510 | 1.912 | 8.690 | 62.788 |
| 7. | 1.048 | 4.762 | 72.272 | 1.048 | 4.762 | 72.272 | 1.632 | 7.417 | 70.205 |
| 8. | 1.007 | 4.576 | 76.848 | 1.007 | 4.576 | 76.848 | 1.461 | 6.643 | 76.848 |
| 9. | .850 | 3.864 | 80.712 | | | | | | |
| 10. | .769 | 3.495 | 84.208 | | | | | | |
| 11. | .638 | 2.901 | 87.108 | | | | | | |
| 12. | .536 | 2.436 | 89.544 | | | | | | |
| 13. | .435 | 1.979 | 91.523 | | | | | | |

*(Contd...)*

**Total Variance Explained**

| | Initial Eigenvalues | | | Extraction Sums of Squared Loadings | | | Rotation Sums of Squared Loadings | | |
|---|---|---|---|---|---|---|---|---|---|
| Component | Total | % of Variance | Cumulative % | Total | % of Variance | Cumulative % | Total | % of Variance | Cumulative % |
| 14. | .375 | 1.704 | 93.227 | | | | | | |
| 15. | .352 | 1.600 | 94.827 | | | | | | |
| 16. | .326 | 1.480 | 96.307 | | | | | | |
| 17. | .226 | 1.029 | 97.336 | | | | | | |
| 18. | .160 | .726 | 98.062 | | | | | | |
| 19. | .138 | .625 | 98.688 | | | | | | |
| 20. | .125 | .567 | 99.254 | | | | | | |
| 21. | 9.377E-02 | .426 | 99.680 | | | | | | |
| 22. | 7.029E-02 | .320 | 100.000 | | | | | | |

Extraction Method: Principal Component Analysis.

KMO Measures of Sample Adequacy = 0.590

Chi-Square = 3088.97*

Table 6.5 (B): Results of Factor Analysis (Public Banks-Expectations)

Rotated Component Matrix

| | Component | | | | | | | |
|---|---|---|---|---|---|---|---|---|
| | 1 | 2 | 3 | 4 | 5 | 6 | 7 | 8 |
| E1 | -.123 | .439 | -.247 | -5.607E-02 | .477 | .126 | .501 | 6.389E-02 |
| E2 | .247 | .211 | -.179 | 1.147E-02 | .577 | -2.630E-02 | .350 | 7.781E-02 |
| E3 | 8.264E-02 | -7.099E-03 | .140 | 6.880E-02 | .866 | 5.519E-02 | 8.477E-03 | -5.869E-02 |
| E4 | .523 | .122 | .179 | -.227 | .616 | -8.452E-02 | -1.312E-02 | 5.337E-02 |
| E5 | .839 | .272 | -.120 | 3.178E-02 | .135 | 6.052E-02 | 1.807E-02 | -1.376E-02 |
| E6 | .840 | .132 | 1.142E-02 | .145 | 6.812E-02 | 2.236E-02 | 9.304E-03 | -3.325E-02 |
| E7 | 8.102E-02 | -.129 | .140 | 7.475E-02 | .151 | -.199 | .802 | 6.642E-02 |
| E8 | .704 | 4.957E-02 | -3.078E-02 | -.143 | .152 | .146 | .389 | .316 |
| E9 | 2.744E-02 | 6.117E-02 | -9.786E-02 | -3.350E-02 | -5.204E-03 | -6.654E-02 | 1.836E-02 | .909 |
| E10 | .274 | .165 | .259 | 9.442E-02 | -.180 | .450 | .516 | -.136 |
| E11 | .212 | 3.442E-02 | .534 | .139 | -7.966E-02 | .589 | -7.121E-02 | .297 |
| E12 | .206 | .446 | .190 | .190 | -8.596E-02 | .699 | 8.620E-02 | -2.104E-02 |
| E13 | -.117 | -.270 | 3.468E-02 | .175 | .232 | .737 | -.229 | -.188 |

*(Contd...)*

**Rotated Component Matrix**

| | Component | | | | | | | |
|---|---|---|---|---|---|---|---|---|
| | 1 | 2 | 3 | 4 | 5 | 6 | 7 | 8 |
| E14 | .284 | .486 | -3.511E-02 | -.323 | 3.771E-03 | -.123 | .230 | .393 |
| E15 | 3.253E-02 | .913 | -1.578E-02 | -8.982E-02 | 7.616E-02 | 3.232E-02 | 5.474E-02 | 6.316E-02 |
| E16 | .411 | .683 | .148 | 9.128E-02 | .147 | .248 | 1.392E-02 | -.177 |
| E17 | .217 | .740 | 1.128E-02 | .183 | 4.045E-02 | -8.365E-02 | -.125 | 8.843E-02 |
| E18 | -3.931E-02 | -4.155E-02 | .857 | .239 | .105 | .146 | 9.452E-02 | -.122 |
| E19 | -7.977E-02 | 7.326E-02 | .830 | .270 | 2.690E-02 | 7.574E-02 | 5.771E-02 | -5.307E-02 |
| E20 | -6.800E-02 | 2.696E-02 | .297 | .757 | -.129 | .289 | 6.044E-02 | -2.929E-02 |
| E21 | .211 | 5.108E-02 | .197 | .844 | -1.734E-02 | -2.410E-02 | -7.651E-02 | -.227 |
| E22 | -5.637E-02 | 2.206E-02 | .251 | .633 | .186 | .197 | .193 | .321 |

Extraction Method: Principal Component Analysis.

Rotation Method: Varimax with Kaiser Normalization.

The KMO measures of sampling adequacy is 0.590 and $\chi^2$ is significant at 0.000 level indicates the suitability of PCA method for identifying the important components of expectations of respondents of public sector banks. Eight factors have been extracted by the method explaining 76.848 per cent of the variances in customers' expectations, taking the cut off point in the Eigen value as '1'. Here, the 1st factor comprising three items explains 12.74 per cent of the total variations. Again, the 2nd factor comprising four items explains 12.55 per cent of the variations. Similarly, the other factors explain their relative contributions in explaining the variations in perception of the respondents.

Further, Table 6.6 (c) makes a comparison of the factors extracted through PCA from the sample with the original dimensions identified by Zeithmal et al (1988). It is observed that out of the five dimensions of reliability (original model), three comprises Factor 1 in the extraction; and one more with Factor 7 along with tangibility and responsiveness and the rest are as a separate dimension explaining 6.64 per cent of the total variations. Similarly, Factor 3 and 4 taken together comprises the assurance dimension of the original model. In the consumers' expectation domain, tangibility is not so important explaining the influence of people factor as more important informing customers' expectations in public sector banks.

Similarly, the analysis of perception of respondents of public sector banks suggests five factors extracted through PCA explain 66.582 per cent variations taking the cut off point of eigen-value as '1'. Further, 1st and 2nd factors combined explain 40.456 per cent of the variations. Here, the first factor comprised of nine out of the 22 items of service quality and second factor has clubbed seven factors. Again, the content of the five factors extracted is different from the initial dimensions suggested in the model.

Table 6.5 (C): Results of Factor Analysis (Public Banks)

| Expectation | | | | |
|---|---|---|---|---|
| Factors | Variables | Components | Loadings | Variance Explained |
| Factor – 1 | 5. Keeping Promises | Reliability | 0.839 | 12.738% |
| | 6. Sincere in Solving Customer Problems | | 0.840 | |
| | 8. Provide Services as Promised | | 0.704 | |
| Factor – 2 | 14. Customers' Confidence on Employees | Assurance | 0.486 | 12.549% |
| | 15. Safe Feeling of Customers in Transaction | | 0.913 | |
| | 16. Courteous Employees | | 0.683 | |
| | 17. Adequate Support to Employees | | 0.740 | |
| Factor – 3 | 18. Individual Attention by Bank | Empathy | 0.857 | 10.070% |
| | 19. Personal Attention by Employees | | 0.830 | |
| Factor – 4 | 20. Understanding Specific Needs of the Customers | Empathy | 0.757 | 09.878% |
| | 21. Customers' Best Interests at Heart | | 0.844 | |
| | 22. Convenient Operating Hours | | 0.633 | |
| Factor – 5 | 2. Visually Appealing Physical Facilities | Tangibility | 0.577 | 08.864% |
| | 3. Neat Appearance of Employees | | 0.866 | |
| | 4. Visually Appealing Materials | | 0.616 | |

*(Contd...)*

| Expectation | | | | |
|---|---|---|---|---|
| **Factors** | **Variables** | **Components** | **Loadings** | **Variance Explained** |
| Factor – 6 | 11. Prompt Service from Employees | Responsiveness | 0.589 | 08.690% |
| | 12. Employees' Willingness to Help | | 0.699 | |
| | 13. Employees' Response to Request | | 0.737 | |
| Factor – 7 | 1. Modern Looking Equipment | Tangibility/ Reliability/ Responsiveness | 0.501 | 07.417% |
| | 7. Dependable | | 0.802 | |
| | 10. Inform when service will be performed | | 0.516 | |
| Factor – 8 | 9. Keeping Accurate Records | Reliability | 0.9.9 | 06.643% |

*(Contd...)*

**Perceptions**

| Factors | Variables | Components | Loadings | Variance Explained |
|---|---|---|---|---|
| Factor - 1 | 10. Inform when service will be performed | Responsiveness/ Empathy | 0.722 | 22.076% |
| | 11. Prompt Service from Employees | | 0.679 | |
| | 12. Employees' Willingness to Help | | 0.768 | |
| | 13. Employees' Response to Requests | | 0.629 | |
| | 18. Individual Attention by Bank | | 0.622 | |
| | 19. Personal Attention by Employees | | 0.746 | |
| | 20. Understanding Specific Needs of the Customers | | 0.825 | |
| | 21. Customers' Best Interests at Heart | | 0.772 | |
| | 22. Convenient Operating Hours | | 0.681 | |
| Factor – 2 | 1. Modern Looking Equipment | Reliability/ Tangibility | 0.723 | 18.380% |
| | 2. Visually Appealing Physical Facilities | | 0.734 | |
| | 3. Neat Appearance of Employees | | 0.807 | |
| | 4. Visually Appealing Materials | | 0.742 | |
| | 5. Keeping Promises | | 0.609 | |
| | 8. Provide Services as Promised | | 0.573 | |
| | 9. Keeping Accurate Records | | 0.625 | |

*(Contd...)*

**Perceptions**

| Factors | Variables | Components | Loadings | Variance Explained |
|---|---|---|---|---|
| Factor – 3 | 14. Customers' Confidence on Employees | Assurance | 0.774 | 12.103% |
| | 15. Safe Feeling of Customers in Transaction | | 0.898 | |
| | 16. Courteous Employees | | 0.539 | |
| Factor – 4 | 6. Sincere in Solving Customer Problems | Reliability | 0.459 | 07.454% |
| | 7. Dependable | | 0.826 | |
| Factor – 5 | 17. Adequate Support to Employees | Assurance | 0.696 | 06.560% |

Table 6.6 (A): Results of Factor Analysis (Public Banks-Perceptions)

| Total Variance Explained | | | | | | |
|---|---|---|---|---|---|---|
| | Initial Eigen-values | | | Rotation Sums of Squared Loadings | | |
| Component | Total | % of Variance | Cumulative % | Total | % of Variance | Cumulative % |
| 1. | 6.396 | 29.074 | 29.074 | 4.857 | 22.076 | 22.076 |
| 2. | 4.288 | 19.492 | 48.566 | 4.044 | 18.380 | 40.456 |
| 3. | 1.577 | 7.168 | 55.734 | 2.663 | 12.103 | 52.559 |
| 4. | 1.272 | 5.783 | 61.517 | 1.640 | 7.454 | 60.013 |
| 5. | 1.114 | 5.065 | 66.582 | 1.445 | 6.570 | 66.582 |
| 6. | .932 | 4.237 | 70.819 | | | |
| 7. | .830 | 3.775 | 74.594 | | | |
| 8. | .755 | 3.432 | 78.026 | | | |
| 9. | .608 | 2.762 | 80.788 | | | |
| 10. | .559 | 2.539 | 83.327 | | | |
| 11. | .498 | 2.265 | 85.592 | | | |
| 12. | .448 | 2.035 | 87.627 | | | |

*(Contd...)*

Total Variance Explained

| | Initial Eigen-values | | | Rotation Sums of Squared Loadings | | |
|---|---|---|---|---|---|---|
| Component | Total | % of Variance | Cumulative % | Total | % of Variance | Cumulative % |
| 13. | .433 | 1.967 | 89.594 | | | |
| 14. | .375 | 1.703 | 91.297 | | | |
| 15. | .336 | 1.528 | 92.825 | | | |
| 16. | .322 | 1.465 | 94.290 | | | |
| 17. | .296 | 1.346 | 95.635 | | | |
| 18. | .252 | 1.144 | 96.780 | | | |
| 19. | .240 | 1.092 | 97.872 | | | |
| 20. | .185 | .841 | 98.712 | | | |
| 21. | .147 | .668 | 99.380 | | | |
| 22. | .136 | .620 | 100.000 | | | |

Extraction Method: Principal Component Analysis.

KMO Measures of Sample Adequacy = 0.803

Chi-Square = 2948.64*

Table 6.6 (B): Results of Factor Analysis (Public Banks-Perceptions)

| Rotated Component Matrix(a) | | | | | |
|---|---|---|---|---|---|
| | Component | | | | |
| | 1 | 2 | 3 | 4 | 5 |
| P1 | .132 | .723 | .129 | -2.490E-02 | .369 |
| P2 | 4.657E-03 | .734 | .143 | -4.762E-02 | .239 |
| P3 | 9.182E-02 | .807 | 1.985E-02 | 4.018E-02 | -8.975E-03 |
| P4 | 4.790E-02 | .742 | -8.761E-02 | .247 | -.204 |
| P5 | .147 | .609 | .373 | .335 | .130 |
| P6 | 6.401E-02 | .475 | .274 | .459 | .118 |
| P7 | 1.319E-02 | .167 | .113 | .826 | 7.353E-02 |
| P8 | .206 | .573 | .564 | .132 | -8.671E-03 |
| P9 | .165 | .625 | .446 | 9.846E-02 | .136 |
| P10 | .722 | .187 | 1.601E-02 | 1.570E-02 | -4.214E-02 |
| P11 | .679 | -8.575E-02 | -.155 | .427 | .204 |
| P12 | .768 | .226 | 6.607E-02 | -.275 | 6.045E-02 |

*(Contd...)*

**Rotated Component Matrix(a)**

| | Component | | | | |
|---|---|---|---|---|---|
| | 1 | 2 | 3 | 4 | 5 |
| P13 | .629 | -.164 | -3.860E-02 | -.349 | .125 |
| P14 | -.210 | 9.736E-02 | .774 | 8.693E-02 | 5.278E-02 |
| P15 | -3.087E-02 | 7.889E-02 | .898 | -2.361E-02 | 1.285E-02 |
| P16 | .181 | .325 | .539 | .235 | .395 |
| P17 | 5.200E-02 | .384 | .294 | .188 | .696 |
| P18 | .622 | -4.480E-02 | .128 | -1.304E-02 | -.578 |
| P19 | .746 | .102 | 7.954E-02 | .165 | -.299 |
| P20 | .825 | .143 | -1.306E-03 | -1.504E-02 | 1.862E-02 |
| P21 | .772 | .102 | 8.290E-02 | 8.453E-02 | .136 |
| P22 | .681 | 6.282E-02 | -.180 | .169 | -8.199E-02 |

Extraction Method: Principal Component Analysis.

Rotation Method: Varimax with Kaiser Normalization.

(a) Rotation converged in 6 iterations.

## SUMMARY

Delivering customer satisfaction is at the heart of modern marketing, which is a post-purchase judgement of the consumers. The study on service quality in banks is measured in five dimensions by using the SERVQUAL scale developed by Parsuraman et al (1988). The analysis of responses clearly reveals that there exists a small perceptual difference among customers regarding overall service quality with their respective banks. The expectations exceeding performances are clearly visible with Indian banks. However, the results of principal component analysis indicate that though the dimensions suggested in the model are comparable with the sample results, but the contents of the factors are different. The respondents of both the banks mostly focus on people (staffs of the banks) factor for improving customer satisfaction; while the banks are focusing on tangible factors such as computerisation, ATMs, etc. to attract customers.

## REFERENCES

Web sites: www.sba.muohio.edu

www.emeraldinsight.com

www.managementjournals.com

Adrian, Pyne (1995); *The Essence of Service Marketing*, Prentice-Hall of India, New Delhi, pp. 224-226.

Andaleeb, S.S. and Basu, A.K, (1994); "Technical Complexity and Consumer Knowledge as Moderators of Service Quality Evaluation in the Automobile Service Industry," *Journal of Retailing*, 70(4), 367-381.

Anderson, E.W., Fornell, C. and Lehmann, D.R. (1994); "Customer Satisfaction, Market Share and Profitability: Findings from Sweden," *Journal of Marketing*, 58(3), 53-66.

Anderson, C. and Zeithaml, C.P. (1984); "Stage of the Product Life Cycle, Business Strategy, and Business Performance," *Academy of Management Journal*, 27 (March), 5-24.

Angur, M.G. Natarajan, R. and Jahera, J.S. (1999); "Service Quality in the Banking Industry: An assessment in a Developing Economy", *International Journal of Bank Marketing*, Vol. 17, No. 3, pp. 116-123.

Aurora, S. and Malhotra, M. (1997); "Customer Satisfaction: A Comparative Analysis of Public and Private sector Banks", *Decision*, 24(1-4), (January-December); pp. 109 -130.

Babakus, E. and Boller, G.W. (1992); "An Empirical Assessment of the Servqual Scale," *Journal of Business Research,* 24(3), 253-68.

Babakus, E. and Mangold, W.G. (1989); "Adapting the Servqual Scale to Hospital Services: An Empirical Investigation," *Health Service Research,* 26(6), 767-780.

Babakus, E. and Inhofe, M. (1991); "The Role of Expectations and Attribute Importance in the Measurement of Service Quality" in Gilly M.C. (ed.), Proceedings of the Summer Educator's Conference, Chicago, IL: American Marketing Association, 142-44.

Barking up the Wrong Tree – Factors Influencing Customer Satisfaction in Retail Banking in the UK; Available at www.managementjournals.com

Bhat, M.A. (2005); "Service Quality Perceptions in Banks: A Comparative Analysis", *Vision – The Journal of Business Perspective,* Vol. 9, No.1, (January-March), pp. 11-20.

Bolton, R.N. and Drew, J.H. (1991a); "A Multistage Model of Customer's Assessment of Service Quality and Value," *Journal of Consumer Research,* 17(March), 375-85.

Bolton, R.N. and Drew, J.H. (1991b); "A Longitudinal Analysis of the Impact of Service Changes on Customer Attitudes," *Journal of Marketing,* 55 (January), 1-9.

Boulding, W., Kalra, A, Staelin, R. and Zeithaml, V.A. (1993); "A Dynamic Process Model of Service Quality: From Expectations to Behavioural Intentions," *Journal of Marketing Research,* 30 (February), 7-27.

Brady, M.K. and Robertson, C.J. (2001); "Searching for a Consensus on the Antecedent Role of Service Quality and Satisfaction: An Exploratory Cross-National Study," *Journal of Business Research,* 51(1) 53-60.

Brady, M.K., Cronin, J. and Brand, R.R. (2002); "Performance—Only Measurement of Service Quality: A Replication and Extension," *Journal of Business Research,* 55(1), 17-31.

Brown, T.J., Churchill, G.A. and Peter, J.P. (1993); "Improving the Measurement of Service Quality," *Journal of Retailing,* 69(1), 127-139.

Brown, S.W. and Swartz, T.A. (1989); "A Gap Analysis of Professional Service Quality," *Journal of Marketing,* 53 (April), 92-98.

Buzzell; R.D. and Gale, B.T. (1987); *The PIMS Principles,* The Free Press, New York.

Carman, J.M. (1990); "Consumer Perceptions of Service Quality: An Assessment of the SERVQUAL Dimensions," *Journal of Retailing,* 66(1), 33-35.

Churchill, G.A. (1979); "A Paradigm for Developing Better Measures of Marketing Constructs," *Journal of Marketing Research,* 16 (February), 64-71.

Churchill, C.A. and Surprenant, C. (1982); "An Investigation into the Determinants of Customer Satisfaction," *Journal of Marketing Research*, 19(November), 491-504.

Cronin, J. and Taylor, S.A. (1992); "Measuring Service Quality: A Re-examination and Extension," *Journal of Marketing*, 56 (July), 55-67.

Cronin, J. and Taylor, S.A. (1994); "SERVPERF versus SERVQUAL: Reconciling Performance-based and Perceptions— Minus— Expectations Measurement of Service Quality," *Journal of Marketing*, 58 (January), 125-131.

Cronin, J., Brady, M.K. and Hult, T.M. (2000); "Assessing the Effects of Quality, Value and Customer Satisfaction on Consumer Behavioural Intentions in Service Environments," *Journal of Retailing*, 76(2), 193-218.

Dabholkar, P.A., Shepherd, D.C. and Thorpe, D.I. (2000); "A Comprehensive Framework for Service Quality: An Investigation of Critical, Conceptual and Measurement Issues through a Longitudinal Study," *Journal of Retailing*, 76(2), 139-173.

Dhananjayan, G. (2005); "Services Marketing: Integrating People, Technology and Strategy", *Marketing Mastermind*, February, pp. 17-23.

Finn, D.W. and Lamb, C.W. (1991); "An Evaluation of the SERVQUAL Scale in a Retailing Setting" in Holman, R. and Solomon, M.R. (eds.), Advances in Consumer Research, UT: Association for Consumer Research, Provo, pp. 480-493.

Garvin, D.A. (1983); "Quality on the Line," *Harvard Business Review*, 61 (September-October), 65-73.

Gotlieb, J.B., Grewal, D. and Brown, S.W. (1994); "Consumer Satisfaction and Perceived Quality: Complementary or Divergent Constructs," *Journal of Applied Psychology*, 79(6), 875-885.

Gronroos, C. (1982); *Strategic Management and Marketing in the Service Sector*, Swedish School of Economics and Business Administration, Finland.

Hartline, M.D. and Ferrell, O.C. (1996); "The Management of Customer Contact Service Employees: An Empirical Investigation," *Journal of Marketing*, 69 (October), 52-70.

Howcroft, J.B. (1991); "Customer Satisfaction in Retail Banking", *Service Industry Journal*, (Jan.); pp. 11-17.

Iacobucci, D., Grayson, K.A. and Ostrom, A.L. (1994); "The Calculus of Service Quality and Customer Satisfaction: Theoretical and Empirical Differentiation and Integration," in Swartz, T.A; et al (eds.), *Advances in Services Marketing and Management*, Greenwich, CT: JAI Press. pp. 1-67.

Jain, S.K. and Gupta, G. (2004); "Measuring Service Quality: SERVQUAL vs. SERVPERF Scales", *Vikalpa*, 29 (2), (April-June); pp. 25-37.

Kassim, N.M. and Bojci, J. (2002); "Service Quality: Gaps in the Telemarketing Industry," *Journal of Business Research*, 55(11), 845-52.

Kotler, P. (2003); *Marketing Management*, Prentice Hall of India, New Delhi.

Krishnaveni, R. and Divya Prava, D. (2004); "Measuring Service Quality in Banking Sector", *Prajnan: Jr. of Social and Management Sciences*, XXXIII (1), pp. 47-55.

Lewis, R.C. (1987); "The Measurement of Gaps in the Quality of Hotel Service," *International Journal of Hospitality Management*, 6(2), 83-88.

Lewis, B (1991); "Service Quality: An International Comparison of Bank Customer's Expectations and Perceptions," *Journal of Marketing Management*, 7(1), 47-62.

Levitt, T. (1981); "Marketing Intangible Products and Product Intangibles", *Harvard Business Review*, May-June, pp. 94-102.

Miller, J.A. (1977); "Exploring Satisfaction, Modifying Modes, Eliciting Expectations, Posing Problems, and Making Meaningful Measurements", in Hunt, K. (ed), *Conceptualisation and Measurement of Consumer Satisfaction and dissatisfaction*, Marketing Science Institute, Cambridge, pp. 72-91.

Mishra, B.B. and Sarangi, M.K. (2000), "Customer needs and Satisfaction: A Comparative Analysis of Public and Private Sector Banks in Orissa", *Advantage South Asia;* Published by AMDISA, Hyderabad; pp. 386-394.

Parasuraman, A., Berry, L.L. and Zeithami, V.A. (1990); "Guidelines for Conducting Service Quality Decrease," *Marketing Research*, 2(4), 34-44.

Parasuraman, A. Berry, L.L. and Zeithaml, V.A. (1991); "Refinement and Reassessment of the SERVQUAL Scale," *Journal of Retailing*, 67(4), 420-450.

Parasuraman, A., Zeithaml, V.A and Berry, L.L. (1985); "A Conceptual Model of Service Quality and Its Implications for Future Research," *Journal of Marketing*, 49 (Fall), 41-50.

Parasuraman, A., Zeithaml, V.A and Berry, L.L. (1988); "SERVQUAL: A Multiple Item Scale for Measuring Consumer Perceptions of Service Quality," *Journal of Retailing*, 64(1), 12-40.

Parasuraman, A., Zeithaml, V.A. and Berry, L.L. (1994); "Reassessment of Expectations as a Comparison Standard in Measuring Service Quality: Implications for Further Research," *Journal of Marketing*, 58 (January), 111-124.

Peter, J.P. Churchill, C.A. and Brown, T.J. (1993); "Caution in the Use of Difference Scores in Consumer Research," *Journal of Consumer Research*, 19 (March), 655-662.

Pitt, L.F. Oosthuizen P. and Morris, M.H. (1992); *Service Quality in a High Tech Industrial Market: An Application of SERVQUAL,* American Management Association, Chicago.

Radon, G.H. (1987); "Quality Service—A Low Cost Profit Strategy", *Bank Marketing,* Vol. 19, No. 9; pp. 10-12.

Ravichandran, M. and Thyagarajan, V. (1998); "Consumer Satisfaction – Determinants and Measurement", *The Journal of NMIMS,* (July-December); pp. 42-55.

Rust, R.T. and Oliver, R.L. (1994); *Service Quality — New Directions in Theory and Practice,* Sage Publications, New York.

Sharma, R.D. and Kaur, G. (2004); "Strategy for Customer satisfaction in Rural Banks", *Prajnan: Jr. of Social and Management Sciences,* XXXIII (1), pp. 23-45.

Smith, R.A and Houston, M.J (1982); "Script-based Evaluations of Satisfaction with Services," in Berry, L, Shostack, G. and Upah, G (eds.), *Emerging Perspectives on Services Marketing,* American Marketing Association, Chicago, pp. 59-62.

Sousa, Cristina (1999); "Customer Expectations and Perceptions of Service Quality in Retail Banking: A Comparative Study of Macau and Guangzhou Banking Consumers", Available in www.sab.muhio.edu. pp. 1-7.

Spreng, R.A. and Singh, A.K. (1993); "An Empirical Assessment of the SERVQUAL Scale and the Relationship Between Service Quality and Satisfaction," in Peter, D.W. Cravens, R. and Dickson (eds.), *Enhancing Knowledge Development in Marketing,* American Marketing Association, Chicago, pp. 1-6.

Srivastava, A.K. (1994); "Customer Service in banks: Need for a Marketing Approach", in Bidhi, C. (1994) *Marketing of Services,* Rawat Publications, New Delhi, pp. 25-38.

Sureshchandar, G.S., Chandrasekharan, R. and Anantharaman, R.N. (2003); "Customer Perceptions of Service Quality in the Banking Sector of a Developing Economy: A Critical Analysis", *International Journal of Bank Marketing,* Vol. 21, No. 5, pp. 233-242. available at www.emeraldinsight.com

Teas, K.R. (1993); "Expectations, Performance Evaluation, and Consumer's Perceptions of Quality," *Journal of Marketing,* 57 (October), 18-34.

Teas, K.R. (1994). "Expectations as a Comparison Standard in Measuring Service Quality: An Assessment of Reassessment," *Journal of Marketing,* 58 (January), 132-139.

Woodruff, R.B, Cadotte, E.R. and Jenkins, R.L. (1983); "Modelling Consumer Satisfaction Processes Using Experience-based Norms," *Journal of Marketing Research,* 20 (August), 296-304.

Young, C., Cunningham, L. and Lee, M. (1994); "Assessing Service Quality as an Effective Management Tool: The Case of the Airline Industry," *Journal of Marketing Theory and Practice*, 2 (Spring), 76-96.

Zeithaml, V.A., Parasuraman, A. and Berry, L.L. (1990); *Delivering Service Quality: Balancing Customer Perceptions and Expectations*, The Free Press, New York.

Zeithaml, V.A., Parasuraman, A. and Berry, L.L. (1993); "The Nature and Determinants of Consuner Expectations of Services", *Journal of Academy of Marketing Science*, Vol. 21, No. 1, pp. 1-12.

Zeithaml, V.A. and Parasuraman, A. (1996); "The Behavioural Consequences of Service Quality," *Journal of Marketing*, 60 (April), 31-46.

Zeithaml, V.A. and Bitner, Mary Jo (2003); *Services Marketing: Integrating Customer Focus Across the Firms*, 3rd Edition, Tata McGraw Hill, New Delhi.

# CHAPTER–7

# SUMMARY AND CONCLUSION

## INTRODUCTION

Bank marketing is the creation and delivery of financial services suitable to meet the customers' needs at a profit to the bank. The need for bank marketing also arises due to increasing sophistication of bank customers, improvement in technology, and increased cost of meeting the customers' needs. The 1970s was the great era of transition in bank marketing field. In today's competitive world, bank marketing is becoming increasingly necessary. With a string of incentive packed non-banking saving instruments entering the market in a big way, increasing the market share apart, even retention of the varied market segments call for innovative and aggressive marketing strategies. In early 1980s, banks in India started thinking in terms of product innovation, market penetration, and strategy development. Today all the banks including foreign banks operating in India offer many innovative financial services.

For effective marketing, it is essential to know the marketing strategy designed specifically for the bank. Marketing strategy is essentially the firm's product-market choice, which is guided by environmental necessities and firm's objectives and capabilities. The service-marketing triangle is built with employees, technology, and the service strategy as the corner points and customers at the heart of that triangle. This make the task of marketing services more complicated and stressed the marketers to be more customers centric. Service companies should, therefore, pay particular attention to the product – planning stage of their marketing programmes. Very often the service providers face a fluctuating demand, which aggravates the marketing scenario. From marketing point of view, the same technique can not be applied to both product and services. Successful marketing of both requires marketing research, designing the product/services and adopting a marketing strategy to market them. However, for marketing of services, especially in the Banks, the marketing manager must understand the nature of the characteristics of services and the manner in which they impinge upon the marketing strategy.

Quality is a buzzword in marketers' dictionary. Poor quality places a firm at a competitive disadvantage. If customers perceive quality as unsatisfactory, they may be quick to take their businesses else where. Thus, it is clear that service quality offers a way of achieving success among competing services, particularly in the case of firms that offer nearly identical services, such as banks, where establishing service quality may be the only way of differentiating oneself. Such differentiation can yield a higher proportion of consumers' choices and, hence, mean the difference between financial success and failure.

The present study aims at providing better understanding of the customers' needs, which will help in designing a better marketing strategy to retain existing customers and attracting new customers. Till the end of 20$^{th}$ century, public sector banks dominated the banking scene with reach and trust. With the entry of new generation tech-savvy private banks and expansion of operations by foreign banks in India, the monopoly of the public sector banks are at stake. Now customers will prefer the banks, which provide them hassle free services. In a fiercely competitive market, a non-price factor like customer service has become more important. The awareness has already dawn that prompt, efficient and speedy customer service alone will tempt the existing customers to continue and induce new customers to try the services offered by the banks.

The study is a unique one, as no such study has been done earlier on bank customers of Orissa. The main objective of the present study is to understand the banking behaviour of customers of Orissa. The study has been conducted to understand the factors that influence the customers' choice of one bank over the other and also examines the expectations and perceptions of the customers regarding banking services. Further, on the basis of study results, ways and means to be suggested for improving service quality in banks with a view to make overall banking service more effective and efficient.

The study is mainly based on field survey and is exploratory in nature. The sources of data are mainly primary. Data are collected through three tailor-made questionnaires, i.e., Customer Survey, Banker Survey and SERVQUAL, with a view to measure the perceptions about the quality of service delivered to the customers. Respondents (bank officials and bank customers) were asked to give their opinion about the level of quality of service delivered/received on a five-point/seven-point Likert scale. The sample for the study comprises of 337 bank customers and 157 bank officials selected randomly.

The data collected through various instruments are processed through SPSS. Cross tabulations are made to understand the underlying relationships among the variable keeping the broad objectives in mind. In order to test the significance of the means of two variables, 't' test has been used. Chi-square test has been used to test the independence between two cross-tabulated variables, which are categorised into two or more groups. Further, Factor analysis is primarily used for data reduction and summarization.

## MAJOR FINDINGS

Bank marketing is becoming increasingly necessary in today's competitive world. A large string of incentive packed non-banking saving instruments are entering the market in a big way. Therefore, apart from increasing the market share, even retention of the varied market segments call for innovative and aggressive marketing strategies focusing on the customers. At this backdrop, the followings are the major findings of the study as perceived by the customers and bankers.

**Customers' View**

- Respondents prefer public sector banks to operate fixed-deposit accounts. Savings bank account dominates the type of account in all categories of respondents. Current accounts are not very popular among the sample customers.
- Proximity, either to home or office, convenient location and overall reputation are the principal determinants of choice of opening an account in public sector banks. For private banks, service quality is the most important reason for opening a deposit account.
- The sample respondents give relatively low weight to customer service for opening of an account. The probable reasons for this may be due to tangible and automated services rendered by the banks.
- Young respondents transact more with public sector banks. Less educated customers have a preference for public sector banks. Post-graduates are more inclined to private sector banks as the private banks are offering a large number of value-added services and have adopted class banking approaches for the special group of customers.
- With regard to having bank accounts in other banks, about 90 per cent of the respondents have only savings accounts with the second bank. All the respondents above 60 years and retired persons have their second accounts with public sector banks.
- Convenient working hour, ATM network and proximity to home are the major reasons for opening an account with other banks. People with higher age group, retired, businessmen and higher income group wants to bank with public sector banks because of their overall reputation.
- 50 per cent of the respondents hardly have any visit to the branch. The numbers of visits are substantially reduced due to the availability of the ATMs.
- The most often used/availed services are ATM and phone banking, followed by remittances and debit/credit cards as evident from the study.

- Customers groups of above 40 years of age are searching for more loan facilities compared to the younger ones. The younger people have shown their interest only in vehicle loans and (or) educational loans, while the elder ones have a need for housing and other loans.
- Customers with deposit accounts are satisfied with their banks in respect of opening of accounts, updating the pass book, issue of cheque books, standing instructions, nomination facility and renewal of nomination. They are not satisfied with the banks for other factors like quick transaction of cash, clearance of outstation cheques, intimation of maturity and settlement of death claims.
- The customers of public sector banks are satisfied with their banks in respect of 14 out of 15 factors under study, except transparency in service charges with regard to value added services.
- The customers of public sector banks are dissatisfied with regard to physical facilities like adequacy of premises, waiting place, location of the branch, enquiry counters and adequacy of lighting and parking facilities.
- The customers of private sector banks are dissatisfied with regard to physical facilities like waiting place, location of the branch, enquiry counters, availability of stationary and adequacy of lighting and parking facilities.
- The extents of dissatisfaction for public sector banks with regard to physical facilities are higher in comparison to private sector banks, although the factors of dissatisfaction are almost same. The major reasons for overall dissatisfaction of the public sector banks rest with ATM network, while delay in transaction processing are for private banks.
- Both public and private sector banks suffer from staff attitude to provide services to the customers. The private sector banks are little ahead of the public sector banks in respect of courteous and polite language. Slightly more number of complaints was lodged against private banks compared to public banks.

- Customers expect a large number of new services, which varies across customer profile. Customers of private banks are expecting more new services than their counterparts in public banks.
- 82.49 per cent of the customers are happy with their banks and they will recommend the bank to others. Respondents in lower income group recommend the public sector bank more to others since these banks have wide network and provide better customer care and services.
- Customers' view private sector banks as progressive, while public sector banks as systematic and methodical.
- For choosing a particular bank, customers view public sector banks better than the private ones on the factors like company transactions with bank, customised services and distance from home/office. The reasons for such trend may be that public banks are widely located indicating its convenient locations. While private banks are preferred as they offer specialised services like *'zero balance'* with salary accounts and usually more transactions through ATMs.
- Out of the five dimensions of service quality (measured through SERVQUAL), gaps in tangibility and reliability are positive indicating customers' satisfaction and rest three, i.e., responsiveness, assurance and empathy are negative indicating customer dissatisfaction. The levels of satisfaction with private bank are significant for reliability dimension, where as they are dissatisfied with assurance dimension.
- Highest level of satisfaction is associated with sincerity in solving customer problems, while highest level of dissatisfaction with safe feeling of customers in transactions and customer's best interests at heart.

**Bankers' View**

- All private banks have excellent locations from business point of view compared to 35.59 per cent for public banks. Again, smaller branches in rural areas find unsuitability of locations for the branch from business point of view.

- About 71 per cent of public sector banks and 76 per cent of private banks have adequate floor space, while less than 8 per cent of the banks have inadequate floor space. Again, more than 30 per cent of public sector banks and about 15 per cent in private banks have just sufficient staff.
- Half of the public sector banks have reported to be either inadequate or just sufficient counters or ATMs, which is about 40 per cent in private banks.
- Considering different amenities available inside the bank, private banks reported to be much ahead of public banks. A big gap exists among the large, medium and small sized branches in respect of physical facilities like 'floor space', 'number of ATMs/counters', and 'air cooling'. Smaller rural branches are in a disadvantageous position compared to their urban counter parts in terms of physical facilities.
- Private Banks has a cutting edge over their counterparts in terms of standards of services rendered, attitude of staff and types of customers. The attitude of service personnel of middle sized banks is better than large and small size categories. Similarly, urban branches are able to provide better services and better employee's attitude compared to the rural branches.
- Strategies suggested by the bankers to improve their performances are physical facilities, use of information technology, concern for customers and appointing more service personnel (staff).
- Rural branches emphasized more on physical facilities, developing customer relationship and improving technology for better customer satisfaction, while their urban counterparts on product innovation.
- The small branches focus on business through referral, personalised service, developing customer relationship and physical facilities and market rapport to get more business. Large banks put forth creating goodwill, product innovations and operating through franchises for cost-effectiveness as important factors. The medium sized banks emphasised

heavily on retaining customers and proving customer satisfaction as the most important factors of improving service quality.

- Technology integration is a major problem for the old public sector banks, as they have to integrate the old practices with new technology.
- Poor quality of the staff has been identified by the bankers as the major weakness except the private banks. This problem is more acute in rural small branches.
- Medium-sized urban public sector banks have attributed inadequate facilities like floor space, parking space, and number of computers as the major problems. Staff attitude in general is one of the major weaknesses of the sample banks.
- Large banks in public sector operating in urban areas face the problem of ageing, as no young men are joining them and adjusting themselves to the changing environment is difficult. Frequent absent without prior intimation of the staffs is a major weakness with small sized rural branches. Their efficiency is further affected by shortage of staff.
- The major problem identified by the private bankers is increasing competition. But this has been refuted by public sector bankers. Private Banks ask for more funds for marketing and promotion from their headquarters, while public sector banks require more young and dynamic staffs.
- Adequate facilities, proper technology, more support staff, and cooperation from the controlling office are major supports that public sector bankers expect from their organizations.
- The large sized banks indicated adequate facilities as number one support they need followed by proper technology, adequate staff members and new products. But the smaller banks hinted upon cooperation from controlling office as most important support, followed by funds for marketing and promotion. Similarly, the smaller branches focus on training of employees, adequate staff, and sufficient product knowledge to improve business performance.

- 23.08 per cent private banks do not want any support, as they are self-sufficient and capable enough to withstand competition, while all the public sector banks need support in one form or other from their organization.
- Mechanization/computerization are the most significant steps taken by all groups of bankers for providing improved services to their customers. Public sector banks have miles to go to match with the private banks in terms of tangible factors like computers, ATMs, physical evidences, etc. to meet customers' expectation.
- Public sector banks have highlighted introduction of innovative products and extended business hours as significant steps, while he private banks highlighted steps like providing services at multi-locations, introduction of personal banking, addressing to the needs of the customers, etc. have been taken by them during the last three years.
- All the respondent bankers, except those from smaller banks have acclaimed introduction of new products as a significant step that they have taken. Rural small branches have adopted aggressive marketing strategy as an important step towards achieving business targets.
- The major competitors for public sector banks are the private banks as perceived by the sample respondents. The private banks feel other private banks as their major competitors. The private banks are competitors to all sized urban branches, while the rural banks feel other public sector banks as their competitors.
- 66.10 per cent of the public sector banks describe the levels of competition is moderate, while 61.54 per cent of the private banks level it as fierce. Smaller banks are more exposed to threat. Only 21.21 per cent of the rural branches described competition level as low, as they are the virtual monopolist in their segment. Only they are facing little challenges from the local post-office savings banks and other non-banking institutions.

- Only a smaller portion of the public sector banks operating in urban areas feels helpless due to intense competition. Most of the sample banks did not have the experiences of customer drop-outs and loss of business during the last two years.
- Smaller rural branches and the private banks do not feel handicapped due to competition. Rather some of them opined that they gained out of competition as they resort to aggressive marketing activities and entering into the fortress of the public sector banks.
- The major strategies adopted by the banks to counter competition are improving product range, improving service level, aggressive marketing, better facilities, focus on customers, and appropriate and timely decisions.
- All categories of banks focus on setting individual targets, building relationship with the customer and putting personal efforts as major strategies to achieve the business targets. The achievement of targets by the private bankers is 100 per cent, which is about 86 per cent in case public sector banks.
- Levels of dissatisfaction regarding pay are more among the public sector bankers compared to the private ones. The smaller banks operating in rural areas have felt mostly the inadequacy of the pay.
- All most all banks are taking sufficient care to improve the job knowledge of the employees to meet the growing demands of the customers.
- Adoption to technological changes is not at all a problem for new generation private banks as they have started with a technological platform. A small percentage of public sector banks (8.5%) found it difficult to adapt to new technology because of stereotype attitude of the staffs (aged one) and proper training given by the banks.
- The rate of vanishing customers is higher in case of urban large sized public sector banks. This may be due to (i) more attractive private banks, (ii) dissatisfactions experienced by the customers, and (iii) apathetic attitude of the staffs.

- Most of the customers are happy with the existing products and the banking still dominates around deposit and withdrawal of money.
- Personal contact, personal attention to consumer needs and improving service quality are most important methods of attracting new business irrespective of the size of the bank.
- Private Banks are resort to aggressive sales promotion and door-to-door campaign to attract new customers than their public sector counterparts.
- Rural branches focus more on distributing bulletins, motivating employees and door-to-door campaign as methods to attract new business apart from personal contact, personal attention to customer needs and improving service quality.
- Advertisements like information dissemination, reaching out people about offerings for building mass awareness, telling people about offerings and attracting and retaining customers are important for attracting new business. The smaller rural banks are far behind in terms of using the front office personnel in attracting and retaining customers.
- Most of the sample banks hold their banker-customer meet regularly either on monthly or quarterly basis. Almost all categories of sample bankers have given access to customers as a part of frequent Banker Customer meet. Large sized branches, mostly in public sector, failed to implement the suggestions given by the customers.
- The public sector banks of different sizes and different locations have achieved the social objectives as have been entrusted to them from time to time. In this regard the private banks are lagging far behind, even some of them do not feel concern about it.
- The public sector banks have largely focus on large network of ATMs and branches to capture more business, followed by better B-C relationship and technological advancement (like introduction of BPR) for faster and appropriate transactions.

- The private banks mostly focus on banker-customer (B-C) relationship, introduction of cheaper and new variety of products, and more promotion is required. The large banks focus more on use of advanced technology, B-C relationship and searching for new business.
- The major reasons for dissatisfaction of the customers of public sector banks are rigid policy, while for the private banks it is mostly service related factors like service charges, interest rates on loans and term deposit and matching to customer's attitude are important.

## SUGGESTIONS

The emerging changes in the Indian economy, especially, in the Indian banking system calls for adoption of efficient and effective marketing strategies. The strategic decisions should take into account the relevant competitive, economic, political, regulatory, legal, technological and socio-cultural factors, in addition to the strengths and weaknesses of the Banks, among other factors. The efficient and effective marketing strategy should encompass market innovation (improving the mix of market segments), product innovation (improving the mix of services offered to the customers), and process innovation (improving efficiency of internal operations). In the light of the research findings, the followings are suggested for better market strategies for both public and private sector banks in Orissa.

- It is important for the banks to improve the service attitude of the staff and reduce the transaction time to improve customer satisfaction and stop the negative feelings of the customers, which may spread as words-of-mouth of the disappointed customers.
- Complaints always bring dissatisfaction with the customers. Hence, the bankers should have to gear up themselves to handle the grievances more quickly and efficiently.
- The customers directly come in contact with the front office personnel, who are observed not to be in the proper mood to listen to the customers. Improvement in the staff factor is common requirement of the banks in general to improve business performance.

- In the changing environment the bankers are depending more on physical and technological factors on one hand and the functional (staff) factors on the other as they represent the functional quality and human touch to make the service better satisfying. Hence, by giving attention to the above factors, the present level of service delivered can be improved.
- The middle-sized public sector banks operating in rural areas realised that the existing products are insufficient to cover the needs and expectations of the customers. Hence, it is advisable for the banks to keep on innovating new products.
- The advancement of information technology (IT) creates a large opportunity before banking sector in India, which should be optimally exploited keeping the customers' action in mind for business growth.
- Not only customer satisfaction, but the concept of customer delight is now the emerging area in Indian banking system, by which the service providers should prepare themselves to offer more than what their customers expect from them.
- The public sector banks should pay more attention to quick transaction of cash, clearance of outstation cheque, intimation of maturity, settlement of death claims, and procedure and paper work in order to take care of the dissatisfied customers. They should also pay more attention to service factors, like services rendered, attitude of the officers, attitude of other staffs, level of customer, and customer retention.
- The private sector banks should pay more attention to nomination facility, quick transaction of cash, clearance of outstation cheque, intimation of maturity, renewal of nomination and settlement of death claims, and guidance and counselling in order to take care of the dissatisfied customers. With regard to value added services, they should give more attention to factors like safety and security, issue if credit/ debit cards, renewal of credit cards, accuracy of statements, timely receipt of statements, transparency in service charges and wide acceptability of credit/debit cards.

- Customer satisfaction and attracting and retaining customers, as evident from the study are two major service qualities that bring improvement in business. The next important factors are satisfied customers as the advertisers and creating goodwill. The public as well as private sector banks should give more attention to these factors.
- More attention should be focussed on the factors like, proper technology, more support staff, adequate facilities, cooperation, mechanization, product knowledge, developing customer relationship and improving technology for the public sector banks operating in rural areas.
- Service quality offers a way of achieving success among competing service providers, particularly in the case of firms that offer nearly identical services, such as banks, where establishing service quality may be the only way of differentiating oneself. Such differentiation can yield a higher proportion of consumers' choices and hence, mean the difference between financial success and failure for the banks.
- In order to compete in the e-commerce world, financial service providers will need to invest heavily in customer relationship management systems and in brand identity. In the fast-track Internet world, it may be the only way to survive. The staff in the banks particularly the public sector banks must have an open mind and accept the fundamental changes brought about by the information technology and internet revolution for better delivery of customer service and appreciate the more efficient way of accounting transactions and generating an array of MIS reports both for the bank management and the Regulator.
- Training and acquiring new skills becomes absolutely essential in the era of new tech-savvy banking products. Adequate training should be provided to the staffs of the banks to meet the competition and deliver the type of services demanded by the customer in the present and futuristic IT environment.

## SCOPE FOR FUTURE RESEARCH

The present study is concerned with a broad picture of customer attitude and perceptions of banking services provided by the public as well as private sector banks in Orissa. Similarly, the bankers' views in this aspect are considered. But there is no comparison of how the bankers perceive the customers expectations relating to various parameters of banking services. This would have provided a better understanding of customers' expectations and perceptions, which needs further research. For analysis of service qualities of banks, SERVQUAL has been used for a broad set of five dimensions to understand expectations and perceptions of customers. But this instrument can also be used to categorise customers into several perceived service quality segments on the basis of individual scores, which needs further research. Similarly, another application of SERVQUAL can be studied by grouping the customers with varying quality images. Further, an analysis of bank/branch characteristics in different clusters may reveal attributes that are critical for ensuring high service quality in designing a marketing strategy.

## THE EPILOGUE

The banks in their own interest should tune up the customer service with a view to retaining the existing customers and to expand their business by winning new customers. It is not easy to cultivate new customers, as the competitors also will be after them. In an attempt to develop new customers, if the existing customers are neglected, they are sure to lose the existing customers also. The banks should remember the old adage "the known devil is better than the unknown angle". Managing customer relationship is an art, without which no organisation can hope to succeed. When the bank makes an attempt to excel, it should not miss out customer relationship. It is not enough if the top management stresses the importance of managing customer relationship, but it should be percolated to the ground level to achieve the desired results. Cultivating and excelling in customer relationship should not only be a good business strategy, but should be the corporate mission. Building value for the customers is more important than building value to the shareholders. Hence bank's operational activities, service quality, customer satisfaction, customer loyalty and profitability create a continuum in giving service to customers. Each of the components of this continuum has to be monitored and managed by the bankers in today's competitive world.

At the end, the saying of Mahatma Gandhi should be remembered: "By entering into your premises, the customer is giving an opportunity to serve him, but you are not doing any favour by serving him. He is the purpose of your business."

# Bibliography

**BOOKS**

Anderson, K. and Carol, K. (2002); "Customer Relationship Management", New Delhi: Tata McGraw Hill.

Andrew, Kenneth (1986); *Bank Marketing Handbook*, England: Woodhead – Faulkner Ltd.

Athreya, N.H. (2003); "The Corporate Art of Caring for the Customer", New Delhi: Tata McGraw Hill.

Balchandran, S. (2001); "Excellence in Services", New Delhi: JAICO Publishing House.

Bandyopadhyay, R.(ed.) (1984), *Emerging Challenges in Indian Banking and Policy Implications*, Bombay: National Institute of Bank Management.

Batra, Pramod (2002); "Simple Ways to make Your Customers Happy", New Delhi: Thinc Inc.

Bhatt, Atul (1990), *Study of Market Research in Banking*, Pune: National Institute of Bank Management.

Black, Sheila et al. (1985), *Handbook of Marketing and Selling Bank Services*, England: MCB University Press.

Bowden, Elbert V. (1980), *Revolution in Banking*, Virginia: Robert F. Dame Inc.

Candilis, W.O. (1975) (ed), "The Future of Commercial Banking", New York: Praeger Publishers.

Chawla, A.S. (1988), *Nationalisation and Growth of Indian Banking*, New Delhi: Deep & Deep Publications.

Clifford, Martin (1999); "Building Better Customer Relations", New York: Martin Clifford Publications.

Compton, Eric N. (1983), *Inside Commercial Banking, 2ed.*, New York: John Wiley & Sons.

Compton, Eric N. Inside Commercial Banking, 2nd Edn. New York: John Wiley & Sons Int., 1983.

Cowell, Denald, The Marketing of Services, London: CAM Foundation & thc Institute of Marketing, 1984.

Cowell, Donald (1984), *The Marketing of Services*, London: CAM Foundation & Institute of Marketing.

Das, Kallol (2004); "h-CRM – The Key to Lifelong Business Relationship", New Delhi: Vision Books.

Das, Tusar K. (1976), *Marketing in Banks*, Bombay: National Institute of Bank Management.

Desai, Vasant (1987), *Indian Banking: Nature and Problems*, Bombay: Himalaya Publishing House.

Freeland, John G. (2004); "The Ultimate CRM Handbook", New Delhi: Tata McGraw Hill.

Gandhi, J.C. (1993), *Marketing: A Managerial Introduction*, New Delhi: Tata McGraw Hill Publishing Co. Ltd.

Ghosh, B.K. (ed.) 1990, *Banking Industry in the 1990s*, Pune: National Institute of Bank Management.

Hodges, L.H. & Tillman, R. (1978), *Bank Marketing: Text and Cases*, Addison – Wesley Publishing Co.

Kothari, C.R. (ed.) 1991, *Indian Banking (Vol 1 & II)*, Jaipur: Arihant Publishers.

Kothary, C. R. (Ed), Indian Banking Vo. I and II, Jaipur: Arihant Publishers, 1991.

Kotler, Philip & Armstrong, Gary (2003), *Principles of Marketing*, New Delhi: Prentice-Hall of India Pvt. Ltd.

Kotler, Philip (2003), *Marketing Management: Analysis, Planning & Control*, New Delhi: Prentice-Hall of India Pvt. Ltd.

Kotler, Philip; and Armstrong, Gery, Principles of Marketing, 5th Edn. New Delhi: Prentice-Hall of India Pvt. Ltd., 1991.

Low, Edgar (2002); "The Bottom line to Better Banking", IBM Financial Services, Singapore: Asia Pacific Sector Publication.

Madhukar, R.K. (1990), *Dynamics of Bank Marketing*, Bangalore: Sri Sudhindra Publishing House.

Mather, L.C. (1977), *Banker and Customer Relationship and the Accounts of Personal Customers*, London: Waterlow Ltd.

McGuire Jr.,E.E. (1971), *Market Segmentation—An Alternative Bank Marketing Strategy*, North Carolina: The Bank of Asheville.

McGuire, Jr., Earl E. Market Segmentation – An alternative Bank Marketing Strategy, North Carolina: The Bank of Asheville, 1971.

Mehra, Dalip (1999); "Indian Financial System and Commercial Banking", New Delhi: Sultan Chand & Sons Publications.

Mehra, Mona (1976), *Bank Advertising in India*, Bombay: Indian Banks Association.

Meidan, Arthur (1984), *Bank Marketing Management*, Hong kong: Macmillan Publishers Ltd.

Murty, Y. Sree Rama, Bank Deposits: Estimation and Forecasting, Pune: National Institute at Bank Management, 1989.

Pai, M.R. Banks and Customer Service, Bombay: All India Depositors' Association (Bombay Branch), 1976.

Patankar, V.N.; and Godse, V.T. Survey of Customer Attitude to Banking System. Bombay: National Institute of Bank Management, 1985.

Paul, R. Timm, (2004); "50 Powerful IDEAS to Keep Your Customers"; New Delhi: JAICO Publishing House.

Pezzullo, M.A. Marketing for Bankers, Washington: American Bankers Association, 1982.

Rangarajan, C. Innovations in Banking: The Indian Experience, New Delhi: Oxford and IBH Publication Co., 1982.

Rangaswamy, B. Public Sector Banking in India, New Delhi: Ministry of Information and Broadcasting, Government of India, 1985.

Rao, B. Rama Chandra, Current Trends in Indian Banking, New Delhi: Deep and Deep Publications, 1984.

Ross, W. Ogen, Marketing in Commercial Banks, Michigan: Masterco Press, Inc., 1968.

Sahoo, S.C.; and Sinha, P.K. Emerging Trends in Indian Marketing, Delhi: Academic Foundation, 1991.

Saxena, K.K.Bank Marketing: Concepts and Applications, New Delhi: Skylark Publications, 1988.

Sen, A. K.; Gupta, M.; and Chakrabarti, S. Banking in the 1990s. Bombay: Himalaya Publishing House, 1990.

Singh, S.P. Banking in India: Achievements and challenges, Bangalore: Bangalore University, 1980.

Singhal, Sushils, Bank and Customers – A Behavioural Analysis, New Delhi, Shri Ram Centre for Industrial Relations and Human Resources, 1988.

Stanton, William J.; and Futrell, Charles, Fundamentals of Marketing, 8th Edn., New York: McGraw-Hill Book Company, 1987.

Varde, S.D.; Singh S.P.; and Bandyopadhyay R. Banking in India: Futuristic Approach, Bombay: National Institute of Bank Management, 1978.

Varde, V.; and Singh, S.P. (Ed). Forecasting in Banking Industry, Pune: National Institute of Bank Management, 1981.

Venkata Ramana, V. and Somayajulu, G. (2003); "Customer Relationship Management – A Key to Corporate Success", New Delhi: Excel Books.

Walker, Michael C. An Introduction to Bank Marketing Research, A Bank BRMA Research Publication.

Weyer, D.V. Bank Marketing, London: The Institute of Bankers, 1969.

## JOURNALS & PERIODICALS

Akber, S.V. "Bank Marketing-Some Issues" Monthly News Review, Indian Overseas Bank, (December 1990), 20-21.

Arora, Kalpana (2003); "Indian Banking – Managing Transformation through Technology", *IBA Bulletin;* Vol. XXV, No. 3, March.

Aurora, S & Malhotra, M. (1997); "Customer Satisfaction: A Comparative Analysis of Public and Private Sector Banks", *Decision,* Vol. 24, No.1-4, January-December.

Avadhani, V.A.; Motwani, V.M.; and Angadi, V.B. "Mobilisation of Rural Savings – Banking Experience", RBI Occasional Paper, (September, 1987).

Berry, L.L.; Kehoe, W.J.; and Lindgren, Jr. J.H. "How Bank Marketers View their Jobs", The Bankers Magazine, (November-December, 1980), 35.

Bettinger, Cass "Developing Marketing Strategy"' The Bankers Magazine, (January-February, 1987), 64-70.

Bhandary, Bhaskar M. "Need for Publicity in Banking Industry", IBA Bulletin, (February, 1985), 111-112.

Bhatnagar, Deepti, "A Model for Managing Innovation in Banks", Vikalpa, (October-December, 1986), 321-327.

Bhatt, Atul (1991), "Bank Marketing, Market Research and Indian Banks", *Prajnan,* January-March.

Bhatt, Atul, "Bank Marketing, Market Research and Indian Banks", Prajnan, (January-March, 1991), 45-55.

Bhattacharya, S.K. "Designing Optimal Management Structures and Control Systems for Commercial Banks: A Market Segmentation Approach", Vikalpa, (January, 1977), 41-57.

Bhattacharyay, B.N "Marketing Approach to Promoting Banking Services", Vikalpa, (April-June, 1989), 35-38.

Bhattacharyay, B.N and Ghose B.K. "Marketing of Banking Services in the 90s: Problems and Perspectives", Economic and Political Weekly, (February 25, 1989), M.27-M.32.

Bhattacharyay, B.N. "Is Customer Service Deteriorating in Indian Banking Industry", Vikalpa, (July-September, 1990), 23-29.

Bolest, Mark, "The Competitor's View", Banking World, (October, 1987), 33-34.

Bortree, William H. "Positioning Bank Products", The Bankers Magazine, (July-August, 1986), 12.

Brown, Sharon Hanes, "Competitive Banks Capitalise on Customer Complaints", Bank Marketing, (February, 1987), 20-22.

Carroll, Daniel T. "Ten Commandments for Bank Marketing", The Bankers Magazine, (Autumn, 1970), 74-80.

Casey, David C. "The Bank Marketing Imperative", The Bankers Magazine, (Autumn, 1974), 115.

Chandra, A. Sarat. "Quality Circle—A Concept in Application", UCO Bank Review, (June, 1990), 16.

Channon, Derek, "Through the Eyes of the Customers", Banking World, (October, 1987), 26-29.

Chorney, Harold F. "Take a Fresh Look at Financial Planning and Forge New Alliances", Bank Marketings, (May, 1987), 29-31.

Clarke, Paul, et al., "Strategic Marketing", Banking World. (October, 1987), 16-20.

Cox, Edwin B. "The Competition in Retail Banking", The Bankers Magazine, (July-August, 1979), 24-31.

Davis, Jan L.; and Cohn, Jonathan, "Marketing Financial Services in a Fragmented Market", Bank Marketing, (January, 1989), 25-27.

Deo, V.P. "Know thy Customer", The Banker, (April 1982), 13.

Desai, Yogesh I. "Win Your Customers: A 20-Point Approach", IBA Bulletin, (February, 1990), 45-46.

Dibbert, Michael T. "Practical Aplications of Personal Banking", The Bankers Magazine, (July-August, 1986), 7.

Dixon, Jeane, "New Directions in Banking", The Bankers Magazine, (Autumn, 1976), 44-48.

Duffy, Helene, "The New Face of Retail Banking", Bank Management, (December, 1990), 26-37.

Dutta, S.K. "Customer Service of Banks", SBI Monthly Review, (January, 1991), 15-22.

Flemington, Roger. "At Heart it's a People Business", Banking World, (December, 1988), 27-28.

Fuller, Donald. "Adding Segmentation Power to your MCIF through Survey Research", Bank Marketing, (April, 1989), 37.

Furash, Edward E. "Targeting the New Customers", The Bankers Magazine, (January-February, 1989), 05-09.

Furlong, Carla, "Magic and Myths of Customer Service", Canadian Banker, (May-June, 1991), 13-17.

Ganguli, Siddhartha, "Deposit Mobilisation in Banks: Harnessing Customer Service", Capital, (February 7, 1983), 32.

Garg, I.K. (1997); "Perspective on Banking in the Emerging Environment in India", *State Bank of India Monthly Review*, Vol. XXXVI, No. 9, September.

Garg, I.K. (1998); "Future of Banking in India – Key Issues", *State Bank of India Monthly Review*, Vol. XXXVII, No. 9, March.

Garg, I.K. (2003); "Indian Banking in Transition: Some Challenges", *IBA Bulletin;* Vol. XXV, No. 3, March.

Gavaghan, Kevin, "To Market to Market ...", Banking World, (March, 1990).

Gavini, A.L. & Athma, P. (1997); "Customer Service in Commercial Banks – Expectations and Reality", *Indian Journal of Marketing*, Vol. XXVII, No. 5,6 & 7.

Gelli, Ramesh. "Financial Sector Reforms: Some Perceptions on Banking Industry", The Journal of Indian Institute of Bankers, (October-December, 1991), 190-198.

German, Donald R.; and German. Joan W. "Bank Promotional Programs that Works", The Bankers Magazine, (July-August, 1979), 47-51.

Goiporia, M.N. "Banks to Make Aggressive Marketing Efforts", IBA Bulletin, (May, 1987), 85-86.

Gopal Sundaram, C.R. (2001); "The Emerging Challenges for Banking Industry", *IBA Bulletin;* Vol. XXIII, No. 3, March.

Goyel, R.P. "Improving Quality of Banking Services", Commerce, (July 30, 1983), 03-05.

Green, Andrea "Bank Marketers Focus on Focus Groups", Bankers Monthly, (April, 1990), 32-35.

Green, Andrea "The Bank Marketing Hotshots", Bankers Monthly, (June, 1990), 15-21.

Green, Andrea. "Bank Products with Pizzazz", Bankers Monthly, (September, 1990), 65-70.

Greenbaum, Thomas L. "A New Perspective on Marketing", The Bankers Magazine, (January-February, 1987), 51-53.

Gupta, R.P. (2001); "Banking in the New Millennium – Strategic Management Issues", *IBA Bulletin;* Vol. XXIII, No. 3, March.

Haas, R.W. "Bank Marketing in the Age of Consumerism", The Bankers Magazine, (Winter, 1972), 39-40.

Jha, Dr. S.M. "Innovative Marketing for the Banking Services", Pigmy Economic Review, (July, 1989), 01-08.

John, August G. St. "A Changing Future for Retail Banking", The Bankers Magazine, (July-August, 1979), 52-56.

Kaura, Mohinder N. "A Blue Print for Aplication of Zero Base Budgeting to Indian Banks", Vikalpa, (October-December, 1988), 23-29.

Kohli, S.S. (2001); "Indian Banking Industry: Emerging Challenges", *IBA Bulletin;* Vol. XXIII, No. 3, March.

Kohn, Stephen J. "Bank Marketing Strategy for the 70's", The Bankers Magazine, (Spring, 1971), 41-48.

Kshirsagar, S.S. "Improving Customer Service of Banks: Organisational Implications", Prajnan, (April-June, 1976), 145-166.

Kulkarni, R.V. and Paranjape, A.M. (2000); "Changing Face of Banking – From Brick and Mortat to E-Banking", *IBA Bulletin;* Vol. XXII, No. 1, January

Kumar, Pawan (1999), "Private Sector Banks in India", *Indian Management,* October.

Kurup, N.P. "The Impact of Interest Rate Changes on Maturity Distribution of Term Deposits – March 1986 to September 1989", PNB Monthly Review, (July, 1990), 403-412.

Lakshminarayanan, P. (2001), "Indian Banking – Preparedness for Emerging Challenges", *IBA Bulletin;* Vol. XXIII, No. 3, March.

Larranage, Bob. "The More You Tell, the More you Sell", Bank Marketing, (January, 1989), 31-32.

Laurent, C.R "Image and Segmentation in Bank-Marketing", The Bankers Magazine, (July-August, 1979), 32-37.

Laurent, C.R. "Marketing's Role in Banking", The Bankers Magazine, (July-August, 1982), 26-30.

Leeladhar, V. (2003); "Branch Banking—Its Future in India", *IBA Bulletin;* Vol. XXV, No. 3, March.

Levy, Sidney J. "Consumer Views of Bank Services", Journal of Bank Research, (Summer, 1973), 100-104.

Liswood, Laura A. "Service Customers before they run the other way", Bank Marketing, (November 1987), 24-26.

Long, Robert H. "Planning for Tomorrow's Customer", Journal of Bank Research, (Summer, 1973), 93-99.

Loud, James F. "Organising for customer Service", The Bankers Magazine, (November-December, 1980), 41.

Madhukar, R.K. (1987), "Indian Banking – The Next Phase", *The Journal of Institute of Bankers,* Bombay.

Mathur, A.N. "Customer Service – New Strategy", Commerce, (July 30, 1983), 35.

Mathure, P.H. (1999), "TQM in Banking", *Indian Management,* May.

McCall, Alan S. "The Impact of Bank Structure on Bank Service to Local Communities", (Summer, 1980), 101-109.

Miller, Richard B. "Bank Marketing – A symposium", The Bankers Magazine, (Autumn, 1973), 17-21.

Mills, Carolyn J. "Selling Bank Services through Telemarketing", The Bankers Magazine, (September-October, 1985), 62.

Murray, James G. "The Importance of Internal Marketing", The Bankers Magazine, (July-August, 1979), 38-40.

Murthy, G.R.K. and Panda, N.R. (2002); "CRM in Banks – A tool to edge-out Competition", *IBA Bulletin;* Vol. XXIV, No. 7, July

Murthy, NRN. (2003); "Reinventing Banking in India", *Bank Quest, The Journal of Indian Institute of Banking and Finance,* Vol. 74, No. 3, July-September.

Murty, Y. Sree Rama; and Haresh G. "Regional Variations in Banking Business: A Study Based on ANOVA Technique", Prajnan, (January-March, 1991), 31-43.

Nadler, Paul S. "What Happened to Traditional Banking", The Bankers Magazine, (Spring, 1971), 32-40.

Nair, K.R.S. (1999), "Universal Banking", *Indian Management*, May.

Nelson, Roger R. "Strategic Marketing", The Bankers Magazine, (July-August, 1982), 43-46.

Noakes, C. Thomas, "How to Mount an Effective Direct Mail Campaign", The Bankers Magazine, (January-February, 1989), 24-26.

Ojha, P.D. (1987), "Banking and Economic Development of India", *RBI Bulletin, 41: 11*

Pai, D.T. (2001); "Indian Banking – Changing Scenario", *IBA Bulletin;* Vol. XXIII, No. 3, March.

Pitman, Brian, "The Weakest Will Go to Wall", Banking World, (October, 1987), 31-32.

Pool, A.A. "Attitude Towards Consumer Banking Packages: An Empirical Analysis", Journal of Bank Research, (Spring, 1976), 88-92.

Pope, N.W. "A Philosophy of Bank Advertising", Marketing for Bank Executives, L.L. Berry and L.A. Capaldini, New York: Petrocelli Books, (1974), 222-238.

Prasad, B.R. (2001), "Improving Strength and Competitiveness of Indian Banks – Some Strategic Issues", *IBA Bulletin;* Vol. XXIII, No. 3, March.

Prasad, Bandi Ram. "Innovative Banking", IBA Bulletin, (February, 1991).

Prasad, S.G. (1999), "Getting Personal", *Outlook,* Vol. V, No. 40, October.

Purushottaman, A. (2004); "Relationship Banking holds the Key to Beat Competition in the Emerging Banking Scenario", *Bank Quest, The Journal of Indian Institute of Banking and Finance,* Vol. 75, No. 1, Jan.-March.

Rados, David L. "Developing New Bank Services", The Bankers Magazine, (Autumn, 1971), 85.

Rai, A., Kamat, V. & Maakan, A. (1999), "More Bang from your Bank", *Intelligent Investor*, Vol. III, No. XVIII, September.

Rajashekara, K.S. (2004), "Application of IT in Banking", *Yojana, July*

Raju, B.Y. (1999), "Looming Challenges to Banking", *Indian Management, November.*

Ramachandra, S.T. (2002); "Customer Relationship Management: Emerging Strategies", *IBA Bulletin;* Vol. XXIV, No. 9, September.

Ramachandran N. "Banking: Challenges of Nineties", Yojana, (November 30, 1991), 11-15.

Ramaswamy, T. "Salesmanship for Banks Services", Monthly News Revies, 108, (August, 1989), 01-02.

Rao, M.S.A. (1998), "A Better Future for Banks", *Indian Management, April.*

Rayudu, Dr. C.S. "Banks Social Marketing and Market Segmentation", Marketology Quarterly, (Vol. 22, No. 2, 3, & 4, 1990), 39-40.

Reed, Barry, "Banker and Retailer", Banking World, (June, 1988), 30-33.

Robertson, Dan, H.; and Bellenger, Danny N. "Identifying Bank Market Segments", Journal of Bank Research, (Winter, 1977), 276-283.

Roderique, Ronald J. "Begin with the Basics", ABA Banking Journal, (October, 1986), 33-38.

Roll, Richard J. "Targeting Markets in Consumer Banking", The Bankers Magazine, (January-February, 1986), 45-46.

Sadare, A.M. "Sources of Information on Banking" IBA Bulletin, (May, 1990).

Samal, B. (2001); "Indian Banking: Phases of Transition", *IBA Bulletin;* Vol. XXIII, No. 3, March.

Satyanarayana, Dr. K. "Cost-Benefit Analysis of a Collection Account", PNB Monthly Review, (February, 1991), 75-84.

Scheffler, Ken, "The Nations Most Lucrative Deposit Market", Bank Management, (December, 1990), 42-46.

Seth, Ashok Kumar, "Interest Rate Sensitivity of Deposits of Banking Sector in a Partial Equilibrium Framework, 1955-1985", Indian Journal of Finance and Research, (July, 1991), 139-151.

Shah, S.G. (2001); "Indian Banking: Obstacles and Opportunities-Strategies and Solutions", *IBA Bulletin;* Vol. XXIII, No. 3, March.

Shah, S.G. "Opportunities for New Services", Commerce, (July 30, 1983), 31-33.

Shastri, R.V. (2001); "Technology for Banks in India – Challenges Ahead", *IBA Bulletin;* Vol. XXIII, No. 3, March.

Shastri,R.V. (2003); "Towards a New Banking Order", *IBA Bulletin;* Vol. XXV, No. 3, March.

Shenoy, B.S. (2001); "Indian Banking, Emerging Challenges – Some key Issues", *IBA Bulletin;* Vol. XXIII, No. 3, March.

Sherden, William S. "Practical Strategies for Cross-Selling", The Bankers Magazine, (January-February, 1989), 12-17.

Shostack, G.L. "Banks Sell Services – Not Things", The Bankers Magazine, (Winter, 1977), 40-42.

Singh, O.N. (2001); "Indian Banking – Emerging Challenges and strategies", *IBA Bulletin;* Vol. XXIII, No. 3, March.

Siraramakrishnayya, Y.V. "Widening the Range of Services in Banks", Commerce, (July 30, 1983), 11-12.

Slater, Robert Bruce, "Bankers Binge on Bank Ads", Bankers Monthly, (June, 1990), 63-65.

Smith, A.G. (2003); "Acquiring a Cuting Edge", *Business Standard Banking Annual,* October 2003.

Srinivasan. "Tree Deposit and Discrete Deposit Account", Prajnan, (April-June, 1991), 185-188.

Stevens, Robert L. "Marketing Serves as Primary Catelyst behind Quality Service", Bank Marketing, (September, 1987), 24-28.

Swain, B.K. (2004); "Indian Banks in 2010: Emerging Scenario", *IBA Bulletin;* Vol. XXVI, No.1, January.

Sweeny, Margaret A. "New Competitive Weapon: Speedy Service", Bank Marketing, (April, 1989), 36-37.

Tejyan, P.K. "Customer Service Centres: Machinery for Redress of Grievances", IBA Bulletin, (February, 1987), 21-22.

Thingalaya, N.K. (1999), "A to Z Bank Management", *Indian Management, June.*

Thingalaya, N.K. (2001); "Indian Banking – Need for a long-term Perspective for Growth and Stability", *IBA Bulletin;* Vol. XXIII, No. 3, March.

Trigg, Michael N. "Sales and Service Cultures are Interchangeable – Not Mutually Exclusive", Bank Marketing, (September, 1987), 30-34.

Vagul, N. "Employee Development for Efficient Customer Service", Prajnan, (April-June, 1976), 167-183.

Varde, S.D. "Customer Service of Banks", Prajnan, (April-June, 1976), 123-143.

Velayudham, T.K. (2002); "Developments in Indian Banking: Past, Present and Future", *Bank Quest, The Journal of Indian Institute of Banking and Finance,* Vol.73, No.4, Oct.-December (Platinum Jubilee Issue).

Velayudham, T.K. (2003), "Banking for Corporates – New Directions", *Bank Quest, The Journal of Indian Institute of Banking and Finance,* Vol. 74, No. 3, July-September.

Venkajah, V. "Bank Marketing – A Systems Approach", Institute of Public Enterprise Journal, (October-December, 1987), 59-75.

Venkitaramanan, S. "Some Aspects of Banking in India", RBI Bulletin, (March, 1992), 495-500.

pa, Kamesan (2001); "Developments in the Indian Banking Industry and the Emerging Challenges", *IBA Bulletin;* Vol. XXIII, No. 3, March.

## NEWSPAPERS

Bakshi, R. K.: "Marketing Concepts in Banks", The Economic Times, (September 1, 1988), 7.

Bhatt, Sanjeev,: "Bank Marketing", The Economic Times, (September 1, 1988), 05.

Bhattacharya, T.S.; "Marketing & Personal Banking", Business Standard (August 2-3, 2005).

Chatterji, B.K. "Chasing Deposits", The Economic Times, (December 29, 1982), 09.

Elumalai, K. "Relevance of Marketing Strategies: A Rejoinder", The Economic Times, (June 30, 1988), 05.

Gops La. "Banks, Companies Tussle for Funds", Financial Express, (June 12, 1982), 05.

Joshi, Navin Chandra, "Relevance of Marketing Strategies in Banks", The Economic Times, (March 17, 1988), 07.

Kumar, P. "Bank Management – towards 21st Century", The Economic Times, (January1, 1987), 06.

Nigam, R. "Marketing Strategies in Banks – I", Financial Express, (May 19, 1988), 04.

Nigam, R. "Marketing Strategies in Banks – II", Financial Express, (June1, 1988), 04.

Radhakrishnan, T.R. "Banks Need Not Ditch Customers", Financial Express, (May 15, 1991), 07.

Ramaswamy, C.V. "II – Marketing Techniques and Bank Deposits", Financial Express, (February 24, 1980), 04.

Ramaswamy, C.V. "I – Marketing Techniques and Bank Deposits", Financial Express, (February 23, 1980), 04.

Ramchandra, B. "Dealing with Public Complaints", Financial Express, (May 8, 1989), 07.

Rao, B. Ramachandra, "Resource Mobilisation – Woes of Banks", financial Express, (May 1, 1991), 07.

Shrikhande, F. "Marketing of Banking Services", The Economic Times, (April 14, 1988), 07.

Varshney, P.N. "Banks and Customer Protection Act", Financial Express, (March 8, 1991), 07.

## DISSERTATIONS

Bal, R.K. (1992); "Promotion of Services and Deposit Mobilisation in Indian Banking Industry: A Marketing Approach", Unpublished Doctoral Thesis submitted to Utkal University.

Bihari, S.C. (2005); "Management of Customer Relations in Commercial banks After Mechanization of Services: A Case Study of Bhubaneswar City", Unpublished Doctoral Thesis submitted to Utkal University.

Ganapathy, A. "A Diagnostic Study of Growth in Deposit of Bank of Baroda in Bombay Metropolitan City", National Institute of Bank Management, 1983.

# Index

❑❑❑